WILDFLOWERS OF
THE MIDWEST

HELP US KEEP THIS GUIDE UP-TO-DATE

Every effort has been made by the author and editors to make this guide as accurate and useful as possible. However, many things can change after a guide is published.

We would appreciate hearing from you concerning your experiences with this guide and how you feel it could be improved and kept up-to-date. While we may not be able to respond to all comments and suggestions, we'll take them to heart, and we'll also make certain to share them with the author. Please send your comments and suggestions to the following address:

FalconGuides
Reader Response/Editorial Department
246 Goose Lane
Guilford, CT 06437

Thanks for your input!

WILDFLOWERS OF
THE MIDWEST

A Field Guide to Over 600 Wildflowers in the Region

DON KURZ

FALCONGUIDES

GUILFORD, CONNECTICUT
HELENA, MONTANA

FALCONGUIDES®

An imprint of The Rowman & Littlefield Publishing Group, Inc.
Falcon, FalconGuides, and Outfit Your Mind are registered trademarks of The Rowman & Littlefield Publishing Group, Inc.

Distributed by NATIONAL BOOK NETWORK

British Library Cataloguing-in-Publication Information Available

Library of Congress Cataloging-in-Publication Data
Names: Kurz, Donald R., author.
Title: Wildflowers of the midwest : a field guide to over 600 wildflowers
  in the region / Don Kurz.
Description: Guilford, Connecticut : FalconGuides, [2020] | Includes
  bibliographical references and index. | Summary: "America's Midwest is
  home to some of the most abundant and beautiful wildflowers in the
  country. Now, with Wildflowers of the Midwest, readers will be able to
  locate and identify the many gorgeous flowering species blooming in the
  heartland. The newest guidebook from wildflower authority Don Kurz
  contains detailed, full-color photographs and concise descriptions of
  approximately 600 of these wildflowers. Written by a wildflower expert
  for the casual wildflower observer, Wildflowers of the Midwest is
  organized by color for easy access out on the trail and includes
  information on blooming season and range as well as a glossary of terms
  and a reference section"— Provided by publisher.
Identifiers: LCCN 2020030823 (print) | LCCN 2020030824 (ebook) | ISBN
  9781493046249 (paperback) | ISBN 9781493046256 (epub)
Subjects: LCSH: Wild flowers—Middle West—Guidebooks. | Middle
  West—Guidebooks.
Classification: LCC QK128 .K87 2020 (print) | LCC QK128 (ebook) | DDC
  582.130977—dc23
LC record available at https://lccn.loc.gov/2020030823
LC ebook record available at https://lccn.loc.gov/2020030824

∞™ The paper used in this publication meets the minimum requirements of American National Standard for Information Sciences—Permanence of Paper for Printed Library Materials, ANSI/NISO Z39.48-1992.

THIS BOOK IS DEDICATED TO WILDFLOWER
ENTHUSIASTS, AND TO THE LAND MANAGERS,
AGENCIES, AND ORGANIZATIONS THAT ALL WORK
TO PROTECT AND MANAGE NATURAL COMMUNITIES
WHERE WILDFLOWERS LIVE, AND TO THE
NATURALISTS THAT INTERPRET THEIR WONDERS.

CONTENTS

THE MIDWEST

Area covered in guide

NORTH DAKOTA

MINNESOTA

SOUTH DAKOTA

WISCONSIN

MICHIGAN

NEW YORK

IOWA

NEBRASKA

PENNSYLVANIA

ILLINOIS

INDIANA

OHIO

WEST VIRGINIA

KANSAS

MISSOURI

KENTUCKY

VIRGINIA

NORTH CAROLINA

TENNESSEE

OKLAHOMA

ARKANSAS

SOUTH CAROLINA

MISSISSIPPI

ALABAMA

GEORGIA

LOUISIANA

TEXAS

FLORIDA

INTRODUCTION

The 447,128 square miles in the north-central part of the United States, known as the Midwest, contains a wide diversity of habitats or natural communities and an incredible array of wildflowers. With blooming beginning as early as late February in the southern part, with the diminutive but interesting harbinger of spring, to the asters in October, there is always something to see, learn about, and appreciate!

Because of the great expanse in the Midwest, particularly going from south to north, there is also a significant difference in the growing season, which greatly influences what is flowering. In the south, the growing season starts a month earlier in the spring and ends a month later in the fall. There is a point, however, when the lengths of the seasons overlap. It is most noticeable with wildflowers that can be found to grow across the region. Around the end of July, those wildflowers are in flower at the same time in the Minneapolis area as they are in the St. Louis area. Beyond that period, the growing season accelerates in the northern part, and is most noticeable in prairies, where the peak of the russet to gold color of the prairie grasses occurs around Labor Day, while the peak is not experienced in the southern part until a month later, in October.

The Midwest is a region of geographic contrasts, from unbroken forests and remnant prairies to crop fields and pastures; from broad, slow-moving rivers to swift, mountain-like streams; from the nearly level plateaus and river valleys to dramatically rugged terrain; and from the sloughs, swamps, and bogs to some of the driest forests in eastern North America.

These habitats or natural communities are based on what types of geology, soils, topography, and local climate are found in a particular region. Many plants have adapted to growing in specific types of soils derived from limestone, dolomite, chert, shale, sandstone, or igneous rock. By learning to recognize plants with the aid of this book, one can get a general understanding of what types of habitats or natural communities are found in the Midwest region. Because there are well over 100 recognized natural communities, it is beyond the scope of this book to describe each one. They can, however, be placed into general categories, which are described in the following pages.

Midwest Natural Communities

Upland forests across the Midwest region vary greatly as to composition, density, diversity, and location. These natural communities or habitats occur on well-drained soils, sometimes rocky, on ridges, slopes, valleys, and plains. Canopy cover is usually more than 50 percent, and plants, especially wildflowers, have adapted over time to live in conditions where light is reduced. These shade-tolerant

Upland Forest

plants found on the forest floor offer a diverse array of sizes, colors, and shapes that appear throughout the growing season. Threats to forest natural communities include conversion, degradation, exotic species, and introduced diseases.

Bottomland forests are primarily found in lowland floodplains along large rivers and lakes. The landscape is relatively flat, but there are some subtle changes in the form of terraces and depressions that increase the diversity of trees, shrubs, vines, and herbaceous plants found in bottomland forests. Wildflowers are fewer in number and variety compared to upland forests due primarily

Bottomland Forest

to increased canopy cover and occasional flooding, but they are well adapted to such conditions. Threats to bottomland forests include conversion to agriculture and alterations in water levels.

Savannas occur in a transition zone between prairies and forests where fire plays a critical role. A higher frequency and intensity of fires tends to favor the prairie, while the opposite allows trees to expand and eventually succeed to forest. Savannas occur on loamy or sandy soils and, in the northern part of the Midwest region, include bur oak and black oak trees, while post oak and black oak trees dominate in the southern region. The canopy cover is usually less than 50 percent, which provides enough sunlight for prairie grasses and wildflowers to flourish. Few remaining savannas exist today due to fire suppression, logging, and grazing.

Savanna

Upland prairies can generally be divided into dry and mesic (moist) prairies.

Dry prairies occur in a wide range of well-drained substrates and are found on broad hills, steep hills, bluffs, slopes, and plains. Soils in dry prairies can be moderately deep to shallow, and vary from glacial till, silt loam, sand, clay, chert, or gravel. Both the topography

Dry Prairie

and soil greatly influence the types of vegetation and animals that are found living on dry prairies. Some dry prairies contain over 250 species of wildflowers and provide outstanding displays throughout the growing season.

Mesic prairies occupy moderately well-drained sites. They are found on broad, level hills, plains, and lower, gentle slopes. Relatively high soil-moisture content and deep soils composed of silt and clay loams allow for lush growing conditions and a wide diversity and density of wildflowers. Like dry prairies, mesic prairies are rich in wildflower displays throughout the season, with some containing more than 300 species of wildflowers.

Dry and mesic prairies have greatly declined throughout their range due to agricultural practices, invasion by exotic species, cattle grazing, woody encroachment, and fire suppression.

Bottomland prairies or wet prairies occur on floodplains of rivers and sometimes in small depressions of upland prairies. The soils are poorly drained and become saturated with standing water during the spring and winter or after heavy rains. Perennial grasses, often up to 7 feet tall by midsummer, dominate the prairie, along with a mixture of

Bottomland Prairie

prairie wildflowers and sedges. Agricultural practices, wetland drainage, channelization, and woody encroachment have drastically reduced the occurrence of bottomland prairies across their range.

Glades generally occur on south- and southwest-facing slopes. Their soils are thin, with bedrock at or near the surface, and they are usually surrounded by woodlands. Some glades have developed on limestone or dolomite bedrock, which produce alkaline soils. Other

Glade

glades can be found on chert, sandstone, shale, or igneous rock, where the soils are more acidic. Certain plants have adapted to growing in the harsh, desert-like environment. Glades contain a wide variety of interesting and showy wildflowers that bloom primarily from spring to midsummer. Fire plays an important role in keeping the glades open, although today, prescribed or controlled fire—not wildfire—is needed to keep woody plants (especially eastern red cedar) from overgrowing glades.

Wetlands is a general term that describes relatively poorly drained sites that include edges of ponds, lakes, and springs; marshes, swamps, bogs, fens, and seeps; and depressions in prairies and bottomland forests. The soil is at least saturated and sometimes covered with water for long periods of time. A wide variety of wildflowers are found,

Wetland

with some specializing in certain types of wetland natural communities. While some of the more commonly encountered wildflowers found in wetlands are represented in this book, it is by no means an all-inclusive list.

Wetlands have declined extensively over the past 200 years due to conversion to agriculture land, water impoundments, urbanization, channelization, sedimentation, and the spread of exotic species.

Plant Identification

Sometimes recognizing wildflowers by their color and shape alone is not enough. There may be more-subtle differences that distinguish one plant from another, so some knowledge of basic plant parts and terms is helpful. In this wildflower guide, technical terms are kept to a minimum; however, a list of terms used is included in the glossary in the back of this book.

Many plants are **perennial**, which means they can live from a few years to well over 100 years. Perennial plants can be divided into **woody** plants, such as trees and shrubs, and **herbaceous** plants, which die back to the underground roots or stems by winter. The perennial wildflowers in this book are the herbaceous type, except for New Jersey tea, leadplant, and roses, which are all woody (but could be taken for herbaceous upon first glance). **Biennials** have a two-year life cycle. The plant, in its first year, usually produces a basal set of leaves. During the second year, the plant sends up a stalk that produces flowers and fruits and then dies; its seed then produces future plants. **Annuals** complete their life cycle in one growing season. Some annuals produce seeds that germinate in the spring, whereas some species, called **winter annuals**, germinate in the autumn, overwinter as small leafy rosettes, and continue their growth in the spring. Having a head start, they are usually some of the first plants to flower in the spring.

Sometimes it is difficult to determine which plants are perennial. These usually have well-developed underground roots in the forms of bulbs or tuberous roots, often with next year's growing buds visible. Annual plants typically have a small system of fibrous roots. All of the wildflowers in this book are perennial unless otherwise noted.

Leaves are important in identifying wildflowers. A variety of technical terms is used to describe leaf shapes, but simple terms are used in this book. Features to note about leaves include: Are the leaves **opposite** each other (figure 1), or **alternate** along the stem (figure 2), or **whorled** at a particular point on the stem (figure 3). Are the leaves

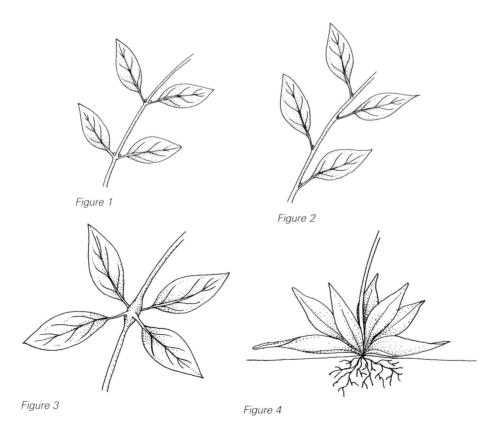

Figure 1

Figure 2

Figure 3

Figure 4

pointed at the tip, or blunt? Are the leaf bases tapering, heart-shaped, rounded, or clasping the stem? Is the leaf texture thick, leathery, or thin? Are the leaf margins smooth, toothed, lobed, or wavy? Do the leaves have stalks attaching them to the stem, or are they stalkless? Are there leafy **wings**, which are thin strips of tissue, attached edgewise along the stalk or stem? Note also that many plants produce **basal** leaves that form rosettes at the base of the plant (figure 4). These leaves are often larger than the leaves along the stem.

Leaves are characterized as either simple or compound. A **simple** leaf has a blade that is usually in one piece and may or may not be attached to a leaf stalk (figure 5). A **compound** leaf has a blade that is attached to a leaf stalk and is divided into leaflets that are either opposite each other or spreading like the fingers of a hand (figures 6–7).

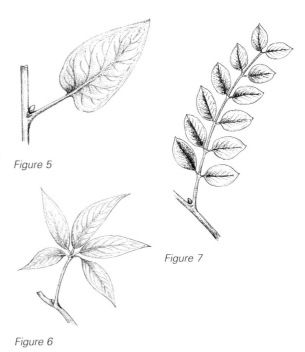

Figure 5

Figure 7

Figure 6

Sometimes where the leaf stalk attaches to the stem, there is a pair of appendages called **stipules**. These leaf-like structures may be large, or tiny and scale-like, and they may fall off soon after the leaf opens.

Bracts are another kind of leaf-like structure, and they are often associated with and usually found just below the flowers. Some are miniature versions of the leaves, whereas others may be colored and resemble the petals of a flower.

Becoming familiar with flower parts is important in the identification of plants. The characteristic of flower color is less reliable than the actual floral structures, because one species of wildflower may have flowers in two or more different colors, and the colors of flowers sometimes change with age. A diagram of a generalized flower is given in figure 8. The variation and number of lower parts are key characters for the identification of most plants. Flowers generally have an outer series of flower parts, called **sepals**, that surrounds the base of the flower. The sepals together are called the **calyx**.

Inside the calyx of most flowers is a series of usually showy parts called **petals**. Petals also vary in size, shape, and color, and may be separate or fused. The petals together, whether separate or fused, form the **corolla**. Depending on the kind of plant, there may be no petals, with only sepals present, or the petals and sepals may look exactly alike.

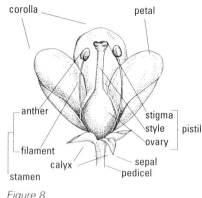

Figure 8

Within the corolla are the **stamens**, which are the pollen-producing structures. The stamens have long, thread-like stalks called **filaments**, each of which support a club-like or elongated structure—the **anther**—which holds the pollen. Stamens vary in number from 1 to over 100 per flower, depending on the species.

Also within the corolla is the seed-producing part of the flower—the **pistil**—which normally consists of the stigma, style, and ovary. The **stigma** receives the pollen; it is supported by a column called the **style**. Below the style, the **ovary**, which is usually swollen, contains the developing seed after it is fertilized. In some plants the style may be absent. Whereas most plants have both male (stamen) and female (pistil) parts in the same flower, some species have separate male and female flowers on the same plant, while others may have male and female flowers on separate plants.

Two families of plants that occur quite often in the Midwest deserve special attention: the bean family (Fabaceae) and the aster family (Asteraceae). The bean family has five modified petals, shown in figure 9.

The **banner** is erect, spreading, and usually the largest of the five. The two side petals, or **wings**, closely surround the **keel**, which are the two fused lowest petals.

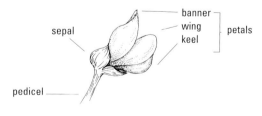

Figure 9

Members of the aster family (Asteraceae) have **flower heads** that look like single flowers but are actually composed of a cluster of a few to several hundred tiny flowers. This head of flowers is

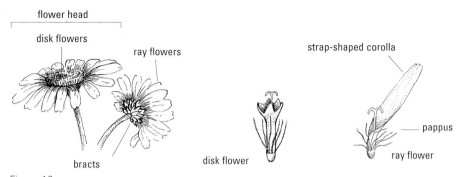

Figure 10

usually surrounded at the base by a series of **bracts**; these bracts are usually tightly clus-tered and overlap each other in rows. The calyx for each tiny flower is absent or reduced to bristles, scales, or hairs. In general, each flower head can produce two kinds of flower: **ray flowers** and **disk flowers**. A typical aster family flower head is illustrated in figure 10. Each outer ray flower has a single colorful petal that is strap-like. The central disk flower has a small, tubular corolla, usually with five lobes on the end. Depending on the species, a flower head may have all ray flowers, all disk flowers, or a combination of both.

HOW TO USE THIS GUIDE

Within the large and varied landscape of the Midwest region is a great diversity of plant life, including well over 2,000 species of native plants. Within this group, a lesser number are considered wildflowers, a term that lacks a precise definition. It is generally under-stood, however, that certain plants have flowers that are eye-catching because of their color, shape, and/or size. In this book 625 wildflowers are represented. These include wildflowers that are more commonly encountered in the Midwest region, as well as a few uncommon types that are particularly showy and characteristic of an area. Also, a few rare or uncommon plants are represented that are of conservation concern, to help bring aware-ness to their situation.

When a closely related species might be encountered, it is briefly described in the Comments section, which adds another 185 species to this guide. Also, a selection of more prevalent exotic or weedy plants is included in the Weeds section. Although their flowers can be showy, it is important to distinguish them from the native flora so one can gain a better understanding of native plants and the habitats in which they are found.

For ease and speed in identifying plants, wildflowers with similar color are grouped together. This is not a perfect method, however, because some wildflowers vary in color shades, especially where lighter pinks and blues sometimes grade into white. When a plant has flowers with two colors, the most noticeable color is the one determining its place-ment in this book. Within each color group, plants are arranged by their family and then by genus, all in alphabetical order, except for a few, mostly asters and goldenrods, where some have been reclassified and placed in a new or different genus. In those cases, the plants are moved out of alphabetical order in the chapter so they can be placed with former related species in the older genus. This results in fewer pages to flip through and a faster identification.

Each photograph is accompanied by text, beginning with the plant's **common name**. Often each wildflower has several common names, so an attempt was made to select the name most widely used in a majority of the Midwest region. Because of the general confu-sion surrounding multiple common names, the scientific name is also presented. These names, rendered in Latin and Greek, are more reliable and universally accepted. The sci-entific name consists of two words that appear in italics. The first word, the **genus**, is the name of a group of plants with similar general characteristics, such as sunflowers, which are in the genus *Helianthus*. Note the first letter of the genus name is always a capital let-ter. The second part of the scientific name is the **specific epithet**, or species name, which identifies the particular species of a plant, such as the species *mollis*. Note that the first letter of the species name is always a lowercase letter. So the correct presentation would be *Helianthus mollis*. The specific epithet may honor a person who may have first found the plant; it could refer to a geographic location; or it could describe some characteristic of the plant.

In a few instances, a plant has a scientific name with a third part, preceded by **vari-ety**, which is typically listed with the abbreviation **var.** In either case, italics are not used. The variety is added when a set of plants differs slightly but consistently from other plants of the same species; these plants often have distinct ranges. The scientific names used in this book are from the most recently published references for these plants.

Next, the **family** name is listed. For example, the milkweed family has the scientific name of Asclepiadaceae. (Family names always end with the suffix *–aceae*.) Families are grouped according to similarities in their structure and biology. As one becomes more familiar with plants, this grouping by family characteristics becomes more obvious.

Each plant has a brief **Description** section that provides information on size and shape of the plant and important characteristics of leaves, flowers, and sometimes fruits. It is not intended to describe a plant completely, but rather to provide those features that readily distinguish it from other plants without getting very technical. Sometimes identifica-tion, especially when examining flower parts and hairs, can be aided by the use of a mag-nifying glass or hand lens, preferably with a magnification power of 10.

The **Habitat/Range** section provides information on the relative abundance of plants, using such terms as *common*, *locally frequent*, *uncommon*, or *rare*. This gives the reader a general perspective on the plant's status in the Midwest region. Many of the plants selected for this book have a wide range of distribution. A few, however, are found only in a part of the region, especially those that may be on the edge of their range and are found more commonly elsewhere, such as in the Great Plains region.

Finally, the **Comments** section provides an opportunity to describe closely related species and mention alternative common names, as well as scientific names by which the plant may have once been known. In addition, to increase interest and appreciation of plants, historical information on how plants have been used for food or medicine is pre-sented. This information is based on written reports and should not be read as promotions for using wild plants as a food source or for medical or herbal prescriptions for self-healing.

Those interested in historical or modern herbalism, homeopathy, or flower essences can search on the Internet. As you probably know, there is an amazing amount of information out there.

This section includes flowers that are mostly white. Off-white flowers can grade into light colors of yellow, green, pink, and blue, so those sections should also be checked.

ANGELICA
Angelica atropurpurea
Parsley family (Apiaceae)

Description: Tall plants, up to 8', with hollow purple stems at maturity and large leaves. The leaves are up to 2' long and as wide, divided into 3–5 leaflets, each up to 4" long, 2" wide, toothed along the margins, and with surfaces generally smooth but sometimes with fine hairs on the underside. At the base of each leaf stalk, there is a large papery sheath that surrounds the stem. The flowers are in umbrella-like heads, 4–9" across, that are made up of 20–50 smaller, round flower clusters, each with 20–40 star-shaped, white to greenish-white flowers. Each flower is about ⅛" across with 5 tiny petals and 5 longer petals.

Bloom Season: Summer

Habitat/Range: Occasional in low moist woods, edges of streams, wet meadows, and ditches; found through the Midwest region, but absent in the lower quarter.

Comments: Native Americans used leaf tea for stomachache, indigestion, fever, colds, flu, coughs, and rheumatism. Early American settlers boiled parts of the plant to make into candy and added it to cakes.

COW PARSNIP
Heracleum maximum
Parsley family (Apiaceae)

Description: A tall, stout, hairy-stemmed plant, up to 6', with large alternate, compound leaves with stalks that clasp the stem at their wide papery bases. Each palm-shaped leaf is up to 15" long and about as wide, with 3 or more leaflets, each with teeth along the margins. Flowers are in flat, umbrella-like heads up to 10" across, with 15–30 flower clusters in each head. Each flower is about ¼" across with 5 white petals that are often notched at the tips.

Bloom Season: Late spring–summer

Habitat/Range: Occasional in low, moist woods, thickets, stream banks, and partially shaded roadsides; found throughout the Midwest region.

Comments: Also known as *Heracleum lanatum*. Native Americans used the stalks as a food source, and root tea was used for colds, cramps, headache, sore throats, colds, coughs, and flu; it was also applied externally for sores, bruises, and swellings. The foliage is poisonous to livestock, and skin contact with the sap can cause blisters among some individuals when handled.

WOOD ANGELICA
Angelica venenosa
Parsley family (Apiaceae)

Description: This tall member of the parsley family is an unexpected find in the woods. The plant can grow to a height of 5' and has fine hairs on the upper portion of the purplish stem, giving it a gray cast. The leaves are on stalks up to 8" long and are divided into smaller leaflets, with the margins finely toothed. The flowers are in clusters from 2–6" across, with each cluster containing numerous, tiny, white to yellowish flowers.

Bloom Season: Late spring–early summer

Habitat/Range: Occasional in dry, rocky woodlands, prairie edges, low, moist woods along streams, and along some roadsides; found in the Midwest region from southern Missouri, southern Illinois, southern Indiana, and south and eastern Ohio, southward.

Comments: Wood angelica is considered poisonous when eaten and the sap can cause dermatitis.

WILD CHERVIL
Chaerophyllum procumbens
Parsley family (Apiaceae)

Description: A low-growing annual with stems, smooth, weak, spreading, and branched, up to 15" long. The leaves are so deeply cut that they appear fern-like. Numerous minute white flowers occur at the ends of stalks.

Bloom Season: Mid-spring–early summer

Habitat/Range: Common in rich or rocky woods, alluvial soils along streams and in valleys, glades, roadsides, and along railroads; found primarily in the Midwest from Iowa and Missouri east to Illinois, Indiana, and Ohio.

Comments: Wild chervil sometimes forms a nearly solid mat of fern-like leaves, sharing the forest floor with more-showy spring wildflowers. A similar plant, southern chervil (*Chaerophyllum tainturiari*), differs by having moderately to densely hairy stems; found in upland prairies, glades, forest openings, and disturbed sites; occurring in the southern half of the Midwest region, but absent in Ohio.

3

WATER HEMLOCK

Cicuta maculata
Parsley family (Apiaceae)

Description: A biennial, hairless plant, up to 6' tall, with several branches holding umbrella-shaped clusters of tiny white flowers. The stem is streaked or spotted with purple and is hollow toward the base. The leaves are alternate on the stem, up to 12" long, and divided into numerous, sharply toothed leaflets. The umbrella-shaped flower heads contain tiny, 5-petaled, white flowers, each less than ⅛" wide.

Bloom Season: Mid-spring–fall

Habitat/Range: Common in wet sites along edges of streams and ponds, in roadside ditches, in marshes, and in wet depressions in prairies; found throughout the Midwest region.

Comments: This plant is highly poisonous. Members of many Native American tribes used the root to commit suicide. Children have been poisoned by using the hollow stems as peashooters. A walnut-sized piece of the root is enough to kill a cow.

HONEWORT

Cryptotaenia canadensis
Parsley family (Apiaceae)

Description: A smooth plant, 1–3' tall, that branches toward the top. The leaves are alternate, on long stalks, with a sheath at the base and compound in groups of 3. Each leaflet is up to 4" long, 2" wide, with pointed tips, bases that abruptly narrow, and densely toothed margins. The stalked flowers are in clusters, 2–3" across, divided into smaller clusters, each with 3–10 white flowers that are less than ⅛" across. There are 5 white petals that often curve inward toward the tips, and 5 tiny stamens.

Bloom Season: Early summer–midsummer

Habitat/Range: Common in moist woods, bottom-land forests, at the base of bluffs, and along banks of streams; found throughout the Midwest region.

Comments: The common name, honewort, is derived from *wort*, which means "plant," and *hone*, a swelling in the cheek, which honewort plants purportedly will cure. Young stems and leaves have been added fresh to salads (like parsley) as a flavoring, or may be boiled as greens.

HARBINGER OF SPRING
Erigenia bulbosa
Parsley family (Apiaceae)

Description: A small, delicate plant with flowering stems, up to 6" tall. The fern-like leaves are divided into numerous small lobes and may not appear until after flowering has started. The flowers are in clusters at the end of stalks with white petals and dark reddish anthers, giving it another common name, "pepper and salt."

Bloom Season: Late winter–mid-spring

Habitat/Range: Common in moist woods near the bases of slopes and in alluvial soils in wooded valleys and along streams; found through the Midwest region, but absent in Minnesota and Iowa, and rare in Wisconsin.

Comments: True to its name, this is the first wildflower to bloom in spring. It may often be overlooked because of its small stature and partial concealment by fallen leaves.

RATTLESNAKE MASTER
Eryngium yuccifolium
Parsley family (Apiaceae)

Description: This stout-stemmed, hairless plant can grow to a height of 5', with bluish-green leaves at the base that resemble a yucca. The leaves are up to 2' long, 1½" wide, with pointed tips, and small, soft, needle-like bristles scattered along the margin. The flowers, each with 5 tiny, white petals, are tightly packed in round balls up to 1" across. Whitish bracts stick out sharply from the flowers, which gives the flower head a rough, prickly feel and appearance.

Bloom Season: Summer

Habitat/Range: Occasional in prairies and savannas; found throughout the Midwest region, but uncommon to rare in Minnesota, Wisconsin, Michigan, and Ohio.

Comments: The Meskwaki used the leaves and fruit in their rattlesnake medicine song and dance. They used the root for treating bladder problems and poisons, including rattlesnake bites. They also used the roots mashed in cold water to make a drink for relieving muscular pains.

SWEET CICELY
Osmorhiza claytonii
Parsley family (Apiaceae)

Description: An upright, branching plant, up to 3' tall, with white hairs along the stem. The large, hairy leaves—as much as 1' across on lower parts of the plant—are divided into 3 parts, and then either further subdivided or deeply toothed to appear somewhat fern-like. The tiny, white flowers are carried in loose, umbrella-shaped sprays. The 5 petals are curved at the tip. The 5 stamens may extend just beyond the petals, but the styles are shorter than the petals.

Bloom Season: Mid-spring–early summer

Habitat/Range: Common in rich woods and on lower slopes of hills, ravines, and in valleys; found throughout the Midwest region.

Comments: The carrot-like root contains anise oil and has been used as a flavoring for cookies, cakes, and candies. The Miami-Illinois Indians used sweet cicely to treat eye ailments. The Ojibwa used a root extract for treating sore throats. Settlers used the root to relieve colic, gas, and indigestion and to improve the appetite. Another species, anise root (*Osmorhiza longistylis*), differs by having stems that are mostly hairless, leaves, less deeply divided, and the style, slightly longer than the petals. Its roots have been reported to be higher in anise oil content, and it's also found throughout the Midwest region in similar habitat as sweet cicely.

COWBANE
Oxypolis rigidior
Parsley family (Apiaceae)

Description: A slender, hairless plant, up to 5' tall, with alternate leaves along the stem that are divided into 5–9 narrow leaflets. These leaflets are smooth and up to 5" long and 1½" wide on the lower part of the stem, and smaller toward the top. The leaflets can be smooth or irregularly toothed along the margins. The flowers are in flat, dome-shaped clusters, up to 6" wide. Each tiny white flower has 5 petals.

Bloom Season: Mid- to late summer

Habitat/Range: Common in marshes, wet prairies, depressions in mesic prairies, fens, and in wet soils along streams and spring branches; found through the Midwest region, but absent in the northern third.

Comments: The roots and leaves of cowbane are poisonous and have been known to poison cattle. Skin contact with the plant can cause dermatitis among some individuals. Cowbane has smooth to irregularly toothed leaflets, while water parsnip has finely and regularly toothed leaflets.

WATER PARSNIP
Sium suave
Parsley family (Apiaceae)

Description: A tall plant, up to 6', with a sturdy, smooth stem that is hollow toward the base. The alternate leaves are divided into 7–17 leaflets, each up to 4" long. The leaflets are toothed along the margin and with a pointed tip. Each leaf has a wide stipule sheathing the base of the leaf stalk. There are several umbrella-shaped flower clusters, up to 3" across, at the top of the stems. Each small flower is about ⅛" across, with 5 white petals.

Bloom Season: Summer

Habitat/Range: Shallow water of marshes, ponds, wet ditches, along streams and spring branches, shallow water in wet prairies, and wet depressions in upland prairies; found throughout the Midwest region.

Comments: Native Americans boiled the root and leaves for food. Because of its similarity to cowbane and poison hemlock, water parsnip should be avoided as a food plant.

INDIAN HEMP
Apocynum cannabinum
Dogbane family (Apocynaceae)

Description: The shrub-like plants are up to 4' tall, often with reddish stems, milky sap, and upright leaves with white to red veins. The leaves are opposite, widest at the middle, pointed at the tip, with smooth margins, and up to 6" long and 3" wide. The flower clusters are usually overtopped by the side branches. The flowers are small, less than ¼" wide, and bell-shaped with 5 tiny, white lobes. The seed pods are in pairs, slender, long-pointed at the tip, and up to 6" long, with seeds that have silky hairs attached at one end.

Bloom Season: Late spring–midsummer

Habitat/Range: Common in prairies, woods, old fields, pastures, and along roadsides; found throughout the Midwest region.

Comments: Also known as *Apocynum sibiricum.* Indian hemp fibers have been found in fabric from the early Archaic period, from 3,000 to 4,000 years ago. The fibers were also used for rope and nets. Root tea was used to treat colds, dropsy (an abnormal accumulation of blood in the body; edema), fever, headache, and sore throat.

WILD SARSAPARILLA
Aralia nudicaulis
Ginseng family (Araliaceae)

Description: An umbrella-like plant that spreads by creeping underground stems, with compound leaves on long, bare stalks, up to 2' tall. The leaves are divided into leaflets, with each leaflet up to 6" long, oval-shaped, toothed along the margins, and with pointed tips. Below the leaves, 2–3 flower clusters on long stalks contain numerous small, greenish-white flowers. Each flower is about ⅛" across, with 5 petals that curve back and downward. The fruits are small, dark purple berries.

Bloom Season: Late spring–early summer

Habitat/Range: Occasional in moist woods, and wooded slopes; found in the northern half of the Midwest region.

Comments: The spicy, aromatic roots have been used to make tea and root beer. Native Americans used root tea as a beverage, a "blood-purifier," and to treat stomachaches and coughs. Wild sarsaparilla was widely used in "tonic" and "blood-purifier" patented medicines of the late 19th century.

SPIKENARD
Aralia racemosa
Ginseng family (Araliaceae)

Description: A bushy-looking plant, up to 5' tall and nearly as wide, with broad, spreading leaves divided into large leaflets, each up to 6" long. Flowers are arranged in branched clusters. Each flower is about ⅛" wide, with 5 greenish-white petals and 5 protruding stamens; the fruit grows in clusters of dark purple berries, each about ⅛" across.

Bloom Season: Late spring–midsummer

Habitat/Range: Occasional in moist woods and wooded ravines; found throughout the Midwest region.

Comments: Spikenard can send rhizomes long distances, up to 50', to initiate new plants. Native Americans used the spicy-aromatic root to improve the flavor of other medicines. The unusual name "spikenard" comes from the Latin *spica*, a spike, and *nardus*, an aromatic root.

GINSENG
Panax quinquefolius
Ginseng family (Araliaceae)

Description: Plants up to 1½' tall, with a whorl of 3 to 4 leaves, each divided into 5 stalked, toothed leaflets. A leafless stem arises from the ground supporting a cluster of small, greenish-white flowers, each less than ⅛" across. Bright red berries develop in late summer.

Bloom Season: Early summer–midsummer

Habitat/Range: Occasional to uncommon in moist woods; found throughout the Midwest region, but rare in both the upper half and in Indiana.

Comments: The roots of ginseng have long been known to have medicinal properties that aid in mental efficiency and physical performance. However, large doses are said to raise blood pressure. Overcollecting of the roots has decreased populations over many areas, which has led to harvest regulations and quotas nationwide. A similar species, dwarf ginseng (*Panax trifolius*), is a smaller plant, less than 7" tall, with stalkless leaflets, white flowers ⅛" across, and yellow berries; it's found in the northern half of the Midwest region.

TALL GREEN MILKWEED
Asclepias hirtella
Milkweed family (Asclepiadaceae)

Description: Stout-stemmed plants, up to 3' tall, with white, milky sap. The leaves are mostly alternate, hairy, and narrow, up to 6" long and 1" wide, with pointed tips. Several flower clusters arise on stalks up to 1½" long from the upper leaf axils. Each flower is up to ½" long and greenish-white, with 5 petals bent backwards that are sometimes white-edged or purple-tipped, and 5 greenish-white structures called "hoods." The seed pods are smooth, slender, and up to 4" long and 1" thick.

Bloom Season: Late spring–summer

Habitat/Range: Occasional in upland prairies and glades; found through the Midwest region, but rare to absent in the northern third.

Comments: Although not as showy as some of the other milkweeds, this tall, narrow-leaved milkweed casts a stately appearance. The flowers are pollinated mostly by long-tongued bees and wasps.

MEAD'S MILKWEED
Asclepias meadii
Milkweed family (Asclepiadaceae)

Description: Short, slender plants usually with a single stem, less than 2' tall, and white, milky sap. The leaves are opposite along the stem, up to 3" long and up to 1½" wide, broadest at the base, tapering to a pointed tip. The leaves are stalkless, smooth, sometimes with wavy margins. There is one drooping flower cluster at the tip of the stem with up to 23 greenish-white flowers, each less than ½" long. The flowers have 5 reflexed petals and 5 cup-like hoods. The seed pods are slender, up to 4" long and ½" thick.

Bloom Season: Late spring–early summer

Habitat/Range: Rare and local in dry and mesic prairies; found in the Midwest region in Iowa, Illinois, and Missouri, and also in eastern Kansas.

Comments: Mead's milkweed is a very rare prairie plant and is federally listed as a threatened species due to habitat destruction throughout its former range. Unfortunately, even in protected sites, this milkweed continues to decline.

WHORLED MILKWEED
Asclepias quadrifolia
Milkweed family (Asclepiadaceae)

Description: A slender, single-stemmed plant, with whorled leaves and up to 18" tall. The long-pointed, smooth leaves are usually in 1 or 2 whorls of 4, plus 1 or 2 pairs along the upper stem. The flowers are in 1–4 clusters at the end of the stem, often causing it to bend. Each flower is about ¼" across on slender stalks up to 1" long, causing them to turn downward. The 5 petals are white to pink and turned back, displaying the 5 cup-like hoods characteristic of milkweeds. The seed pods are smooth, slender, and up to 5" long.

Bloom Season: Mid- to late spring

Habitat/Range: Common in dry or rocky, open woods; found throughout the southern half of the Midwest region.

Comments: This is the first milkweed to bloom in the spring. Like that of most milkweeds, the sap is milky.

POKE MILKWEED
Asclepias exaltata
Milkweed family (Asclepiadaceae)

Description: Plants with light green to purplish stems, 3–5' tall, with milky sap and flowers in drooping clusters. The leaves are opposite, smooth, up to 6" long and 3" wide, oval- to egg-shaped, tapering at both ends, and on stalks ¼–1" long. The white to pinkish flowers are about ½" long and ⅜" wide, with 5 petals that bend back away from the 5 hoods. The pods are thin, 4–6" long, ¾" wide, and covered in downy hairs.

Bloom Season: Summer

Habitat/Range: Occasional to uncommon in mesic upland forests and forest edges; found throughout the Midwest region, but absent in Missouri.

Comments: The common name refers to the similarity of its leaves to those of pokeweed (*Phytolacca americana*) (see page 85).

OVAL-LEAF MILKWEED
Asclepias ovalifolia
Milkweed family (Asclepiadaceae)

Description: A shorter milkweed, 8–20" tall, with milky sap, oval-shaped leaves, and covered in fine downy hairs. The leaves are opposite, 2–3" long and ½–1" wide, slightly broader at the base, narrowing at the tip, and with a leaf stalk about ¼" long. The flowers are in 1–3 clusters, each about 1½–2" across that emerge from leaf axils near the top of the stem. Each flower is about ½" long and ¼" wide, with 5 white petals that often have a pinkish tone toward the tip, and 5 white hoods. The pods are 2–3" long and are upright at maturity.

Bloom Season: Early summer–midsummer

Habitat/Range: Occasional in sandy soils of prairies, savannas, and open woods; found in the northwest quarter of the Midwest region.

Comments: The genus name, *Asclepias*, refers to the Greek god of medicine, Askepios, while the species name, *ovalifolia*, refers to the oval-shaped leaves. A similar-looking species, woolly milkweed (*Asclepias lanuginosa*), differs by having spreading woolly hairs on both leaf surfaces and along the stem, and one single flower cluster arising at the top of the stem. A very rare milkweed, it occurs on dry, rocky prairies and open woods; found in the northern quarter of the Midwest region.

NARROW-LEAVED MILKWEED

Asclepias stenophylla
Milkweed family (Asclepiadaceae)

Description: A graceful, slender-stemmed plant, up to 3' tall, with milky sap and very long, narrow leaves. The leaves are mostly opposite, up to 8" long, and less than ½" wide. The flowers are in rounded clusters that arise from the leaf axils along the upper part of the plant. Each cluster has up to 25 white flowers, each less than ½" long, with 5 spreading petals surrounding 5 hoods. The seed pods are smooth, up to 5" long, and less than ½" wide.

Bloom Season: Early summer–midsummer

Habitat/Range: Occasional in dry prairies and glades; found in the southwestern part of the Midwest region and westward.

Comments: The Lakota fed the root to their children when they refused to eat in order to help them regain their appetite.

VARIEGATED MILKWEED

Asclepias variegata
Milkweed family (Asclepiadaceae)

Description: This attractive, large-flowering milkweed has a stout purple stem, up to 3' tall. The leaves are 3–6" long and 1–3" wide, opposite on the stem, but some may be whorled. The leaf base tapers to a stalk, and the leaf margins are smooth but often wavy. The large vein running the length of the leaf is yellow and sometimes red. The flowers are in clusters of 1–4. Each flower is about ⅜" across, with 5 white petals that are turned back, revealing purple markings at their base. The 5 cup-like hoods in the center are characteristic of milkweeds. The sap is milky.

Bloom Season: Late spring–midsummer

Habitat/Range: Occasional in dry or rocky woods, ravine bottoms, at the edges of woods, and along roadsides; found in the southern quarter of the Midwest region, and southward.

Comments: Variegated milkweed has bright white flowers with purple centers, which makes this a particularly showy milkweed.

WHORLED MILKWEED
Asclepias verticillata
Milkweed family (Asclepiadaceae)

Description: Slender plants, sparingly branched, up to 2½' tall, with milky sap. The soft, thread-like leaves, up to 3" long and less than ⅛" wide, are mostly in whorls along the stem. The flowers are arranged in clusters of 2–14, with less than 20 flowers in each cluster. There are 5 reflexed, greenish-white petals and 5 white hoods. The seed pods are smooth, narrow, and about 3" long.

Bloom Season: Mid-spring–late summer

Habitat/Range: Common in dry prairies, savannas, old fields, pastures, and along roadsides; found throughout the Midwest region.

Comments: A tea from the whole plant was given to Lakota mothers who were unable to produce milk. The theory behind this practice is similar to the medieval concept of the "doctrine of signa-tures"—the belief that certain characteristics of a plant signify its uses. In this case, the milky sap was thought to signify that the milkweed would promote the production of milk. This milkweed is poisonous to cattle but is rarely taken in enough quantity to cause problems.

GREEN MILKWEED
Asclepias viridiflora
Milkweed family (Asclepiadaceae)

Description: Plants with unbranched, hairy stems, up to 2' tall, with milky sap and opposite leaves. The leaves are thick, and vary from narrow to broadly oval, up to 5" long and 2½" wide, with wavy margins. There are from 1 to several dense flower clusters arising from the leaf axils. Each greenish-white flower is about ½" long, with 5 pet-als bent backward and 5 erect hoods. The smooth, narrow seed pods are up to 6" long and 1" wide.

Bloom Season: Late spring–midsummer

Habitat/Range: Occasional in dry or sandy prairies, savannas, glades, and at the edges of woods; found throughout the Midwest region.

Comments: The Lakota gave the pulverized roots of green milkweed to children with diarrhea. The Blackfeet chewed the root to relieve sore throat, and also applied the root to swellings and rashes. In the nonflowering vegetative state, stems of green milkweed can sometimes be mistaken for the very rare Mead's milkweed.

SPIDER MILKWEED
Asclepias viridis
Milkweed family (Asclepiadaceae)

Description: A large, somewhat sprawling plant, up to 2' tall, with thick stems and milky sap. The leaves are alternate, fleshy, up to 5" long and 2" wide, with wavy margins. The flowers appear in a large cluster, up to 5" across, at the top of the stem. Each flower has 5 whitish-green petals, ½–⅝" long, that spread upward, unlike other milkweeds, where the petals are reflexed. Inside the flower are 5 purple hoods arranged in a star-like fashion that together are taller than they are wide. The seed pods are relatively smooth, up to 6" long and 1" thick, with each seed tipped with a tuft of long, white hairs.

Bloom Season: Late spring–midsummer

Habitat/Range: Common in dry or rocky prairies, glades, and along roadsides; found in the southwest part of the Midwest region and southern Ohio, and also westward.

Comments: Spider milkweed has the largest flowers of the milkweeds found in the Midwest region. The common name is given for the presence of crab spiders hunting for insect prey around the flowers.

CLIMBING MILKWEED
Cynanchum leave
Milkweed family (Asclepiadaceae)

Description: A climbing vine, up to 15' long, with hairy, light green to reddish-green stems. The leaves are opposite, up to 6" long and 2½" wide, pointed at the tip, broadest toward the base, which is deeply heart-shaped. The leaf stalk is up to 3" long and often reddish-green. The flowers are in clusters emerging from axils of the middle to upper leaves. Each flower cluster is about ¾–1½" wide and attached to a stalk 1–3" long. The flowers are white to pinkish-white and about ¼" long, with 5 narrow lobes surrounding a crown-like center. The seed pods are smooth, up to 4" long and 1" wide, and turn from green to reddish-green to brown with age.

Bloom Season: Summer–fall

Habitat/Range: Common in bottomland forests, and banks of streams, ponds, and lakes; also crop fields, roadsides, gardens, and open, disturbed areas; found in the southern half of the Midwest region.

Comments: Also known as *Ampelamus albidus*. Another common name, honeyvine, refers to the flowers, which have a strong, honey-like fragrance. Climbing milkweed is sometimes planted as an ornamental and is recommended by beekeepers as an excellent honey source.

YARROW
Achillea millefolium
Aster family (Asteraceae)

Description: Single-stalked, strongly scented, hairy plants, up to 2' tall, with alternate fern-like leaves and flat-topped flower clusters. The lower leaves are up to 10" long on stalks; the upper leaves are smaller and without stalks. Numerous flower heads are arranged in a branching, flat-topped flower cluster. Each flower head is about ¼" across with 4–6 white ray flowers surrounding a central disk of up to 20 yellow disk flowers.

Bloom Season: Mid-spring–fall

Habitat/Range: Common in prairies, open woods, fields, pastures, disturbed sites, and along roadsides; considered a native of both Europe and North America, yarrow is found throughout the Midwest region.

Comments: Fossil records reveal yarrow pollen in Neanderthal burial caves. More recently, yarrow has been used in a wide variety of medicinal treatments by at least 58 Native American tribes as a stimulant, laxative, painkiller, diuretic, wound healer, antiseptic, and tonic, to name a few.

PEARLY EVERLASTING
Anaphalis margaritaceae
Aster family (Asteraceae)

Description: Plants that arise from creeping underground stems to a height of up to 3', but usually less. The stems and leaves are covered with white woolly hairs. The leaves are 3–5" long and up to ¾" wide, toothless, often with wavy or rolled edges, sharply pointed at the tip, and with no leaf stalks. The flowers are in a compact cluster at the top, each about ¼–⅜" wide, with separate male and female flowers, usually on different plants. The numerous tiny white petals surrounding the flower heads are bracts. There are no petal-like ray flowers, only yellow disk flowers.

Bloom Season: Midsummer–fall

Habitat/Range: Common in dry, sandy, or gravelly soils in open woods, old fields, pastures, and roadsides; found in the northern half of the Midwest region.

Comments: Pearly everlasting is a sweet-smelling plant, and as its name suggests, its flowers retain their shape and are used in dried flower arrangements. Native Americans used a tea made from the plant for colds, bronchial coughs, and throat infections. A poultice (moist, warm plant material applied to the skin) was used for rheumatism, burns, sores, bruises, and swellings. Leaves were smoked to treat throat and lung ailments.

SWEET EVERLASTING
Pseudognaphalium obtusifolium
Aster family (Asteraceae)

Description: An annual to biennial plant, up to 2½′ tall, with felt-like hairs on the stems and undersides of leaves that give it a whitish cast. The leaves are alternate, narrow, up to 4" long and ½" wide, green on the top, white below, and lacking teeth along the margins. Numerous small flower heads occur on branches near the top. Each flower head is about ¼" tall, with white, papery bracts surrounding a narrow tubular head of yellowish-white disk flowers. There are no petal-like ray flowers.

Bloom Season: Midsummer–fall

Habitat/Range: Common in prairies, degraded prairies, sandy soil, old fields, pastures, and roadsides; found throughout the Midwest region.

Comments: Dried plants have a maple or balsam fragrance. Pillows filled with dried flowers were used to quiet coughing. Plants laid in drawers and wardrobes kept away moths. Meskwaki burned sweet everlasting as a smudge to restore consciousness or to treat insanity. Other tribes used it for colds, fever, and other infirmities. When chewed, it increases saliva flow. A similar species, clammy cudweed (*Pseudognaphalium macounii*), differs by having broader, clasping leaves; common in woodland clearings, open sandy woods, fields, pastures, and other disturbed sites; found in the northern quarter of the Midwest region.

17

FIELD PUSSYTOES
Antennaria neglecta
Aster family (Asteraceae)

Description: A slender plant, spreading by underground runners to form large colonies. The densely hairy stems can eventually reach up to 8" when the fruit develops. The basal leaves are ½–2½" long and less than ¾" wide, with smooth edges, pointed tips, and narrowing bases. The lower surface is silvery white from dense matted hairs and with a single prominent vein along its length. Flower stalks are white-hairy, with small, alternate, hairy leaves. There are separate male and female flowers on separate plants. The female flowers are white, about ⅜" long, and look like shaving brushes. The male flowers are also white, somewhat smaller, and have brown stamens.

Bloom Season: Spring

Habitat/Range: Common in dry prairies, savannas, and open woods; found throughout the Midwest region.

Comments: The woolly, female flower heads account for the plant's common name. Early folk medicine sometimes prescribed a tea of pussy-toe leaves taken every day for two weeks after childbirth to keep the mother from getting sick. An extract from the plant was once used to treat stomach disorders, and the flowers have been used to make cough syrup.

PARLIN'S PUSSYTOES
Antennaria parlinii
Aster family (Asteraceae)

Description: A slender plant, spreading by underground runners to form large colonies. The densely hairy stems can eventually reach up to 12" when the fruit develops. The basal leaves are 1–3¾" long and up to 1¾" wide, with smooth edges and rounded tips. The lower surface is silvery white from dense matted hairs and the upper surface is gray-green and hairless to woolly hairy. There are 3–5 prominent veins on the lower surface. Flower stalks are white-hairy, with small, alternate, hairy leaves. There are separate male and female flowers on separate plants. The female flowers are white, about ½–¾" long, and look like shaving brushes with pink to yellowish tips. The male flowers are also white and somewhat smaller, with brown stamens.

Bloom Season: Spring

Habitat/Range: Fairly common in dry prairies, savannas, and open woods; found throughout the Midwest region.

Comments: A similar species, plantain-leaved pussytoes (*Antennaria plantaginifolia*), differs by usually having a woollier and gray-green upper leaf surface. The flowers are also smaller, with female and male flowers around ¼" long. They occur less frequently in prairies and savannas than Parlin's pussytoes, and prefer open woods. Plantain-leaved pussytoes is found in the western half of the Midwest region. The easiest identifiable field character that differentiates between field pussytoes and the other two species is that the former has 1 prominent vein on the leaf undersurface, while the latter two have 3–5 prominent veins. Past medicinal uses for both of these pussytoes are similar to field pussytoes.

PALE INDIAN PLANTAIN
Arnoglossum atriplicifolium
Aster family (Asteraceae)

Description: This plant has a smooth, whitish cast and widely spaced leaves, growing to a height of 4–6', but sometimes to 8'. The leaves are alternate on the stem and have a whitish coating on the underside. The lower leaves are long-stalked, large, 8" long and 6–8" wide, and broadly triangular, with shallow lobes and large teeth. Numerous flower heads form a somewhat flattened top, with the flower head in the center of the cluster opening first. Each flower head is less than ¼" wide, lacks petal-like ray flowers, and features 5 whitish, tubular disk flowers.

Bloom Season: Summer–early fall

Habitat/Range: Occasional in upland and rocky woodlands, prairies, and savannas; found through the Midwest region, but absent in the northern third.

Comments: The common name, Indian plantain, also refers to another species in this genus, *Arnoglossum plantagineum*, which has plantain-shaped leaves. "Pale" refers to the whitish cast of the plant. The leaves have been used as a poultice for cuts, bruises, and cancers, and to draw out blood or poisonous materials.

PRAIRIE INDIAN PLANTAIN
Arnoglossum plantagineum
Aster family (Asteraceae)

Description: This plant has large, thick, distinctive basal leaves and a flowering stalk, up to 5' tall but usually less. The single stem is smooth and angled and grooved along the surface. The basal leaves are large, up to 8" long and 4" wide, with smooth but sometimes shallow-toothed margins and distinct parallel veins along the leaf and long leaf stalks. The leaves along the stem are few, alternate, small, and lack teeth along the margins. The flower heads are numerous in open branches forming a flat-topped cluster. Each flower head is up to 1" tall, containing 5 white, tubular disk flowers. There are no petal-like ray flowers.

Bloom Season: Late spring–midsummer

Habitat/Range: Common to occasional in wet to mesic prairies, moist open areas along streams, and other wet areas; found throughout the Midwest region, but rare in the eastern and northern parts.

Comments: The name of the plant refers to the similarity of its leaves to that of a plantain. Native Americans applied mashed leaves to the skin to treat cancers, cuts, and bruises, and to draw out blood or poisonous substances.

GREAT INDIAN PLANTAIN

Arnoglossum reniforme
Aster family (Asteraceae)

Description: Plants with a stout central stem, 3–4' tall but sometimes up to 8'. The stem is hairless, angled, and grooved, often with longitudinal veins that are red. The leaves are alternate, with a thick succulent texture, up to 15" wide on the lower stem and with stalks up to 10" long. The upper leaves are smaller, up to 7" long and 4" wide, broadest toward the base, and broadly toothed to smooth along the margins. The leaf stems are up to 2" long. The flowers are in clusters up to 10" across, with each flower head about ½" long and less than ¼" wide, with 5 whitish disk flowers. There are no petal-like ray flowers.

Bloom Season: Summer

Habitat/Range: Uncommon in mesic upland forests, bottomland forests, bases of cliffs and prairies, and banks of rivers and streams; found in scattered locations across the Midwest region, but rare to absent in the northeast quarter.

Comments: The species name, *reniforme*, means "kidney-shaped," which refers to the shape of the leaves.

WHITE SAGE
Artemisia ludoviciana
Aster family (Asteraceae)

Description: Narrow, strongly aromatic when bruised, densely white-hairy plants, up to 3' tall, with branching occurring above the upper half of the stems. The leaves are very narrow, stalkless, pointed at the tips, and up to 4" long and ¾" wide. The leaves are smooth along the margins but occasionally may have teeth, or even lobes. The underside of the leaves is densely hairy, giving the plant a bright white appearance. The flowers are numerous and occur in small clusters along the upper parts of the stem. Each flower head is less than ⅛" across, tubular, and contains several disk flowers.

Bloom Season: Summer–fall

Habitat/Range: Common in dry to mesic upland prairies, sand prairies, hill prairies, pastures, old fields, and roadsides; found in the western half of the Midwest region; introduced eastward.

Comments: White sage has been used extensively by Native Americans for medicinal and ceremonial purposes. Its properties and powers were used to treat sore throat, coughs, stomach troubles, and several other ailments, and to drive away mosquitoes, evil spirits, and bad luck. A similar species, wormwood (*Artemisia campestris*), differs by being biennial, having smooth leaves, densely packed along the lower part of the stem, with leaves divided into toothless, linear lobes that are thread-like; occurs in sand prairies, sand savannas, and in sandy soils of fields and roadsides; found in the northern half of the Midwest region.

FALSE ASTER
Boltonia asteroides
Aster family (Asteraceae)

Description: A much-branched plant, smooth, up to 6' tall, with alternate leaves along the stem. The leaves are narrow, up to 6" long and ¾" wide, reduced in size upward along the stem. The flower heads are numerous, each about ¾" across, with about 60 white, petal-like ray flowers surrounding numerous yellow disk flowers.

Bloom Season: Midsummer–fall

Habitat/Range: Common in wet prairies, areas subject to flooding, stream banks, and marshes; found throughout the Midwest region, but rare in the eastern third.

Comments: The genus name is in honor of James Bolton, an 18th-century English naturalist, botanist, mycologist, and illustrator. The seeds are commonly eaten by waterfowl. A related species, decurrent false aster (*Boltonia decurrens*), differs by having leaf bases running down the stem as wings of green tissue along the stem ridges; rare in wet prairies, banks of rivers, and margins of ponds and lakes; found along the Illinois River basin and just below where it enters into the Mississippi River.

FALSE BONESET
Brickellia eupatorioides
Aster family (Asteraceae)

Description: One or more often-reddish stems emerge from the base of this whitish or cream-colored plant, up to a height of 3'. The somewhat hairy leaves are alternate, up to 4" long and 1½" wide, with prominent raised veins and one central vein on the underside. The 7–21 small, yellowish-white disk flowers occur in clusters at the tips of branches. There are no petal-like ray flowers. The styles extend beyond the flower, giving them a fringed look.

Bloom Season: Summer–early fall

Habitat/Range: Frequent in dry prairies, as well as rocky or sandy prairies, hill prairies, savannas, and open woods; found throughout the Midwest region.

Comments: Great Plains Indians used false boneset to reduce swelling. Its bitter taste restricted its use as a medicine or food plant. The dried seed head has been used in winter flower arrangements. False boneset is sometimes confused with tall boneset (*Eupatorium altissimum*) (see page 27); false boneset has alternate leaves with one central vein, whereas tall boneset has opposite leaves with 3 veins.

HORSEWEED
Conyza canadensis
Aster family (Asteraceae)

Description: A tall annual with a single stem, up to a height of 7'. The slender leaves are 2–3" long and ¼–½" wide, alternate along the stem, and hairy. The flower heads are small, numerous, and up to ¼" long. There are 20–40 white, petal-like ray flowers surrounding 8–28 disk flowers.

Bloom Season: Summer–fall

Habitat/Range: Common in upland prairies, sand prairies, banks of streams and rivers, pastures, fallow fields, crop fields, and along roadsides; found throughout the Midwest region.

Comments: Native Americans and early settlers boiled the leaves and drank the liquid to treat dysentery. Native Americans also used the tops in their sauna bath, sprinkling them on the hot rocks. An oil obtained by distilling the plant has been used to treat diarrhea, hemorrhoids, and pulmonary problems. The pollen is an irritant to some hay fever sufferers, and the plant can cause skin irritation.

FIREWEED
Erechtites hieracifolius
Aster family (Asteraceae)

Description: An annual plant up to 8' tall, with a grooved, often hairy stem. The leaves are alternate, somewhat lance-shaped, with ragged to deeply cut teeth along the margins, and stalkless, with the midvein of the leaf sometimes whitish. The flower heads are surrounded by cylindrical green bracts that contain numerous small, creamy-white disk flowers that are barely visible.

Bloom Season: Midsummer–fall

Habitat/Range: Common in rocky, open woods, eroding slopes, thickets, disturbed ground, and along roadsides; found throughout the Midwest region.

Comments: The common name "fireweed" refers to the plant's tendency to grow in recently burned-over areas.

ROBIN'S PLANTAIN
Erigeron pulchellus
Aster family (Asteraceae)

Description: This plant often forms small colonies by sending out leafy runners at its base. The stems are unbranched, up to 15" tall, hollow, with long, soft hairs. The leaves at the base of the stem are very hairy and spoon-shaped with shallow lobes; the leaves along the stem are scattered, smaller toward the top, and clasp the stem. The flower heads are loose and showy on long stalks, about 1" across, and white or lilac. The flower heads have 50–75 thread-like, white ray flowers surrounding a circle of densely packed yellow disk flowers.

Bloom Season: Mid-spring–early summer

Habitat/Range: Common in rocky or open woods and clearings, and along streams and roadsides; found throughout the Midwest region.

Comments: A similar species, Philadelphia fleabane (*Erigeron philadelphicus*), differs by lacking leafy runners at the base of the plant, taller stems, smaller flowers, and having 100–200 thread-like white ray flowers; common in upland and bottomland forests, prairies, savannas, open wet areas, and disturbed sites; found throughout the Midwest region.

DAISY FLEABANE
Erigeron strigosus
Aster family (Asteraceae)

Description: An annual or rarely biennial plant, with stems up to 2½' tall, with small, daisy-like flowers. The stems have scattered hairs lying flat against the stem. Leaves are narrow, less than 1" wide; the basal leaves are toothed and on stalks, while the stem leaves are alternate, without teeth, and stalkless. The flowers are in spreading clusters at the top of branched stems. The flower heads are about 1" across, with over 40 white, thread-like ray flowers surrounding a yellow center of densely packed disk flowers.

Bloom Season: Mid-spring–early fall

Habitat: Common in dry to mesic prairies, pastures, old fields, and along roadsides; found throughout the Midwest region.

Comments: A closely related species, annual fleabane (*Erigeron annuus*), differs by having spreading, rigid hairs on the stem and wider, sharply toothed leaves. It occurs in more-disturbed prairies, fields, and pastures, and is common throughout the Midwest region. Annual fleabane was used by the Lakota to make tea to treat children who had sore mouths and adults who had difficulty urinating.

WHITE SNAKEROOT
Ageratina altissima
Aster family (Asteraceae)

Description: A plant growing up to 4' tall, with branching stems toward the top. The leaves are up to 6" long, opposite, long-stalked, and somewhat heart-shaped, with large teeth along the margins. The network of veins is conspicuous, giving the leaf a slightly crinkled appearance. The flower heads are arranged in branching, flat-topped clusters 2–3" across. Each flower head has small, white flowers with extended styles that give them a tufted look.

Bloom Season: Summer–fall

Habitat/Range: Common in moist or rocky woods, at the base of bluffs, woodland borders, and disturbed sites; found throughout the Midwest region.

Comments: Formerly known as *Eupatorium rugosum*. Native Americans used a root tea for treating diarrhea, painful urination, fever, and kidney stones, and as an application for snakebite. White snakeroot was responsible for "milk sickness," a deadly disease encountered during early settlement by Europeans. When cows eat the plant, the toxin tremetol is released into their milk. The cattle themselves develop a disease called "trembles" for its chief symptom. In 1818, Abraham Lincoln's mother, Nancy Hanks Lincoln, died from a brief, agonizing bout of milk sickness. Research has shown that the active ingredient in white snakeroot, eupatorin, may have anticancer properties.

TALL BONESET
Eupatorium altissimum
Aster family (Asteraceae)

Description: Hairy plants, 3–6' tall, with a single stem that branches toward the top. The opposite leaves are narrowly tapering at the base and typically stalkless. The leaves are up to 5" long and 1½" wide, with 3 prominent veins along the length of the blade and a few widely spaced small teeth on the upper half of the leaf. Narrow, flattish clusters of flower heads branch at the top of the stem. Each flower head has 5–7 white, tubular flowers, each about ⅛" wide. There are no petal-like ray flowers.

Bloom Season: Late summer–fall

Habitat/Range: Common in prairies, hill prairies, savannas, open woods, pastures, old fields, and roadsides; found through the Midwest region, but absent in the northern quarter.

Comments: The genus *Eupatorium* is named for the Greek Mithridates VI Eupator, king of Pontus from about 120–63 BC. There are up to approximately 60 species in this genus worldwide.

LATE BONESET
Eupatorium serotinum
Aster family (Asteraceae)

Description: Plants up to 4' tall, densely short-hairy in the upper part, with opposite leaves that are coarsely toothed along the margins. The leaves are 5" long and 2" wide, widest near the base, tapering to long pointed tips, with stalks ⅜–1¼" long. There are numerous branched flower clusters near the top. Each flower head is about ⅛" wide, with 9–15 white, tubular disk flowers. There are no petal-like ray flowers.

Bloom Season: Midsummer–fall

Habitat/Range: Occasional in dry prairies, hill prairies, pastures, old fields, roadsides, and disturbed areas; found through the Midwest region, but absent in the northern half.

Comments: The species name, *serotinum*, is Latin for "late" (flowering).

COMMON BONESET
Eupatorium perfoliatum
Aster family (Asteraceae)

Description: A plant up to 4' tall, with noticeable spreading hairs on the stem and leaves. The leaves are up to 8" long and opposite, with their bases joining and circling the stem. Infrequently, some plants will have leaves in whorls of 3 rather than opposite. The leaves taper toward the end, and the margins are toothed. The dome-shaped flower clusters have white flower heads each about ¼" tall that contain 9–23 small disk flowers, but no petal-like ray flowers.

Bloom Season: Midsummer–fall

Habitat/Range: Common in wet prairies, moist depressions of upland prairies, and marshes, as well as along streams and moist roadsides; found throughout the Midwest region.

Comments: Early settlers called boneset "Indian sage" because it was widely used by Native Americans, who considered it a panacea for all ills, aches, and pains. The settlers' use of the name "boneset" is confusing, because it refers to its use in treating flu rather than in treating bones (a flu that caused severe body aches was called a "breakbone fever").

WILD QUININE
Parthenium integrifolium
Aster family (Asteraceae)

Description: The sometimes-branched stems are smooth in the lower portion; rough, with a few hairs, in the upper portion; and up to 3' tall. The basal leaves are up to 8" long and 4" wide and taper into long stalks; the stem leaves are alternate, smaller, lacking stalks, hairy, and toothed along the margin. The flowers are numerous in flat-topped or slightly rounded clusters. Each individual flower head is ⅓" wide, with 5 tiny, white, petal-like ray flowers with stamens that surround a thick head of sterile disk flowers.

Bloom Season: Late spring–summer

Habitat/Range: Common in dry to mesic prairies and savannas; found in the central and southwest part of the Midwest region.

Comments: This plant is also known as American feverfew. The flowering tops of wild quinine were once used to treat intermittent fever, such as with malaria. This plant served as a substitute when the tropical supply of quinine from the bark of the cinchona tree was cut off during World War I. The roots were used as a diuretic for kidney and bladder ailments. A close relative, also known as wild quinine (*Parthenium hispidum*), has somewhat shorter stems with noticeable spreading rough hairs, and long hairs on the lower surfaces of leaves. Occasional in dry prairies, open woodlands, glades, and bluff ledges; found primarily in the southern quarter of the Midwest region.

LEAFCUP

Polymnia canadensis
Aster family (Asteraceae)

Description: A tall, very hairy, branching plant, up to 5' in height, with large, soft leaves that are aromatic when crushed. The leaves are opposite, 3–5 lobes, with small teeth scattered along the margin. The base of the leaf tapers onto the upper part of the leaf stalk. The flower heads are few, small, with 5 white, petal-like ray flowers, usually 3-lobed, that surround the yellow disk flowers.

Bloom Season: Late spring–fall

Habitat/Range: Occasional in moist woods on slopes and ravines; found throughout the Midwest region.

Comments: A closely related species, bear's foot or yellow-flowered leafcup (*Smallanthus uveda-lius;* formerly *Polymnia uvedalia*), differs by having yellow ray flowers, leaf tissue that extends down the length of the leaf stalk, and leaves that are 3-lobed. They are found in low, moist, level woods in the southern quarter of the Midwest region.

TALL WHITE LETTUCE

Prenanthes altissima
Aster family (Asteraceae)

Description: A slender plant, up to 6' tall, with the upper branches supporting hanging, cream-colored flowers. The thin leaves are 4–6" long, alternate, smooth, on stalks, and variable in shape. The lower leaves are deeply 3- to 5-lobed, while the upper leaves are commonly arrowhead-shaped to more oval. The long, slender flower heads are about ¾" long and ½" wide, with each containing 5–6 cream-colored, petal-like ray flowers. There are no disk flowers.

Bloom Season: Midsummer–fall

Habitat/Range: Occasional in moist woods and ravines and banks of rivers and streams; found throughout the Midwest region, but absent in the northwestern part.

Comments: Also called *Nabalus altissimus.* Known also as "rattlesnake root," because Native Americans used the leaves and roots for treating snakebite, as well as bites by dogs. A tea was drunk for dysentery. A similar species, white let-tuce (*Prenanthes alba*), also called *Nabalus albus*, differs by having 7–13 petal-like ray flowers per head; found throughout the Midwest region, but less common in the southern half.

ROUGH WHITE LETTUCE
Prenanthes aspera
Aster family (Asteraceae)

Description: Tall, slender plants, up to 6' in height, with unbranched, hairy leaves and stems, and milky sap. The leaves are alternate, up to 4" long and 1¾" wide, and somewhat toothed along the margins. The lower leaves are stalked, whereas the upper leaves are smaller and lack stalks, with the leaf bases often clasping the stem. The flowers are clustered along the upper portion of the stem. Each cylindrical flower head is up to ¾" tall and ¾–1" across, with 10–14 creamy-white, fragrant, petal-like ray flower heads, each with 5 small teeth at the tip. There are no disk flowers.

Bloom Season: Summer–early fall

Habitat/Range: Occasional in prairies, savannas, glades, and openings in mesic to dry upland forests; found throughout the Midwest region, but rare in the northern and eastern parts.

Comments: Also called *Nabalus asperus*. The Choctaw made a tea of the roots and tops of rough white lettuce to increase urine flow and to relieve pain. The bitter roots of this plant were once used to treat snakebite; hence, its other name, "rattlesnake root."

WHITE UPLAND ASTER
Oligoneuron album
Aster family (Asteraceae)

Description: Slender, branching plants, up to 2' tall. The leaves are narrow, alternate, and widely spaced along the stem. The lower leaves are up to 8" long and ½" wide, often with 3 fine veins running along the length of the leaf. The flower heads form an open, flat-topped cluster, with each head about ¾" across, containing up to 25 white, petal-like ray flowers, and a pale yellow central disk.

Bloom Season: Midsummer–fall

Habitat/Range: Occasional in dry prairies, hill prairies, rocky, open woods, pastures, railroads, and roadsides; found in the northern half of the Midwest region and in the southern half of Missouri.

Comments: White upland aster was once thought to be an aster because of its appearance, but it is now considered to be more closely related to other flat-topped goldenrods in the genus *Oligoneuron*, because it has been found to hybridize with them. It is also known as *Solidago ptarmicoides*.

FLAT-TOPPED ASTER
Doellingeria umbellata
Aster family (Asteraceae)

Description: Plants, usually with one stem, are up to 5' tall, with mostly hairless stems. The leaves are alternate along the stem, up to 3" (and rarely, 6") long and less than 1½" wide, broadest at the middle, with toothless margins. Flower heads are numerous at the ends of branches, forming a nearly flat-topped crown. Each flower head is about 1" across, with 4–12 white, petal-like ray flowers surrounding a yellow disk.

Bloom Season: Midsummer–fall

Habitat/Range: Occasional in moist to wet areas, including wet depressions and low thickets in prairies; found through the Midwest region, but absent in the southwestern quarter.

Comments: *Doellingeria* is a genus of flowering plants in the aster family. It contains species formerly included in aster, but now considered to be a distinct genus. It was formerly known as *Aster umbellatus.*

FORKED ASTER
Eurybia furcata
Aster family (Asteraceae)

Description: A small aster, 1–3' tall, often forming dense colonies from long, sometimes relatively stout, fleshy rhizomes. The stems are often zigzag and slightly to moderately hairy. The leaves at the base are usually absent at flowering time, but the lower stem leaves are long-stalked, heart-shaped, and hairy, up to 6" long, coarsely toothed, and shortly tapering at the tip. The leaves toward the top of the stem are smaller, with much shorter stalks, coarsely toothed, broadest near the base, and tapering to a pointed tip. The flower heads are in a flat-topped to rounded cluster at the top of the stem. Each flower head is 1–1½" across with 12–20 white, petal-like ray flowers that often become pinkish to lavender with age, and 25–40 yellow disk flowers.

Bloom Season: Midsummer–fall

Habitat/Range: Rare in mesic and bottomland forests, edges of forests, bases and ledges of moist cliffs, and along banks of streams; found in scattered locations through the Midwest region, but absent in the northwest quarter.

Comments: Although forked aster has a broad distribution across the Midwest region, it is rare throughout its range, and classified as threatened or endangered in the states in which it occurs.

LARGE-LEAVED ASTER
Eurybia macrophylla
Aster family (Asteraceae)

Description: Although ranging from 1–4' tall, this aster is typically low-growing, often forming patches of basal leaves only, and may not flower in a given year. The leaves are on long stalks with lobes that clasp the stem. The lowest leaves are large and heart-shaped, up to 8" long and 6" wide, coarsely toothed, and densely hairy, and they become progressively smaller ascending the stem. The flower heads are in branching clusters on stalks up to 1½" long, with gland-tipped hairs. Each flower head is up to 1½" across, with 10–20 white to pale blue to violet, petal-like ray flowers that surround a cluster of tiny, 5-lobed yellow disk flowers.

Bloom Season: Midsummer–fall

Habitat/Range: Common in dry to mesic forests, open woods, lightly shaded slopes, and forest edges; found primarily in the northern half of the Midwest region, but with scattered populations in the southern half.

Comments: The Algonquin people cook and eat the large, thick young leaves. The Ojibwa bathe their heads with an infusion of this plant to treat headache and smoke it as a hunting charm to attract deer. They also consume the young leaves as both food and medicine, and use the roots to make soup.

HEATH ASTER
Symphyotrichum ericoides
Aster family (Asteraceae)

Description: A low, compact plant, up to 3' tall, with very leafy branches. The leaves are alternate, small, narrow, pointed, smooth along the edges, and less than 2" long and ¼" wide. The branches have numerous flower heads, with each flower head on a short stalk. The stalks have several small, leaf-like bracts. Flower heads are about ½" wide, with up to 20 white, petal-like ray flowers surrounding a small yellow disk.

Bloom Season: Late summer–fall

Habitat/Range: Scattered to common in prairies, hill prairies, bluffs, pastures, old fields, and along roadsides; found throughout the Midwest region, but less common in the eastern third.

Comments: Heath aster can commonly be found growing together in clumps, giving it a bushy appearance, with densely packed and overlapping flowers that resemble a heath or heather shrub.

TALL WHITE ASTER
Symphyotrichum lanceolatum
Aster family (Asteraceae)

Description: A plant usually appearing in colonies connected by long, slender, branched rhizomes. Stems are up to 5' tall, with sparse to moderate hairs toward the tips of numerous branches or panicles. The leaves are alternate, up to 6" long and 1½" wide, narrow, tapering to a tip, and sometimes irregularly toothed along the leaf margin. The flower heads are in leafy clusters at the top of the plant. Each flower head is about 1" wide, with 20–45 white, petal-like ray flowers surrounding a yellow disk.

Bloom Season: Midsummer–fall

Habitat/Range: Common in moist depressions in upland prairies, wet prairies, bottomland forests, mesic upland forests, swamps, fens, along streams, pastures, roadsides, and open, disturbed areas; common throughout the Midwest region.

Comments: The Zuni people used this plant to treat wounds and nosebleeds. The Iroquois used it to treat fever.

HAIRY ASTER
Symphyotrichum pilosum
Aster family (Asteraceae)

Description: A widely branched, spreading aster, up to a length of 4', with many thin, needle-like, alternate leaves along the upper stems and flowering branches. The basal leaves are up to 4" long and usually die back before the flowers emerge. The stem leaves are alternate, thin, and needle-like. There are usually many flower heads scattered along the side branches and upper stems on flower stalks ¼–1¼" long. The flower heads are numerous, about ½" wide, with 15–30 white, petal-like ray flowers and a central yellow disk with 20 or more disk flowers.

Bloom Season: Late summer–fall

Habitat/Range: Common in disturbed or over-grazed prairies, savannas, edges of woods, banks of streams and rivers, old fields, and roadsides; found throughout the Midwest region.

Comments: Several Native American tribes thought the smoke from burning aster plants was helpful in reviving a person who had fainted. Some tribes brewed a tea of aster plants for headache. Other similar small, white-flowered asters that occupy similar ranges and habitats are: small-headed aster (*Symphyotrichum parviceps*), which has shorter flower heads about ¼–⅜" across and fewer than 13 disk flowers; calico aster (*Symphyotrichum lateriflorum*), which has leaves with short hairs only along the midvein, 9–15 ray flowers, and a pale yellow central disk; and bottomland aster (*Symphyotrichum ontarionis*), which has densely hairy stems and short flower stalks less than ⅓" long.

ARROW-LEAVED ASTER
Symphyotrichum urophyllum
Aster family (Asteraceae)

Description: Numerous, short-stalked flower heads are arranged in a somewhat loose cylindrical cluster at the top of a stem, up to 4' tall. The leaves are alternate, lacking hairs, with a heart-shaped base, small teeth along the margins, and a long and winged stalk. Leaves on the upper part of the stem are narrow and taper at the base. The flower heads are typically white, but shades of pale blue or lilac are also possible. Each flower head is ½–¾" wide, with 8–15 petal-like ray flowers surrounding the pale yellow disk flowers.

Bloom Season: Late summer–fall

Habitat/Range: Common in rocky or sandy woods, ravines, savannas, and edges of glades; found throughout the Midwest region.

Comments: Formerly known as *Aster sagittifolius*. A similar species, heartleaf aster (*Symphyotrichum cordifolium*), is also hairless, or sometimes with hairs along the veins on the leaf undersurface. The heartleaf aster has more of a widely branching cluster of flower heads; leaf stalks wingless, or, less commonly, only slightly winged; flower heads about ½" wide, with 8–15 petal-like ray flowers nearly white to pale blue to lavender, and surrounding a creamy-yellow central disk; found in similar habitat throughout the Midwest region.

DRUMMOND'S ASTER
Symphyotrichum drummondii
Aster family (Asteraceae)

Description: The plant produces 1 or more leafy stems, up to 4' tall, with short, downy hairs covering the upper stems, underside of leaves, and flower clusters. The leaves are alternate, 1–4" long, ½–3" wide, heart-shaped on the lower part of the stem and more lance-shaped with rounded bases on the upper part, coarse teeth along the margins, and leaf stalks that have narrow wings along the edges. Often secondary smaller leaves are present at the axils of the leaves. The flower heads are in branching clusters, numerous, each about ½" wide, with 10–15 white to pale blue to lavender, petal-like ray flowers and 10–15 yellow disk flowers.

Bloom Season: Fall

Habitat/Range: Common in dry upland forests, bottomland forests, forest edges, savannas, and banks of streams; found throughout the Midwest region.

Comments: The main distinguishing characteristic that separates Drummond's aster from arrow-leaved aster and heartleaf aster is the presence of short downy hairs that cover the upper stems, undersides of leaves, and flower clusters. The species name, *drummondii*, honors Thomas Drummond (1790–1835), a Scottish naturalist who collected plant specimens in the western and southern United States in the early 1830s.

WHITE CROWNBEARD
Verbesina virginica
Aster family (Asteraceae)

Description: Stout plants with leafy wings along the stem and up to 7' tall. The leaves are alternate and lance-shaped to 7" long, with widely spaced, small teeth. The flower heads are about 1–1½" across and clustered at the end of the stem on branches. Each flower head has 3–5 white, petal-like ray flowers that surround each white disk.

Bloom Season: Late summer–fall

Habitat/Range: Common in open woods, valleys, and streamsides; found in the southwest quarter of the Midwest region.

Comments: In late autumn, during hard freezes, white crownbeard produces "frost flowers." These are ribbons of ice oozing out of cracks at the base of the stem. Sap from still-active roots freezes as it emerges from the dead stem, growing like a white ribbon as more fluid is pumped out. Another name for this plant is "frostweed."

MAYAPPLE
Podophyllum peltatum
Barberry family (Berberidaceae)

Description: This distinctive plant has extensive underground rhizomes that form colonies and can grow to a height of 2'. The large, umbrella-like, usually smooth, paired leaves are up to 14" across and have 5–9 deeply cut lobes. Plants with single leaves are young and do not flower. At the base of the leaf stalks, a single, slightly nodding flower is produced with 6 sepals and 6 petals, all cream-colored. The flower is up to 2" across and has 12 yellow stamens. The large green fruit turns yellow when ripe and is up to 2" wide.

Bloom Season: Spring

Habitat/Range: Common in moist or dry open woods and in pastures at the edges of woods, usually in colonies; found throughout the Midwest region.

Comments: The Cherokee used a root tea for treating constipation, deafness, rheumatism, sores, and ulcers, and for expelling intestinal parasites. The Osage used an infusion as an antidote for poisons. Early settlers used the powdered rhizomes in an infusion to treat a wide range of common diseases. The active component, podophyllum, still is the most widely used treatment for venereal warts. Ripened fruits lose their toxicity and are edible, but the rest of the plant is considered a powerful intestinal irritant, acting as an emetic (an agent that causes vomiting) and a purgative (a medicine stronger than a laxative). If misused, it can be fatal.

HELIOTROPE
Heliotropium tenellum
Borage family (Boraginaceae)

Description: Slender, wiry, much-branched annual plant, up to 10" tall, with stems and leaves covered with dense, white hairs. The leaves are alternate, very narrow, up to 1" long and ⅛" wide, with their margins often rolled, and lacking stalks. The flowers are small, about ¼" wide, white, 5-lobed, and solitary to numerous on short, small branches.

Bloom Season: Summer

Habitat/Range: Common on glades, dry open woods, and blufftops; found in the southwest quarter of the Midwest region.

Comments: Heliotrope endures some of the harshest living conditions. It seems quite suited to the thin soils over dolomite bedrock, where it can reach over 110 degrees Fahrenheit in the summer months. The leaves are narrow and densely covered by white, reflective hairs, and have margins that become strongly curled under times of extreme drought.

SPRING FORGET-ME-NOT
Myosotis verna
Borage family (Boraginaceae)

Description: An annual or sometimes biennial plant, ½–1½" tall, with stems and leaves densely covered with both spreading and appressed hairs. Leaves are alternate and stalkless, with the basal leaves withering away by flowering time. Each leaf is up to 2" long and ⅓" wide, with the margins and surfaces densely hairy. The flowers are at the tips of branching stems, stalked, with each cluster tightly curled at the tip, with flowers opening in succession as the tip unfurls and elongates. Each flower is about ⅛" wide, with 5 white, spreading lobes.

Bloom Season: Late spring–early summer

Habitat/Range: Common in wet, mesic, and dry prairies, sand prairies, savannas, open woods, and open, disturbed areas; found through the Midwest region, but absent in the northern quarter.

Comments: Also known as early scorpiongrass, which refers to the tight curling of the flower cluster similar to the tail of a scorpion.

MARBLESEED

Onosmodium molle
Borage family (Boraginaceae)

Description: A hairy-stemmed plant, up to 4' tall, with numerous leaves along the stem. The leaves are alternate, hairy, and narrow, about 5" long and ½" wide. Both the upper and lower leaf surfaces are densely hairy. The flowers are tightly coiled at the ends of the upper branches, with flowers opening in succession as the tip unfurls and elongates. The tube-like flowers are dull white to greenish-white, each about ½" long, with 5 lobes.

Bloom Season: Mid-spring to early summer

Habitat/Range: Occasional in mesic to dry prairies, hill prairies, savannas, pastures, and sandy soil; found throughout the Midwest region.

Comments: Also known as *Onosmodium bejariense* and *Lithospermum occidentale*. Marbleseed is named for the hard, white nutlet or seed. Another common name, false gromwell (meaning "gritty meal"), refers to its resemblance to nutlets of the genus *Lithospermum*.

LYRE-LEAVED ROCK CRESS

Arabidopsis lyrata
Mustard family (Brassicaceae)

Description: A biennial or short-lived perennial, 4–15" tall, that forms a small rosette of basal leaves that typically wither away by flowering time. The leaves at the base are hairy, up to 2" long and ¼–½" wide, with a large lobe at the tip and 1–2 pairs of shorter side lobes. Along the stem, there are a few widely spaced, narrow leaves, each 1" long. The flowers are loosely arranged on elongated clusters with each stalked flower about ¼" across, and 4 rounded, white petals and 6 yellow stamens.

Bloom Season: Late spring–summer

Habitat/Range: Common in sandy soils of prairies, savannas, upland woods, sand dunes, and cliffs; found primarily in the northern half of the Midwest region and in Missouri.

Comments: Also known as mouse-ear cress and *Arabis lyrata*. This native is not to be mistaken for the nonnative mouse-ear cress (*Arabidopsis thaliana*), which has smaller flowers, broader stem leaves, and unlobed basal leaves. A native of Asia and Europe, it prefers disturbed soil and is found throughout the Midwest region, but absent in the northwest quarter.

SMOOTH ROCK CRESS
Boechera laevigata
Mustard family (Brassicaceae)

Description: A single, leafy stem, up to 3' tall, arises from a cluster of leaves at the base. The smooth leaves clasp the stem by their eared bases and are somewhat toothed along the margins. The small white or yellowish-white flowers have 4 petals, each about ¼" long. The fruit forms pods, up to 4" long, which spread outward and downward.

Bloom Season: Spring–summer

Habitat/Range: Common in moist woods, ravines, and bluffs; found throughout the Midwest region.

Comments: Formerly known as *Arabis laevigata*. The overwintering leaves at the base of the plant are often purplish. Another species that shares similar habitats and range is sicklepod (*Boechera canadensis*; formerly *Arabis canadensis*), which has hairy leaves along the stem, and lacks the eared flaps at the base.

SPRING CRESS
Cardamine bulbosa
Mustard family (Brassicaceae)

Description: A smooth, sparingly branched plant, up to 18" tall. The leaves at the base are round, up to 2½" long, on long stalks, and usually wither by flowering time. The stem leaves are scattered, mostly without stalks, up to 2" long and 1" wide, longer than broad, and irregularly toothed. The flowers are small, about ½" wide when fully open, white, 4-petaled, and appear in clusters at the end of a stalk.

Bloom Season: Spring–early summer

Habitat/Range: Occasional in bottomland forests, banks of streams, and moist soils; found throughout the Midwest region.

Comments: Pioneers used the young shoots and leaves of spring cress to give a peppery-pungent taste to salads, and as cooked greens. The base of the stem and the roots were used as a mild horseradish. Another species with similar habitats and range is Pennsylvania bitter cress (*Cardamine pensylvanica*), which differs by having stem leaves divided into leaflets, with the end leaflet distinctly larger, and with smaller flowers, less than ¼" across.

TOOTHWORT
Cardamine concatenata
Mustard family (Brassicaceae)

Description: A plant with an unbranched, smooth, upright stem, up to 10" tall. The leaves appear in whorls of 3 about midway up the stem, and each leaf has 3–5 deeply cut segments with teeth along the margins. Young leaves are often tinged with purple, and another set of leaves develops at the base of the plant after flowering. Nonflowering plants produce a single, palmately lobed leaf. The 4-petaled, white flowers are up to ¾" long and are sometimes tinged with pink as they get older. The flowers are often nodding and may only partially open on cloudy days.

Bloom Season: Spring

Habitat/Range: Common on lower wooded slopes and in valleys; found through the Midwest region, but absent in the northeast part.

Comments: Formerly known as *Dentaria laciniata*. The common name may come from the toothlike shape of the fleshy root; it was also used as a folk remedy for toothaches. Pioneers gathered the little tuberous roots in early spring and used them throughout the year for seasoning soups, stews, meats, and other dishes. Eaten raw, the little tubers have the flavor of a radish or mild horseradish. A similar species, broad-leaved toothwort (*Cardamine diphylla*), differs by having only a pair of leaves at the middle of the stem, each divided into 3 broad leaflets, with shallow, rounded teeth along the margins; found only in the northeast part of the Midwest region.

SMALL-FRUITED WHITLOW GRASS
Draba brachycarpa
Mustard family (Brassicaceae)

Description: A winter annual, with multiple to single stems, each up to 4" tall, with seeds that germinate in the fall, producing leaves that overwinter. The hairy flower stalk appears in early spring with leaves clustered at the base and a few along the stem. Leaves are hairy and up to ½" long. Flowers have 4 notched, white petals, each about ¼" long.

Bloom Season: Spring

Habitat/Range: Occasional in prairies, dry upland forests, lawns, fields, often in sparse areas with little competition; found in the Midwest region in Missouri, southern Illinois, and southern Indiana.

Comments: The name *whitlow* derives from the ancient belief that some species could cure "whitlows," which are sores that develop around finger- or toenails, or in the hooves of horses. The common name erroneously implies that this plant is a grass.

WHITLOW GRASS
Draba cuneifolia
Mustard family (Brassicaceae)

Description: A winter annual, its seeds germinate in the fall, producing leaves that overwinter. The stems appear in early spring and are single or branched at the base, hairy, and up to 10" tall. Leaves are mostly at the base, hairy, toothed along the margins, stalkless, up to 1" long, and wedge-shaped. Its flowers have 4 notched, white petals, each about ¼" long.

Bloom Season: Late winter–spring

Habitat/Range: Common along edges of dolomite, limestone, sandstone, and igneous bluffs and glades, usually on bare ground, and in rocky, open woods; found in the Midwest region primarily in Missouri, southwest Illinois, and southern Ohio.

Comments: A similar species, Carolina whitlow grass (*Draba reptans*), differs by having stems that are hairless, leaves that are smooth along the margins, and branching hairs on both surfaces; occurs in dry sandy or rock soil in prairies, dry upland forests, and rock outcrops; found throughout the Midwest region, but absent in the northern third.

LEAVENWORTHIA
Leavenworthia uniflora
Mustard family (Brassicaceae)

Description: A winter annual, its seeds germinate in the fall, producing leaves that overwinter. This early flowering diminutive plant produces flower stalks up to 5" tall. The deeply cut leaves with 7–15 lobes occur at the base of the plant and are up to 3" long. The small, 4-petaled, white flowers are solitary and about ⅜" long. The distinctive fruits are up to 1¼" long, narrow and flattened, with up to 10 segments ending in a small, pointed tip.

Bloom Season: Spring

Habitat/Range: Occasional on dolomite and limestone glades, usually on thin, bare soil over bedrock; found in the southwest part of the Midwest region, rare in the southeast part.

Comments: The flowers are noticeably showy for their small size, with the dark green rosette of deeply cut leaves often turning red as the plant begins to die in late spring. Leavenworthia is named for Henry Leavenworth (1783–1834), the famous American frontier military officer.

FIELD CHICKWEED
Cerastium arvense
Pink family (Caryophyllaceae)

Description: The stems are slender, sprawling, and up to 15" tall. The narrow, opposite leaves are about 1" long and ⅛" wide. The main stem leaves have tufts of smaller leaves at their base. Flowers are in branched clusters on slender stalks at the top of the plant. Flowers are ½" wide with 5 white petals, each notched about half their length.

Bloom Season: Late spring–early summer

Habitat/Range: Uncommon in open woods, sandy prairies, rock outcrops, low grassy areas, and riverbanks; scattered across the Midwest region.

Comments: There are four species of native chickweeds and eight species of nonnative chickweeds that occur in the Midwest region. Field chickweed is by far the showiest of the native chickweeds.

STIFF SANDWORT
Minuartia michauxii
Pink family (Caryophyllaceae)

Description: Dense clusters of stems arise up to 8"
tall above a dense mat of stiff, leathery leaves with
spine-like tips. Leaves are opposite along the stem,
with smaller leaves clustered in the leaf axils. Each
leaf is ½–¾" long and thread-like in width. The stiff
leaves are flat on the upper surface and increas-
ingly convex toward their bases. The number of
flowers varies from 5–50, arranged at the top of the
stems, with the upper flowers blooming first. Flowers are about ⅛" across, with 5 white, spreading
petals, 5 green sepals, and 10 stamens.

Bloom Season: Late spring–midsummer

Habitat/Range: Occasional in sandy soils of woodlands, savannas, prairies, glades, ledges of cliffs,
and dunes; found scattered across the Midwest
region, but absent in the northwest quarter.

Comments: A related species, slender sandwort
(*Minuartia patula*), differs by being an annual that
has a rosette of basal leaves that overwinter;
stems lack smaller leaves clustered in the axils of
the main leaves; leaves are softer, more succulent
and round; typically blooms earlier; and occurs
primarily in Missouri, along with a few populations in northeast Illinois, Indiana, and Ohio, where
slender sandwort is classified as threatened or
endangered.

STARRY CAMPION
Silene stellata
Pink family (Caryophyllaceae)

Description: Several stiff, slender stems emerge
from the base, up to 3' tall. The leaves are in
whorls of 4 along the stem, with pointed tips, and
up to 3" long. Showy, bell-shaped flowers are
about ¾" wide, with 5 white petals, each with
8–12 linear lobes and 10 stamens.

Bloom Season: Summer

Habitat/Range: Common in dry to mesic upland
forests, bottomland forests, savannas, wet
prairies, and banks of streams; found across the
Midwest region.

Comments: The lacy fringe of the petals produces
the "starry" appearance from which the common
name is derived. The Potawatomi and Meskwaki
tribes used the roots as a poultice (plant material
mashed and applied warm) to dry up infected
sores. Starry campion is related to the carnations
and pinks familiar to flower gardeners.

HEDGE BINDWEED
Calystegia sepium
Morning glory family (Convolvulaceae)

Description: A twining vine that creeps along the ground or climbs, with smooth, branching stems, up to 9' long. The long-stalked leaves, up to 4" long and 1–2" wide, are alternate along the stem and triangular, with 2 squarish lobes at the base. The long-stalked flowers arise singly from leaf axils. The flowers are funnel-shaped, large, up to 2½" across, with 5 broad lobes, and white to pink in color, with yellow throats.

Bloom Season: Late spring–fall

Habitat/Range: Occasional in disturbed portions of upland prairies, margins of wet areas, pastures, fencerows, and roadsides; found throughout the Midwest region.

Comments: On sunny days the flowers close by midday. The pulpy roots have historically been used as a purgative; also used to treat jaundice and gall bladder ailments. A similar species, low bindweed (*Calystegia spithamaea*), differs by having shorter, non-twining, finely hairy stems, up to 2' long, with short leaf stalks and heart-shaped leaf bases. Uncommon in prairies and open woods, and dry sandy or rocky soils; found throughout the Midwest region, but more frequently in the northern part.

DODDER
Cuscuta spp. (several species)
Morning glory family (Convolvulaceae)

Description: Leafless annual plants, with stringy, orange stems that twine around and over other plants. Because dodder lacks chlorophyll, which is needed to produce food from sunlight, these parasitic plants attach to a host plant with special roots called "haustoria" that penetrate the host plant's stem and absorb its nutrients. The flowers appear in dense clusters scattered along the stems. Each flower is small, about ¼" across, with 5 spreading white lobes.

Bloom Season: Summer–fall

Habitat/Range: Occasional in upland prairies, wet prairies, stream banks, wetlands, fields, and along railroad tracks; occurs throughout the Midwest region.

Comments: There are eleven species of dodder found in the Midwest region, and all are difficult to identify. Most dodder species have specific host plants, such as members of the aster family, including goldenrods, asters, sunflowers, ragweeds, and fleabanes, along with milkweeds, penstemons, smartweeds, and others. A yellow dye can be made from dodder.

WILD POTATO VINE
Ipomoea pandurata
Morning glory family (Convolvulaceae)

Description: A trailing or climbing vine, 10–15' long. The leaves are alternate, heart-shaped, smooth, and up to 6" long and nearly as wide. The leaf veins, margins, and leaf stalks are often purplish. There are 1–7 flowers on long stalks that emerge at the junction of the leaf and stem. The flowers are funnel-shaped, about 3" wide, with red or purple centers. The flowers close about midday.

Bloom Season: Late spring–summer

Habitat/Range: Occasional in mostly disturbed prairies, edges of prairies bordering woodlands, fencerows, pastures, and roadsides; found in the southern half of the Midwest region.

Comments: The large root, which can weigh over 20 pounds, was used as a food source by Native Americans. The root was heated and applied to the skin to treat rheumatism and "hard tumors." Root tea was used by early settlers as a diuretic and a laxative, and as a treatment for coughs, asthma, and the early stages of tuberculosis. Because the root is a strong laxative when eaten raw, it was often boiled like a potato to neutralize its effect before consuming. The taste is said to be somewhat bitter.

WILD STONECROP
Sedum ternatum
Stonecrop family (Crassulaceae)

Description: A low, spreading succulent, up to 6" tall, with creeping stems that form a mat. The leaves are in whorls of 3 with the lower leaves somewhat rounded, about ¾" long and ½" across, while the upper leaves are narrower and near cylindrical, ½" long and ¼" across. Each plant produces several leafy, sterile shoots and one leafy flowering stem, up to 7" tall. The flowers are clustered on top, each about ½" across with 4 spreading, narrow, white petals and 8 stamens, with anthers that are initially white but turn red to purple with age.

Bloom Season: Mid-spring–early summer

Habitat/Range: Occasional in moist wooded ravines and slopes, open places in woods, and partially shaded banks along rivers and streams; found across the southern half of the Midwest region.

Comments: Wild stonecrop makes an attractive ground cover and can be propagated from cuttings that will root when in contact with the ground.

WILD CUCUMBER
Echinocystis lobata
Gourd family (Cucurbitaceae)

Description: An annual, high-climbing, 2–10' vine, with angled stems and branching tendrils that entwine on nearby vegetation. The leaves are widely spaced along the vine, up to 7" in diameter, with 5 triangular lobes that have widely spaced teeth along the edges. There are both male and female flowers on the same plant. Both types are about ½" across with 6 narrow, white petals that are sometimes covered in short, glandular hairs. Male flowers are in upright clusters with pale yellow–tipped stamens. Female flowers are located at the base of the male flower cluster with a blunt stigma and a round spiny ovary beneath the petals. The inflated fruit is up to 2" long and covered with soft spines.

Bloom Season: Summer–fall

Habitat/Range: Locally common in large patches in moist ground, thickets, bottomland forests, banks of streams, and disturbed ground; found throughout the Midwest region, but less common in the southern quarter.

Comments: Also known as balsam apple, wild cucumber has been used medicinally by Native Americans. The Taos Pueblo of New Mexico used it to treat rheumatism, while the Menominee of Wisconsin made a bitter extract from the roots for use as a love potion and as a painkiller. The powdered root has been used to prepare a poultice to relieve headache, and the pitted, dark brown, mottled seeds have been used as beads. As the bristly fruit ages, it bursts at the tip and the seeds are propelled explosively under hydrostatic pressure.

BUR CUCUMBER
Sicyos angulatus
Gourd family (Cucurbitaceae)

Description: An annual, low-climbing vine up to 25' long that develops multiple stems with branching tendrils, and often sprawls across the ground. The stems are light green, ribbed, and hairy. The leaves are alternate, finely hairy underneath, 4–8" across, with 3–5 shallow lobes and widely spaced teeth along the edges. There are both male and female flowers on the same plant. The male flowers are about ½" across, in clusters at the end of a long, hairy stem that is opposite a leaf. Each male flower has 5 white lobes that surround a column of pale yellow–tipped stamens. The female flowers are smaller, more bell-shaped, and are in a round cluster at the tip of a long stalk. Each female flower has a large ovary about ½" long, with the surface covered by sharp spines and long white hairs. The bur-like fruit contains a single seed that is brown and flattened.

Bloom Season: Summer–fall

Habitat/Range: Locally common in sometimes-large patches in the moist soil of bottomland forests, thickets, banks of streams, and disturbed ground; found throughout the Midwest region, but less common in the northern third.

Comments: The fruit of the bur cucumber appear in small clusters and are covered with spines that easily break off, embedding themselves in skin and clothing that can result in a painful experience!

INDIAN PIPE
Monotropa uniflora
Heath family (Ericaceae)

Description: Small, single-flowered plants with single stems or in clusters arising from the base, up to 8" tall. The fleshy stem has rudimentary, scale-like leaves. The flowers droop to form the pipe, then become erect as the fruit forms. The flowers are about 1" long, with 4–6 whitish petals that slightly flare at the end.

Bloom Season: Summer–fall

Habitat/Range: Occasional in upland woods, ravines, on slopes or ridges, usually in dense leaf mulch; found throughout the Midwest region.

Comments: The plants are white, and lack the green chlorophyll needed to produce their own food. They obtain their nutrients from fungi in the soil that are connected to the roots of other plants. Native Americans and early settlers used the juice of Indian pipe for treating sore eyes. According to one Indian legend, this plant always appeared on the exact spot where some Indian had knocked the white ashes of his pipe to the forest floor.

HOGWORT
Croton capitatus
Spurge family (Euphorbiaceae)

Description: Annual plants, up to 3' tall, but much shorter on dry, thin soil, with a dense, white, woolly layer of tiny, star-shaped hairs on the stems and leaves. The leaves are alternate, stalked, up to 4" long and 1" wide, smooth along the margins, and with rounded bases. The flowers are in short, compact clusters near the ends of branches. Tiny male and female flowers are in each cluster. The female flowers lack petals, whereas the male flowers have 5 tiny, white petals.

Bloom Season: Summer–fall

Habitat/Range: Frequent in often-disturbed upland prairies, sand prairies, and glades, as well as pastures, idle fields, and other disturbed areas; found in the southwest part of the Midwest region.

Comments: The oil in hogwort is toxic, and cattle have been poisoned from eating hay containing the plants. There are five species of crotons found in the Midwest region.

PRAIRIE TEA
Croton monanthogynus
Spurge family (Euphorbiaceae)

Description: An annual plant, up to 2' tall and branching freely up to 3' wide, but much smaller on dry, thin soil, and with a dense, white layer of tiny, star-shaped hairs on the stems and leaves. The leaves are alternate, stalked, up to 2" long and ¾" wide, smooth along the margins, and with rounded bases. The tiny flowers are in short compact clusters in the axils of the upper leaves. There are both male and female flowers in each cluster. The female flowers lack petals, whereas the male flowers have 5 tiny, white petals.

Bloom Season: Summer–fall

Habitat/Range: Frequent in dry, often-disturbed prairies, open woods, and glades, as well as pastures, idle fields, and other disturbed areas; found in the southern half of the Midwest region.

Comments: As the common name implies, a leaf tea was made from various species of crotons by Native Americans. The Lakota, Kiowa, and Zuni made a tea to relieve stomach pains. While croton oil was rarely used in medicine in the United States, it was used medicinally in Europe. Croton oil has now been reported to be a carcinogen. It can also cause skin dermatitis and is no longer used in Europe. Twenty drops of the oil are considered lethal.

49

FLOWERING SPURGE
Euphorbia corollata
Spurge family (Euphorbiaceae)

Description: Slender, erect plants, with a pale bluish or yellowish-green cast, white, milky sap, and widely branching flower clusters. The narrow, smooth-edged leaves are alternate on the stem but sometimes opposite or whorled near the flower clusters. The flower heads are numerous, each about ½" across, with 5 chalky white false petals surrounding a cup of tiny, yellow male flowers and a single female flower. The fruit is a 3-parted ball on a tiny stalk.

Bloom Season: Mid-spring–fall

Habitat/Range: Common in dry and mesic prairies and open woods, as well as in old fields, pastures, roadsides, and other disturbed sites; found throughout the Midwest region.

Comments: Native Americans used a leaf or root tea to treat chronic constipation, rheumatism, and diabetes. The root was mashed and applied to the skin to treat snakebite. The flowers, fruits, and leaves are eaten by wild turkeys. The seeds are eaten by greater prairie-chickens, bobwhite quail, and mourning doves. White-tailed deer feed upon the plants in spring and summer.

TOOTHED SPURGE
Euphorbia dentata
Spurge family (Euphorbiaceae)

Description: An annual plant, up to 2' tall, with hairy stems and milky sap. The leaves are opposite but sometimes alternate toward the upper nodes, stalked, ½–3" long and ¼–1½" wide, with toothed margins. Flowers are small cups emerging in clusters at the tops of stems, with numerous tiny male flowers, each with a single stamen and a single larger female flower, with a stalked pistil. There are 1–2 green, kidney-shaped glands around the lip of each cup. Sepals and petals are lacking, but leaves just below the flowers are light green to white at their base. The fruit is stalked and 3-lobed, with each lobe bearing a bumpy white, brown, or dark-gray seed.

Bloom Season: Summer–fall

Habitat/Range: Locally common in dry, rocky prairies, hill prairies, sand prairies, pastures, and open disturbed areas; found in the southern half of the Midwest region.

Comments: Like other plants in the *Euphorbia* genus, the sap can be irritating to the skin and eyes. A related species, painted leaf—also known as fire-on-the-mountain (*Euphorbia cyathophora*)—differs by having alternate leaves and attractive red or yellow patches near the bases of the upper leaves; found in open woods, floodplains, and disturbed soils in the western half of the Midwest region.

SNOW-ON-THE-MOUNTAIN
Euphorbia marginata
Spurge family (Euphorbiaceae)

Description: An annual plant with finely hairy stems, up to 3' tall, and white, milky sap. The leaves are alternate and up to 4" long and 2½" wide, stalkless, with rounded bases and pointed tips. Toward the top of the stem, there is a whorl of leaves under 3–5 leafy branches, which are themselves branched. Leaves on the flower branches are often densely clustered and have broad white to sometimes pinkish bands along the margins. The flower heads are less than ½" wide, with 5 white, petal-like structures surrounding a single female flower and several smaller male flowers.

Bloom Season: Summer–fall

Habitat/Range: Locally common in dry prairies and hill prairies, as well as fields, pastures, railroads, and roadsides; found in the western third of the Midwest region, and introduced in scattered locations eastward.

Comments: When the stem is broken, it exudes a white, milky sap that can be irritating to the skin of some people. This spurge can spread across large areas, often seeming to blanket the landscape with what appears from a distance to be snow; hence, the origin of the common name. The Lakota made a tea for mothers with insufficient breast milk. This may have been suggested by the plant's milky sap. The Lakota used crushed leaves as a liniment (liquid or semi-liquid) for swellings.

HOG PEANUT
Amphicarpaea bracteata
Bean family (Fabaceae)

Description: An annual to short-lived perennial, this vine grows to about 8' long and, lacking tendrils for clinging, entwines its hairy stem around other plants for support. The leaves are divided into groups of 3 at the end of a long stem. The leaflets are hairy, broadest toward the base, and tapering to a sharply pointed tip. The middle leaflet is larger than the two side leaflets, up to 3" long and 2½" wide, and long-stalked, with the 2 side leaflets stalkless (or mostly so). The flowers, up to 15, are in a compact cluster at the end of a stem arising from a leaf axil. Each flower consists of 5 white to violet to two-toned purple petals typical of those in the bean family, with an upright banner, 2 lateral wings, and a keel that is curved upward. The fruit is a green pod up to 1½" long that contains 3–4 relatively large seeds that are flattened and kidney-shaped.

Bloom Season: Midsummer–fall

Habitat/Range: Occasional in bottomland forests, wooded banks along streams, moist thickets, and sandy open areas; found throughout the Midwest region.

Comments: The hog peanut produces two types of flowers and fruit. The flowers on the stem produce pods with seeds that are not edible. The flowers at ground level do not open, lack petals, self-fertilize, and produce pods from stolons (runners) with seeds that are edible, like peanuts; hence, the common name.

CANADIAN MILK VETCH
Astragalus canadensis
Bean family (Fabaceae)

Description: Sturdy plants, up to 5' tall, with compound leaves alternating along the stem. The compound leaves are divided into 11–31 leaflets that are narrowly oval, smooth along the edges, and each 1–1½" long and ⅜–½" wide. The creamy-white to pale yellow, ½"-long flowers are crowded along a stalk that emerges above the leaves. Each flower has a hood-like upper petal over 2 smaller side petals flanking a lower lip. The pods are numerous, crowded, erect, and up to ¾" long.

Bloom Season: Summer

Habitat/Range: Occasional in prairies, hill prairies, sand prairies, prairie/woodland edges, moist thickets, and along streams; found throughout the Midwest region, but uncommon to rare in the eastern third.

Comments: Young Omaha-Ponca boys used the stalks with persistent dry pods as rattles in games where they imitated the tribal dances. Milk vetches, in general, had a reputation for increasing a cow's or a goat's milk yield.

WHITE WILD INDIGO
Baptisia alba var. *macrophylla*
Bean family (Fabaceae)

Description: A smooth, shrubby-looking plant, up to 5' tall, often with a thin, white, waxy coating on the stems and leaves. The branched stems have alternate leaves that are each divided into 3 leaflets, 1–3" long, round at the tip and tapering at the base. Stems emerge above the leaves with showy, white flowers, each about 1" long, having the structure of similar flowers in the bean family. The black seed pods are thick, pointed, and less than 2" long.

Bloom Season: Late spring–midsummer

Habitat/Range: Common in mesic and dry prairies, savannas, stream edges, fields, and roadsides; found through the Midwest region, but absent in the northern quarter.

Comments: These deep-rooted plants can persist in converted pastures and fields long after native prairie has been destroyed. Plants in the genus *Baptisia* have been used medicinally by Native Americans and early settlers as a tea for internal cleansing and, externally, for treating skin wounds. White wild indigo has been known to poison cattle if eaten in large quantities.

SESSILE-LEAVED TICK TREFOIL
Desmodium sessilifolium
Bean family (Fabaceae)

Description: Plants up to 4' tall, hairy, and typically unbranched below the flowers. Leaves are widely spaced along the stem, alternate, compound, with 3 narrow leaflets. Each leaf is stalkless, with the central leaflet 1–3" long and ¼–½" wide and slightly longer than the 2 side leaflets. Flowers are numerous, small, white to pinkish, about ¼" long, and having the structure of similar flowers in the bean family. The seed pods are flattened, hairy, about 1" long, and carrying 2–4 smooth brownish seeds.

Bloom Season: Summer

Habitat/Range: Common in upland prairies, sand prairies, savannas, old fields, fencerows, and roadsides; found through the lower part of the Midwest region, but absent in the northern half.

Comments: Like other tick trefoils, the seeds are eaten by bobwhite quail, wild turkey, and mammals, such as deer, rabbits, groundhogs, and white-footed mice. Also, like other tick trefoils, the seed pods are covered with hooked hairs that easily stick to the fur of mammals and the clothing of humans, which aids in their dispersal.

WHITE PRAIRIE CLOVER
Dalea candida
Bean family (Fabaceae)

Description: A finely leaved plant having a single to a few stems arising from a common base, up to 2' tall. The leaves are smooth, divided typically into 7 narrow leaflets, each up to 1¼" long and less than ¼" wide. The flowers are crowded into cylindrical spikes 1–3" long at the tips of the stems. The small flowers, each about ¼" long, bloom first at the bottom and progress upward along the column, forming a skirt of 5 white petals and 5 white stamens.

Bloom Season: Late spring–summer

Habitat/Range: Occasional in high-quality mesic and dry prairies, savannas, and glades; found through the Midwest region, but absent in the eastern quarter.

Comments: White prairie clover is sensitive to disturbance, especially grazing; its presence, in addition to that of other highly selective plants, is an indicator of high-quality habitat. Some Native Americans used the leaves for tea. The Ponca chewed the root for its pleasant taste. The Pawnee used the tough, elastic stems to make brooms. They also drank root tea to keep away disease.

ILLINOIS BUNDLE FLOWER
Desmanthus illinoensis
Bean family (Fabaceae)

Description: Smooth, bushy plants, up to 5' tall. The angled stem supports alternate, highly dissected leaves with numerous paired leaflets that appear fern-like. At the axil of the leaves, slender stalks emerge that support small, round flower clusters about ½" across, with each flower containing 5 small, white petals. The fine, long stamens projecting from each flower give the cluster a fuzzy appearance. The fruit is a round cluster, up to 1½" across, with twisted or curved pods, each one containing 2–6 smooth seeds.

Bloom Season: Summer

Habitat/Range: Common and occasionally weedy in disturbed prairies, rocky prairies, along prairie edges, pastures, and roadsides; found primarily in the central and southwest quarter of the Midwest region.

Comments: The children of some Native American tribes used the dried seed pods as rattles. The boiled leaves were used by the Pawnee as a wash to relieve itching. The leaves and seeds are considered an important source of protein for both wildlife and livestock.

ROUND-HEADED BUSH CLOVER
Lespedeza capitata
Bean family (Fabaceae)

Description: A slender, unbranched legume that grows up to 5' tall and is covered with fine, silvery hairs. The leaves are alternate along the stem and divided into 3 narrow leaflets, each up to 3" long and 1" wide. The flowers occur in dense, rounded heads up to 1½" in diameter. Each flower is less than ½" long, creamy-white, with a reddish to purplish spot at the base and an upper petal, 2 side petals, and a lower lip.

Bloom Season: Midsummer–fall

Habitat/Range: Occasional to common on prairies, hill prairies, sand prairies, and savannas; found throughout the Midwest region.

Comments: The Comanche used the leaves to make a tea. The Omaha and Ponca moistened one end of a short piece of the stem so it would stick to the skin, then lit the other end and allowed it to burn down to the skin. This was used to treat sharp pain associated with nerves and rheumatism. The leaves and seeds are eaten by wild turkeys. The seeds are eaten by a wide variety of wildlife. A related species, prairie bush clover (*Lespedeza leptostachya*), is federally listed as a threatened species. It is rare and occurs in the northwest part of the Midwest region on dry prairies. The plant has open flower clusters and much narrower leaflets.

HAIRY BUSH CLOVER
Lespedeza hirta
Bean family (Fabaceae)

Description: A largely unbranched plant below the midpoint, 1½–3' tall, with stems densely hairy. The leaves are alternate, compound, with 3 leaflets, and a short hairy leaf stalk with a pair of short leafy appendages at its base. The leaflets are hairy, each up to 2" long and 1½" wide, oval to broadest at the base and with smooth margins. The flowers are densely crowded in upright clusters. Each flower is about ⅓" long and cream-colored, typically with a purple spot at the base. The flower has a typical bean-shaped structure with a banner, keel, and wings.

Bloom Season: Midsummer–fall

Habitat/Range: Occasional in upland prairies, sand prairies, glades, savannas, dry upland forests, and blufftops; found throughout the southern half of the Midwest region and Michigan.

Comments: Cream-colored flowers, long stalks that support the flower clusters, broad leaves, and very hairy stems help to distinguish hairy bush clover from other *Lespedeza* species.

BUFFALO CLOVER
Trifolium reflexum
Bean family (Fabaceae)

Description: Plants are annual but sometimes biennial, with low-sprawling stems, up to 1' long. The alternate leaves are on stalks, up to 2½" long, with 2 prominent stipules at the base of each stalk where it joins the stem. Leaves are divided into 3 oval leaflets, each ¾–1" long and ⅓–¾" wide, with minutely toothed edges. The flowers are clustered in a ball shape, about 1" across and on stalks ¾–2½" long. Each flower is creamy-white to pale yellow and about ½" long, with a spreading upper petal, and 2 smaller side petals that surround a keel-like lower lip.

Bloom Season: Late spring–midsummer

Habitat/Range: Uncommon to rare in mesic to dry prairies, savannas, and open woodlands; found primarily in the southwestern part of the Midwest region, and rare in the central and southeastern part.

Comments: Populations of buffalo clover are known to respond to disturbances such as fires and logging; they also appear along logging roads, foot trails, and, once, probably along bison trails; hence, the common name. Without continued disturbance, they usually disappear after a few years, although the seeds lay dormant in the soil until the next disturbance.

WOOD VETCH
Vicia caroliniana
Bean family (Fabaceae)

Description: A climbing or trailing plant, up to 3' long. Each leaf has 5–9 pairs of narrowly oval leaflets, each up to ¾" long, with forked tendrils at the tip. There are 7–20 flowers in long-stalked clusters arising from where the leaf stalk meets the stem. Each flower is about ½" long and white, but sometimes a light violet or blue. The flower has a typical bean-shaped structure with a banner, keel, and wings. The fruits are small pods up to 1" long.

Bloom Season: Mid-spring–early summer

Habitat/Range: Common to occasional in woods, woodland borders, and rocky, open woods; found primarily in the southwest and northeast parts of the Midwest region.

Comments: The Cherokee used this plant for a variety of medicinal purposes, including the treatment of back pain and local pain; to toughen muscles; for muscular cramps; and for twitching. The seeds and leaves of wood vetch are eaten to a limited extent by birds and rodents, including mourning dove, ruffed grouse, bobwhite quail, wild turkey, white-footed mouse, and eastern wood rat.

SQUIRREL CORN
Dicentra canadensis
Fumitory family (Fumariaceae)

Description: Similar in appearance to Dutchman's breeches, with smooth, slender stems, up to 12" long. The leaves are compound and fern-like, 5–9" long and 2½–5" wide, divided into 3 primary leaflets, with each divided again into 3 secondary leaflets that are finely dissected, smooth, and emerging from the base on long stalks. Single compound leaves appear on flowerless plants. The 4–8 nodding, fragrant, heart-shaped, white flowers are up to ¾" long and ½" wide, notched at the top and spreading at the bottom. At the base of the flower is a pair of small, yellowish lobes that open like wings, revealing short stamens and a 2-horned stigma. A pair of long, vertical ruffles is at right angles to the wings.

Bloom Season: Spring

Habitat/Range: Locally common in moist woods, especially on lower slopes and in ravines; found throughout the Midwest region, but uncommon in the western quarter.

Comments: Squirrel corn can be found flowering about two weeks after Dutchman's breeches, and often in the same habitat. The roots of squirrel corn are yellow, kernel-like tubers that resemble something a squirrel would have buried.

AMERICAN COLUMBO

Frasera caroliniensis
Gentian family (Gentianaceae)

Description: Stiff, smooth plants, with single purple stems, up to 8' tall. The large leaves are whorled at the base and along the stem, broadest at the tip, narrowing toward the stem, and up to 16" long. The whitish-green flowers are in a large cluster at the top of the stem. Each flower is up to 1" across, with brownish-purple dots and a large gland on each of the 4 petals.

Bloom Season: Late spring–early summer

Habitat/Range: Locally common in rocky, open woods and borders of glades; found through the Midwest region, but absent in the northwest part.

Comments: The plant produces large basal leaves annually before sending up a flowering stem up to 25 years later. After blooming, the plant dies and spreads its seed to begin new seedlings. A root tea was formerly used for colic, cramps, dysentery, diarrhea, stomachache, lack of appetite, and nausea, and as a general tonic.

DUTCHMAN'S BREECHES

Dicentra cucullaria
Fumitory family (Fumariaceae)

Description: Stems are smooth and slender, often leaning, up to 10" long. The gray-green, fern-like leaves are compound, 3–7" long and 3–7" across, divided into 3 primary leaflets, with each divided again into 3 secondary leaflets that are finely dissected, smooth, and emerging from the base on long stalks. Single leaves appear on flowerless plants. The 4–14 flowers are on leafless stalks and hang in a one-sided cluster. The V-shaped or "breeches-shaped" petals are up to ¾" long and sometimes tinged with pink. There are 2 pale yellow lobes at the base of the flower that open like wings, revealing the stamens and style.

Bloom Season: Spring

Habitat/Range: Common in moist woods near the bases of slopes and in wooded valleys; found throughout the Midwest region.

Comments: The Iroquois used Dutchman's breeches in an ointment to make athletes' legs more limber. Settlers used a tea from the early bulb as a diuretic to treat urinary problems and to promote sweating. It is poisonous and can cause skin rashes. The plant, especially the bulb, contains an alkaloid toxic to cattle.

57

PALE GENTIAN
Gentiana alba
Gentian family (Gentianaceae)

Description: Stems are stout and up to 2' tall, usually unbranched. Leaves are smooth, opposite, attached to the stem without a stalk, up to 4" long, and about 1" wide at the base. The flowers are greenish-white or yellowish-white, bottle-shaped, with 5 short-toothed lobes that are closed to slightly open at the tip, and up to 1½" long.

Bloom Season: Late summer–fall

Habitat/Range: Occasional on rocky, wooded slopes, ledges along bluffs, dolomite glades, and openings in woods; found in the western half of the Midwest region, but rare in the eastern half.

Comments: Also known as *Gentiana flavida*. The bitter-tasting root of several species of gentian was used to increase the flow of gastric juice, promoting the appetite and aiding digestion. The bumblebee is one of the few insects strong enough to open the bottle-shaped flower and achieve pollination.

PENNYWORT
Obolaria virginica
Gentian family (Gentianaceae)

Description: A diminutive plant, up to 6" tall, that is mycoheterotrophic—which means it gets much of its nutrients through a symbiotic relationship with fungi, instead of through its small purplish-green leaves. The leaves are opposite, purplish-green, spatula-shaped to broadest toward the tip, up to ⅝" long, and reduced to scales below. The flowers are small, white, ¼–½" long, funnel-shaped, with 4 ascending to slightly spreading lobes that are about as long as the tube. There are 4 stamens, and they do not extend beyond the petals.

Bloom Season: Spring

Habitat/Range: Uncommon in mesic upland forests and bottomland forests; found in the southern quarter of the Midwest region and further south.

Comments: *Obolaria virginica* is monotypic, which means there are no other species in the genus *Obolaria*. Due to its small stature, it is difficult to see, and is often buried under leaf litter.

CAROLINA CRANESBILL

Geranium carolinianum
Geranium family (Geraniaceae)

Description: A summer annual, 8–12" tall, that branches at its base and along its stems. The green stems are covered with white hairs and often become reddish-brown as they mature. Leaves are opposite, about 3" long and wide, hairy, and deeply divided into 3–9 lobes with coarse teeth or secondary lobes that are pointed. The flowers are about ¼" wide and in tight clusters, each with 5 white to pink petals and 5 sepals that are often longer than the petals. The fruit is an erect, capsule-like structure about 1" long that looks like the beak of a crane; hence, the common name. Eventually the beak splits open and flings the seeds some distance from the mother plant.

Bloom Season: Summer

Habitat/Range: Common in sandy or gravelly soil of prairies, glades, tops of ledges, and banks of streams; also pastures, idle fields, roadsides, and other disturbed areas; found throughout the Midwest region, but less common in the northern third.

Comments: A related species, northern cranesbill (*Geranium bicknellii*), has deep pink flowers about ½" wide and with the leaf lobes rounded at the tips; frequent in dry areas in open woods, rocky slopes, and burned or disturbed sites; found in the northern third of the Midwest region.

PRAIRIE BLUE-EYED GRASS

Sisyrinchium campestre
Iris family (Iridaceae)

Description: Small, clump-forming plants, with stems not branching at the top, up to 12" tall, with pointed, upright, grass-like leaves. The flower stems are flat, about ⅛" wide, with 2 narrow wings, and typically longer than the leaves. Several flowers, each on a slender stalk, emerge from two long-pointed, leaf-like bracts at the top of the stem. Each flower is white or light to dark blue (see page 299 for the blue version), about ½" across, with a yellow center, and 3 sepals and 3 petals, which all look like petals. The tips of the sepals and petals vary, from rounded with a hair-like point, to notched, to shallowly toothed.

Bloom Season: Mid-spring–early summer

Habitat/Range: Common in dry upland prairies, savannas, rocky, open woods, and glades; found throughout the Midwest region, but absent in the eastern third.

Comments: A similar species, eastern blue-eyed grass (*Sisyrinchium albidum*), has 3–4 leaf-like bracts surrounding a single flower cluster at the top of the stem. Flowers are white or pale violet. Habitat is similar to prairie blue-eyed grass; found throughout the Midwest region, but absent in the western third.

AMERICAN BUGLEWEED
Lycopus americanus
Mint family (Lamiaceae)

Description: Plants up to 2' tall, with square stems. The leaves are opposite, up to 3½" long, with the leaf cut into coarse lobes or teeth along the margins. Flowers are in dense stands surrounding the stem at the bases of the leaves. Each flower is white, less than ¼" long, with 4 lobes, and stamens that extend beyond the tube. This plant does not have the aromatic foliage often found with many other mints.

Bloom Season: Early summer–fall

Habitat/Range: Common in wet prairies, moist swales of upland prairies, margins of wet, marshy areas, fallow fields, and along roadsides; found throughout the Midwest region.

Comments: The plant has been used as an astringent (a substance that causes contraction of the tissues and stops bleeding), a mild sedative, and as a treatment for hyperthyroidism. It is also used in the treatment of coughs. Because the leaves are bitter-tasting, they are often not eaten by mammalian herbivores. The plant is also called "common water horehound." There are five other species of bugleweeds in the Midwest region, but American bugleweed is the most widespread.

HAIRY MOUNTAIN MINT
Pycnanthemum pilosum
Mint family (Lamiaceae)

Description: Aromatic plants with square stems that are moderately to densely hairy and up to 4' tall. The numerous leaves are opposite, up to 3" long and ¾" wide, with bases rounded and stalkless. There are often small, leafy branches emerging from where the main leaves join the stem. The flowers are in dense clusters near the top of each branch. Each flower is less than ¼" long, tube-shaped, and with a 3-lobed lower lip and a single upper lip. The flowers are white to pale lavender, with small purple spots.

Bloom Season: Midsummer–fall

Habitat/Range: Occasional in mesic to dry prairies, savannas, old fields, pastures, and roadsides; found in the lower half of the Midwest region.

Comments: Also known as *Pynanthemum verticillatum* var. *pilosum*. Like other mountain mints, the numerous flowers are good nectar sources for a variety of bees, wasps, flies, beetles, moths, and butterflies.

SLENDER MOUNTAIN MINT
Pycnanthemum tenuifolium
Mint family (Lamiaceae)

Description: Aromatic plants with smooth, square stems growing to a height of 3'. The stem, with numerous pairs of leaves, branches toward the top. The narrow, pointed leaves are up to 2" long and ¼" wide. Flower heads are densely packed, with each flower about ⅛" wide, and a white to pale lavender upper lip, and a lower lip with 3 lobes. Both lips often have small purple spots.

Bloom Season: Late spring–summer

Habitat/Range: Common in mesic to dry prairies, savannas, glades, old fields, pastures, and roadsides; found throughout the southern half of the Midwest region, and rare northward.

Comments: The genus *Pycnanthemum* is commonly known as mountain mint, but that is something of a misnomer, because species in this group do not usually occur in mountainous habitats. Native Americans used slender mountain mint, with its alluring scent, to bait mink traps and to make a tea for treating a run-down condition. The tea has been used as a seasoning in cooking.

VIRGINIA MOUNTAIN MINT
Pycnanthemum virginianum
Mint family (Lamiaceae)

Description: Often bushy-looking plants, up to 3' tall, with green or reddish square stems and scattered white hairs along the ridges. The leaves are opposite, stalkless, up to 2½" long and ½" wide, hairless, with smooth margins, a rounded base, and tapering to a pointed tip. The flowers are densely packed in flat clusters with each head about ¾" across and containing up to 50 flowers. The flowers in a head do not all flower at the same time. Each flower is about ⅛" long, tubular, with 2 lips. The upper lip has 2 lobes while the lower lip has 3 lobes. The lobes are white with purple spots. The outside of the tube is covered with fine hairs.

Bloom Season: Midsummer–fall

Habitat/Range: Frequent in mesic prairies, wet prairies, moist sand prairies, and moist open areas; found throughout the Midwest region.

Comments: Mountain mints attract many insects to its flowers, including various bees, wasps, flies, small butterflies, and beetles. The leaves are very fragrant; when crushed, they have a strong minty odor. The long bloom time, a month or more in the summer, makes it a great garden choice, especially for feeding pollinators.

61

COLIC ROOT
Aletris farinosa
Lily family (Liliaceae)

Description: A smooth, single-stemmed, wand-like plant, up to 2½" tall. The leaves are found at the base of the plant, with each strap-like leaf up to 8" long. The flowers are clustered at the top of a mostly bare stem. The white, tubular flowers are about ¼" long, with 6 lobes, and covered with a rough surface.

Bloom Season: Summer

Habitat/Range: Occasional in moist, sandy prairies, sandy flats, open woods, marshes, and roadsides; found in the central part of the Midwest region.

Comments: The outside of the flowers have an unusual rough texture, giving rise to the species name, *farinosa*, meaning "mealy." *Colic* is a Greek word meaning "relative to the colon." Colic (or cholic) is a form of pain that starts and stops abruptly. It occurs due to muscular contractions of the colon as it tries to relieve an obstruction by forcing content out. Native Americans used the root to treat stomach and bowel disorders, as well as rheumatism, jaundice, and lung disease. However, the fresh root is mildly poisonous.

WILD LEEK
Allium tricoccum
Lily family (Liliaceae)

Description: An onion odor is detected with this plant, along with its pair of leaves arising at its base that are 6–12" long and 1–4" wide. The leaves have reddish stalks and appear in early spring, only to wither away before flowering time. The numerous white flowers are clustered at the tops of bare stems, which are up to 18" tall. Each flower is about ¼" long, with 3 sepals and 3 petals that are similar in appearance.

Bloom Season: Early summer–midsummer

Habitat/Range: Locally common, often forming dense colonies in moist woods, typically on north- or east-facing slopes; found throughout the Midwest region, but rare in the southwest part.

Comments: Also called "wild ramp," the onion-like flavor of the leaves and bulbs have a long history of being eaten by North American Indians and pioneers, as well as modern-day enthusiasts. There are two varieties of wild leek. *Allium tricoccum* var. *tricoccum* has broader leaves that are commonly reddish at the base and up to 50 flowers in a cluster. *Allium tricoccum* var. *burdickii* has narrower leaves that are green at the base and shorter-stalked, with 20 or fewer flowers per cluster.

WHITE DOGTOOTH VIOLET
Erythronium albidum
Lily family (Liliaceae)

Description: A single-flowering plant originating from a corm (a bulb-like underground structure), with stalks up to 6" tall. Flowering plants have a pair of flat to slightly folded leaves emerging from the base, whereas the more-numerous nonflowering plants produce only single leaves. The leaves, up to 6" long, are mottled with brown and resemble the pattern on a trout; hence, the other common name, "trout lily." The 3 sepals and 3 petals are similar and curve backward as the flower ages. The flowers are about 1" wide, with large yellow stamens.

Bloom Season: Spring

Habitat/Range: Common in moist woods and lower wooded slopes and valleys, usually in colonies; found throughout the Midwest region.

Comments: Dogtooth violet is named for the shape of its underground corm. Large colonies often can be found with few plants in flower. The deeply buried corm can send out side shoots to produce new plants, each with a single leaf. Native Americans used root tea for fever, and a warm mass of leaves was applied to the skin for hard-to-heal ulcers. A similar species, prairie dogtooth violet (*Erythronium mesochoreum*), has strongly folded leaves lacking mottling and spreading flowers that do not bend back; they are found on mesic to dry prairies in the west-central and southwest part of the Midwest region.

CANADA MAYFLOWER
Maianthemum canadense
Lily family (Liliaceae)

Description: A short plant, 3–6" tall, with zigzag stems between the alternately attached leaves. There are typically 2 leaves—but sometimes 3—on fertile plants, and with single leaves on immature or sterile plants. Each leaf is up to 3" long and 2" wide, with heart-shaped bases and pointed tips. There are faint parallel veins along the length of the leaf. Flowers are in elongated clusters, 1–2½" long, along the upper part of the stems. Each flower is about ¼" wide with 4 white, petal-like segments and 4 stamens surrounding a flask-shaped ovary. The fruit is a green berry about ¼" wide, a mottled dull pale red that turns dark red in late summer.

Bloom Season: Mid-spring–early summer

Habitat/Range: Common in dry to wet forests, and in bogs and swamps; found throughout the northern half of the Midwest region.

Comments: The seeds are produced infrequently and most plants in a location are vegetative clones. The plants are spreading by their rhizomes, which are shallow, trailing, and white. A tea made from the plant has been used in the treatment of headache and as a kidney tonic for pregnant women. It has also been used as a gargle for sore throats and as an expectorant (induces the removal [coughing-up] of mucous secretions from the lungs). Another species, false mayflower (*Maianthemum trifolium*), has 3 long, narrow leaves, up to 6" long and 1½" wide, and a flower cluster more loosely arranged; locally common in bogs, wet conifer forests, and shaded wet soils; found in the northern third of the Midwest region.

FALSE SOLOMON'S SEAL
Maianthemum racemosum
Lily family (Liliaceae)

Description: The slightly zigzag stem stiffly arches to a length of up to 3'. The firm, spreading leaves alternate along the finely hairy stem. The leaves are 3–6" long and 3" wide, with parallel veins, smooth margins, and very short stalks. There are up to 80 tiny, creamy-white, star-shaped flowers, each about ⅛" across, with 3 petals and 3 sepals that are similar in size and shape, and 6 yellow stamens. The flowers are borne in a branched cluster at the end of the stem. Clusters are up to 4" long and 2" across. The fruits are ruby-red berries about ¼" across and often speckled with brown or purple.

Bloom Season: Late spring–early summer

Habitat/Range: Occasional in woodlands and moist woods toward the bases of slopes, ravines, and valleys; found throughout the Midwest region.

Comments: Formerly known as *Smilacena racemosa*. The Meskwaki tribe burned the root as a smudge to quiet a crying baby and to return someone to normal after temporary insanity. They also used the root with food during times of plague to prevent sickness. The plant was also used for its internal cleansing effect. The young shoots, when boiled, are said to taste like asparagus, while the starchy rootstocks can serve as a substitute for potatoes. The berries are edible but prompt a cathartic (laxative) action. Ruffed grouse, some songbirds, white-footed mice, and eastern wood rats are known to eat the berries.

STARRY FALSE SOLOMON'S SEAL
Maianthemum stellatum
Lily family (Liliaceae)

Description: The slightly zigzag stem stiffly arches to a length of up to 3'. The firm, spreading, somewhat curved leaves alternate along a smooth to finely hairy stem. Each slightly folded leaf is up to 6" long and 2" wide, stiff in shape, with pointed tips and clasping bases, parallel veins along the length, and a slightly hairy underside. At the tip of the stem, up to 20 creamy-white, star-like flowers are arranged, each about ⅜" across, with 3 petals and 3 sepals that are similar in size and shape, and 6 yellow stamens. The fruit is a small berry, about ¼" across, that is initially green with purple stripes and ripens to a reddish-purple.

Bloom Season: Mid- to late spring

Habitat/Range: Locally frequent in open to partially shaded prairies, savannas, and edges of woods; found across the northern two-thirds of the Midwest region.

Comments: Formerly known as *Smilacena stellata*. The Paiute dried the root and pounded it into a powder; this was applied to a wound, causing blood to clot almost immediately. The roots were also used to treat stomach problems, menstrual disorders, and venereal disease. The fruit is bitter-tart but edible.

BUNCHFLOWER
Melanthium virginicum
Lily family (Liliaceae)

Description: Erect, stout plants, up to 5' tall, with long, grass-like leaves at the base, which alternate up the stem. The leaves are up to 20" long and up to 1" wide, with upper leaves being much shorter. The flowers occur along long branches at the top, up to 18" tall. Individual stalked flowers are ½–1" across, creamy-white, with 3 petals and 3 sepals that are similar in size and shape.

Bloom Season: Late spring–midsummer

Habitat/Range: Occasional in mesic to wet prairies and degraded remnant prairies along railroads and roadsides; found in the southern half of the Midwest region, but rare in the central and eastern parts.

Comments: Also known as *Veratrum virginicum.* The towering plumes of white flowers are very conspicuous in open areas, making their identification from a distance very easy. The roots and stems contain alkaloids that are poisonous to livestock, and the root has been used to kill intestinal parasites. The flower turns black with age.

FALSE GARLIC
Nothoscordum bivalve
Lily family (Liliaceae)

Description: A slender plant that grows from a bulb, producing leafless stems, up to 12" tall. The smooth, grass-like leaves that emerge from the base are long and narrow. The 5–12 fragrant flowers, each about ½" across, are on stalks that arise from a common point on top of the stem. There are 3 petals and 3 sepals, all about the same size and shape, and white to slightly yellow in color. The 6 stamens are yellow.

Bloom Season: Spring; sometimes again in fall

Habitat/Range: Common in mesic to dry prairies, glades, and open woodlands; found in the southwest and south-central part of the Midwest region.

Comments: Also called "crow poison," the Cherokee harvested the bulbs of this plant to poison crows that were eating their corn. False garlic is a favorite nectar source for small butterflies, such as the falcate orangetip. This plant is related to the wild onion, but there is no characteristic onion odor.

SOLOMON'S SEAL
Polygonatum biflorum var. *commutatum*
Lily family (Liliaceae)

Description: A gracefully arching plant with alternate leaves that may reach up to 5' in length. The stems are smooth, unbranched, and stout, supporting several leaves up to 7" long and 3" wide. The leaves are stalkless, almost clasping at the base, and have parallel veins and pale undersides. The tubular, greenish-white flowers are about ¾" long, ending in 6 short lobes, and hang from slender stalks in clusters, each containing up to 12 flowers. The fruits are dark blue berries about ½" in diameter.

Bloom Season: Mid-spring–early summer

Habitat/Range: More common as a woodland plant, but sometimes occurring in mesic prairies along thicket edges and stream banks; found throughout the Midwest region.

Comments: Native Americans used the rhizome in a tea for treating internal pains. Externally, it was used as a wash for poison ivy, skin irritations, and hemorrhoids. Settlers used root tea for rheumatism, arthritis, and skin irritations. The young shoots, when boiled, are said to taste like asparagus, while the starchy rootstocks can serve as a substitute for potatoes. However, like many plants in the lily family, they are not common enough to be collected in the wild. Ruffed grouse, some songbirds, white-footed mice, and eastern wood rats are known to eat the berries. A related species, hairy Solomon's seal (*Polygonatum pubescens*), differs by being generally smaller, having short hairs on the underside of leaves, and 1–3 hanging flower in the leaf axils, each ½" long; found throughout the Midwest region except for the southwest part.

WHITE MANDARIN
Streptosus amplexifolius
Lily family (Liliaceae)

Description: The plants are freely branched and spreading from a single stem, up to 3' tall. The leaves are alternate, 2–6" long and 1–2½" wide, broadly rounded, with smooth margins, a base that often clasps the stem, and a pointed tip. The flowers dangle along the stem and are attached to the leaf axils by an often bent or twisted stalk, up to 2" long. Each bell-shaped flower is about ⅜–½" long, with 6 greenish-yellow to white, narrow, flaring lobes. The fruit is about ½" across and ripens to a yellow-orange to red color.

Bloom Season: Late spring–early summer

Habitat/Range: Occasional in moist shaded sites in ravines and seeps, on slopes, and along stream banks; found in the northern quarter of the Midwest region.

Comments: Also known as clasping-leaved twisted stalk. A related species, rose mandarin or rose twisted stalk (*Streptopus lanceolatus*), has pinkish-purple flowers about ⅜" long with 6 lobes that curve outward at their tips; shorter stems, up to 16" in size; and leaves with a fringe of hairs along the margins. Common in rich, moist sites in woods, and found across the northern third of the Midwest region.

FEATHERBELLS
Stenanthium gramineum
Lily family (Liliaceae)

Description: A large pyramidal cluster of small, white, nodding flowers arises on a stem, 2½–5' tall. The leaves form a basal rosette of flat, smooth, grass-like leaves, 8–20" long. The few leaves on the stem are greatly reduced and mostly bract-like. The numerous flowers on the lower branches are mostly male, while the upper branches hold female and perfect (male and female) flowers. The flowers are on short stalks, with 3 sepals and 3 petals of equal length, about ⅜" each.

Bloom Season: Summer–early fall

Habitat/Range: Uncommon to rare in mesic upland and bottomland forests, wet-mesic prairies, at the base of bluffs, and along banks of streams; found in the southern third of the Midwest region.

Comments: The genus name, *Stenanthium*, is from the Greek *stenos* (narrow) and *anthos* (flower), which refers to the narrow, pointed sepals and petals. The species name, *gramineum*, means grass-like.

FALSE ASPHODEL
Triantha glutinosa
Lily family (Liliaceae)

Description: Single-stemmed plants, up to 1½'
tall, with narrow, grass-like leaves clustered at
the base, and with small, dark, sticky spots along
the upper part of the stem. Leaves are up to 7"
long and ¼–½" wide, erect, stalkless, and pointed
at the tip. There are 1–3 much smaller leaves
arranged up to about mid-stem. There are small,
white flowers that form dense clusters at the top
of the stem, with 1–3 stalked flowers at each
point. The flowers are about ¼" wide, with 3 tiny
bracts at the base and 6 narrow, petal-like segments surrounding 6 stamens.

Bloom Season: Summer

Habitat/Range: Local in wet soil of meadows,
fens, seeps, wet sands, and moist rocky areas;
found in the northern third of the Midwest region.

Comments: The species name, *glutinosa*, means
sticky or gluey, which describes the tactile
sensation experienced when lightly tapping the
glandular stem. The stickiness is probably a
defense mechanism to discourage small insects
from climbing the stem in order to eat or pierce the
stem, flowers, or fruit.

NODDING TRILLIUM
Trillium cernuum
Lily family (Liliaceae)

Description: A whorl of 3 leaves sits above
a bare stem that is 8–20" tall. The leaves are
broadly rounded, short-stalked, each 2½–5" long
and nearly as wide, and tapering to a sharply
pointed tip. Margins are smooth but sometimes
wavy, and the base is broadly rounded. The single
nodding flower is on a stalk up to 1½" long that
droops below the leaves. The flower is 1½–2"
wide and has 3 green, pointed sepals, 3 broad,
pointed, white petals, and 6 large, white to pinkish
stamens.

Bloom Season: Mid-spring–early summer

Habitat/Range: Frequent in mesic forests and
moist shaded slopes and stream banks; found in
the northern half of the Midwest region.

Comments: The genus *Trillium* is comprised of 38
species in North America, especially in the eastern
United States, with another 12 species found in
Asia. There are 10 species of Trillium that occur in
the Midwest region.

WHITE TRILLIUM
Trillium flexipes
Lily family (Liliaceae)

Description: A showy spring wildflower and one of the largest of the Midwest trilliums. The unbranched stems rise up to 2' tall and spread a whorl of 3 very broad leaves that are up to 5" across and about as long. A single, nodding flower about 3" across is attached to an arched stalk up to 4" long. There are 3 white petals, 3 green sepals, and 6 creamy-white stamens. The fruit, which is 1" in diameter, turns a rose color during summer.

Bloom Season: Spring

Habitat/Range: Occasional in moist woods on lower slopes and in wooded valleys or ravines; found through the Midwest region, but absent in the northern quarter.

Comments: Also known as drooping trillium. White trillium may form small colonies from spreading rhizomes, but scattered, solitary flowers are common. Various Native American tribes used trillium to treat open wounds and sores, menstrual disorders, menopause, internal bleeding, to induce childbirth, and as an aphrodisiac. Settlers called it "birthroot" because of its labor-inducing properties.

LARGE-FLOWERED TRILLIUM
Trillium grandiflorum
Lily family (Liliaceae)

Description: A single-flowered plant, up to 18" tall, with a single whorl of 3 leaves at the top of each stem. Leaves are glossy on the upper surface, and up to 6" long and half as wide to nearly as wide. The large flower, which is about 3" across, has 3 white petals emerging from the leaves on a stalk 1–3" long. The wavy-edged petals turn pinkish with age. There are 6 yellow stamens.

Bloom Season: Mid-spring–early summer

Habitat/Range: Moist woods; found through the Midwest region, but absent in the southwest quarter.

Comments: Large-flowered trillium tends to grow in large patches, which makes for an attractive display on the forest floor, especially with its large flowers and glossy leaves. A slow-growing plant, often taking 6 years to flower, it is rarely grown from seed in the nursery trade. Plants offered for sale are probably root-dug from the wild, which is not an ethical practice and should be avoided.

SNOW TRILLIUM
Trillium nivale
Lily family (Liliaceae)

Description: As the name implies, this early spring wildflower sometimes appears through the snow. The unbranched stems rise up to 6" tall, ending with a whorl of 3 rounded leaves up to 2" long and 1¼" wide. Nonflowering plants are generally smaller and may have only 1–2 leaves. The flowers are 1–2" wide, with three showy petals each about 1" long. The edges of the petals are often wavy. There are 6 yellow stamens and the fruit is 3-sided.

Bloom Season: Early spring

Habitat/Range: Uncommon in moist woods; found in the middle third of the Midwest region and rare elsewhere.

Comments: Also known as dwarf white trillium in some states, snow trillium often appears in large colonies, with the plants shriveling and disappearing by late July. The species name, *nivale*, is Latin for "snow." Another small, white flowering species, Ozark trillium (*Trillium pusillum* var. *ozarkanum*), is up to 12" tall, with 3 narrow leaves each about 3" long and 1" wide, and 3 petals each about 1" long that turn pink with age; rare; found in woods in the extreme southwestern part of the Midwest region.

WHITE CAMASS
Zigadenus elegans
Lily family (Liliaceae)

Description: The hairy stalk is up to 2½" tall, with grass-like leaves that are up to 12" long and less than ½" wide. The stems are often bluish-green with a white waxy coating. Individual flowers are stalked and alternate along the upper stem. Each creamy-white flower is about ½" across and composed of 6 petal-like segments. Each segment has a greenish, 2-lobed gland at the base.

Bloom Season: Early summer–midsummer

Habitat/Range: Occasional in prairies and moist soil in open areas; found in the northern half of the Midwest region.

Comments: Also known as death camass. All parts of this plant are poisonous, from alkaloids more toxic than strychnine. Humans have been poisoned by mistakenly eating the bulbs, believing they were eating wild onions.

GLADE MALLOW
Napaea dioica
Mallow family (Malvaceae)

Description: Stems are ridged, sparsely hairy, often covered with a waxy bloom, 3–9' tall, and may form colonies from spreading rhizomes. The leaves are long-stalked up to 8", alternate, and quite large, up to 18" long and wide, becoming smaller as they ascend the stem. The leaves have 5–9 palmate lobes, which can be further divided into additional lobes that are coarsely lobed and sharply pointed. The flowers are in tight, branching clusters and on stalks up to 1" long. Each flowering plant has either all male or all female flowers. Individual flowers are ½–¾" across with 5 white, oval petals. The male flowers have a cluster of stamens in the center that are fused together in a column, with pinkish anthers in a ball at the tip. The female flowers have a cluster of curly, thread-like styles above a white ovary.

Bloom Season: Summer

Habitat/Range: Uncommon to rare in wet prairies, openings in bottomland forests, banks of streams, and low areas along streams; found across the central section in the Midwest region.

Comments: When in bloom, glade mallow produces a fragrant aroma. It does well in cultivation and the compact cluster of flowers, and the interesting large, coarsely toothed leaves, make it desirable for a garden setting if the soil has adequate moisture, like in a rain garden.

ENCHANTER'S NIGHTSHADE
Circaea canadensis
Evening primrose family (Onagraceae)

Description: Single-stemmed plants, 1–2' tall, with opposite leaves, the pairs at right angles to the pairs below. The leaves are up to 5" long and 3" across, widest toward the base, loosely toothed along the edges, and tapering to a pointed tip. The leaf stalk is up to 1½" long. The flowers are sparse but evenly arranged along the upper stem. Each flower, which is on a ½"-long stalk, is about ¼" in diameter, with 2 white to pinkish petals that are deeply notched, 2 long, white stamens projecting from the center, and 2 green to purple sepals that bend back away from the flower. The upper stem, flower stalk, flowers, and fruit are all hairy.

Bloom Season: Summer

Habitat/Range: Occasional to locally common in mesic upland forests, bottomland forests, and at the base of bluffs; found throughout the Midwest region.

Comments: Also known as *Circaea lutetiana* var. *canadensis*. A related species, small enchanter's nightshade (*Circaea alpina*), is a much smaller plant, up to 10" tall, with flowers clustered at the top rather than scattered along the upper stem; common in moist shaded sites in woods, swamps, and edges of bogs; found in the northern third of the Midwest region. The genus name, *Circaea*, comes from the enchantress Circe of Greek mythology, and even though its common name is nightshade, it is not especially toxic, although it does contain a large amount of astringent tannin.

LARGE-FLOWERED GAURA
Oenothera filiformis
Evening primrose family (Onagraceae)

Description: A tall annual or biennial plant reaching a height of 7' tall, branching toward the top, with curved hairs lying flat along the stems. The leaves are alternate on the stem, up to 6" long and ⅜" wide, with widely spaced teeth along the margins, and fine silky hairs along both surfaces. The flowers are about 1" long and ¾" wide, and scattered along the upper stem, with 4 white petals that fade to pink with age. The petals are arranged in an upward-pointing, semicircular fan shape. Below are 8 downward-pointing stamens and a thread-like style, with 4 narrow lobes at the tip.

Bloom Season: Summer–early fall

Habitat/Range: Locally frequent in dry and rocky prairies, sand prairies, old fields, pastures, disturbed sites, and roadsides; found in the central and southwest parts of the Midwest region.

Comments: Formerly known as *Gaura longiflora*. A closely related species, biennial gaura (*Oenothera gaura*, formerly known as *Gaura biennis*), is usually shorter, less than 6' tall, with straight hairs spreading away from the stem, instead of lying flat along the stem, like large-flowered gaura; found in similar habitat throughout the Midwest.

WHITE LADY'S SLIPPER
Cypripedium candidum
Orchid family (Orchidaceae)

Description: Short plants, less than 1' tall, which can form large colonies. The 3–4 leaves along the stem are finely hairy, up to 6" long and 2" wide, and slightly pleated along their length. There is typically a single flower at the top of the stem in front of an erect, leaf-like bract. The flower has a broad, white "slipper" about 1" long, with two twisted, greenish-brown lateral petals that slant downward and away from the slipper. There are 2 lateral sepals of similar color fused behind the lip, while the upper sepal is broader and erect above the lip. The petals and sepals are typically yellowish-green, streaked purplish-brown.

Bloom Season: Mid-spring–early summer

Habitat/Range: Rare in seepage areas in mesic prairies and glades, fens, meadows, and marshes; found scattered across the Midwest region.

Comments: With the destruction of most of its former habitat, finding the white lady's slipper is a special occasion. Fortunately, there are protected public lands where this delicate jewel of the wildflower world can still be admired.

RATTLESNAKE PLANTAIN
Goodyera pubescens
Orchid family (Orchidaceae)

Description: An orchid with a finely hairy, slender stalk, 9–14" tall, with an attractive rosette of bluish-green basal leaves that overwinter. The 5–7 basal leaves are from 1½–2" long and about 1" wide, with a prominent network of silvery-white veins. The flowers appear in an alternate, spiral-like pattern toward the top of the stem, with 28–52 flowers. Each white flower is ⅜" long, with 3 petal-like sepals, 2 slightly smaller petals, and a pointed, sac-like lower lip.

Bloom Season: Summer

Habitat/Range: Not common in dry to moist woods; found primarily in the northern half of the Midwest region, and with scattered populations in the southern half.

Comments: The genus name is in honor of John Goodyer, a 17th-century English botanist. The common name "rattlesnake" is for the similarity of the leaf shape and venation pattern to the head of a snake, while another source states that the name is derived from the early belief that the leaves, when chewed and applied to a rattlesnake bite, would provide antidotal relief. The name "plantain" is for the similarity of the leaves to that of the common plantain. Another species, tessellated or checkered rattlesnake plantain (*Goodyera tessellata*), is 7–13" tall, has over 25 flowers on one side along the stem, each ⅛" long, with an elongated lip; found in sandy upland forests in the northern quarter of the Midwest region. And, there's lesser rattlesnake plantain (*Goodyera repens*), with stems 2–7" tall, with less than 25 flowers, also on one side along the stem, each ⅛" long, with a rounded lip; found in wetter habitats, also in the northern quarter of the Midwest region.

75

GREEN WOOD ORCHID
Platanthera clavellata
Orchid family (Orchidaceae)

Description: A small, single-stemmed plant, 4–12"
tall, with a principal leaf that is located near the
base. The leaf is broadest above the middle, 2–5"
long, and narrows to a base that clasps the stem.
There are also several small, bract-like leaves
along the stem. The flowers are alternate along
the upper part of the stem, with each creamy- to
greenish-white flower about ¼" across. An upper
sepal and 2 petals form a hood over the flower
center, and 2 small lateral sepals spread out at
the sides. The dangling lower lip is somewhat
rectangular, with a blunt tip with 3 minute lobes.
At the base of the flower, a swollen ovary twists
to display the flower horizontally.

Bloom Season: Summer

Habitat/Range: Rare to occasional in acid seeps,
wet forests, swamps, bogs, meadows, and margins of sinkhole ponds; found in the northern and
southern thirds of the Midwest region.

Comments: Because of their diminutive size, green
wood orchids can often be overlooked. The flowers
are apparently self-pollinated throughout much of
their range, a process by which the pollen masses
crumble and fall onto the flowers' stigmatic
surface.

TUBERCLED REIN ORCHID
Platanthera flava var. *herbiola*
Orchid family (Orchidaceae)

Description: Smooth, single-stemmed plants,
7–18" tall, with alternate leaves that clasp the
stem at their tapering bases. There are 2–3 main
leaves, up to 6" long and ¾" wide, with pointed
tips. The whitish-green flowers are alternate along
the upper part of the stem, each ¼" wide, with an
upper sepal and 2 side petals that form an upper
hood, 2 lateral sepals spreading outward, and a
broad lower lip, with a round tip and 2 small side
lobes at the base. Near the center of the base, a
small tubercle (bump) blocks insects from entering
into the middle and forces them to enter from the
sides. A stout spur, about ¼" long, extends below.

Bloom Season: Summer

Habitat/Range: Uncommon to rare in floodplains,
wet-mesic prairies, wetland edges, and meadows;
found in scattered locations across the Midwest
region.

Comments: The similar-looking long-bracted orchid
(*Coeloglossum viride*) has a notched lip instead of
rounded, a purple mark at the base of the lip, and
a short, sac-like spur underneath; occasional in
moist woods, meadows, and bogs; found throughout the northern half of the Midwest region.

RAGGED FRINGED ORCHID

Plantanthera lacera
Orchid family (Orchidaceae)

Description: A smooth, slender plant, up to about 2' tall, with 10–40 white to greenish-white flowers. The 2–5 leaves are alternate, 3–10" long, lance-shaped, longest near the base of the stem, and reduced in size upward. The flowers are less than 1" long and ½" wide, with a lip that has 3 lobes that are deeply divided into thread-like segments. The upper sepal and two upper petals are greenish and form a hood. The lateral sepals are also greenish, similar in shape, but spread outward. The spur is about ½" long.

Bloom Season: Late spring–midsummer

Habitat/Range: Occasional in mesic to dry prairies; also in moist soil in wetlands; found throughout the Midwest region, but absent in the west-central part.

Comments: The species name, *lacera*, is Latin for "torn," in reference to the fringed lip of the flower. The fragrant flowers are pollinated primarily by moths, including noctuid moths and sphinx moths.

EASTERN PRAIRIE FRINGED ORCHID

Platanthera leucophaea
Orchid family (Orchidaceae)

Description: A smooth, single-stemmed orchid, growing up to 2½' tall. The 3–6 leaves are alternate along the stem, up to 10" long and 1" wide, and clasp the stem. The 18–30 creamy-white flowers are located along the top of the stem. The lip of the flower is about ¾" long, with 3 lobes, each cut into narrow fringes. The upper sepal and two upper petals are creamy-white and form a hood. The lateral sepals are also creamy-white, similar in shape, but spread outward. The spur is ¾–1½" long.

Bloom Season: Early summer–midsummer

Habitat/Range: Very rare in mesic to wet prairies, sand prairies, and marshes; found primarily in the central and east-central part of the Midwest region.

Comments: The eastern prairie fringed orchid is listed as threatened by the US Fish and Wildlife Service under the federal Endangered Species Act. Unfortunately, this orchid has been eliminated throughout a large portion of its former range, due to the plowing of many prairies and the heavy grazing of other sites by livestock. The plants emit a sweet fragrance, particularly around sunset, and are pollinated by hawk moths. The eastern prairie fringed orchid is similar to the western prairie fringed orchid, but the latter has a less-dense flower cluster, fewer flowers, and the flowers tend to be larger.

77

WESTERN PRAIRIE FRINGED ORCHID
Platanthera praeclara
Orchid family (Orchidaceae)

Description: A smooth, single-stemmed orchid, growing up to 2½' tall. The 3–6 leaves are alternate along the stem, up to 10" long and 1" wide, and clasp the stem. The flowers are in clusters along the tops of the stems, with 8–18 creamy-white flowers. The lip of the flower is about ¾–1¼" long, with 3 lobes, each cut into narrow fringes. The upper sepal and two upper petals are creamy-white and form a hood. The lateral sepals are also creamy-white and similar in shape, but spread outward. The spur is 1¼–2" long.

Bloom Season: Early summer–midsummer

Habitat/Range: Very rare in mesic to wet prairies; found in the western third of the Midwest region.

Comments: The western prairie fringed orchid is listed as threatened by the US Fish and Wildlife Service under the federal Endangered Species Act. Unfortunately, this orchid has been eliminated throughout a large portion of its former range, due to the plowing of many prairies and the heavy grazing of other sites by livestock. The plants emit a sweet fragrance, particularly around sunset, and are pollinated by hawk moths. The western prairie fringed orchid is similar to the eastern prairie fringed orchid, but the latter has a denser flower cluster, more flowers, and the flowers tend to be smaller.

NODDING LADIES' TRESSES
Spiranthes cernua
Orchid family (Orchidaceae)

Description: A slender orchid, up to 10" tall, with fine hairs on the stem and flowers. The 3–4 basal leaves are grass-like, up to 9" long, and often die back at the time of flowering. The upper stem leaves are reduced to scales. The white flowers are in a spiraled arrangement of 2–3 rows on the upper part of the stem. Each flower is up to ½" long, slightly nodding, with the sepals and petals forming a tube around the lip. The side sepals stay close to the flower and do not arch up and away. The mouth of the flower is sometimes light yellow. The flowers have a light vanilla-like scent.

Bloom Season: Midsummer–fall

Habitat/Range: Frequent to occasional in prairies, glades, pastures, and old fields; found throughout the Midwest region.

Comments: Important characteristics that separate nodding ladies' tresses from Great Plains ladies' tresses are that the former has lateral sepals that do not spread upward and away from the rest of the flower. Also, the mouth of the orchid has a white to faint yellow center and the flowers emit a weak vanilla-like scent. Another species, Case's ladies' tresses (*Spiranthes casei*), has a spiral arrangement of a single row of flowers, a creamy-yellowish flower, and wider basal leaves; found in the northern quarter of the Midwest region.

GREAT PLAINS LADIES' TRESSES
Spiranthes magnicamporum
Orchid family (Orchidaceae)

Description: A smooth, single-stemmed orchid, up to 2½' tall. The 3–4 basal leaves are 5½" long and ½" wide, and usually die back before the flowering period. The upper stem leaves are reduced to scales. The white flowers are in a spiraled arrangement of 2–3 rows on the upper part of the stem. Each flower is up to ½" long, with the sepals and petals forming a tube around the lip. The side sepals are free to the base, spreading, the tips arching upward and angling away from the rest of the flower. The mouth of the flower is yellow to yellowish-tan. The flowers have a strong vanilla-like scent.

Bloom Season: Midsummer–fall

Habitat/Range: Frequent to occasional in prairies, hill prairies, and glades; found throughout the Midwest region, but absent in the northeast quarter.

Comments: Important characteristics that separate Great Plains ladies' tresses from nodding ladies' tresses are that the former has lateral sepals that spread upward and away from the rest of the flower. Also, the mouth of the orchid has a noticeable yellow center and the flowers emit a strong vanilla-like scent. Another orchid similar to both Great Plains and nodding ladies' tresses, hooded ladies' tresses (*Spiranthes romanzoffiana*), differs by having the upper and lateral petals and sepals fused to form a broader hood; occasional in swamps, wet meadows, and fens; found in the northern third of the Midwest region.

SLENDER LADIES' TRESSES
Spiranthes lacera
Orchid family (Orchidaceae)

Description: This slender, delicate orchid has a single stalk that grows up to 1' tall. There are 2–3 round basal leaves, with the stem leaves reduced to scales. The upper part of the stalk twists with a graceful spiral of evenly spaced flowers along the spike. The flowers are about ¼" long and white, with green on the center of the lip. The sepals and petals form a tube surrounding the ragged-edged lip.

Bloom Season: Late summer–fall

Habitat/Range: Occasional in dry, rocky, or sandy upland forests, ridgetops and bluffs, open meadows, stream banks, old fields, roadsides, and other disturbed sites; found throughout the Midwest region.

Comments: Some references cite two varieties of slender ladies' tresses. Northern ladies' tresses (*Spiranthes lacera* var. *lacera*) has more loosely packed flowers, hairs on the stem, and basal leaves persisting during flowering time; found more commonly in the northern half of the Midwest region. Southern ladies' tresses (*Spiranthes lacera* var. *gracilis*) has more densely packed flowers, hairless stems, and basal leaves that are absent by flowering time; found more commonly in the southern half of the Midwest region.

LITTLE LADIES' TRESSES
Spiranthes tuberosa
Orchid family (Orchidaceae)

Description: One of the most delicate of ladies' tresses in the Midwest region, with its very slender stem, from 6–12" tall. The 2–3 basal leaves are oval, up to 1" long and ⅜" wide, appearing in early spring but withering away by midsummer, and not present at flowering time. The flowers are in a single loose, graceful spiral of 10–20 white, tiny flowers, each from ⅛–¼" long. Two petals and one sepal form the hood, the 2 lateral sepals are slightly spreading, and the flared lip has a waxy appearance at the tip.

Bloom Season: Late summer–fall

Habitat/Range: Uncommon on dry sites with little competition in dry upland forests, ridges, slopes, and blufftops; found in the Midwest region in Missouri, southern Illinois, southern Indiana, eastern Ohio, southern Michigan, and further south.

Comments: The species name, *tuberosa*, references a single tuberous root, instead of multiple roots, as found in other orchids. Although the clear white flowers are extremely small, when viewed close-up with a hand lens, the cell structure takes on a jewel-like appearance.

YELLOW-LIPPED LADIES' TRESSES
Spiranthes lucida
Orchid family (Orchidaceae)

Description: A smooth, single-stemmed orchid, 4–15" tall, with shiny leaves. The 3–5 basal leaves are 1¼–4¼" long, ⅜–¾" wide, stalkless, and broadest at or below the middle. The flowers are in a dense spike at the top of the stem and arranged in 2–4 spiraling ranks. The flowers are white, tubular, small, ⅛–¼" long, with a squarish lip and a bright orange-yellow center. The 2 lateral sepals are slightly spreading.

Bloom Season: Late spring–early summer

Habitat/Range: Uncommon to rare in calcareous seeps along creeks, moist limestone outcrops, and fens; found in scattered locations throughout the Midwest region, but absent in Minnesota.

Comments: Yellow-lipped ladies' tresses is the only ladies' tresses orchid in the Midwest region that flowers in the spring. Also, the basal leaves are present at flowering time, and not withered away, as with most other ladies' tresses.

OVAL LADIES' TRESSES
Spiranthes ovalis
Orchid family (Orchidaceae)

Description: A small, single-stemmed orchid, 6–15" tall, with 1–2 basal leaves and a few alternate leaves near the base. The basal leaves are up to 6" long and ¼–¾" wide, widest below the middle, or oval in shape. The lower stem leaves are generally smaller. The flowers are arranged in a double spiral along the upper ¾–4" of the stalk, with each flower containing a small bract about ⅜" long. Flowers are white, about ⅛" long, with an upper hood comprised of a central petal and 2 lateral sepals, and a lip that is somewhat recurved downward, broadest at the base to oval in shape, with its margins slightly toothed.

Bloom Season: Fall

Habitat/Range: Uncommon to rare in mesic upland forests and wet to mesic bottomland forests, where they prefer filtered light and not dense shade; found in scattered locations across the southern half of the Midwest region, and further south.

Comments: A combination of the flowers' extremely small size, the downward recurved lip, and the preference for shade rather than full sun help to distinguish this ladies' tresses from others in the Midwest region.

NODDING POGONIA

Triphora trianthophora
Orchid family (Orchidaceae)

Description: A short, delicate orchid, often found growing in small colonies, with a smooth stem, 3–12" tall. The stem leaves are alternate, about ½" long and ⅜" wide, broadest at the base, and clasping the stem. There are typically 3 white to pinkish flowers, upright or nodding, each lasting but a day. The flowers are about ½" long, with a 3-lobed lip that is somewhat crinkled and irregular along the tip.

Bloom Season: Late summer–fall

Habitat/Range: Uncommon to occasional in moist woods; scattered throughout the Midwest region, but absent in the northern third.

Comments: Also called "three-birds orchid," for its tendency to produce 3 flowers. This small, slender orchid is easily overlooked on the forest floor.

SPRING LADIES' TRESSES

Spiranthes vernalis
Orchid family (Orchidaceae)

Description: The stem is finely hairy, up to 3' tall, with a single spiral of 30–40 flowers. The 4–6 leaves are basal, up to 10" long, and often withered at flowering time. The flowers are white, about ⅜–½" long, somewhat nodding, tubular, with the two upper petals and 1 sepal forming a hood, while the 2 lateral sepals are somewhat spreading and enrolled along their length. The lip has irregular teeth along the tip and a yellowish throat.

Bloom Season: Late spring–midsummer

Habitat/Range: Uncommon in mesic to somewhat dry prairies; found in the southern third of the Midwest region.

Comments: Spring ladies' tresses is the tallest of the ladies' tresses in the Midwest region and the second to bloom of the season, preceded only by yellow-lipped ladies' tresses. As with many other orchids, the frequency of flowering plants varies greatly from year to year. In general, often after flowering, orchids may not appear again for two or more years, mainly due to the large amount of energy it takes to produce flowers and fruits, and the time it takes to replenish food reserves.

BEECHDROPS

Epifagus virginiana
Broomrape family (Orobanchaceae)

Description: A parasitic annual plant found on the roots of American beech trees, with wiry, brown stems having several branches up to 20" tall. Minute leaf scales are alternate along the stem. The white flowers, each about ⅜" long, have 4 lobes at the tip, and purplish-brown stripes along their length. The lower flowers along the stem, which don't open, are fertile (produce fruit).

Bloom Season: Last summer–fall

Habitat/Range: Common on American beech roots in moist woods; found in the eastern half of the Midwest region; also, in southern Illinois and southeast Missouri.

Comments: The plants lack the green chlorophyll necessary for food production, so they attach to the roots of beech trees in order to obtain nutrients. A highly bitter tea was once used for diarrhea, dysentery, mouth sores, and cold sores.

ONE-FLOWERED CANCER ROOT

Orobanche uniflora
Broomrape family (Orobanchaceae)

Description: Several branchless, hairy stalks emerge from this plant up to a height of 8". Brownish scales, which are rudimentary leaves, are found at the base of the stalks. The flowers, which are about 1" long, are solitary at the tip of the stems. The 5 sepals are united to form a hairy cup. The 5 petals are united into an elongated, curved tube, with 5 lobes, and 4 yellow stamens found within. The flowers range from white to lavender.

Bloom Season: Mid-spring–early summer

Habitat/Range: Uncommon in rocky or dry open woods, upland slopes, ridges, and glades; found throughout the Midwest region.

Comments: Also known as one-flowered broomrape. This plant lacks chlorophyll (the green pigment associated with photosynthesis), so it must rely on other plants for its food. It parasitizes the roots of oaks, asters, goldenrods, and others. The common name probably comes from its having been used as a folk remedy for cancer.

BLOODROOT
Sanguinaria canadensis
Poppy family (Papaveraceae)

Description: This showy, low-growing plant, 3–10" tall, produces a single flower that normally blooms for 1–3 days. A single, light-green leaf, paler underneath, emerges from the ground, wrapped around the flower stalk. The leaf may open with the flower or shortly after to a width of 3–5", with 3–9 lobes. The fragrant flower opens to 1½" wide and usually has 8 white petals, 4 of which are slightly longer, and 24 yellow stamens that surround the single pistil.

Bloom Season: Spring

Habitat/Range: Common in moist woods, lower slopes of moist or rocky woods, and in wooded valleys; found throughout the Midwest region.

Comments: The large, fleshy root emits a red sap, as does the rest of the plant. Native Americans used bloodroot as a dye for fabrics, tools, and war paint. The red sap was mixed with oak bark, which is a source of tannin, to set the color, making it more permanent. The plant was used by Native Americans and settlers to treat hemorrhages, fever, rheumatism, poor digestion, colds, and coughs. Today bloodroot is used commercially as a plaque-inhibiting agent in toothpaste and mouthwashes.

DITCH STONECROP
Penthorum sedoides
Ditch stonecrop family (Penthoraceae)

Description: Plants 6–24" tall, with small, gland-tipped hairs along the upper flowering stems. The leaves are alternate, stalkless, finely toothed along the margins, up to 5" long and 1½" wide, and tapering at both ends. The flowers are typically on one side of the stem in branched clusters that fan out. Individual flowers are about ¼" across, with petals absent, 5 white, narrow sepals, and 10 stamens with creamy-white tips that turn brown with age.

Bloom Season: Summer–early fall

Habitat/Range: Common in open muddy places, wetlands, bottomland forests, depressions in prairies, and along shores and ditches; found throughout the Midwest region.

Comments: Ditch stonecrop has moved around, from the stonecrop family (Crassulaceae), then the saxifrage family (Saxifragaceae), to the ditch stonecrop family (Penthoraceae), which includes a few Asian species. Although the flowers are not very attractive in bloom, the fruit turns a showy red in the fall.

POKEWEED

Phytolacca americana
Pokeweed family (Phytolaccaceae)

Description: Tall, smooth, red-stemmed plants with hollow stalks, up to 10' in height. The leaves are stalked, smooth, broadest in the middle, and up to 12" long and 3–6" wide. The small, greenish-white flowers are arranged along a drooping cylindrical cluster, with each flower individually stalked, and 5 lobed, white to pink sepals that flare outward, but no true petals. The purple to black berries have a juice that stains. Each berry is about ¼" wide and contains 10 glossy black seeds that are smooth and lens-shaped.

Bloom Season: Late spring–fall

Habitat/Range: Occasional in wood openings and edges of woods, and common in disturbed soil around farm lots, dwellings, fields, and along roadsides; found through the Midwest region, but absent in the northwestern part.

Comments: The leaves of young plants are cooked and served as "poke salad." The purple juice has been used to color foods such as frostings, candies, and beverages; also used as a red dye, and as ink. The root and stem are poisonous. The berries are quickly eaten by birds.

WHITE TURTLEHEAD

Chelone glabra
Plantain family (Plantaginaceae)

Description: An upright, usually unbranched plant, up to 3' tall, with angled stems. The leaves are opposite along the stem, broadest at the middle, toothed along the margin, and up to 6" long and 1½" wide. The white flowers are clustered at the top, each about 1" long. The upper lip of the flower has two lobes, which extend over the 3-lobed lower lip. There are 5 hairy stamens, 4 of which are fertile, while the remaining stamen is sterile and green. The lower interior of the flower has abundant white hairs. Flowers bloom from the bottom of the cluster up.

Bloom Season: Midsummer–fall

Habitat/Range: Uncommon in wet woods and wetlands; found throughout the Midwest region, but with fewer locations along the western edge.

Comments: The common name is very fitting, especially when viewing the profile of the flower. A leaf tea was said to stimulate an appetite, also a folk remedy for worms, fever, jaundice, and as a laxative.

CLAMMY HEDGE HYSSOP
Gratiola neglecta
Plantain family (Plantaginaceae)

Description: An annual plant covered in short, fine hairs, 4–12" tall, with an erect stem and many short side branches. The leaves are opposite, stalkless, ¾–2" long and ½" wide, broadest near the middle and tapering at each end, with sparse teeth toward the tip. The flowers emerge from the axils of the leaves on stalks up to 1" long. Each flower is about ⅓" long, white, tubular, with 4–5 lobes, 3 of which are notched. Fine yellow hairs are at the base of the upper lobes.

Bloom Season: Mid-spring–summer

Habitat/Range: Common in bottomland forests, wet swales in sand prairies, swamps, marshes, wet meadows, and ditches; found throughout the Midwest region.

Comments: A similar species, round-fruited hedge hyssop (*Gratiola virginiana*), has stems that are smooth, often inflated, spongy or nearly so, and short flower stalks less than ⅛" long; occurs in similar habitat, and found primarily in the southern half of the Midwest region.

FOXGLOVE BEARDTONGUE
Penstemon digitalis
Plantain family (Plantaginaceae)

Description: A sturdy, somewhat glossy plant with unbranched stems to a height of 4'. The basal, up leaves are on long stalks and arranged in a rosette. The stem leaves are up to 4" long and 2½" wide, opposite, without stalks, with their edges curved inward and toothed. The flowers are on spreading, branched stalks at the top of the stem. The white tubular flowers are ¾–1¼" long, often hairy on the outside, with 2 upper lobes and 3 lower lobes. There are purple lines running down the white throat of the flower. At the mouth of the flower is a large, sterile stamen with bright yellow hairs.

Bloom Season: Mid-spring–midsummer

Habitat/Range: Common in mesic prairies, sand prairies, savannas, pastures, and roadsides; found throughout the Midwest region, but considered introduced in the northwest quarter.

Comments: The common name "foxglove" and the species name *digitalis* refer to the similarity of the flower to *Digitalis purpurea*, the foxglove from England used to treat ailments.

PALE BEARDTONGUE
Penstemon pallidus
Plantain family (Plantaginaceae)

Description: Slender, unbranched, hairy-stemmed plants, up to 2' tall, with opposite leaves that tend to point upward. The leaves are firm, pale, and velvety-hairy on both sides, with the margins randomly toothed. The leaves partly clasp the stem at the base and taper to a point on the end. The flowers are in branched clusters at the end of the stalk. Each tubular flower is about 1" long and marked inside with fine purple lines. The flower has a 2-lobed upper lip and 3-lobed lower lip. At the mouth of the flower is a large, sterile stamen with bright yellow hairs.

Bloom Season: Mid-spring–midsummer

Habitat/Range: Common in prairies, savannas, old fields, and roadsides; found throughout the Midwest region, but rare in the northern half.

Comments: The genus name, *Penstemon*, comes from the Greek words *penta*, meaning "5," and *stemon*, meaning "stamen," in reference to each flower having 5 stamens (4 are fertile, and 1 is sterile). The species name, *pallidus*, comes from Latin, meaning "pale," in reference to the pale white flowers and pale green leaves. Penstemons are called "beardtongue" because the unusual sterile stamen contained in the mouth of each flower has a tuft of small hairs.

WHITE WAND BEARDTONGUE
Penstemon tubaeflorus
Plantain family (Plantaginaceae)

Description: Smooth, single-stemmed plants, up to 3' tall, with narrow, opposite leaves. The stem leaves are up to 5" long and less than 1" wide, with broadly rounded bases, pointed tips, and lacking teeth along the margins. The flowers are clustered around the stem in tiers. Each tubular flower is up to 1" long, with sticky hairs on the inside, a relatively flat-faced opening, and a 2-lobed upper lip and a 3-lobed lower lip. At the mouth of the flower is a large, sterile stamen with bright yellow hairs.

Bloom Season: Mid-spring–midsummer

Habitat/Range: Occasional in mesic to dry prairies, savannas, and roadsides; found in the southwest quarter of the Midwest region; rare in Illinois and Iowa.

Comments: Native Americans used plants of this genus as a remedy for chills and fever. To treat toothache, they chewed the root pulp and placed it in the painful cavity.

CULVER'S ROOT
Veronicastrum virginicum
Plantain family (Plantaginaceae)

Description: A tall, graceful plant growing to a height of 6', with branching flower stems that resemble candelabra. The leaves are in whorls of 3–8, with each up to 6" long and 1" wide. The leaf margins are finely toothed. The flowers are in dense clusters on spikes 3–9" long. Each tubular flower is about ¼" long, white, and with 4 lobes. The stamens have noticeable yellow to brownish-red tips.

Bloom Season: Summer

Habitat/Range: Occasional in mesic prairies, moist depressions in upland prairies, and savannas; found throughout the Midwest region.

Comments: The Cherokee drank a root tea for treating backache, fever, hepatitis, and typhus. The Seneca made a root tea to use as a mild laxative. For the Menominee, Culver's root served as a strong physic, a reviver, and as a means of purification when they had been defiled by the touch of a bereaved person. Early doctors used the root to treat a variety of ailments, including liver disorders, pleurisy, and venereal diseases.

SENECA SNAKEROOT
Polygala senega
Milkwort family (Polygalaceae)

Description: Several unbranched stems emerge from one base, up to 20" tall. The leaves are alternate along the stem and up to 3½" long and less than 1" wide. The lower stem leaves are usually very small. The small, white flowers, about ¼" wide, are clustered along the upper part of the stem. Each flower has 3 small petals, with one of them usually fringed.

Bloom Season: Mid-spring–summer

Habitat/Range: Occasional in mesic to dry prairies, hill prairies, and open woodlands; found throughout the Midwest region.

Comments: Seneca snakeroot was used by the Seneca Indians to treat snakebite. It was for this use that the colonists gave the plant its name. It was one of the first plants whose medicinal use was learned from the Indians. A root tea was used for respiratory ailments, rheumatism, heart troubles, convulsions, etc. A related species, whorled milkweed (*Polygala verticillata*), differs by being an annual, 6–12" tall, having leaves in whorls of 3–7, with each leaf about 1" long; occurring in prairies, loess hill prairies, sand prairies, savannas, and open disturbed sites; found throughout the Midwest region.

CLIMBING FALSE BUCKWHEAT

Fallopia scandens
Smartweed family (Polygonaceae)

Description: A climbing, twining, annual or perennial plant, up to 16', often forming curtain-like masses of flowers and leaves. The red stems support round- to heart-shaped leaves up to 6" long and 3" wide. Numerous small flowers, each about ⅛" long, with 5 white petals forming showy clusters. The fruit hangs down, and has a green center and 3 large, white, ruffled wings.

Bloom Season: Summer–fall

Habitat/Range: Common in moist, open, or shaded bottomlands, floodplains, and thickets; found throughout the Midwest region.

Comments: Formerly known as *Polygonum scandens*. This is the only climbing member of the smartweed family that is commonly found throughout the Midwest region. The black, shiny seeds look and taste like buckwheat.

JUMPSEED

Persicaria virginiana
Smartweed family (Polygonaceae)

Description: Erect, often arching stems, 1–4' tall, with broad leaves and a long flower stalk. The leaves are alternate, stalked from ¼–1¼" on the lower leaves, and stalkless (or nearly so) on the upper leaves. Each leaf is 2–6" long and 1–4" wide, oval-shaped, and often hairy, with a rounded base and sharp-pointed tip. The flowers are loosely arranged along a spike, 4–16" long, with each flower white or sometimes pinkish, about ⅛" long, with 4 pointed petals and 4 stamens that protrude slightly beyond the petals. The fruit has an oval, dry seed with a remnant style at the tip.

Bloom Season: Summer–fall

Habitat/Range: Common in mesic upland forests, bottomland forests, stream banks, and along shaded roadsides; found throughout the Midwest region, but rare to absent in the northern quarter.

Comments: Also known as Virginia knotweed. There are 13 native and 6 nonnative species in the genus *Persicaria* in the Midwest region. Jumpseed has an interesting seed dispersal mechanism. As the fruit ripens, tension builds at the joint of the seed stalk that springs the seed up to 10'. The action is often triggered by a passing animal, and the hooked beak of the seed becomes tangled in the fur, thereby giving it a free ride to new habitat.

SPRING BEAUTY
Claytonia virginica
Purslane family (Portulaceae)

Description: Plants arise from tuberous roots, with flower stalks up to 6" tall. One pair of opposite, grass-like leaves, up to 6" long and ¼" wide, occurs about halfway up the stem. A single, strap-like leaf up to 7" long is produced at the base. Not all plants flower in a year, but a single leaf identifies their presence. Flowers, usually less than ½" across, vary from white to pink, with distinctive darker pink veins running the length of the 5 petals. There is a pair of green sepals below the petals. The 5 anthers are typically pink.

Bloom Season: Late winter–late spring

Habitat/Range: Common in dry to moist woods, and occasional in dry prairies, sand prairies, and savannas; found throughout the Midwest region.

Comments: Both Native Americans and early settlers dug the small, round tuberous roots and ate them raw or boiled as a potato substitute. Their bland flavor has often been likened to that of chestnuts. The succulent leaves were used in salads. Deer are known to browse on the leaves when they first appear, and rodents eat the bulbs. A similar species, Carolina spring beauty (*Claytonia caroliniana*), differs by having shorter, wider leaves, about 3" long and ½–¾" wide, and found only in the northern quarter of the Midwest region.

STARFLOWER
Trientalis borealis
Primrose family (Primulaceae)

Description: A short plant that grows in colonies, each 4–8" tall, with a single stem that supports a whorl of 5–9 leaves at the top. The leaves are divided into leaflets of unequal size ranging from 1–4" long and ¼–1½" wide, broadest in the middle, with a pointed tip and tapering at the base. The 1–2 flowers are on stalks ¾–2½" long, with each flower about ½" across and 5–9 (typically 7) star-shaped, white petals, and 5–9 yellow-tipped stamens.

Bloom Season: Mid-spring–early summer

Habitat/Range: Common to occasional in sandy woodlands along swamps, hummocks in sandy swamps, bogs, and ravines leading out of bluffs; found throughout the northern half of the Midwest region, and in a few scattered locations in the southeast quarter.

Comments: Also known as *Lysimachia borealis*. This delicate-looking wildflower is unusual because it typically has flowers with 7 petals.

DOLL'S EYES
Actaea pachypoda
Buttercup family (Ranunculaceae)

Description: This stately plant is bushy in appearance and grows to about 2' tall. The large leaves are divided twice, ending in 3–5 leaflets, each up to 4" long and 2¼" wide that vary in shape. The leaflets, especially the end ones, may have 3 irregular lobes. The leaf margins are sharply toothed. The flowers appear in a tight rounded shape on the end of a stout stalk. The small sepals and petals fall away early, leaving a mass of creamy-white stamens, giving the flower its basic color. The fruits are a loose cluster of oval, shiny, white berries, each about ⅓" wide and marked with a dark purple spot at one end, which accounts for the common name.

Bloom Season: Late spring–early summer

Habitat/Range: Uncommon to occasional in moist woods; often on north-facing slopes, ravines, and at the base of bluffs in the southern part; found throughout the Midwest region.

Comments: Also called "white baneberry." Both Native Americans and settlers made a tea of the root for relieving the pain of childbirth. Settlers also used the plant to improve circulation and to cure headache or eyestrain. The plant is poisonous, and all parts may cause severe gastrointestinal inflammation and skin blisters. A related species, red baneberry (*Actaea rubra*), is similar in appearance but has hairy leaves and red berries; found in the northern half of the Midwest region.

BLACK COHOSH
Actaea racemosa
Buttercup family (Ranunculaceae)

Description: A stately plant with a skirt of finely cut, fanlike leaves and a tall-flowered stem, 3–7' tall. The leaves are divided 2–3 times to produce numerous small leaflets, up to 4" long and 3" wide; they are shallowly lobed, coarsely toothed along the margins, and with bases that are flat or slightly indented. At the top of the wand-like stem, 1–3 branches produce a cylindrical spray of showy white flowers, each about ½" wide. The flowers lack petals, and the sepals drop away early; it is the numerous stamens that account for the color.

Bloom Season: Late spring–summer

Habitat/Range: Uncommon to rare in moist woods on lower slopes and at the base of bluffs and ravines; found in the southern third of the Midwest region and eastward.

Comments: Formerly known as *Cimicifuga racemosa*. Black cohosh was an important medicinal herb to Native Americans. The Cherokee, for example, used the roots for treating menstrual cramps, difficult deliveries, rheumatism, tumors, backache, respiratory disorders, constipation, fatigue, hives, and insomnia. This herb was also of much value to settlers, who used it for snakebite, malaria, nervous disorders, yellow fever, bronchitis, and dropsy. A related species, Appalachian bugbane (*Actaea rubifolia*; formerly known as *Cimicifuga rubifolia*), differs by having bases of leaflets that are heart-shaped. This plant is rare, found in the Midwest region at the southern edge of the southeast part, and southward.

MEADOW ANEMONE
Anemone canadensis
Buttercup family (Ranunculaceae)

Description: Hairy leaves on long stalks are clustered at the base of the plant, with a branching stem up to 2' tall supporting 1–3 flowers on long, hairy stalks. Deeply cut leaves occur in whorls at the base, and with a whorl of 3 stalkless leaves at the top of the stem, where the flower stalks emerge from the center. The white, flowers are up to 2" across, with 5 white petal-like sepals and numerous yellow stamens. The seed head is a bur-like cluster of flattened fruits with beaks.

Bloom Season: Late spring–midsummer

Habitat/Range: Locally frequent in moist depressions in prairies, and along streams and roadsides; found throughout the Midwest region, but uncommon to absent in the southern third.

Comments: Also called "Canada anemone," it often occurs in large, matted colonies. Native Americans used a preparation of the roots and leaves to treat wounds, sores, and nosebleed.

CAROLINA ANEMONE
Anemone caroliniana
Buttercup family (Ranunculaceae)

Description: A short-stemmed plant, 3–6" tall, with several basal leaves that are long-stalked, and deeply divided. The leaves, up to 2" long, are divided into 3 sections, further divided at the tip, with 2–3 lobes. There is a whorl of 3 stalkless, lobed leaves on the stem below the flower. Flowers are solitary on the stem, about 1–1½" wide, with 8–20 white, to pink, to blue, to deep violet, petal-like sepals, and numerous yellow stamens.

Bloom Season: Early spring–mid-spring

Habitat/Range: Infrequent in dry, often sandy, or rocky prairies and open rocky woods; found in scattered locations across the western half of the Midwest region.

Comments: The flowers of Carolina anemone are highly variable throughout its range. They only bloom for a short period of time, and close at night and on cloudy days. They are most easily located where vegetation is short and sparse.

WOOD ANEMONE
Anemone quinquefolia
Buttercup family (Ranunculaceae)

Description: A small plant, covered in fine hairs, that tends to grow in colonies, spreading by way of rhizomes, with each plant 4–8" tall. The leaves are stalked and divided into 3 leaflets that are again divided into 2–3 parts. Leaflets are up to 2" long, coarsely toothed at the tip, and with narrow, tapering bases. A single flower arises from the whorl of leaves on a hairy stalk. Each flower is ¾–2" wide, with 4–9 (typically 5) white, occasionally pink, petal-like sepals and numerous white-tipped stamens.

Bloom Season: Spring–early summer

Habitat/Range: Frequent in mesic woods, swampy woods, and along stream banks; found throughout the northern half of the Midwest region, and in scattered locations in the southeast quarter.

Comments: The plants have been known to take as long as five years to flower. When not flowering, the plant puts out a single basal leaf that is long-stalked and divided into 3 parts, similar to those of a flowering plant. Wood anemone has been used as a topical application in the treatment of rheumatism, gout, and fever.

THIMBLEWEED
Anemone cylindrica
Buttercup family (Ranunculaceae)

Description: Plants up to 2½' tall with hairy unbranched stems. There are basal leaves and 2 or 3 sets of opposite leaves (sometimes a whorl of 3) on the flowering stems. The leaves are stalked, divided into 3 leaflets, up to 4" long, hairy, and deeply lobed in 3–5 parts. Several tall flower stalks arise above the main whorl of leaves, with one flower on each stalk. Flowers are ¾" across, white, with 5 pointed, hairy, petal-like sepals and numerous yellow stamens around a greenish, cone-shaped cylinder that is twice as tall as it is wide. The fruits develop on a cylinder up to 1½" tall and about ½" wide that resembles a thimble; hence, the common name.

Bloom Season: Summer

Habitat/Range: Frequent in mesic and dry prairies, loess hill prairies, sand savannas, edges of woods, and other sandy areas; found throughout the Midwest region, but absent or rare in the southern quarter.

Comments: The fruit develops into seeds with dense, woolly hairs that resemble small white tufts of cotton. Mammalian herbivores tend to avoid the leaves because they are toxic and cause a burning sensation in the mouth and irritation of the gastrointestinal tract. Thimbleweed is similar to tall thimbleweed (*Anemone virginiana*), but differs by having 3 or more leaves in the main whorl of stem leaves, while the latter usually has 2, and sometimes 3. Also, thimbleweed has a central head that is more than twice as long as it is wide, while tall thimbleweed has a shorter, central head that is less than twice as long as it is wide.

TALL THIMBLEWEED
Anemone virginiana
Buttercup family (Ranunculaceae)

Description: Plants up to 3' tall with hairy, unbranched stems. There are basal leaves and a pair of 2, or sometimes 3, compound leaves on the flowering stems. The leaves are stalked, divided into 3 leaflets, up to 4" long, hairy, and deeply lobed in 3–5 parts. Several tall flower stalks arise above the main whorl of leaves, with one flower on each stalk. Flowers are ¾" across, white, with 5 pointed, hairy, petal-like sepals and numerous yellow stamens around a greenish, cone-shaped cylinder. The fruits develop on a cylinder ¾–1" tall and about ½" wide that resembles a thimble; hence, the common name.

Bloom Season: Summer

Habitat/Range: Occasional in prairies, savannas, and open woods; found throughout the Midwest region.

Comments: The fruit develops into seeds with dense, woolly hairs that resemble small white tufts of cotton. Mammalian herbivores tend to avoid the leaves because they are toxic and cause a burning sensation in the mouth and irritation of the gastrointestinal tract. Tall thimbleweed is similar to thimbleweed (*Anemone cylindrica*), but differs by having only 2, and sometimes 3, leaves in the main whorl of stem leaves, while the latter has 3 or more leaves. Also, tall thimbleweed has a central head that is shorter and less than twice as long as it is wide, while with thimbleweed, it is more than twice as long as it is wide.

GOLDTHREAD
Coptis trifolia
Buttercup family (Ranunculaceae)

Description: A fast bloomer, the petal-like sepals do not last very long. This delicate plant is 3–6" tall, with evergreen basal leaves and string-like, golden-yellow, creeping roots. The leaves arise from slender stalks and are divided into 3 shiny leaflets, each up to 1" long, with notched tips or shallow lobes. The flower has a stalk with small bracts scattered along its length. Each flower is ½" wide, with 5–7 petal-like sepals and golden-yellow, club-shaped petals that are shorter than the stamens. The stamens are white-tipped and surround the bright green styles that are curled at the tip.

Bloom Season: Mid-spring–early summer

Habitat/Range: Common in moist, mossy forests and wet areas, including swamps and bogs; found in the northern third of the Midwest region.

Comments: The common name comes from the long, string-like, golden-yellow roots, which Native Americans used to produce a yellow dye. The roots also have antibacterial properties and were chewed to relieve canker sores, which is the source of another common name, canker-root.

FALSE RUE ANEMONE
Enemion biternatum
Buttercup family (Ranunculaceae)

Description: A delicate plant with branched, smooth stems, up to 10" tall. The leaves are compound, divided into 3 leaflets, with each leaflet about 1" long and ¾" wide, with 3 lobes. The leaves at the base are on stalks, the upper leaves, nearly stalkless. The flowers have 5 petal-like sepals about ½" across, with numerous stamens; there are no petals. The sepals are always white.

Bloom Season: Spring

Habitat/Range: Common in moist woods, and low, rich woods of valleys and river floodplains; found throughout the Midwest region.

Comments: Formerly known as *Isopyrum biternatum*. The white flowers of false rue anemone are among the earliest of spring. Pearl-like buds give the plant an unusual beauty even before the flowers open. False rue anemone is similar to rue anemone (*Thalictrum thalictroides*), but the latter occurs on drier sites in woods, grows more solitarily, has a whorl of 6 leaflets below the flowers, has 5–9 petal-like sepals, and varies in color from white to pink to lavender.

RUE ANEMONE
Thalictrum thalictroides
Buttercup family (Ranunculaceae)

Description: A plant with upright, smooth, unbranched stems, up to 8" tall. The leaves at the base are compound, divided into 3 sections, with each division further divided into 3 leaflets; a whorl of 6 leaflets occurs just below the flower stalks. Each leaflet is smooth, 3-lobed, and up to ¾" across. There are usually 1–4 flowers, each about 1" across, occurring at the end of a stalk; each flower has 5–9 petal-like sepals and numerous stamens; there are no petals. The sepals vary in color from white to pink to lavender.

Bloom Season: Spring–early summer

Habitat/Range: Common in dry open or rocky woods; also on slopes and in valleys. Found throughout the Midwest region, but uncommon to absent in the northern quarter.

Comments: Formerly known as *Anemonella thalictroides*. Rue anemone is sometimes confused with false rue anemone (*Enemion biternatum*), but the latter occurs in moister sites in valleys, grows in colonies, and has leaflets more numerous on the stem, with their lobes more deeply cut.

PURPLE MEADOW RUE
Thalictrum dasycarpum
Buttercup family (Ranunculaceae)

Description: A sometimes purplish, stout-stemmed plant, up to 5' tall, with compound leaves. The leaves are divided into 2–3 leaflets, each up to 2", with 3 pointed lobes at the tip. The small flowers are in branching clusters, with male and female flowers on separate plants. There are no petals, and the sepals drop early. The male flowers have many showy, white, thread-like stamens; the female flowers have a bur-like head of pistils.

Bloom Season: Late spring–early summer

Habitat/Range: Occasional in mesic prairies, wet prairies, wet meadows, edges of woods, and moist stream banks; found throughout the Midwest region.

Comments: The Dakota broke off fruits when they were approaching maturity and stored them away for their pleasant odor, later rubbing and scattering them over their clothing. The hollow stems were used by small boys to make toy flutes. The Pawnee used this plant as a stimulant for horses by mixing plant material with a certain white clay and applying it as a snuff on the muzzle of horses. This was done when making forced marches of three or more days' duration in order to escape enemies. A closely related species, waxy meadow rue (*Thalictrum revolutum*), occurs in similar habitats. The leaves have a bad odor when crushed and have gland-tipped hairs on their undersides. Found in the central and southwest quarters of the Midwest region, and in widely scattered areas elsewhere. Another species, early meadow rue (*Thalictrum dioicum*), is shorter, 8–30" tall, and blooms in spring before the others in mesic woods; found throughout the Midwest region.

GOLDENSEAL
Hydrastis canadensis
Buttercup family (Ranunculaceae)

Description: The attractive, coarsely textured leaves easily identify this woodland wildflower. Hairy, unbranched stems up to 10" tall support a pair of broad, 5- to 9-lobed leaves. The leaves, up to 6" across, are hairy and irregularly toothed along the margins. One leaf, about 9" across, is found at the base. A small, single flower emerges at the top of the uppermost leaf. The flower, about ½" across, has 3 whitish sepals that fall away early; there are no petals. The numerous white stamens give the flower its color. The distinctive red fruit, resembling a red raspberry, persists for some time.

Bloom Season: Spring

Habitat/Range: Occasional in moist woods on lower slopes, in ravines, and on the floor of wooded valleys; occurs throughout the Midwest region, but rare to absent in the northern quarter, and rare in Indiana.

Comments: Goldenseal is declining throughout its range due to root diggers; the plant can be cultivated for commercial use. The perennial rhizome, with its distinctive yellow sap, was used by Native Americans and settlers as a tonic, stimulant, and astringent. The herb is believed to possess some measure of anti-inflammatory, antidiarrheal, antibacterial, and immune system–enhancing properties.

PASQUEFLOWER
Pulsatilla patens
Buttercup family (Ranunculaceae)

Description: One of the first prairie wildflowers to bloom in the spring, often appearing while there is still snow on the ground. The plants are 2–16" tall, with basal leaves on long stalks that appear after the flowers bloom. The basal leaves have long, silky hairs and are deeply divided into several narrow, lobed, and toothed segments. The whorl of stem leaves below the flower is similar to the basal leaves, but stalkless and smaller. A single flower emerges from a long stalk, with 5–8 showy, white, pale lavender, or purple, petal-like sepals, each up to 1½" long, and with numerous parallel veins. Each seed has a long, feather-like plume.

Bloom Season: Early spring–mid-spring

Habitat/Range: Occasional in prairies, hill prairies, open slopes, and dry, rocky, gravelly, or sandy sites; found in the northwest quarter of the Midwest region.

Comments: Also known as *Anemone patens*. Native Americans used crushed leaves to treat rheumatism, boils, burns, and sore eyes, and to promote the healing of wounds.

NEW JERSEY TEA
Ceanothus americanus
Buckthorn family (Rhamnaceae)

Description: A small, wildflower-like shrub, up to 3' tall, with spreading branches. The stem is woody, with greenish-brown bark that becomes brown and flaky on older stems. The upper branches are mostly herbaceous, often dying back in winter. The leaves are alternate, stalked, up to 4" long and 2½" wide. The leaf margin is toothed, the surface hairy above and gray with velvety hairs below. The flowers are on branched clusters arising on long stalks from the bases of leaves of the current year's growth. The flowers are about ⅛" wide, with 5 white, hooded petals, usually notched, each resembling a miniature ladle. There are 5 white stamens.

Bloom Season: Late spring–early summer

Habitat/Range: Common in prairies, savannas, and open woods; found throughout the Midwest region.

Comments: The leaves were used by Native Americans to make a tea. Tribes along the Atlantic Coast probably taught the colonists the use of New Jersey tea, used as a patriotic substitute for black tea during the American Revolution, after black tea was dumped into Boston Harbor. Native Americans also used a root tea for treating colds, fever, snakebite, stomach disorders, diarrhea, lung ailments, and constipation, and as a blood tonic. A similar species, prairie redroot (*Ceanothus herbaceous*), has narrower leaves and flatter flower clusters mostly at the ends of leafy branches of the current year's growth. Found in prairies, hill prairies, and open woods throughout the northern and western parts of the Midwest region.

GOAT'S BEARD
Aruncus dioicus
Rose family (Rosaceae)

Description: A bushy plant with showy, branching plumes that reaches a height of 6'. The single stalk is smooth, with few (but very large) leaves up to 20" long. The compound leaves are divided into 5–7 leaflets. The lower leaflets may be further divided. Each leaflet is up to 6" long, pointed at the tip and finely toothed along the margin. The flowers are numerous, small, less than ⅛" across, white, and appear in plume-like clusters. The male and female flowers occur on separate plants. All flowers have 5 petals and 5 sepals, but the male flowers have 15 or more stamens, and the female flowers have 3 pistils and 15 or more incompletely developed stamens.

Bloom Season: Late spring–midsummer

Habitat/Range: Occasional along lower wooded slopes, at the base of bluffs, and in moist woodlands; found primarily in the southern half of the Midwest region.

Comments: Although the male and female flowers are on separate plants, they are easily distinguished by the showier stamens on the male plant. The foliage turns yellow in the fall. The somewhat scraggly appearance of the spikes of flowers accounts for the plant's common name. The Cherokee applied pounded root on bee stings. Root tea was used to diminish bleeding after childbirth and to reduce profuse urination. Tea was also used externally to bathe swollen feet.

WILD STRAWBERRY

Fragaria virginiana
Rose family (Rosaceae)

Description: This low, ground-hugging plant spreads by runners, often forming large colonies. Along the runners, hairy stalks up to 6" long support leaves, each of which is divided into 3 leaflets, up to 2½" long and 1½" wide, with teeth along the margins. The flowers, about 1" across, are in small clusters on stalks with spreading hairs, leafless, and contain 5 white petals, 5 green sepals alternating with 5 leaf-like bracts, and numerous stamens. The fruit has an attractive scarlet color and grows to about ½" in length.

Bloom Season: Spring; sometimes in fall

Habitat/Range: Common in mesic to dry prairies, open woodlands, pastures, and old fields; found throughout the Midwest region.

Comments: Some say wild strawberries are sweeter than the typical garden-variety strawberries, which are hybrids between the wild strawberry and the Chilean strawberry. Wild strawberries were greatly appreciated by Native Americans, and later, by early travelers and settlers. They are also nutritious, having more vitamin C than an equal weight of oranges. Another species, woodland strawberry (*Fragaria vesca*), has flower stalks with appressed hairs, not spreading, smaller flowers, about ½" across, and with the tooth on the tip of the leaf of equal size as the side teeth (whereas on wild strawberry, the end tooth is noticeably shorter). Occasional in open, rocky woods, slopes, and low woods; found in the northern half of the Midwest region, and rare in the central part.

WHITE AVENS
Geum canadense
Rose family (Rosaceae)

Description: Often several slender stems emerge from the base to form spreading branches, up to 2½' tall. The basal leaves are on long stalks, with the leaf margins sometimes cut into 3–7 deep lobes. The stem leaves have 3 leaflets and a very short stalk, or are stalkless. The leaf margins are toothed, and the tip, pointed. The basal leaves are green all winter. The flowers are few, about ¾" across, and on velvety stalks. The 5 white petals are interspersed with 5 green sepals. Stamens are from 10 to many. The fruit has numerous hooked ends that attach to clothing and fur, which aids in the plant's dispersal.

Bloom Season: Late spring–fall

Habitat/Range: Common in rich or rocky woods, hillsides, ravines, and in valleys along streams; found throughout the Midwest region.

Comments: The leaves are browsed by white-tailed deer, and wild turkey eat the seeds in autumn and winter. Another species, rough avens (*Geum laciniatum*), has flowers about ½" across, with petals much shorter than the sepals, and the flower stalks densely covered with long hairs. Occasional in moist to wet soils in floodplains and thickets; found throughout the Midwest region, but absent in the lower quarter.

INDIAN PHYSIC
Gillenia stipulata
Rose family (Rosaceae)

Description: A leafy, branching plant with thin, soft-hairy stems, up to 3' tall. The basal leaves are divided several times into small leaflets and appear fern-like. The leaves along the stem appear to be divided into 5 leaflets, but the bottom 2 are large, leaf-like stipules. The leaflets are lance-shaped, sharply toothed, and up to 3" long. The flowers are ¾–1¼" wide, on long stalks, with 5 very narrow, spreading, white petals and about 20 stamens.

Bloom Season: Late spring–midsummer

Habitat/Range: Occasional, but can become locally common in dry, rocky, or upland and open woods; found in the southern third of the Midwest region.

Comments: Formerly known as *Porteranthus stipulatus*. Another common name is American ipecac. Both common names refer to Native American use of this plant for internal cleansing, a widespread ceremonial custom. An "ipecac" is an emetic (an agent that causes vomiting), in this case derived from certain dried roots. The roots are potentially toxic. The foliage is attractive in autumn, varying from yellow to red.

AMERICAN BURNET
Sanguisorba canadensis
Rose family (Rosaceae)

Description: Plants with usually unbranched stems, smooth, up to 5' tall, with alternate compound leaves up to 1½' long. The leaves are located mostly along the lower half of the stem and divided into 7–15 individually stalked leaflets, each up to 3" long. The leaflets are widest near the middle and toothed along the margins. The flowers are in dense, cylindrical clusters at the tops of the stem, with each white flower about ¼" wide, with 4 petal-like sepals and 4 long stamens, each about ½" long. Petals are absent.

Bloom Season: Mid- to late summer

Habitat/Range: Rare in wet to mesic prairies; found in the east-central part of the Midwest region, and eastward.

Comments: The first part of the genus name, *Sanguis*, originates from the Latin words for *blood*, and *sorba*, which translates to "to drink up," as many years ago, the plant sap was believed to be a remedy to stop bleeding.

CLEAVERS
Galium aparine
Madder family (Rubiaceae)

Description: A spreading, sprawling annual plant, up to 3' long, with a 4-sided stem. The leaves occur along the stem in whorls of 6–8, each up to 3" long and about ¼" wide. The stem and leaves have recurved hairs that cling ("cleave") to animal hair, as well as to the clothing of hikers; hence, the name. The small flowers, each about ⅛" wide, have 4 pointed, white petals that are attached on long stems arising from leaf axils.

Bloom Season: Late spring–midsummer

Habitat/Range: Common in moist woods, wooded valleys, and in shaded, disturbed areas; found throughout the Midwest region.

Comments: The other common name, "bedstraw," refers to settlers' use of the aromatic plants as "hay" to fill bedding. Another species, forest bedstraw (*Galium circaezans*), has leaves whorled in groups of 4, with each leaf ¾–2" long and about 1" wide; leaves and stems are densely hairy. Occasional to common in mesic to dry upland forests, upland prairies, savannas, and banks of streams; found throughout the Midwest region, but absent in the northern quarter.

NORTHERN BEDSTRAW
Galium boreale
Madder family (Rubiaceae)

Description: Plants 1–3' tall, with leaves whorled in groups of 4 along the stem. Leaves are ¾–2" long and about ¼" wide, broadest near the base, and with a pointed tip. There are often smaller leaves at the nodes where the main leaves are attached. There are 3 distinct veins along the length of the leaves. The flowers are numerous in branching clusters at the top of the stems. Flowers are ⅛–¼" across, with 4 white lobes, pointed at the tip, and 4 white stamens.

Bloom Season: Late spring–summer

Habitat/Range: Frequent in mesic and dry prairies, moist depressions in prairies, open woods, and along roadsides; found in the northern half of the Midwest region.

Comments: A similar species, wild madder (*Galium obtusum*), differs by having mostly spreading, matted stems instead of being erect, 1 distinct vein in the leaves instead of 3, and tiny flowers, up to ⅛" across. It occurs in wet prairies, wet depressions in upland prairies, woods, and wet soil; found throughout the Midwest region. Another species, stiff bedstraw (*Galium tinctorium*), also has spreading, matted stems, but with even smaller flowers that have 3 lobes instead of 4. It also occurs in wet prairies, wet depressions in upland prairies, and wet woods; found throughout the Midwest region.

LONG-LEAVED BLUETS
Houstonia longifolia
Madder family (Rubiaceae)

Description: Low, slender plants with several stems arising from the base to a height of 8". Leaves at the base of the stem are narrow, long, and present at flowering time; leaves along the stem are opposite, narrow, and smooth, ½–1" long and ¼" wide, with one midvein along the length of the leaf. The flowers are on stalks about ¼" long, white but sometimes tinged with pink, small, about ¼" across, and clustered at the tops of the leaf axils. The corolla is funnel-shaped, with 4 sharply pointed, hairless lobes, and 4 stamens that extend just beyond the lobes.

Bloom Season: Spring–midsummer

Habitat/Range: Occasional in dry prairies, hill prairies, glades, and rocky, open woods; found throughout the Midwest region.

Comments: Long-leaved bluets were formerly known as *Hedyotis longifolia*. A similar species, broad-leaved bluets (*Houstonia purpurea*; formerly known as *Hedyotis purpurea*), has leaves up to 2½" long and 1½" wide, with 3–5 main veins along the length of the stem; flowers, white to light purple; found throughout the southern half of the Midwest region in upland and bottomland forests, glades, and banks along streams. Long-leaved bluets are similar to narrow-leaved bluets, but the former has leaves present at the base during flowering and flower stalks about ¼" long, whereas the latter has leaves absent at the base during flowering and the flowers are stalkless.

NARROW-LEAVED BLUETS

Houstonia nigricans
Madder family (Rubiaceae)

Description: Low, slender plants with several erect, stiff, often-branched stems arising from the base to a height of 8". The leaves at the base are usually absent at flowering time. Leaves are stalkless, opposite, up to 1½" long and ⅛" wide, mostly smooth, with pointed tips, and 1 vein along the length of the leaf. There is a pair of white, papery, pointed stipules at the base of the opposite leaves. The flowers are numerous, stalkless, small, about ¼" across, funnel-shaped, with 4 pointed lobes that are white, pink, or sometimes pale violet. The surface of the lobes is hairy, and the 4 stamens extend just beyond the lobes.

Bloom Season: Late spring–fall

Habitat/Range: Occasional in dry, rocky prairies, hill prairies, and rocky, open woods; found in the southwest quarter of the Midwest region.

Comments: Narrow-leaved bluets is also known as *Stenaria nigricans*, and formerly known as *Hedyotis nigricans*.

SMOOTH FALSE BUTTONWEED

Spermacoce glabra
Madder family (Rubiaceae)

Description: Annual plants with stems upright to loosely ascending or trailing, up to 2' long. The stems are smooth and 4-angled. Leaves are opposite, stalkless, with short stipules, and 5–7 bristles at the leaf base. The leaves are up to 3" long and 1" wide, widest toward the middle, tapering at the base, pointed at the tip, and smooth along the margins. The flowers range from 3–30 in clusters around the stem at the base of the leaves. Each tiny white flower is less than ¼" long and tube-shaped, with 4 lobes.

Bloom Season: Summer–fall

Range/Habitat: Common in wet prairies, moist depressions of sand prairies, banks of streams and rivers, and margins of ponds; found in the southern half of the Midwest region.

Comments: Smooth false buttonweed is similar in appearance to American bugleweed (see page 60), but the former has leaves with smooth margins instead of toothed, as in the latter, and with stipules and bristles at the junction of where the leaves meet the stem, while in the latter, they are lacking.

FALSE TOADFLAX
Comandra umbellata
Sandalwood family (Santalaceae)

Description: A creeping underground rhizome
sends up yellow-green plants that form colonies
to a height of 12". The smooth stems produce
alternate narrow leaves up to 1½" long and about
½" wide, with a pointed or blunt tip, and stalkless.
Flattened clusters of flowers emerge at the top.
Each flower is about ¼" long with 5 sepals; petals
are absent. The fruit is urn-shaped, green, matur-
ing to a chestnut brown or purplish-brown. The
flowers and fruits persist for some time.

Bloom Season: Late spring–early summer

Habitat/Range: Occasional in dry prairies, sandy
sites, savannas, and open woods; found throughout the Midwest region.

Comments: Like other species in the sandalwood
family, false toadflax is parasitic on other plants.
However, it may be considered only partially
parasitic, because the plant has its own green
leaves that photosynthesize and provide energy for
growth. Like mistletoe, false toadflax may need
its host plant only for water. Native Americans
ate the fruits, which are sweet, but consuming too
many could produce nausea.

LATE ALUMROOT
Heuchera parviflora
Saxifrage family (Saxifragaceae)

Description: Small, sparse-looking plants with
flower stalks extending to a height of not more
than 1½' tall. The leaves and flower stalks are covered with gland-tipped hairs. The rounded leaves,
up to 5" across, emerge from the base of the plant
on long stalks. Large, coarse teeth line the margins
of the leaf, and the underside is usually red. The
tiny flowers appear on spreading branches and
have 5 white petals that curl back, revealing yellow stamens.

Bloom Season: Late summer–fall

Habitat/Range: Common on north- and east-
facing, shaded sandstone and dolomite cliffs;
found in the southwest quarter of the Midwest
region, and southeastward.

Comments: The Blackfoot Indians used pounded,
wet roots of late alumroot for rheumatism and
sores, and an infusion of the roots as an eyewash.
They applied a poultice of chewed roots to wounds
and sores, as a styptic, and to cold sores and
children's mouth cankers. The Navajo used the
plant as a panacea (or "life medicine"), and for
rat bites. The common name is derived from the
late flowering time and the puckering, bitter taste
imparted by the root.

PRAIRIE ALUMROOT

Heuchera richardsonii
Saxifrage family (Saxifragaceae)

Description: Hairy plants with tall, leafless flowering stalks, up to 2½' tall, arising from a base of long-stalked leaves. The leaves are round, up to 3½" across, with shallow lobes, toothed edges, and a heart-shaped leaf base. Small flowers are arranged along the top of a long, flowering stem. The flowers are somewhat bell-shaped and droop on individual short stalks that branch from the main flower stalks. Each flower is about ⅜" long, with 5 green sepals and 5 spatula-shaped petals that vary from white to pale green to lavender. The stamens are tipped with brilliant orange and extend just beyond the petals.

Bloom Season: Late spring–summer

Habitat/Range: Common in mesic to dry prairies, hill prairies, sand prairies, and open woods; found throughout the Midwest region.

Comments: Native Americans and early settlers used a root powder as an astringent to close wounds and to treat diarrhea and sore throat. The Meskwaki used the leaves as a dressing for open sores. A similar species, common alumroot (*Heuchera americana*), has smaller flowers, about ¼" long, with the stamens extending well beyond the petals. Occasional in open woods, rocky slopes, ledges, and bluffs; found throughout the Midwest region, but absent in the northern third.

SWAMP SAXIFRAGE

Micranthes pensylvanica
Saxifrage family (Saxifragaceae)

Description: Hairy, leafless stems, 12–40" tall, with a cluster of thick, hairy basal leaves. Leaves are up to 9" long and 3" wide, widest at or above the middle, tapering abruptly at the tops to sharp pointed tips, but with long, tapering bases. The leaf surfaces are covered with sticky hairs and the edges may be toothless or have rounded teeth. The flowers are in dense clusters at the tops of the stems. Flowers are about ¼" across with 5 narrow whitish petals and 10 spreading, orange-tipped stamens.

Bloom Season: Mid-spring–early summer

Habitat/Range: Locally frequent in mesic forests, swamps, open swampy woods, wet meadows, seeps, moist sandy depressions, and moist sandstone cliffs; found throughout the Midwest region, but absent in the western parts of Iowa and Missouri, and the southwest part of Minnesota.

Comments: Formerly known as *Saxifraga pensylvanica*. The genus name, *Micranthes*, is derived from two Greek words: *micros*, meaning "small," and *anthos*, meaning "flower." The species name, *pensylvanica*, means "of Pennsylvania."

107

EARLY SAXIFRAGE
Micranthes virginiensis
Saxifrage family (Saxifragaceae)

Description: Small plants, 4–12" tall, with basal leaves and 1 or more leafless, densely hairy stems. The basal leaves are 1–3" long, oval- to spatula-shaped, sometimes toothed and hairy along the margins, rounded at the tip, and tapering at the base to a short stalk. The flowers are in compact branched clusters at the tops of stems that open and expand as the season progresses. Flowers are about ⅜" across, with 5 triangular sepals and 5 spreading, white petals and 10 yellow stamens.

Bloom Season: Mid-spring–early summer

Habitat/Range: Occasional in rock outcrops in mesic to dry upland forests, cliffs, exposed ledges and outcrops, rocky slopes, and stream banks; found in the Midwest region in southeast Missouri, southern Indiana, eastern Ohio, and disjunct in northern Minnesota and northern Michigan.

Comments: Another species, encrusted saxifrage (*Saxifraga paniculata*), has thick, sharply toothed basal leaves, ¾–1¼" long, stiff, and leathery, with white crusty pores along the edges that secrete lime, and with scattered small alternate leaves on the flower stem. Occurring on rocky ledges and crevices on shady cliffs; found in the northeast corner of Minnesota and the northern edge of Michigan.

BISHOP'S CAP
Mitella diphylla
Saxifrage family (Saxifragaceae)

Description: From a cluster of heart-shaped basal leaves, multiple stems arise 10–18" tall. The basal leaves are 4" long, 3" wide, coarsely toothed, and 3-lobed. There is a pair of opposite leaves on the stem below the flower cluster. The stem leaves are 2½" long and 1½" wide, coarsely toothed, with 3 shallow lobes. All parts of the plant are covered with short hairs. The attractive white flowers, each about ⅛" wide, have 5 deeply dissected petals appearing as snowflakes. The calyx and flower stalks are covered with short, glandular hairs.

Bloom Season: Spring

Habitat/Range: Occasional on moist wooded slopes, especially in deep ravines and shaded ledges; also, in wetlands further north; found throughout the Midwest region.

Comments: One really needs a 10x magnifying lens to better appreciate the delicate pattern of the flowers. Another related species, small bishop's cap (*Mitella nuda*), is smaller, 3–8" tall; the leaves are also smaller, 1–1½" long and wide, usually unlobed, and with rounded teeth along the edges. Frequent in swampy woods, conifer forests, and wetlands; found in the northern quarter of the Midwest region.

SULLIVANT'S COOLWORT
Sullivantia sullivantii
Saxifrage family (Saxifragaceae)

Description: A rather delicate plant, with an interesting history of survival, 2–16" tall, with stems covered in glandular hairs. The leaves are mostly basal, 1–3" long and wide, mostly hairless, long-stalked, kidney-shaped to round, with many shallow lobes along the margin, each with 2–3 teeth, and with a base that is heart-shaped. The flowers are in an open branching cluster at the top of the stem. The branches are loosely arranged, spreading, and somewhat ascending, with flowers at the tips. The flowers are ¼" across, bell-shaped, with 5 white petals and 5 yellow stamens.

Bloom Season: Late spring–summer

Habitat/Range: Uncommon to rare on moist, shaded sandstone, limestone, or dolomite cliffs; found in widely scattered locations in the central and southern part of the Midwest region.

Comments: Sullivant's coolwort is considered a glacial relict (when a cold-adapted species of plant or animal that once survived over a broader range was left behind as an ice age ended). Remnant populations of Sullivant's coolwort are found in unglaciated regions of Missouri, southeast Indiana, and southern Ohio; also, in an area that was not covered by glaciers, known as the "Driftless Area" in southeast Minnesota, southwest Wisconsin, northeast Iowa, and northwest Illinois.

FOAM FLOWER
Tiarella cordifolia
Saxifrage family (Saxifragaceae)

Description: Hairy plants, up to 1' tall, that spread by runners to form dense clumps, 1–2' wide. The long-stalked basal leaves are semi-glossy, heart-shaped, about 4" long and about as wide, with 3–5 lobes and coarse, irregular teeth along the margins. Flowers are at the top of bare stems on horizontal stalks. Each flower is ¼" wide, with 5 small, blunt sepals, 5 delicate, white petals, and 10 slender stamens that are longer than the petals, creating a foamy texture, resulting in the common name.

Bloom Season: Mid-spring–early summer

Habitat/Range: Common in mesic forests, shaded ravines, and swampy areas; found in the Midwest region in northeast Wisconsin, Michigan, and eastern Ohio, and eastward.

Comments: The foliage is evergreen in mild winters, often turning reddish-bronze in autumn and winter. The plants are known to bloom over a period of six weeks, making them a bonus for garden plantings.

109

STINGING NETTLE
Laportea canadensis
Nettle family (Urticaceae)

Description: An upright, branched (or unbranched) plant, with a somewhat zigzagged stem, up to 3' tall. The stem and leaves have numerous stinging hairs. The alternate leaves are broad, up to 6" long and 4" wide, with coarse teeth along the margins, and leaf stalks up to 4" long that are also covered with stinging hairs. The tiny flowers, less than ⅛" across, are crowded into separate branched clusters on the same plant; the male flowers arise in loose clusters from the leaf axils about midway up the plant, while the female flowers are on flat branching clusters at the top. Each flower has 5 narrow, greenish-white sepals and no petals.

Bloom Season: Summer

Habitat/Range: Common in wet or moist, low woodlands, in valleys, and along streams; found throughout the Midwest region.

Comments: The stinging hairs contain formic acid, like that felt in the bite of an ant. One preventive measure when hiking in lowland woods is to wear thick material like fairly new blue jeans, which prevents the needle-like hairs from reaching the skin. Once a person is stung, the juice from the soft stem of spotted touch-me-not (see page 200) or pale touch-me-not (see page 155), when applied to the skin, can reduce the sting. A related stinging species, tall nettle (*Urtica dioica*), differs by having opposite narrower leaves, with a single stem, and shares the same habitat and range with stinging nettle.

HORSE NETTLE
Solanum carolinense
Nightshade family (Solanaceae)

Description: An upright, branched plant, with spiny stems, up to 3' tall. The leaves, up to 6" long and 3" wide, are alternate, short-stalked, pointed at the tip, and tapering at the base. The leaf margins are wavy, with deep lobes. There are straw-colored spines along the veins on the underside of the leaf and along the leaf stalk. The flowers are few, loosely clustered at the end of stalks, and about ¾" across. The 5 white petals are united at the base. There are 5 large, bright yellow stamens. The fruit, about ¾" in diameter, is a smooth, bright yellow berry, like a tiny tomato, which persists through the winter.

Bloom Season: Late spring–fall

Habitat/Range: Common in disturbed prairies, edges of woods, old fields, pastures, sandy ground, roadsides, and disturbed ground; found through the Midwest region, but absent in the northern quarter.

Comments: Horse nettle and other nightshades are closely related to tomatoes and eggplant. However, the attractive bright yellow berries are toxic, and fatalities have been reported in children. Native Americans gargled wilted leaf tea for sore throat, applied wilted leaves to the skin for poison ivy rash, and drank tea for worms. The fruit is eaten by a variety of both birds and mammals.

CORN SALAD
Valerianella radiata
Valerian family (Valerianaceae)

Description: Although a native plant, this small, succulent annual often occurs in disturbed soil and is somewhat weedy. The much-branched stem is angled, has sparse hairs, and grows to 15" tall. The leaves are opposite on the stem, up to 3" long and 1" wide, stalkless, and slightly toothed on the lower margins. The flowers are packed tight at the ends of the branched stalks, forming a flat top. The white flowers are ⅟₁₆" long, with the stamens extending just beyond the petals.

Bloom Season: Spring

Habitat/Range: Common in disturbed ground, idle fields, prairies, moist, open ground, bare soil in valleys, creek bottoms, rocky glades, and along roadsides; found throughout the Midwest region.

Comments: The young, tender leaves gathered before the flowers appear have been used in salads or prepared like spinach. A related species, northern corn salad (*Valerianella umbilicata*), is up to 1½' tall, with flowers each ⅛" long and very fragrant. Occasional in floodplain forests and banks of streams where there is greater light intensity; found in the eastern third of the Midwest region.

EDIBLE VALERIAN
Valeriana edulis
Valerian family (Valerianaceae)

Description: Thick-stemmed plants that are multiple from the base, up to 4' tall, with basal leaves appearing on a short, winged stalk. The basal leaves are up to 12" long and less than 1" wide, and narrowly spatula-shaped. The stem leaves are few, opposite, shorter than the basal leaves, thick, with 3–9 narrow, finger-like lobes that are fringed with tiny hairs along the edges. The flowers are in dense clusters at the top of the plant. Each flower is about ⅛" wide, with 5 creamy-white, fused petals, lobes that spread and curve back, and 3 stamens. The sepals are small at flowering but later expand into 3–10 feathery threads at the top of the fruit that carry the seeds on the wind.

Bloom Season: Late spring–early summer

Habitat/Range: Uncommon to rare in mesic prairies, wet-mesic prairies, wet meadows, and fens; found across the central third of the Midwest region; also found in western states.

Comments: Edible valerian was once common and widespread, but destruction of habitat by agriculture has reduced the population significantly. The root of edible valerian is edible when cooked, then dried and ground into a powder. The raw roots are considered poisonous. Native Americans and pioneers used it extensively. On August 21, 1805, it was noted that George Drouillard collected the roots and used them as flour while on the Lewis and Clark Expedition. The crushed root has been used on parts of the body affected by rheumatism, swollen bruises, painful bleeding cuts, and wounds.

FOG FRUIT
Phyla lanceolata
Vervain family (Verbenaceae)

Description: These moist soil–loving plants mostly creep along, rooting at the nodes (points of leaf attachment to the stem), up to 1½' long. The leaves are opposite, up to 2" long and ½" wide, lance-shaped, pointed at the tip, and coarsely toothed along the margin. Several flowers, less than ¼" long, are clustered on small heads that emerge from the axils of leaves on long stalks. The 4 petals are united into a pair of 2-lobed lips. The flowers are white, with some showing pink or purple.

Bloom Season: Late spring–fall

Habitat/Range: Common along floodplains, muddy or gravelly margins of streams, ponds, sloughs, ditches, and low meadows; found through the Midwest region, but absent in the northern quarter.

Comments: This plant is also known as frog fruit. The small seeds are a source of food for waterfowl.

GREEN VIOLET
Hybanthus concolor
Violet family (Violaceae)

Description: Hairy, unbranched plants, up to 2' tall, often in large colonies. The dark green leaves are alternate, hairy, lance-shaped, up to 4" long and 1¼" wide, tapering at both ends, and usually lacking teeth along the margins. There are 1–3 flowers arising from the leaf axils. Each flower is about ⅜" long, greenish-white, attached to a drooping stalk, with 5 green, narrow sepals and 5 greenish-white petals. One petal is wider than the others and swollen at the base.

Bloom Season: Spring–early summer

Habitat/Range: Occasional in moist upland forests, wooded slopes, and ravines; found throughout the Midwest region, but rare in the northern half.

Comments: Although belonging to the violet family, this plant looks nothing at all like the other violets in the Midwest.

PALE VIOLET
Viola striata
Violet family (Violaceae)

Description: Several stems rise from the base of the plant up to 10" tall. The stems are upright but may recline; they are smooth and angular, bearing fringed, leaf-like stipules where the leaves arise. The leaves are alternate, about 2½" long and 2" across, broadest in the middle, heart-shaped at the base, smooth, with round teeth along the edges. The flowers emerge solitarily from the axils of the leaves on long stalks. The flowers are white or creamy-white, about 1¼" long, with 5 petals, some with purple lines.

Bloom Season: Spring–early summer

Habitat/Range: Common in low or rich, moist woods in valleys along streams; found in the southern half of the Midwest region.

Comments: Pale violet is a rather tall and attractive species that blooms longer and later than most violets.

YELLOW FLOWERS

This section includes yellow, golden, and yellowish-orange to pale, creamy-yellow flowers. Also, multiple-colored flowers that are predominantly yellow are included in this section.

FALSE ALOE
Manfreda virginica
Agave family (Agavaceae)

Description: Tall, smooth plants, up to 6' in height, with fleshy, dark green leaves at the base. The basal leaves are thick, smooth, and succulent, up to 16" long and 2" wide, pointed at the tip, and often purple-blotched across the surface. The stem leaves are much reduced in size. The 10–60 flowers are arranged along a long spike at the top of a wand-like stem. Each greenish to dark yellow, tubular flower is about 1" long, with 6 convex ridges, 6 narrow lobes, and 6 green to brown stamens with large, yellow anthers that extend well beyond the flower.

Bloom Season: Summer

Habitat/Range: Occasional on glades, dry upland ridges or flats, and rocky ledges; found in the southern quarter of the Midwest region, and southward.

Comments: Formerly called *Agave virginica*. The flowers are fragrant, similar to Easter lilies. Native Americans used a root tea for dropsy and a wash for snakebite.

PRAIRIE PARSLEY
Polytaenia nuttallii
Parsley family (Apiaceae)

Description: A stout plant, up to 3' tall, with thick, long-stalked, alternate, highly dissected leaves, with a few coarse teeth along their margins. The leaf stalks have wide, flat, clasping bases. The flowers are clustered in numerous branches that form a flat-topped head. Each cluster is on a long stalk and has 15–25 pale yellow flowers, each about ⅛" wide, with 5 tiny petals.

Bloom Season: Mid-spring–early summer

Habitat/Range: Occasional on upland prairies, savannas, and open woods; found in the central and southwest quarters of the Midwest region.

Comments: Prairie parsley is the tallest wildflower blooming in the prairies in early spring, towering over Indian paintbrush, yellow star grass, hoary puccoon, shooting star, and others. The Meskwaki used tea made from the seeds to treat diarrhea.

GOLDEN ALEXANDERS

Zizia aurea
Parsley family (Apiaceae)

Description: A smooth, branched plant, up to 3'
tall, with alternate leaves divided into 3 leaflets.
The leaflets can sometimes be divided again into
another 1–3 leaflets. The lance-shaped leaflets
are up to 3" long and 1" wide, with teeth along
the margins. The flower heads are flat-topped
and have several branches arising from a common
point on the stem. Each yellow flower is less than
⅛" wide, with 5 tiny, incurved petals. The central
flower within each cluster lacks a stalk, so that the
flower is slightly recessed.

Bloom Season: Mid-spring–early summer

Habitat/Range: Common in mesic prairies, savannas, open woods, wet thickets, and banks along
streams; found throughout the Midwest region.

Comments: The Meskwaki used the root to reduce
fever. Early settlers considered the plant useful
for treating syphilis and for healing wounds. A
closely related species, heart-leaved meadow
parsnip (*Zizia aptera*), also occurs in prairies and
open woods. Found in the Midwest region, but
rare to absent in the central and eastern parts.
The leaves at the base of the stem are not divided
into leaflets and are heart-shaped at the base.
Golden Alexanders is similar to meadow parsnip
(*Thaspium trifoliatum*) (see page 118), but the
latter's central flower in each flower cluster has a
short stalk.

YELLOW PIMPERNEL

Taenidia integerrima
Parsley family (Apiaceae)

Description: Slender, delicate plants with a
whitish-powdered appearance, up to 3' tall.
The leaves are alternate and divided into 2–3
segments, with 3–5 leaflets per segment. The
leaflets are almost rounded, ½–1" long, and lack
teeth along the margins. The flower heads form
a loose, umbrella-shaped cluster up to 3" across.
Each cluster contains 10–20 stalks, tipped with its
own small head of flowers. Each tiny flower has 5
yellow petals that curve inward at their tips.

Bloom Season: Mid-spring–early summer

Habitat/Range: Occasional in upland prairies,
savannas, open woods, and wooded slopes; found
throughout the Midwest region, but uncommon to
absent in the northwest quarter.

Comments: Both Native Americans and early
settlers mixed the root of yellow pimpernel with
other medicines to impart a pleasant aroma. The
Meskwaki used it as a seasoning agent for some
of their foods. In early folk medicine, a root tea
was given for lung ailments.

MEADOW PARSNIP
Thaspium trifoliatum
Parsley family (Apiaceae)

Description: A much-branched plant, up to 2½'
tall and lacking hairs. The basal leaves are simple,
heart-shaped, or sometimes divided into 3 leaflets.
The leaves along the stem are on long stalks and
divided into 3 leaflets, each with a rounded base
and small teeth along the margins. The flower
heads are on stalks forming an umbrella-shaped
cluster, with numerous, tiny flowers, each less
than ⅛" wide, which are yellow but sometimes
dark purple. The flowers are all on short stalks.

Bloom Season: Mid-spring–early summer

Habitat/Range: Occasional in upland prairies,
savannas, mesic to dry upland forests, and blufftops;
found in the southern half of the Midwest region.

Comments: Meadow parsnip can sometimes be
confused with golden Alexanders (*Zizia aurea*) but
differs most noticeably by the latter having the
central flower in a flower head lacking a stalk,
so that the flower is slightly recessed. Another
meadow parsnip, hairy-jointed meadow parsnip
(*Thaspium barbinode*), has stems with hairs at
the nodes, basal leaves (not simple), divided 2–3
times, and with the edges fringed with hairs. Occasional in mesic prairies, bottomland forests, upland
forests, wooded bluffs and slopes, and banks of
streams; found throughout the Midwest region, but
absent in the northern third.

CLUSTERED BLACK SNAKEROOT
Sanicula gregaria
Parsely family (Apiaceae)

Description: Single or multiple stems emerge from
the base up to 3' tall, with branching at the top.
The leaves are palmately compound, with 5 leaflets up to 2" long and 1" wide, coarsely toothed,
smooth, and notched or lobed toward the tip. The
leaf stalks are up to 6" long. The small flowers
are in clusters at the ends of branching stems.
Each cluster is about ½" across and contains a
mixture of 20–60 flowers that are male, female,
and perfect (both male and female parts) in the
same cluster. The greenish-yellow flowers have 5
petals that are much longer than the sepals and 2
long, spreading styles that are much longer than
the bristles on the fruit; the styles cling to fur and
clothing, which aids in the plant's dispersal.

Bloom Season: Early summer–midsummer

Habitat/Range: Common in mesic upland forests,
bottomland forests, and on banks of streams;
found throughout the Midwest region.

Comments: Also known as *Sanicula odorata*. A
similar species, Canadian black snakeroot (*Sanicula
canadensis*), has greenish-white flowers, and the
styles are shorter than the bristles on the fruit;
habitat and range are similar to *Sanicula gregaria*.
Another species, black snakeroot (*Sanicula marilandica*), has 5–7 leaflets, larger flower heads, and
white petals; found in similar habitats, but located
primarily in the northern half of the Midwest region.

GREEN DRAGON
Arisaema dracontium
Arum family (Araceae)

Description: A single, highly dissected leaf with deep, narrow lobes that is attached to a smooth, green stalk, up to 3' tall. The leaf is divided into 5–15 segments, with each segment lance-shaped, up to 10" long and 4" wide, smooth, and lacking teeth along the margins. A flower stalk rises up to 10" from the base to a tubular, green sheath called a "spathe." Inside the spathe, the greenish-yellow flowers are crowded together, and at the top emerges a greenish-yellow, tail-like, cylindrical column called a "spadix," up to 7" long. In the fall, a cluster of shiny orange-red berries is arranged along a thick head.

Bloom Season: Mid-spring–early summer

Habitat/Range: Common on moist, rocky, wooded slopes, bases of ravines, and floodplains; found throughout the Midwest region, but absent in the northern quarter.

Comments: Native Americans first dried the bulb-like corm and used it for food. Fresh corms, however, contain calcium oxalate crystals, which cause intense burning in the mouth and throat.

COMMON RAGWEED
Ambrosia artemisiifolia
Aster family (Asteraceae)

Description: A summer annual, 1–3' tall, which branches frequently and is covered with soft, erect, white hairs. The leaves are egg-shaped, up to 6" long and 4" wide near the base, thin, fern-like, and deeply lobed, with many of the side lobes deeply lobed again. The lower leaves are opposite while the upper leaves are alternate. The flowers are on spikes 1–6" long, greenish-yellow, tiny, about ⅛" long, petal-less, and mostly male, with the female flowers in clusters at the base of the spike.

Bloom Season: Midsummer–fall

Habitat/Range: Common in disturbed soil of prairies, savannas, glades, upland and bottomland forests, banks of streams, pastures, and roadsides; found throughout the Midwest region.

Comments: Common ragweed is native to the United States but is now found worldwide. It is a major contributing factor to the struggles of hay fever sufferers around the globe. The plant does have value to various kinds of wildlife, however: Honeybees collect pollen from the male flowers; many kinds of insect larvae feed on the leaves; and several species of birds eat the oil-rich seeds.

WESTERN RAGWEED
Ambrosia psilostachya
Aster family (Asteraceae)

Description: A colonial plant, 12–30" tall, with widely creeping rhizomes, and hairy stems and leaves. Lower leaves are opposite, but the upper leaves are often alternate, up to 5" long and 2" wide, and deeply divided into many narrow lobes that are again further lobed. The hairy leaves are denser underneath, giving the leaves a gray-green appearance. The flowers are tiny, drab, and greenish-yellow, with the male flowers on spikes that are 1–6" long, while the female flowers are in small clusters at the base of the upper leaves. Petals and sepals are absent.

Bloom Season: Midsummer–fall

Habitat/Range: Common in dry prairies, loess hill prairies, and sand prairies; also, roadsides and sandy, open, disturbed ground; found in the western third of the Midwest and randomly dispersed eastward.

Comments: Western ragweed, along with the other ragweeds, is notorious for causing hay fever with their windborne pollen. The Cheyenne drank a tea made from a pinch of finely ground leaves and stems to treat bowel cramps and colds. The Kiowa boiled small pieces to make a medicine that was rubbed on sores. A tea was a remedy for "worm holes," a skin disease of horses, and for sores that were slow in healing. Another species, lanceleaf ragweed (*Ambrosia bidentata*), is an annual up to 3' tall with leaves mostly unlobed, lance-shaped, and up to 3" long and ½" wide. Common in disturbed soil in a wide range of habitats; found in the southern third of the Midwest region, and southward.

GIANT RAGWEED

Ambrosia trifida
Aster family (Asteraceae)

Description: A branched, hairy, annual plant, up to 15' tall, sometimes forming dense stands in disturbed sites. The leaves are opposite, stalked, deeply 3-lobed, rough, toothed along the margins, with the lower leaves up to 12" across. The upper leaves are unlobed and smaller. The flowers are arranged on long stalks with greenish-yellow, pollen-producing male flowers much more numerous than the female flowers, which are nearly hidden in leaf axils. Petals and sepals are absent.

Bloom Season: Midsummer–fall

Habitat/Range: Common in moist soils in low woods, along floodplains and streams, fields, disturbed sites, and along roadsides; found throughout the Midwest region.

Comments: The seed of giant ragweed has been found in several archaeological sites where it is thought to have been cultivated as a food source. The seeds are an important food for wildlife. Ragweed pollen is a major contributor to hay fever.

PRAIRIE BROOMWEED

Amphiachyris dracunculoides
Aster family (Asteraceae)

Description: A wide-spreading annual, up to 2' tall and 1½' wide, with a single, smooth, angled or grooved stem that branches mostly in the upper half of the stem. Leaves are alternate, narrow, tapering at the base, with a pointed tip, smooth margins, and up to 2" long. The leaf surface is smooth but with moderate to dense, indented, resinous dots, often somewhat sticky to the touch. Many flower heads appear on numerous spreading branches, forming a mound shape. Each yellow flower head has 7–10 ray flowers, each about ⅛" long, and 10–25 disk flowers.

Bloom Season: Midsummer–fall

Habitat/Range: Common in upland prairies, disturbed sites, and roadsides; found in the southwest quarter of the Midwest region.

Comments: Formerly known as *Gutierrezia dracunculoides*. Native Americans and early settlers used these plants as brooms.

TICKSEED SUNFLOWER
Bidens aristosa
Aster family (Asteraceae)

Description: A smooth, much-branched annual, growing up to 3' tall, but sometimes to a height of 6' on rich soils. The leaves are opposite, stalked, and divided into 5–11 narrow, coarsely toothed leaflets. The flower heads are on individual stalks, with each head about 1½–2½" across, with 8 golden-yellow, petal-like ray flowers surrounding a yellow central disk. The seeds resemble ticks and have 2 barbed, bristle-like structures that attach to clothing and fur, aiding in their dispersal.

Bloom Season: Late summer–fall

Habitat/Range: Common in wet prairies, edges of marshes, low depressions, ditches, and fallow fields; found through the Midwest region, but absent in the northern third.

Comments: Tickseed sunflower is also known as beggar-ticks. The Cherokee used a similar species of *Bidens* in leaf tea to expel worms. The leaves were chewed for sore throat. The seeds are eaten by ducks, bobwhite quail, and some songbirds; the plants are eaten by cottontail rabbits. There are nine species of the genus *Bidens* in the Midwest region.

NODDING BUR MARIGOLD
Bidens cernua
Aster family (Asteraceae)

Description: Annual plants 6–36" tall, with widely spaced opposite leaves that clasp the stem. The leaves are smooth, narrow, up to 6" long and 1" wide, tapering to a point, and toothed along the edges. The flower heads are on stalks that arise from leaf axils, each about 1–2" across, with 8 oval, yellow, petal-like ray flowers and a central cluster of tiny, 5-lobed, tubular disk flowers. The petals may not all be the same size, and occasionally are absent altogether. The seeds resemble ticks and have 4 barbed, bristle-like structures that attach to clothing and fur.

Bloom Season: Summer–early fall

Habitat/Range: Common along banks of streams, margins of wetlands, sloughs, swamps, bottomland forests, fens, and roadside ditches; found throughout the Midwest region.

Comments: The flower head nods as it ages— hence, the common name—so the seed head points down. Plants like nodding bur marigold, with its showier flowers, attract an abundance of bees, wasps, butterflies, skippers, moths, and various kinds of flies.

LARGE-FLOWERED COREOPSIS
Coreopsis grandiflora
Aster family (Asteraceae)

Description: Slender, smooth plants, up to 2' tall, with opposite to sometimes alternate leaves. The leaves are about 3" long and 2" wide, and divided into slender, thread-like segments less than ¼" wide. Flower heads are on solitary stalks above the leaves. Each flower head has 6–12 golden-yellow, petal-like ray flowers, each about 1" long, with 3–5 teeth or lobes at the tip. The numerous disk flowers are yellow to yellowish-orange.

Bloom Season: Mid-spring–midsummer

Habitat/Range: Locally frequent in dry prairies; found primarily in the southwest quarter of the Midwest region, but escaped from cultivation elsewhere.

Comments: Through introduction and garden escapes, this coreopsis has become established in the central and eastern United States, well beyond its native range.

LANCELEAF COREOPSIS
Coreopsis lanceolata
Aster family (Asteraceae)

Description: Branching plants with several smooth stems emerging from a clump up to 2' tall. Leaves opposite, mainly near the base, up to 8" long and 1" wide, and lacking teeth along the margins. The showy, golden-yellow flower heads, each up to 2½" wide, are on long stalks. Each head has 8–10 fan-shaped ray flowers with jagged teeth at the tip and numerous yellow to yellowish-orange disk flowers.

Bloom Season: Mid-spring–midsummer

Habitat/Range: Locally common in dry, shallow, rocky to sandy soils in prairies, glades, and along railroads and roadsides; found throughout the Midwest region, but escaped from cultivation in the northwest part.

Comments: This showy, long-blooming perennial is easily grown from seed. Another species, downy coreopsis (*Coreopsis pubescens*), has downy-covered stems and undersurface of the leaves, larger leaves, and flowers about 2" across; occasional in mesic woods, bottomland forests, banks of streams and ravines; found in the southwest quarter of the Midwest region.

PRAIRIE COREOPSIS

Coreopsis palmata
Aster family (Asteraceae)

Description: Narrow, rigid-stemmed plants, usually 1–2½' tall. The leaves are opposite on the stem, with each leaf divided into 3 long, narrow segments. The middle segment can sometimes be divided again for another 1–2 segments. The flower heads are on individual stalks, with each head having 8 yellow, petal-like ray flowers, each up to 1" long, that surround a central yellow disk. The ends of the ray flowers are notched or toothed.

Bloom Season: Late spring–midsummer

Habitat/Range: Frequent in dry prairies, savannas, glades, and open woods; found throughout the central and western parts of the Midwest region.

Comments: The genus name, *Coreopsis*, comes from the Greek words *koris*, meaning "bug," and *opsis*, meaning "like," in reference to the shape of the seed, which resembles a tick. The Meskwaki boiled the seeds and drank the brew. Some tribes applied the boiled seeds to painful areas of the body to relieve ailments such as rheumatism.

PLAINS COREOPSIS

Coreopsis tinctoria
Aster family (Asteraceae)

Description: A multibranched, annual plant, 2–4' tall, with smooth stems and opposite leaves. The leaves are up to 6" long and 4" wide, and divided into very narrow leaflets or lobes. The flower heads are about 1–2" across, numerous, on long stalks, and very showy. The 6–12 petal-like ray flowers are golden-yellow, with a prominent reddish-brown spot at the base, and 3 large teeth at each tip. The central disk is reddish-brown.

Bloom Season: Summer–fall

Habitat/Range: Occasional in glades, sand prairies, open and sandy ground, and along roadsides; found to occur naturally along the southwest border of the Midwest region and westward; also naturalized in scattered locations elsewhere in the Midwest region, having escaped from cultivated gardens.

Comments: Plains coreopsis is a popular ornamental plant. The Lakota boiled the flowers in water, which turned red, and used it as a beverage. The plant tops were used in a tea to strengthen the blood. The Meskwaki boiled the plant to make a drink to treat internal pains and bleeding.

TALL COREOPSIS
Coreopsis tripteris
Aster family (Asteraceae)

Description: Tall, stout stems, sometimes with a whitish coating, up to 8' tall, but typically shorter. The leaves are opposite, with stalks, and divided into 3, and sometimes 5, narrow leaflets. Individual leaflets are up to 5" long and ¾" across. The flower heads are on several slender stalks at the top of the plant. Each head is about 1½" across, with 6–10 yellow, petal-like ray flowers surrounding a brown central disk. The flower heads have an anise scent.

Bloom Season: Summer–early fall

Habitat/Range: Occasional to common in mesic prairies, savannas, open woods, and along banks of streams and rivers; found through the Midwest region, but absent in the northern third.

Comments: The Meskwaki boiled the plant to make a drink to treat internal pains and bleeding.

YELLOW CONEFLOWER
Echinacea paradoxa
Aster family (Asteraceae)

Description: Attractive, smooth, yellow-green plants with stout stems, up to 3' tall. The leaves lack hair and are smooth to the touch, up to 10" long and 1½" wide, tapering at each end, with several parallel veins running along the length of the leaf. The basal leaves are on long stalks, while the stems leaves are few. The flower heads are single on long stems, with several drooping, bright yellow ray flowers each up to 3½" long, surrounding a broad, purplish, conical central disk. The stamens are yellow.

Bloom Season: Late spring–summer

Habitat/Range: Localized in dry, often rocky upland prairies and dolomite glades; found in the southwest quarter of the Midwest region.

Comments: The genus name, *Echinacea*, comes from the Greek word *echinos*, meaning "hedgehog" or "sea urchin," in reference to the spiny center cone found in most flowers of this genus. The species name, *paradoxa*, refers to the paradox of why this species has yellow flowers instead of the usual purple flowers in this genus.

NARROWLEAF GUMWEED
Grindelia lanceolata
Aster family (Asteraceae)

Description: This multibranched, reddish-stemmed plant grows up to 3' tall, with sticky or gummy bracts resembling round burs below the flower heads. The leaves are upturned, alternate, smooth, up to 4" long and 1" wide, with the tip ending abruptly to a point, and scattered bristle-like teeth along the margins. The flower heads are about 1½" across, with 20–30 yellow, slender, petal-like ray flowers that are upturned, forming a cup. The yellow disk at the center of the flower head is flat.

Bloom Season: Late summer–fall

Habitat/Range: Common in dry, rocky upland prairies, glades, pastures, and roadsides; found in the southwest quarter of the Midwest region.

Comments: Also known as spiny-toothed gumweed. Native Americans made a root tea for treating liver ailments. Crushed and soaked plants were applied to relieve the pain and swelling of rheumatic joints. An extraction has been used as a wash to relieve the skin rash of poison ivy.

BITTERWEED
Helenium amarum
Aster family (Asteraceae)

Description: A very leafy, much-branched annual plant, up to 12" tall. The leaves are thread-like, alternate but sometimes whorled on the stem, up to 1½" long. The flower heads are fan-shaped, up to 1" across, with yellow, petal-like ray flowers that have notches on the ends, and a central, dome-shaped, yellow disk.

Bloom Season: Summer–fall

Habitat/Range: Scattered to common in disturbed portions of prairies, woods, stream banks, grazed pastures, and roadsides; native to Louisiana, Oklahoma, and Texas, but introduced and spread throughout the southern half of the Midwest region.

Comments: This plant has a strong, bitter smell. Cattle often avoid it, and those that graze on the plant give milk with a bitter flavor; hence, the common name. There are cases of sheep, cattle, horses, and mules having been poisoned from eating this plant.

SNEEZEWEED

Helenium autumnale
Aster family (Asteraceae)

Description: A very leafy-stemmed plant, up to 5' tall, with branching near the top. The stem has narrow wings of leafy tissue extending downward along the stem from the leaf bases. The leaves are alternate, up to 6" long and 1½" wide, broadest near the middle, and tapering at both ends. There are a few small, widely spaced teeth along the margins. The flower heads are about 2" in diameter, with 10–20 drooping, yellow, broadly fan-shaped, petal-like ray flowers surrounding a rounded, central yellow disk. The ray flowers have 3 lobes at their tips.

Bloom Season: Midsummer–fall

Habitat/Range: Occasional in moist ground in prairies, wet prairies, meadows, and along streams; found throughout the Midwest region.

Comments: The Meskwaki dried the flower heads and used them as an inhalant to treat head colds. To reduce fever, the Comanche soaked sneezeweed stems in water and bathed the patient's body with the liquid. The dried flower heads were reportedly used as a snuff by early settlers. Sheep, cattle, and horses have been poisoned by eating large amounts of the plant, especially the seed heads.

PURPLE-HEADED SNEEZEWEED

Helenium flexuosum
Aster family (Asteraceae)

Description: A single-stemmed plant, up to 3' tall, with branching toward the top. The stem has leafy wings that originate at the base of the leaf and continue down the stem. The leaves are alternate, lacking stalks, up to 3" long and less than 1" wide. The distinctive flower head, about 1½" across, has a round, brownish-purple central disk surrounded by 8–14 fan-shaped, yellow, petal-like ray flowers, each with 3 lobes.

Bloom Season: Summer–fall

Habitat/Range: Occasional in moist ground in prairies, wet prairies, meadows, and along streams; found in the southern half of the Midwest region, and escaped from cultivation elsewhere.

Comments: Sneezeweeds are considered poisonous to cattle if eaten in large enough quantity. This is unlikely to happen, however, because of the plant's bitter taste. The plant is also poisonous to fishes and worms, as well as to insects. Research by the National Cancer Institute has demonstrated significant antitumor activity in this plant's chemistry.

COMMON SUNFLOWER

Helianthus annuus

Aster family (Asteraceae)

Description: A robust annual, with branching stems often up to 9' tall. The stems are stout and coarsely hairy. The leaves are alternate, on long stalks, up to 10" long, heart-shaped, notched at the base, with sandpapery surfaces and coarse teeth along the margins. The flower heads are large, 4–10" across, with 20 or more yellow, petal-like ray flowers, each 1–2" long, that surround a reddish-brown central disk 1" or more in diameter.

Bloom Season: Midsummer–fall

Habitat/Range: Common,found in dry prairies, pastures, roadsides, and disturbed ground throughout the Midwest region. Originally native to the southwest part of the region and westward, but the common sunflower has been introduced to the East Coast and Canada.

Comments: Originally cultivated by Native Americans, the sunflower's seeds were used as food and a source for oil. Today, cultivated varieties with large seed heads and seeds are used to produce oil, food, and birdseed.

PLAINS SUNFLOWER

Helianthus petiolaris

Aster family (Asteraceae)

Description: An annual plant, 2–5' tall, with a tap-root, single to branched stems, and a rough texture throughout. The leaves are long-stalked, alternate, triangle- to narrow-shaped, 1½"–6" long and ½–3" wide, with a rough surface and somewhat wavy edges. Leaves are mostly toothless. Flowers are on stalks 1½–6" long. The flower heads are 1½–3" wide, with 12–25 yellow, petal-like ray flowers and a center, ½–1" in diameter, with numerous dark brown to reddish-purple disk flowers. The center of the disk contains chaffy scales with white-hairy tips, often appearing as a whitish spot.

Bloom Season: Summer–fall

Habitat/Range: Locally common in degraded upland prairies and sand prairies, roadsides, and other areas with disturbed rocky or sandy soil; found in the western third of the Midwest region and westward, but introduced into other parts eastward, where there are open, disturbed areas, often in sandy soil.

Comments: The plains sunflower resembles the common sunflower, but the former has shorter, narrower leaves and smaller flowers. Both sunflowers occupy similar habitats. The Hopi mixed dried, ground petals with cornmeal to use as yellow face powder for ceremonial dances.

BRISTLY SUNFLOWER
Helianthus hirsutus
Aster family (Asteraceae)

Description: Often in colonies, this plant grows up to 4' tall, with stiff hairs along the stem and leaves. The leaves are mostly opposite, on stalks ¼–⅝" long on larger leaves, with a sandpapery texture and small, widely spaced teeth along the margin. The leaves have 1 central vein and 2 side veins. The flower heads are up to 3" across, with 8–15 yellow, petal-like ray flowers surrounding a yellow central disk. The circle of bracts below the flower cluster is about ¾" in diameter.

Bloom Season: Midsummer–fall

Habitat/Range: Common in rocky or dry upland forests, prairies, savannas, thickets, and along roadsides; found throughout the Midwest region, but rare in the northeast quarter.

Comments: A closely related species, woodland sunflower (*Helianthus divaricatus*), differs by having stems that are smooth or hairy only toward the tip, leaves that are stalkless or up to ¼" long, and the circle of bracts below the flower cluster about ½" in diameter. Common in dry upland forests, prairies, savannas, glades, blufftops, and roadsides; found throughout the Midwest region, but rare to absent in the northwest quarter.

PALE-LEAVED SUNFLOWER
Helianthus strumosus
Aster family (Asteraceae)

Description: A relatively smooth-stemmed plant, 2–6' tall, often with a white coating along the stem. The leaves are opposite but often alternate near the upper part, on stalks ⅜–1¼" long. Each leaf is 2½–7" long and ¾–4" wide, rounded or slightly tapering at the base, broadest at the base and narrowing to a pointed tip, with smooth to loosely spaced shallow teeth along the margins, a rough upper surface, and short-hairy and paler in color on the lower surface. The flower heads are 1½–4" wide, with 8–15 yellow, petal-like ray flowers surrounding a central yellow disk.

Bloom Season: Summer–fall

Habitat/Range: Common in open dry and mesic upland forests, bottomland forests, banks of streams, fens, upland prairies, and along roadsides; found throughout the Midwest region.

Comments: The smooth stem (often with a whitish bloom), stalked leaves, and the pale undersides of the leaves help to distinguish this sunflower from bristly and woodland sunflowers.

SAWTOOTH SUNFLOWER
Helianthus grosseserratus
Aster family (Asteraceae)

Description: A tall, many-branched, colony-forming sunflower, up to 9' tall, often with several smooth stems and a whitish bloom, emerging from a single base. The leaves are alternate, on stalks up to 1½" long, large, about 8" long and 2" wide, tapering at each end, with hairs on the underside. The margins are finely to coarsely toothed; hence, the common name. The flower heads are numerous, up to 3½" across, with 10–20 yellow, petal-like ray flowers surrounding a yellow disk.

Bloom Season: Midsummer–fall

Habitat/Range: Common in draws and thickets in wet to dry prairies and pastures, and also along roadsides, ditches, streams, and often disturbed areas; found throughout the Midwest region, but rare to absent in the northeast quarter.

Comments: The Meskwaki mashed the flowers and applied them to burns. In the Southwest, Zuni medicine men cured rattlesnake bites by chewing the fresh or dried root and then sucking the snakebite wound. A similar species, giant sunflower (*Helianthus giganteus*), differs by having a distinctly hairy stem, and its leaves are stalkless; common in moist woods, wet sand prairies, and wetlands; found throughout the Midwest region, but rare to absent in the southwest quarter.

MAXIMILIAN SUNFLOWER
Helianthus maximilianii
Aster family (Asteraceae)

Description: Plants with densely hairy stems, up to 9' tall, with leaves alternate, narrow, and toothed along the margins. The leaves are up to 12" long and 2" wide, and curved and folded along the blade. The leaf surface is rough with minute, often flattened hairs, and the leaf margins have small, widely spaced teeth. Flower heads are on stout stalks along the upper part of the stem. Each head is up to 4" wide, with 10–25 yellow, petal-like ray flowers, each up to 1½" long, surrounding a yellow disk.

Bloom Season: Midsummer–fall

Habitat/Range: Frequent on dry prairies, hill prairies, and savannas; also, old fields, roadsides, and open disturbed areas; found native in the western third of the Midwest region, with more recent introductions, especially those escaped from cultivation, found across the rest of the region.

Comments: Maximilian sunflower is named for Prince Maximilian of Wied-Neuwied (1782–1867), a German explorer, ethnologist, and naturalist, who encountered it on his travels in North America. The thick rhizome is edible and provided a food similar to the Jerusalem artichoke for Native American tribes, such as the Sioux. The showy, attractive plants are widely used in perennial gardens and are a popular nectar source for insects, while the seeds are eaten by a variety of songbirds.

ASHY SUNFLOWER
Helianthus mollis
Aster family (Asteraceae)

Description: Usually growing in colonies, these grayish-green plants reach a height of 4'. The stem and leaves have dense gray hairs that can be rubbed off. The leaves are opposite, stiff, up to 6" long and 3" wide, with rounded to notched, stalkless bases. The flower heads are on long stalks, with each head 2½–4" across. There are up to 30 yellow, petal-like ray flowers surrounding the yellow disk.

Bloom Season: Midsummer–fall

Habitat/Range: Common in upland prairies, savannas, glades, thickets, and along roadsides; found in the central and southwest part of the Midwest region, and rare or absent elsewhere.

Comments: Ashy sunflower is sometimes mistaken for rosinweed (*Silphium integrifolium*) (see page 145), but the latter has leaves with a rough, sandpapery surface and lacks the dense gray hairs on the stems and leaves.

WESTERN SUNFLOWER
Helianthus occidentalis
Aster family (Asteraceae)

Description: A colony-forming sunflower, up to 3' tall, with spreading white hairs along the stem. There are up to 5 sets of opposite or 3-whorled leaves along the stem. The basal stem leaves are on long stalks and are 3–6" long and up to 2½" wide. The stem leaves are smaller, much fewer, and usually lack stalks. The flower heads are on short stalks at the top of plants. The flower heads are 1½–2" across, with 8–15 narrow, yellow, petal-like ray flowers surrounding a ½" central yellow disk.

Bloom Season: Midsummer–fall

Habitat/Range: Occasional in dry, sandy, or rocky prairies, hill prairies, and open woods; found in the southwest and north-central parts of the Midwest region, and rare or absent elsewhere.

Comments: The species name, *occidentalis*, is Latin and means "western." The plant was first described in 1836, when the Great Lakes region was considered the western part of the United States. Of the approximately sixteen species of sunflowers in the Midwest region, western sunflower is distinguished by its almost leafless stem.

PRAIRIE SUNFLOWER
Helianthus pauciflorus
Aster family (Asteraceae)

Description: An often single-stemmed plant, up to 6' tall, with widely spaced, opposite leaves that are progressively smaller toward the top. The leaves are thick, stiff, rough, long-pointed, broadest below the middle, and up to 12" long and 1–2½" wide. Flower heads are often solitary at the top of the stem, with the head 2½–4" wide, and 10–25 yellow, petal-like ray flowers, each about 1½" long, surrounding a purplish-brown to sometimes yellow disk.

Bloom Season: Midsummer–fall

Habitat/Range: Widespread and locally frequent in dry prairies, hill prairies, gravel prairies, and sand prairies; found throughout the Midwest region.

Comments: Also called "stiff sunflower," and formerly known as *Helianthus rigidus*, prairie sunflowers form colonies by spreading rhizomes, and are one of the earliest-blooming sunflowers.

JERUSALEM ARTICHOKE
Helianthus tuberosus
Aster family (Asteraceae)

Description: This stout, reddish-stemmed sunflower is up to 7' tall and covered with rough hairs. The leaves are opposite on the lower stem and usually alternate on the upper part. Rough, sandpapery hairs are also on the leaves, which are up to 10" long, lance-shaped, and stalked. The flower heads are on individual stalks at the tops of branches, with each head up to 4" across. There are 10–20 yellow, petal-like ray flowers surrounding a yellow central disk.

Bloom Season: Late summer–fall

Habitat/Range: Common in prairie draws, at the edges of woods, moist thickets, and along streams; found throughout the Midwest region.

Comments: When the roots of this plant grow in good soil, they form edible tubers that have been grown and marketed commercially for centuries. The tubers are cooked as potatoes, diced, and added to salads, and even pickled.

FALSE SUNFLOWER
Heliopsis helianthoides
Aster family (Asteraceae)

Description: A spreading, branched plant, up to 5' tall. The leaves are opposite, on stalks, shaped like arrowheads, up to 6" long and 3" wide. The margins have coarse teeth. The flower head is 2–4" across and on a long stalk. There are up to 20 pale to golden-yellow ray flowers surrounding a cone-shaped, yellow disk.

Bloom Season: Late spring–fall

Habitat/Range: Common in moist areas on prairies, sand prairies, open thickets in prairies, and at the edges of woods; found throughout the Midwest region.

Comments: Also known as ox-eye sunflower. The genus name, *Heliopsis*, comes from the Greek words *helios*, for "sun," and *opsis*, for "appearance," in reference to the golden-yellow ray flowers. The species name, *helianthoides*, means "resembling the genus *Helianthus*." As the name implies, false sunflower is not a true sunflower. The ray flowers of true sunflowers are sterile and do not produce seeds, while both the ray flowers and disk flowers of this plant are fertile.

SOFT GOLDEN ASTER
Bradburia pilosa
Aster family (Asteraceae)

Description: A branched annual plant, up to 2' tall, with densely spreading hairs along the stem and leaves. The leaves are numerous, stalkless, narrow, less than 3" long and ½" wide, and toothed to mostly smooth along the margins. The flower heads are several, each less than 1" across, with 13–25 yellow ray flowers and 25–60 yellow disk flowers.

Bloom Season: Summer–fall

Habitat/Range: Locally frequent in dry prairies, sand prairies, dry open woodlands, glades, disturbed areas, and often in sandy soil; found in the southwest quarter of the Midwest region.

Comments: Formerly known as *Chrysopsis pilosa* and *Heterotheca pilosa*.

GOLDEN ASTER
Heterotheca camporum
Aster family (Asteraceae)

Description: Plants with taproots and rhizomes, moderately hairy stems and branches, up to 3' tall. Leaves are stalkless, hairy, 1–3" long and about ½" wide, with smooth margins, and shortly tapering to a pointed tip. The flowers are 1½" wide, with 15–35 bright yellow ray flowers and 25–65 darker yellow disk flowers.

Bloom Season: Summer–fall

Habitat/Range: Common in sand prairies and disturbed areas, often in sandy soil; found in the central and southwest parts of the Midwest region.

Comments: Formerly known as *Chrysopsis camporum.*

LONG-BEARDED HAWKWEED
Hieracium longipilum
Aster family (Asteraceae)

Description: Slender, mostly solitary stems, 2–5' tall, with densely covered, stiff hairs, up to 1" long. The basal leaves are numerous, stalked, up to 10" long, about 1" wide, tapering at the base, pointed at the tip, densely hairy, and are often present at flowering time. The stem leaves are also densely hairy and gradually reduced in size going up the stem. Flower heads are 8–20, in an open, cylindrical cluster at the top of the stem. Each flower is about ½" across on short, hairy stalks, with 8–20 yellow, petal-like ray flowers with notched tips. The bracts behind the flower are densely covered in short, dark, glandular hairs. The flowers often close by midday.

Bloom Season: Midsummer–late summer

Habitat/Range: Frequent in dry prairies, sand prairies, open woods, and sandy sites; found throughout the Midwest region, but absent in the southeast quarter.

Comments: A similar species, hairy hawkweed (*Hieracium gronovii*), differs by being less hairy, with hairs up to ¼" long and a more-open cluster of flowers. It occurs in sand prairies, sand savannas, and rocky, open woods; found throughout the Midwest region, but absent in the northwest quarter.

TWO-FLOWERED CYNTHIA
Krigia biflora
Aster family (Asteraceae)

Description: A dandelion-like plant with milky sap and a branching, smooth, bluish-green stem, up to 2' tall. The leaves at the base of the plant are spoon-shaped on a long stalk. The 1–3 stem leaves are much smaller and clasp the stem. There are 2–7 orange-yellow flower heads on each stem, with each head about 1½" across and containing 25–60 petal-like ray flowers.

Bloom Season: Mid-spring–late summer

Habitat/Range: Occasional in upland prairies, rocky, open woodlands, and sandy areas; found throughout the Midwest region.

Comments: The species name, *biflora* ("with 2 flowers"), and common name are misleading, because the plant may have any number of flower heads.

POTATO DANDELION
Krigia dandelion
Aster family (Asteraceae)

Description: A dandelion-like plant with a bulbous underground tuber, a bare single stem topped with a single flower, up to 15" tall, and with milky sap. The leaves are basal, with the margins wavy and widely toothed, up to 8" long and 1" wide. The flower heads are about 1½" across with 25–35 small, yellow-orange, petal-like ray flowers.

Bloom Season: Mid-spring–early summer

Habitat/Range: Occasional in upland prairies, rocky, open woods, and sandy areas; found in the southern quarter of the Midwest region, and southward.

Comments: The genus name, *Krigia*, is in honor of David Krig (or Kreig), a German physician who was among the first to collect the plants in Maryland. Potato dandelion flower heads open during the morning, and only under sunny conditions.

DWARF DANDELION
Krigia virginica
Aster family (Asteraceae)

Description: Small annuals with milky sap, up to 8" tall. Stems are mostly unbranched, with sparsely to moderately gland-tipped hairs. Leaves are all at the base or on the lower parts of stems, up to 4½" long and ½" wide. The margins are often wavy, with scattered pointed lobes. Flower heads are single at the tops of stems, with a yellow-orange head about ½" across, with 14–35 small, petal-like ray flowers.

Bloom Season: Mid-spring–summer

Habitat/Range: Occasional in depressions in upland prairies and sand prairies; also, in pastures, fields, and disturbed sites; found throughout the Midwest region, but absent in the northwest quarter and rare in the southeast quarter.

Comments: A closely related species, western dwarf dandelion (*Krigia occidentalis*), differs by having 8 or fewer ribbed bracts at the base of each flower head, compared to 9 or more flat bracts in dwarf dandelion; locally common in upland prairies and sandy areas; found in the southwest quarter of the Midwest region, and blooming in the spring.

PRAIRIE FALSE DANDELION
Nothocalais cuspidata
Aster family (Asteraceae)

Description: A dandelion-like plant, up to 8" tall, with milky sap. The leaves are clustered at the base, up to 12" long and 1" wide, with wavy margins along the blade. A leafless stalk supports a showy, single flower head up to 2" wide, with 35–80 bright yellow, petal-like ray flowers.

Bloom Season: Spring

Habitat/Range: Uncommon in dry, often rocky prairies and hill prairies with sparse vegetation; found in the northwest quarter of the Midwest region, but rare in the central and southwest quarter.

Comments: Formerly known as *Agoseris cuspidata*. Prairie false dandelion can be found growing with pasqueflower (see page 98).

FALSE DANDELION
Pyrrhopappus carolinianus
Aster family (Asteraceae)

Description: A winter annual or biennial plant, branched, smooth, up to 3' tall, with milky sap. The leaves at the base of the stem are lobed and up to 6" long, while the leaves along the stem are merely toothed or without teeth, and narrow. The flower heads are up to 1½" across, with sulphur-yellow ray flowers and 5 teeth along the tip of the petals. The fruit is similar to that of a dandelion.

Bloom Season: Late spring–fall

Habitat/Range: Occasional in upland prairies, glades, fields, disturbed ground, borders of streams, and along roadsides; found in the southwest quarter of the Midwest region.

Comments: The flowers are open only during the morning hours.

WILD LETTUCE
Lactuca canadensis
Aster family (Asteraceae)

Description: Often multibranched at the tips, this smooth-stemmed biennial grows up to 8' tall and has milky-orange to tan sap. The leaves are alternate, stalkless, and up to 12" long and 6" wide (but usually smaller). The leaves vary from deeply lobed to rounded. The numerous flower heads are small and occur in large branching clusters, with 50–100 heads. Each head is less than ½" across, with 15–22 yellow, petal-like ray flowers. The flower and seed heads resemble miniature dandelions.

Bloom Season: Midsummer–early fall

Habitat/Range: Common in upland prairies, sand prairies, open thickets, woodland edges, and disturbed ground; found throughout the Midwest region.

Comments: Native Americans used a root tea to treat diarrhea, heart and lung ailments, hemorrhaging, and nausea, and to relieve pain. The milky sap from the stems was used for treating skin eruptions. The bruised leaves were applied directly to insect stings. Both Native Americans and early settlers used a leaf tea to hasten milk flow after childbirth. Not to be mistaken for wild lettuce, the nonnative and invasive prickly lettuce (*Lactuca serriola*) has a line of prickles along the midrib on the underside of the leaf, and small teeth and prickles along the leaf margin; found in disturbed sites across the Midwest region.

WESTERN WILD LETTUCE
Lactuca ludoviciana
Aster family (Asteraceae)

Description: A single-stemmed, smooth, biennial plant, up to 6' tall, with brownish sap. The leaves are alternate, stalkless, sometimes clasping, 8–12" long and 2–4" wide, with toothed margins, and often prickly along the midvein on the underside of the leaf. The flower heads are located on the tips of branches with 50–100 heads, each about ¾–1" across. There are 20–30 yellow to pale blue, petal-like ray flowers. The flower and seed heads resemble miniature dandelions.

Bloom Season: Summer–fall

Habitat/Range: Found in prairies, hill prairies, woodland openings, roadsides, and disturbed ground; common and native in the northwest quarter of the Midwest region, and adventive in the central part.

Comments: The genus name, *Lactuca*, is Latin for "milk," referring to the plant's milky sap; the species name, *ludoviciana*, is the Latin version of the word "Louisiana." Native Americans used tea made from members of this genus as a nerve tonic, sedative, and pain reliever. The latex-like sap from the stem has been used for warts, pimples, poison ivy rash, and other skin irritations. Members of this genus may cause dermatitis or internal poisoning.

GOLDEN RAGWORT
Packera aurea
Aster family (Asteraceae)

Description: A smooth, branching plant, up to 2½' tall, with a reddish-brown stem. The leaves are mostly basal, long-stalked, and heart-shaped, with coarse teeth along the margins. The stem leaves are fewer and smaller, with deeply cut lobes. The flower heads are in a somewhat flat-topped cluster. Each flower head is about ¾" wide and has 8–12 golden-yellow ray flowers surrounding a central yellow disk.

Bloom Season: Mid-spring–early summer

Habitat/Range: Occasional in moist ground along spring branches, streams, and in moist, low woods and wooded ravine slopes; found throughout the Midwest region.

Comments: Formerly known as *Senecio aureus*. Native Americans, settlers, and herbalists used root and leaf tea to treat delayed and irregular menstruation and childbirth complications; it was also used for lung ailments, dysentery, and difficult urination. Like many ragworts, this plant is now considered highly toxic.

BUTTERWEED
Packera glabella
Aster family (Asteraceae)

Description: An annual arising from slender roots, with a smooth, unbranched stem, up to 3' tall. The leaves at the base of the stem are deeply divided with lobes and teeth, up to 8" long and 3" wide. The stem leaves are similar and gradually reduced in size upward. The flowers are in a terminal cluster, with numerous flower heads. Each flower head is ¾–1" across, with 12–20 yellow, petal-like ray flowers surrounding a yellow disk.

Bloom Season: Spring–early summer

Habitat/Range: Locally common in bottomland forests, wet prairies, moist depressions in upland prairies and sand prairies, and moist, open disturbed ground; found in the southern half of the Midwest region.

Comments: Formerly known as *Senecio glabellus*. The genus is from the Latin *senex*, meaning "old man," an allusion to the gray-haired tufts of filaments attached to the seeds. The name *Packera* is a New World genus composed of 75 taxa, separated from the Old World genus *Senecio*, based on molecular, morphological, and palynological data (the study of pollen grains). The common name "butterweed" is in reference to the color of the flowers.

ROUNDLEAF GROUNDSEL
Packera obovata
Aster family (Asteraceae)

Description: Unbranched stems, up to 2' tall, with creeping roots that form colonies. The basal leaves are roundish and blunt, 3–6" long, including the stalks, with teeth along the margins and tapering at the base to continue as leafy tissue along the stalks. The 2–3 leaves along the stem are alternate, narrow, ¾–2½" long, with lobes along the margins, and lacking stalks. The flower heads are clustered into an umbrella shape with bright yellow flowers each ½–¾" wide. There are 10–15 petal-like ray flowers that surround the disk flowers.

Bloom Season: Mid-spring–early summer

Habitat/Range: Occasional in mesic or rocky woods at the base of slopes and on borders of glades, bottomland forests, roadsides, and open, disturbed areas; found in the southern half of the Midwest region.

Comments: Formerly known as *Senecio obovatus*. Plants in the genus *Packera* were used to increase perspiration and to treat kidney stones and lung troubles. They were used by Native American women for general health. The plants are poisonous.

139

PRAIRIE RAGWORT
Packera plattensis
Aster family (Asteraceae)

Description: A biennial or short-lived perennial with stems single or rarely 2–3 in a cluster, up to 2' tall, with dense, white, cobwebby hairs on the stem and leaves, but less so when mature. The basal leaves are up to 3" long and 1½" wide, long-stalked, toothed along the margins, and usually divided into lobes. The stem leaves are smaller and stalkless, with the margins usually divided into lobes. Up to 10 (rarely 20) flower heads occur in a flattened cluster at the top of the stem. Each head is ½–1" wide, with 8–13 yellow, petal-like ray flowers, each about ¼" long, surrounding a small, yellow-orange disk.

Bloom Season: Mid-spring–early summer

Habitat/Range: Frequent in dry upland prairies, hill prairies, sand prairies, and in sandy, gravelly, rocky soils; found throughout the Midwest region, but absent in the eastern quarter.

Comments: Formerly known as *Senecio plattensis*. Prairie ragwort foliage is toxic to humans and cattle. It contains pyrrolizidine alkaloids that can damage the liver and cause other health problems. A closely related species, balsam ragwort (*Packera paupercula*; formerly known as *Senecio paperculus*), differs by having few if any cobwebby hairs on the leaves and stem, and mostly unbranched flower stalks. Occurs in upland prairies, hill prairies, open woods, and wet meadows; found throughout the Midwest region, but less common in the southeast quarter.

GRAY-HEADED CONEFLOWER

Ratibida pinnata
Aster family (Asteraceae)

Description: A slender, hairy-stemmed plant, up to 5' tall, often branching toward the top. The leaves are divided into 3–7 slender leaflets, with a few teeth or small side lobes along the margins. The leaves at the base of the stem are on long stalks, with the leaf blade up to 7" long. The leaves on the stem are alternate and smaller. Each flower head has its own long stalk. The 5–10 yellow, petal-like ray flowers droop downward, each about 2" long and less than ½" wide. They surround a conical disk about ¾" tall. Prior to opening, the small disk flowers are ashy gray, but they turn brown as the flowers open. The crushed heads have a distinct anise scent.

Bloom Season: Mid-spring–early fall

Habitat/Range: Common in mesic to dry prairies, savannas, glades, woodland borders, and roadsides, especially in areas that have had some past disturbance; found throughout the Midwest region, but less common in the northern quarter.

Comments: Native Americans made a tea from the flower cones and leaves. The Meskwaki used the root to cure toothache.

PRAIRIE CONEFLOWER

Ratibida columnifera
Aster family (Asteraceae)

Description: A single-stemmed plant, but often in clusters, up to 2' tall. The leaves are up to 6" long and 2½" wide, and divided into 5–13 narrow leaflets. There are from 4–11 drooping, petal-like ray flowers, each about 1½" long, which are yellow or red to reddish-brown, with varying degrees of yellow along the edges and toward the tip. The flower column is cylindrical, up to ½" long, and contains numerous disk flowers that vary from yellow to red to purple.

Bloom Season: Summer–fall

Habitat/Range: Occasional in upland prairies, pastures, roadsides, and often disturbed areas; found in the western quarter of the Midwest region and westward; introduced elsewhere.

Comments: Also known as Mexican hat. The Cheyenne made a tea from the leaves and stems and rubbed it on a rattlesnake bite to relieve the pain; they also used it to treat areas affected by poison ivy rash. Prairie coneflower is sometimes used in garden and wildflower plantings.

ORANGE CONEFLOWER
Rudbeckia fulgida
Aster family (Asteraceae)

Description: A clump-forming plant, 1½–2½'
tall, spreading by rhizomes and producing prolific
blooms over an extended period. The basal leaves
are oval, with teeth along the margins, and
rounded bases. The stem leaves are alternate, up
to 5" long and 2½" wide, broadest at the base or at
the middle and tapering at both ends. The base of
the leaf tapers to a winged stalk that sometimes
clasps the stem. The flower heads are 2–3" across,
with 10–20 petal-like ray flowers that are yellow
to orange-yellow with notched tips. The disk flowers are dark brownish-purple and tubular in shape.

Bloom Season: Midsummer–fall

Habitat/Range: Locally common on banks of
streams and rivers, spring branches, calcareous
seeps, fens, marshes, bottomland forests, moist
woodlands, limestone glades, and moist rocky
ledges; found throughout the Midwest region,
but absent in Iowa and Minnesota, and rare in
Wisconsin.

Comments: Orange coneflower has been known
to flower over a two-month period, which makes
it a popular candidate for wildflower gardens. It
is readily available from plant nurseries that carry
wildflowers.

BLACK-EYED SUSAN
Rudbeckia hirta
Aster family (Asteraceae)

Description: This short-lived perennial grows 1–3'
tall, with rough and hairy leaves and stems. The
basal leaves are up to 5" long and 1" wide. Along
the stem, the leaves are alternate, up to 4" long,
½–1½" wide, widest in the middle, and tapering
toward the tip. Flower heads are single at the top
of each stem branch, with showy heads about 2–3"
across. There are 20–30 yellow to orangish-yellow,
petal-like ray flowers that surround a dark brown
to purple-brown, dome-shaped disk about ½" long.

Bloom Season: Mid-spring–fall

Habitat/Range: Common in mesic to dry prairies,
glades, openings in mesic to dry forests, old fields,
pastures, roadsides, and open, disturbed areas;
found throughout the Midwest region.

Comments: The Potawatomi prepared a root tea
for curing colds. Early settlers used the plant as
a stimulant and a diuretic. A yellow dye is made
from this plant.

MISSOURI CONEFLOWER
Rudbeckia missouriensis
Aster family (Asteraceae)

Description: Slender, hairy plants, up to 20" tall, that grow only on dolomite glades. The leaves are narrow, very hairy, up to 4" long and ½" wide, stalkless, tapering to a pointed tip, and slightly folded along the length of the blade. The leaves do not spread far from the stem. The flower heads are up to 2" across, with 8–12 yellow, petal-like ray flowers surrounding a dome-shaped, brown disk.

Bloom Season: Summer–fall

Habitat/Range: Common on dolomite glades, cliff ledges, rock outcrops in upland prairies, and rocky openings in forests; found in the Midwest region in Missouri and southwest Illinois, and southward.

Comments: Missouri coneflowers are relatively low and slender in stature, often forming large colonies of dense rosettes. Their narrow leaves, dense hairiness, strongly ascending branches, and relatively small heads are characteristics that set them apart from other coneflowers in the Midwest region.

GOLDENGLOW
Rudbeckia laciniata
Aster family (Asteraceae)

Description: A large plant, up to 9' tall, with a smooth, whitish stem that branches near the top. The leaves are alternate, on long stalks, large, up to 10" long and 6" wide, deeply divided into 3–7 segments, and often with teeth along the margins. The flower heads have 6–10 narrow, golden, petal-like ray flowers that angle downward and surround a central green disk, ½–¾" across.

Bloom Season: Midsummer–fall

Habitat/Range: Common in bottomland forests, wet woods along streams, margins of banks of ponds and lakes, and sloughs; found throughout the Midwest region.

Comments: Also known as cut-leaf coneflower. Native Americans used root tea for indigestion and applied a mixture of flowers from goldenglow, blue cohosh, and blue giant hyssop to burns. They also cooked and ate spring greens for "good health." The basal leaves remain green over winter and provide an important source of winter food for white-tailed deer.

SWEET CONEFLOWER
Rudbeckia subtomentosa
Aster family (Asteraceae)

Description: Plants up to 6' tall, branching near the top, often with dense, short hairs along the upper stem. The stem leaves are alternate, with short stalks, or stalkless, have large teeth along the margins, and are often covered with soft, dense hairs. The leaves, at least on the lower part of the stem, are divided into 3 deep lobes, and up to 8" long and 4½" wide. The upper leaves usually lack lobes; they are up to 3" long and 1" across. The flower heads are on long, individual stalks, with each head up to 3" wide. The heads have 6–20, yellow, petal-like ray flowers, surrounding a dome-shaped, brown central disk.

Bloom Season: Summer

Habitat/Range: Locally frequent in mesic prairies, depressions in upland prairies, bottomland forests, mesic upland forests, banks of streams, and roadsides; found in the central and southwest parts of the Midwest region.

Comments: The common name, sweet coneflower, comes from the flower's anise scent. This plant is also known as sweet black-eyed Susan. This showy plant is often cultivated in flower gardens where it tends to be aggressive, and occasionally escapes.

BROWN-EYED SUSAN
Rudbeckia triloba
Aster family (Asteraceae)

Description: A biennial to short-lived perennial with several branches, up to 5' tall, and with spreading hairs on the stems. The leaves are alternate and hairy, with the lower ones 3-lobed; they often shed at the time of flowering. The upper stem leaves are narrow, stalkless, about 4" long, with toothed edges. The flower heads are numerous, with each up to 1¾" across. Each head has 6–12 yellow, petal-like ray flowers surrounding a dome-shaped brown disk. The ray flowers are grooved along their lengths and narrowly notched at the tips.

Bloom Season: Summer–fall

Habitat/Range: Occasional in prairies, savannas, open woods, moist thickets, and along streams; found throughout the Midwest region, but rare to absent in the northern quarter.

Comments: The flower heads of brown-eyed Susan are smaller and much more numerous than those of black-eyed Susan. The plants are also significantly taller and more widely branched, which also helps to differentiate them from black-eyed Susan.

ROSINWEED
Silphium integrifolium
Aster family (Asteraceae)

Description: Often occurring in colonies, these stout, single-stemmed plants grow up to 6' tall. The leaves are opposite but may be slightly alternate, or even whorled. The leaves lack stalks, are up to 6" long and 2½" wide, with a rough, sandpapery texture, and vary in shape from narrow and long to broad and round; teeth may be present along the margins. The flower heads are about 3" wide, with 15–35 yellow, petal-like ray flowers, each 1–2" long, surrounding a yellow central disk of small, sterile flowers.

Bloom Season: Summer–fall

Habitat/Range: Common in mesic prairies, hill prairies, savannas, open woods, and roadsides; found throughout the Midwest region, but absent in the northern third and very eastern part.

Comments: Rosinweed is named for its sticky resin that exudes from the stem when cut or bruised. Plants in the genus *Silphium* resemble sunflowers (*Helianthus* species), but unlike the latter, their ray flowers produce the seeds, whereas in sunflowers, the disk flowers produce the seeds. Native Americans used the root of rosinweed for pain relief.

WHORLED ROSINWEED
Silphium trifoliatum
Aster family (Asteraceae)

Description: A waxy, smooth-stemmed, slender plant, 3–7' tall, with widely spaced leaves in whorls of 3. The leaves are short-stalked, rough in texture, coarsely toothed to sometimes entire, divided into whorls of 3 (occasionally 4), each 3–8" long and ½–1½" wide, broadest at the base and tapering toward a pointed tip. Flower heads are several to numerous in an open branching pattern at the top of the stem. Each flower head is 1½–2" wide, with 12–20 yellow, petal-like ray flowers and numerous yellow disk flowers.

Bloom Season: Midsummer–fall

Habitat/Range: Occasional in open woods, woodland borders, prairies, and disturbed open places; found in the Midwest region in Indiana and Ohio, and southward.

Comments: Some references place whorled rosinweed under starry rosinweed (*Silphium asteriscus*), but the latter has leaves that are opposite or alternate and rough stems and leaves with spreading hairs, among other differences; occasional in openings of dry upland forests, blufftops, pastures, ditches, and roadsides; found in the Midwest region in Indiana, Ohio, and Missouri, and southward.

145

COMPASS PLANT
Silphium laciniatum
Aster family (Asteraceae)

Description: A tall, stout plant, up to 8' in height, with very large basal leaves, sometimes over 1' long. The deeply cut basal leaves are commonly oriented in a north–south direction, in order to take maximum advantage of the sun's rays; hence, the common name. The stem leaves are smaller, alternate, and clasping at the base. The flower heads are along the upper part of a single, long, hairy stalk. Each head is up to 4½" across, with 20–30 yellow, petal-like ray flowers that surround a yellow center, with many sterile disk flowers.

Bloom Season: Summer–fall

Habitat/Range: Common in mesic and dry prairies, sand prairies, savannas, and roadsides; found throughout the Midwest region, but absent in the northern third, and rare in the east-central part.

Comments: The Omaha and Ponca avoided camping wherever compass plant grew abundantly, because they believed the plants attracted lightning. They sometimes burned the dried root during an electrical storm to act as a charm against a lightning strike. The root was used by Native Americans and early settlers to alleviate head colds or pains. The dried leaves were used for treating dry, obstinate coughs and intermittent fever. Many Native American children chewed the resin that exudes from the stem as a chewing gum.

CUP PLANT
Silphium perfoliatum
Aster family (Asteraceae)

Description: Large plants, up to 8' tall, branching near the top, with stout, square stems. The large upper leaves are cupped around the stem tight enough to hold rainwater. The opposite leaves, up to 8" long and 5" across, have wavy margins, large teeth, and are rough to the touch on both sides. The flower heads are at the tops of branches, numerous, and up to 3" across. Each head has 20–30 yellow, petal-like ray flowers that surround a yellow center with sterile disk flowers.

Bloom Season: Summer–fall

Habitat/Range: Common in moist areas in prairies and along prairie streams, low thickets, low-lying woodland edges, and along roadsides; found throughout the Midwest region, but absent in the northern third, and rare in the east-central part.

Comments: The Omaha and Ponca used the root as a smoke treatment, inhaling the fumes for head colds, nerve pains, and rheumatism. Also, the resinous sap that exudes from the stem was chewed as a gum to help prevent vomiting. This plant is also known as carpenter's weed because of its straight, square stem.

PRAIRIE DOCK
Silphium terebinthinaceum
Aster family (Asteraceae)

Description: A tall, wand-like stem rises 3–10′ above a cluster of large, spade-shaped basal leaves. The long-stalked leaves are up to 16″ long and 12″ wide, very rough in texture, with a heart-shaped base and coarse teeth along the margins. The flower heads occur at the top of a smooth, shiny, nearly leafless stalk. The heads are 2–3″ across, with 12–20 yellow, petal-like ray flowers that surround a yellow center with sterile disk flowers.

Bloom Season: Summer–fall

Habitat/Range: Common in mesic prairies, savannas, glades, and rocky and sandy sites; also, along railroads and roadsides; found throughout the Midwest region, but absent in the northwest quarter.

Comments: Native Americans made a root tea to alleviate feebleness and to expel intestinal worms. Leaf tea was used for coughs, lung ailments, and asthma. Like compass plant, prairie dock is also known to align its leaves on a north–south axis in order to take maximum advantage of the sun's rays.

GRASS-LEAVED GOLDENROD
Euthamia graminifolia
Aster family (Asteraceae)

Description: Plants up to 3′ tall, with hairy stems and leaves, and the upper half of the stem branched. The leaves are alternate, up to 5″ long and ⅜″ wide, with 3 distinct parallel veins along the length of the blade, and with minute, resinous spots on the underside. The yellow flowers are in a branched, flat-topped cluster at the top of the stem. Each flower head is about ¼″ across, with 15–25 petal-like ray flowers and 5–10 central disk flowers.

Bloom Season: Late summer–fall

Habitat/Range: Occasional in prairies, sandy fields, and edges of marshes; found throughout the Midwest region, but rare in the southwest quarter.

Comments: Formerly known as *Solidago graminifolia.*

PLAINS GRASS-LEAVED GOLDENROD

Euthamia gymnospermoides
Aster family (Asteraceae)

Description: Rather spindly plants, up to 3' tall, branching in the upper half of the stem. The leaves are alternate along the hairless stem, with leaf blades up to 4" long and less than ⅛" wide, hairless, with minute, resinous spots on the underside. A prominent vein runs down the center of the leaf. Small flower heads are about ¼" wide and are found in small, flattened clusters at the tips of the stem branches. Each head typically has 7–11 yellow, petal-like ray flowers surrounding 4–6 small, yellow disk flowers.

Bloom Season: Late summer–fall

Habitat/Range: Occasional in upland prairies, sand prairies, savannas, meadows along rivers, and sandy fields; found throughout the Midwest region, but uncommon to absent in the eastern third.

Comments: Formerly known as *Solidago gymnospermoides.*

RIDDELL'S GOLDENROD

Oligoneuron riddellii
Aster family (Asteraceae)

Description: A showy plant with somewhat shiny stems and several fine ridges or grooves along its length, up to 3' tall. The leaves, up to 3" long and ½" wide, are loosely alternate along the stem, toothless along the margins, shiny, somewhat folded along the blade, sheathing at the base, and tending to curve away from the stem. Flowers are in a short, dense, domed cluster at the top of the stem, with numerous heads on all sides of the branches. Each small head is up to ⅜" across, with 7–9 yellow, petal-like ray flowers, surrounding 6–10 yellow disk flowers.

Bloom Season: Late summer–fall

Habitat/Range: Occasional in wet to mesic prairies and calcareous wetland seeps; found throughout the Midwest region, but absent in the north-central and northeast parts, and rare in the southwest quarter.

Comments: Also known as *Solidago riddellii.* The rounded, flat cluster of flowers is unique from other goldenrods, except for stiff goldenrod (*Oligoneuron rigidum*). However, the latter prefers dry, sandy habitats, and its stem leaves are noticeably rounder, with rough, hairy surfaces.

STIFF GOLDENROD
Oligoneuron rigidum
Aster family (Asteraceae)

Description: A coarse, stout plant, with stems up to 5' tall, usually hairy, giving the plant a pale to gray-green cast. The large basal leaves are on long stalks and up to 10" long and 5" wide. The stem leaves are alternate, stalkless, and progressively smaller upward. All the leaves are rough and leathery. The flower heads are in a flat-topped to somewhat rounded, densely packed cluster. Each head is about ½" across, with 7–14 yellow, petal-like ray flowers surrounding a yellow central disk.

Bloom Season: Late summer–fall

Habitat/Range: Common in upland prairies, hill prairies, savannas, old fields, roadsides, and open disturbed areas; found throughout the Midwest region, but less common to absent in the eastern third.

Comments: Also known as *Solidago rigida*. Bee stings were once treated with a lotion made from the flowers of stiff goldenrod. Leaf tea was used to treat swollen throats. The rounded, flat cluster of flowers is unique from other goldenrods, except for Riddell's goldenrod (*Oligoneuron riddellii*). However, the latter prefers wet to mesic prairies and calcareous wetland seeps, and its stem leaves are shiny, somewhat folded along the blade, sheathing at the base, and tending to curve away from the stem.

TALL GOLDENROD
Solidago altissima
Aster family (Asteraceae)

Description: A large, hairy-stemmed goldenrod, up to 7' tall, with many alternate leaves, the largest of which occur along the middle part of the stem. The leaves are up to 6" long and 1¼" wide, with some teeth along the margins, especially toward the tip. The upper side of the leaf is rough, while the underside is hairy, with 3 prominent veins. The flower heads are arranged in a pyramidal cluster, with the heads all occurring on the upper side of the branches. Each head is about ¼" across, with 10–16 yellow, petal-like ray flowers. The green bracts under the flower heads are more than ⅛" tall.

Bloom Season: Midsummer–fall

Habitat/Range: Common in upland prairies, hill prairies, sand prairies, and savannas; also, in old fields, pastures, roadsides, and open disturbed areas; found throughout the Midwest region.

Comments: Of the goldenrods, this species is the most commonly infected by the goldenrod gall. This round swelling along the stem is caused by certain moths and flies that lay an egg in the stem. The larva hatches and secretes a chemical that causes the plant tissue to swell around it; the larva then eats the tissue and overwinters in its protected home, emerging in the spring as an adult.

149

CANADA GOLDENROD
Solidago canadensis
Aster family (Asteraceae)

Description: Plants with 1 to several unbranched, hairy stems and leaves, up to 6' tall, which arise from creeping rhizomes. The leaves are alternate, narrow, short-stalked to stalkless, 1–6" long and ¼–¾" wide, with 3 parallel veins running the length of each leaf, and shallow teeth along the margins. The flower heads are arranged in a pyramidal cluster, with the heads all occurring on the upper side of the branches. Each head is less than ¼" across, with 6–12 yellow, petal-like ray flowers. The green bracts under the flower heads are less than ⅛" tall.

Bloom Season: Summer–fall

Habitat/Range: Common in upland prairies, savannas, at the edges of woods, and wetland margins; also, in old fields, pastures, roadsides, and open disturbed areas; found throughout the Midwest region.

Comments: Native Americans used the flowers to make a medicinal tea to treat fever, diarrhea, insomnia, and snakebite. The roots were used for burns. A similar species, giant or late goldenrod (*Solidago gigantea*), has smooth stems, sometimes with a white, waxy coating. Occurs in moist sites, including wet and mesic prairies, banks of streams and rivers, and disturbed areas; found throughout the Midwest region.

BLUE-STEMMED GOLDENROD
Solidago caesia
Aster family (Asteraceae)

Description: A graceful, arching, wand-like plant, up to 3' long, with bluish-green stems and a whitish coating. The leaves are alternate, smooth, stalkless, lance-shaped, 2–5" long and up to 1" wide, and slightly hairy above. The flower heads are small and appear in tufts along the stem, emerging from the leaf axils. The heads have 3–5 yellow, petal-like ray flowers.

Bloom Season: Late summer–fall

Habitat/Range: Common in mesic or rocky woods and at the base of bluffs; found in the southern part of the southwest quarter and the eastern half of the Midwest region.

Comments: The genus name, *Solidago*, comes from the Latin word *solidare*, meaning "to make whole," in reference to the plant's medicinal healing properties. The species name, *caesia*, is Latin for "blue-gray." A similar species, zigzag goldenrod (*Solidago flexicaulis*), differs by having leaves up to 4" wide, broadest toward the base, abruptly ending in a long, winged leaf stalk, with stems that often zigzag toward the tip; found throughout the Midwest region.

CLIFF GOLDENROD
Solidago drummondii
Aster family (Asteraceae)

Description: Usually arching out over cliffs, the soft-haired stems grow 1½–3' long. The basal and lowermost stem leaves, 1–3" long and ¾–2¾" wide, are typically absent at flowering time. The upper stem leaves are broadest in the middle, 1½–3½" long and 1–3" wide, short-stalked, with 3 veins along the leaf, and fine, dense hairs beneath. The very small flower heads are at the end of the arching stem on short branches. Each head has 3–7 yellow, petal-like ray flowers and 4–6 yellow disk flowers.

Bloom Season: Late summer–late fall

Habitat/Range: Common on ledges and cliffs of dry dolomite bluffs; found in the southwest corner of the Midwest region.

Comments: Also known as Drummond's goldenrod. This plant is easy to identify because it only grows on cliffs.

EARLY GOLDENROD
Solidago juncea
Aster family (Asteraceae)

Description: An upright plant, up to 3' tall, with a smooth stem and fine lines or grooves along its length. The basal leaves are up to 8" long and 1" wide. The stem leaves are alternate, smaller, up to 5" long and about 1"wide, linear, tapering at the base and tip, with some small teeth along the margins. A single prominent vein runs the length of the leaves. The flower heads are crowded together on the tops of arching side branches. Each head has about 7–12 very small, yellow, petal-like ray flowers and 8–15 tiny disk flowers.

Bloom Season: Summer–fall

Habitat/Range: Common in upland prairies, sand prairies, gravel prairies, savannas, old fields, and roadsides; found throughout the Midwest region, but absent in the west-central part.

Comments: Early goldenrod, as the name implies, is one of the first goldenrods to flower, doing so in early summer. It is often grown in gardens as an ornamental. Another early bloomer, rough goldenrod (*Solidago radula*), has a rough stem and leaves that are up to 3" long and ¾–1" across, widest at the middle, with 3 prominent veins along the leaf; common in mesic to dry upland forests, woodlands, and glades; found in the Midwest region in western Illinois, Missouri, and southward.

MISSOURI GOLDENROD
Solidago missouriensis
Aster family (Asteraceae)

Description: Smooth-stemmed plants, up to 3' tall, with several fine lines or grooves along its length. Basal and lowermost leaves up to 6" long and less than ½" wide are often absent at flowering time. The stem leaves are alternate, smooth, unstalked, 2–6" long and less than ½" wide, pointed at the tips, with 3 veins running the length of the blades, and with small clusters of leaves at the axils of the main leaves. The flower heads are crowded together on the tops of branches. Each head has about 7–13, yellow, petal-like ray flowers and 6–15 disk flowers.

Bloom Season: Summer–fall

Habitat/Range: Common in dry upland prairies, hill prairies, sand prairies, rocky, open areas, savannas, old fields, and roadsides; found through the Midwest region, but absent in the eastern third.

Comments: Missouri goldenrod is known to colonize disturbed soils. During the Dust Bowl era, it flourished in the dry, cleared soil. As the drought ended and the grasses returned, it became less common, disappearing in many areas. Missouri goldenrod increases in overgrazed pastures, and can be found in soils turned over by burrowing animals and on roadsides and western mining sites.

OLD-FIELD GOLDENROD
Solidago nemoralis
Aster family (Asteraceae)

Description: The stems vary from arching to upright, growing up to 2½' tall, with dense, short, gray hairs on the stems, and leaves that give the plant a gray-green appearance. The basal leaves are present at flowering time, up to 4" long and ¾" wide, with 1 main vein running the length of the blade. The stem leaves are progressively smaller toward the top of the stem. The flower heads are densely packed on the tops of short branches. Each head is less than ¼" across, with 5–9 yellow, petal-like ray flowers and 3–9 disk flowers.

Bloom Season: Summer–fall

Habitat/Range: Common in prairies, open woods, old fields, pastures, and roadsides; found throughout the Midwest region.

Comments: Also known as gray goldenrod. The upright form of old-field goldenrod is easy to identify at a distance by its slightly bent tip. Native American tribes like the Houma used it medicinally to treat jaundice. The Goshute used the seeds for food, and the Navajo used the seeds for incense.

WOODLAND GOLDENROD
Solidago petiolaris
Aster family (Asteraceae)

Description: Erect plants, up to 3' tall, with the stems smooth below and hairy on the upper part. The stem leaves are thick, firm, lance-shaped to nearly oval, ¼–1" wide, somewhat toothed and hairy along the margins, with the upper surface hairy. The showy flower heads are clustered in the upper leaf axils to form a long and narrow column. The heads have 5–6 yellow, petal-like ray flowers and 10–16 disk flowers.

Bloom Season: Summer–fall

Habitat/Range: Common in thickets and in dry, rocky, open woods, glades in acidic soils associated with sandstone, chert, or igneous rock; found in the southwest quarter of the Midwest region.

Comments: The large flower heads and long ray flowers of woodland goldenrod are quite showy. A similar species, Buckley's goldenrod (*Solidago buckleyi*), has thin, not thick, leaves, 1–2" wide, with the margins sharply toothed; also found in similar habitat and range as woodland goldenrod.

SHOWY GOLDENROD
Solidago speciosa
Aster family (Asteraceae)

Description: Sturdy, sometimes red, unbranched smooth stems, up to 4' tall, with alternate, smooth leaves. The lower leaves are large, about 12" long and 4" wide, and wither around flowering time. The upper leaves decrease in size going up the stem. The flowers are densely arranged on branches in an elongate, cylindrical cluster at the top of the stem. Each flower head is about ½" across, with 6–8 yellow, petal-like ray flowers and 4–5 small disk flowers.

Bloom Season: Late summer–fall

Habitat/Range: Occasional in upland prairies, hill prairies, savannas, at the edges of woods, and roadsides; found throughout the Midwest region, but less common in the eastern third.

Comments: A similar species, hairy goldenrod (*Solidago hispida*), has conspicuously hairy stems and leaves; occasional in mesic and upland woods, sandy woods, blufftops, and roadsides; found primarily in the northern half and southwest quarter of the Midwest region. Another species, bog goldenrod (*Solidago uliginosa*), has erect clusters, but not as cylindrical, and it is more of a wetland species; found throughout the Midwest region, but absent in the west-central and southwest parts.

ELM-LEAVED GOLDENROD
Solidago ulmifolia
Aster family (Asteraceae)

Description: A single-stemmed, smooth plant, up to 4' tall, with widely spreading branches. The leaves are alternate, coarsely toothed along the margins, thin, hairy underneath, with broad stalks on the lower leaves, which fall away by flowering time. The lower leaves are up to 5" long and 2" wide, with the upper leaves much reduced in size. The flower heads are on long, arching branches, with crowded heads. Each head has 3–5 yellow, petal-like ray flowers and 4–7 disk flowers.

Bloom Season: Late summer–fall

Habitat/Range: Common in dry or rocky, open woods, along bluffs, in thickets, and along streams; found throughout the Midwest region, but absent in the northern quarter.

Comments: Goldenrods, in general, have been unfairly blamed for the allergic reaction of hay fever. It is the windblown pollen of the ragweeds that is the primary cause for late-summer hay fever. The pollen of goldenrods is distributed by bees, fall wasps, and beetles and is not windblown. A similar species, wrinkle-leaved goldenrod (*Solidago rugosa*), has thick leaves, rough to the touch and somewhat wrinkled in appearance; occasional in bottomland forests, banks of streams and rivers, and other moist soil areas; found in the eastern half and south-central part of the Midwest region.

YELLOW IRONWEED
Verbesina alternifolia
Aster family (Asteraceae)

Description: A tall, coarse, branching plant, up to 7' in height, with narrow wings of leafy tissue extending down the stems from the leaf bases. The leaves are alternate, rough, lance-shaped to broadest in the middle, up to 10" long and 2½" wide, with toothed edges. The flower heads are 1–2" across with 2–8 yellow, drooping, petal-like ray flowers, surrounding a yellow, round disk.

Bloom Season: Late summer–fall

Habitat/Range: Common in low, moist woods in valleys, wooded floodplains, and along streams; found across the southern half of the Midwest region.

Comments: Yellow ironweed is eaten occasionally by white-tailed deer in the summer. In September, yellow ironweed often forms large, dense patches of yellow in bottomland forests.

YELLOW CROWNBEARD
Verbesina helianthoides
Aster family (Asteraceae)

Description: Flaps of leafy tissue or "wings" run down the length of the hairy stem that can reach a height of 3½'. The leaves are alternate, up to 6" long and 2" wide, tapering at the base, with pointed tips and teeth along the margins. There are coarse hairs on the upper surface, while the lower surface is soft-hairy. The flower heads are large, 2–2½" across, with 8–15 yellow, petal-like ray flowers surrounding a yellow disk.

Bloom Season: Late spring–fall

Habitat/Range: Common in dry prairies, savannas, and rocky, open woods; found throughout the southern half of the Midwest region.

Comments: The plant is also known as wingstem. Primarily long-tongued bees visit the flowers for pollen and nectar. Bobwhite quail, songbirds, and small mammals eat the seeds.

PALE TOUCH-ME-NOT
Impatiens pallida
Touch-me-not family (Balsiminaceae)

Description: Annual plants growing up to 5' tall, with branched stems that are weak and watery. The stems are pale green and translucent, with leaves alternate, oval, thin, and bluish-green. The leaves are up to 3½" long and 2" wide, with long stalks and widely spaced teeth along the margins. Flowers are shaped like a cornucopia, up to 1¼" long, and hang on a slender stalk. The smaller end of the flower is a curved spur that holds the nectar. The larger end has 2 round, broad, lower lobes and a much smaller upper lobe. The fruit is a slender capsule about 1" long, which splits and propels the seed when touched.

Bloom Season: Late spring–fall

Habitat/Range: Common in moist, low woodlands, at the base of bluffs, low thickets, and banks of streams; found throughout the Midwest region.

Comments: Water sometimes is exuded along the leaf margins in humid conditions and appears as glistening drops, giving rise to its other name, "jewelweed." The Potawatomi and settlers applied the juice of touch-me-not to relieve the itch of poison ivy. Today the juice is used to relieve the burning sensation of stinging nettle, which is often found occupying the same habitat as touch-me-not. The juice is also thought to neutralize the oil of poison ivy after contact. Livestock have been poisoned by eating large amounts of the fresh green plants.

BLUE COHOSH

Caulophyllum thalictroides
Barberry family (Berberidaceae)

Description: A low, spreading plant, 1–2' tall, with 1 large leaf that is divided into many small leaflets, as well as a smaller, many-divided leaf just below the flowers. The leaflets are 1–3" long, smooth, and irregularly lobed above the middle. The flower clusters arise above the leaves on 1–2 stalks, with each flower about ½" across containing 6 yellowish-green, petal-like sepals and 6 yellow stamens. The 6 glandlike petals are inconspicuous. The round, fleshy fruit is a deep iridescent blue.

Bloom Season: Spring

Habitat/Range: Occasional in moist woods, wooded slopes, and along banks of streams; found throughout the Midwest region.

Comments: *Cohosh* is an Algonquin word meaning "rough," referring to the rhizome with its many old stem scars. A root tea was used extensively by Native Americans to aid in labor and to treat menstruation, abdominal cramps, urinary tract infections, lung ailments, and fever. It is a folk remedy for rheumatism, cramps, epilepsy, and inflammation of the uterus.

HOARY PUCCOON

Lithospermum canescens
Borage family (Boraginaceae)

Description: Single stems, with several emerging from the base of older plants, 6–18" tall, with dense, soft hairs on the stems and leaves that give the plant a gray-green color. The leaves are alternate, stalkless, about 2½" long and less than ½" wide, and lack teeth along the margins. The orange-yellow flowers are in a flattened cluster at the top of the plant. Each flower is about ½" long and ½" wide, tubular-shaped, with 5 spreading, rounded lobes.

Bloom Season: Spring–early summer

Habitat/Range: Common in mesic to dry prairies, hill prairies, savannas, rocky, open woods, but seldom in sandy sites; found throughout the Midwest region.

Comments: Native Americans used leaf tea as a wash for fevers accompanied by spasms, and as a wash rubbed on persons thought to be near convulsions. To the Menominee, the white, ripened seed of this plant was a type of sacred bead used in special ceremonies. A red dye was extracted from the roots.

CAROLINA PUCCOON

Lithospermum caroliniense
Borage family (Boraginaceae)

Description: Single-stemmed plants, 1–2½' tall, with short, bristly hairs. The leaves are stalkless, up to 1½" long and ⅜" wide, linear, with pointed tips and covered with short, stiff hairs. The flowers are single on short stalks arising from the axils of arching branches at the top of the stems. Each flower is about ¾" long and 1" wide, and tubular, with 5 orange-yellow, petal-like lobes. The stamens are hidden inside the tube.

Bloom Season: Spring–early summer

Habitat/Range: Occasional in sandy soils of prairies, hill prairies, savannas, and open woods; found primarily in the northern half of the Midwest region.

Comments: The orange-yellow flowers are very showy and can be seen from a considerable distance. Carolina puccoon is easily mistaken for hoary puccoon (*Lithospermum canescens*), which has smaller flowers and longer, softer hairs on the stems.

FRINGED PUCCOON

Lithospermum incisum
Borage family (Boraginaceae)

Description: Densely hairy plants, up to 15" tall, with narrow, alternate leaves up to 3" long and less than ¼" wide. Flowers are in clusters at the tops of stems, with each lemon-yellow to bright yellow flower up to 1½" long and 1" wide, tubular-shaped, and with 5 spreading lobes that are unevenly toothed to nearly fringed along the margins.

Bloom Season: Mid-spring–early summer

Habitat/Range: Occasional in dry upland prairies, hill prairies, and rocky or sandy open areas; found through the Midwest region, but absent in the eastern third.

Comments: The first flowers are large and sterile, while later in the season, the flowers are much smaller, and self-pollinated (making them easy to mistake for a different species). The Blackfeet made incense from the dried tops, which they burned during ceremonial events. The Cheyenne ground the dried leaves, roots, and stems and applied them to limbs to treat paralysis.

PRICKLY PEAR
Opuntia humifusa
Cactus family (Cactaceae)

Description: A low-growing cactus with enlarged, fleshy, spiny, green stems that often grows in colonies. The stem segments or pads are narrow, up to 5" long and 3" wide. The upper one-third of the pad may have 1–2 needle-like spines, spreading, which emerge from clusters of small bristles, also known as glochidia. These clusters or tufts are scattered across the surface of the pad. The showy flowers are up to 4" across, and open from single buds along the edge of the pad (new pads also emerge along the edge). The 8–12 large, bright yellow petals have a waxy surface, often with a reddish center. Numerous yellow stamens surround a stout central style. The fruit is cylindrical, up to 2" long, and red when ripe.

Bloom Season: Late spring–midsummer

Habitat/Range: Frequent in dry, rocky, or sandy sites, including prairies, savannas, fields, and pastures; found through the Midwest region, but absent in the northern third.

Comments: The spines and bristles are covered with microscopic reflexed barbs at their tips, making them difficult to extract. Native Americans ate the ripe fruit, pads, buds, and flowers, either raw, cooked, or dried. A closely related species, plains prickly pear (*Opuntia macrorhiza*), differs by having more than 2 spines per cluster that are turned backward (reflexed), and the spines are found along the upper two-thirds of the pad. Uncommon to rare in dry prairies in the west-central and southwest parts of the Midwest region, and westward. Another cactus, fragile prickly pear (*Opuntia fragilis*), is short and sprawling, with a more-cylindrical pad, up to 2" long and ½–1" wide; yellow flowers are 1½–2" wide; occurs in dry, rocky, or sandy prairies; uncommon to rare in the northwest part of the Midwest region, and westward.

WESTERN WALLFLOWER
Erysimum capitatum
Mustard family (Brassicaceae)

Description: A biennial or perennial plant, 1–3' tall, with stems covered with appressed, branched hairs. The leaves are alternate, numerous, narrow, ½–4" long and less than ½" wide, with margins smooth or somewhat toothed, and pointed tips. The flowers are on stalks attached to the upper stem. The flowers are ¾" wide, with 4 yellow to yellow-orange petals and 6 stamens.

Bloom Season: Mid-spring–early summer

Habitat/Range: Uncommon in dry open woods and calcareous bluffs and glades, and less commonly, on road cuts; found in the Midwest region, in a broad band through central Missouri and on cliffs along the Ohio River to Ohio; more common in the Great Plains.

Comments: Western wallflower is a very showy species and is cultivated as a garden ornamental, which explains scattered records for it across the Midwest region.

YELLOW-FLOWERED HORSE GENTIAN
Triosteum angustifolium
Honeysuckle family (Caprifoliaceae)

Description: Stems up to 30" tall, covered with moderately to densely, often bristly hairs that are sometimes gland-tipped. The leaves are opposite, 4–7" long and ¾–2" wide, broadest in the middle and tapering at both ends, with hairy surfaces, and stalks that are slightly winged. A single flower emerges at the leaf axil on a short stalk. The flowers are tubular, about ½" long, pale yellow, with the outer surface lined with gland-tipped hairs. The fruit is about ⅜" in diameter, orangish-yellow to pale orange, and moderately to densely hairy.

Bloom Season: Mid- to late spring

Habitat/Range: Occasional in mesic upland forests, bottomland forests, bases and ledges of bluffs, and banks of streams; found in the southern quarter of the Midwest region, and southward.

Comments: The dried and roasted fruits of horse gentians have occasionally been used as a substitute for coffee, but the plant is chiefly valued for its medicinal properties. The roots have been used as an emetic (induces vomiting) and mild cathartic (laxative). The drug is sometimes called Tinker's root, after Dr. Tinker, who first brought it to notice.

NITS AND LICE

Hypericum drummondii
St. John's wort family (Clusiaceae)

Description: Slender annuals, less than 1' tall, with lower stems that are reddish-brown, and many pairs of tiny, pointed, opposite leaves. The stem and leaves are covered with minute, yellowish-brown to dark brown or black, resinous dots, whose appearance inspired the common name of the plant. Each leaf is up to ¾" long and ⅛" wide, needle-like, sharply pointed, and narrowing at the base. The flowers are mostly solitary in the leaf axils, sometimes with small, loose clusters of 3 or 5 flowers at the branch tips. Each flower is up to ⅓" wide, with 5 pointed, green sepals that are slightly longer than the 5 orange-yellow petals.

Bloom Season: Summer

Habitat/Range: Occasional in dry open areas in sand or clay soils in prairies, glades, pastures, and old fields; found in the southern third of the Midwest region.

Comments: The species name, *drummondii*, is named for Thomas Drummond (1790–1835), a naturalist born in Scotland who collected plants and birds primarily in the New Orleans vicinity, and in Texas.

PINEWEED

Hypericum gentianoides
St. John's wort family (Clusiaceae)

Description: Looking like a pine seedling (hence, the common name), this annual plant has a multi-branched, wiry stem, with a powdery blue-green to reddish color, and grows up to 12" tall. The scale-like leaves are extremely small, opposite, and hug the stem. The flowers are stalkless, singly attached at the stem nodes, about ¼" across, with 5 yellow petals that open on bright, sunny days.

Bloom Season: Summer–fall

Habitat/Range: Common in sandy soils in glades and other dry sandy areas; found in scattered locations through the Midwest region, but absent in the northern third.

Comments: Adapted to living in shallow soil over bedrock, pineweed minimizes water loss by having scale-like leaves. Pineweed is the smallest *Hypericum* of the twenty-one species in the Midwest region.

DWARF ST. JOHN'S WORT
Hypericum mutilum
St. John's wort family (Clusiaceae)

Description: A summer annual or short-lived perennial plant, 4–18" tall, with multibranched stems. The stems are smooth, 4-angled, and sometimes narrowly winged. The leaves are opposite, about ½–1½" long and ¼–¾" wide, stalkless, broadest toward the middle or at the base, smooth, with minute, brown to black, resinous dots. The flowers are in clusters at the branch tips. Each flower is about ¼" wide, with 5 bright yellow to lemon-yellow petals and 5–15 stamens.

Bloom Season: Midsummer–fall

Habitat/Range: Occasional in bottomland forests, swamps, banks of streams, sloughs, fens, acid seeps, depressions in sandstone glades and cliffs, and abandoned sandy fields; found through the Midwest region, but absent in Minnesota; also in Mexico, Central America, South America, and the Caribbean Islands.

Comments: Dwarf St. John's wort grows in moist or muddy habitats where its seeds adhere to wading birds. The long-distance migration of these birds is most likely the method by which the species has been introduced to Central and South America.

FALSE SPOTTED ST. JOHN'S WORT
Hypericum pseudomaculatum
St. John's wort family (Clusiaceae)

Description: The sturdy stem of this plant is somewhat branched at the top and up to 3½' tall. The undersides of the leaves, sepals, and petals are covered with numerous tiny black dots. The leaves are opposite, lacking stalks, up to 2½" long and ¾" wide, oval- to somewhat triangular-shaped, and mostly pointed at the tip. The flowers are clustered at the top of the stem and in short side branches. Each flower has 5 yellow petals, each ⅜–½" long, and numerous stamens.

Bloom Season: Summer

Habitat/Range: Locally frequent in prairies, savannas, and dry open woods; found in the southwest quarter of the Midwest region.

Comments: *Hypericum pseudomaculatum* was formerly known as *Hypericum punctatum* var. *pseudomaculatum*, and has been elevated to species level.

SPOTTED ST. JOHN'S WORT

Hypericum punctatum
St. John's wort family (Clusiaceae)

Description: The sturdy stem of this plant is some-what branched at the top and up to 3' tall. The undersides of the leaves, sepals, and petals are covered with numerous tiny black dots. The leaves are opposite, lacking stalks, up to 2½" long and ¼" wide, oval, and rounded at the tip. The flowers are clustered at the top of the stem and in short side branches. Each flower has 5 yellow petals, each ¼–⅜" long, and numerous stamens.

Bloom Season: Summer

Habitat/Range: Common in low areas in prairies, savannas, and open woods, along streams, and in fields and pastures; found throughout the Midwest region.

Comments: A similar species, common St. John's wort (*Hypericum perforatum*), differs by having smaller leaves, ⅛–¾" long and ⅛–¼" wide. Also, the stems are much more branched and there are fewer black dots on the petals, sepals, and stems. Native to Europe, it has been popularized by its use in the treatment of depression. Found in degraded prairies, pastures, old fields, roadsides, and other disturbed areas. (See this similar-looking species in Weeds, page 353.)

GREAT ST. JOHN'S WORT

Hypericum pyramidatum
St. John's wort family (Clusiaceae)

Description: A tall St. John's wort, 3–5' in height, with a somewhat woody rootstock and stem base. The main stem is 4-angled and slightly winged on young plants, becoming 4-lined with maturity. The leaves are opposite, stalkless, up to 3" long and 1" wide, with smooth margins, rounded at the base, and tapering to a pointed tip. The flowers are bright to golden-yellow, 2–2½" across, with 5 petals, numerous yellow stamens, and a pistil with 5 styles.

Bloom Season: Summer

Habitat/Range: Occasional in mesic prairies, wet prairies, and moist open areas; found in the northern half of the Midwest region.

Comments: Also known as *Hypericum ascyron*. The size of the plants and flowers sets great St. John's wort apart from other herbaceous St. John's worts. It is sometimes cultivated in gardens.

ROUND-FRUITED ST. JOHN'S WORT
Hypericum sphaerocarpum
St. John's wort family (Clusiaceae)

Description: The stem is somewhat woody and often branched at the base, up to 30" tall. The leaves are opposite, linear, of equal width throughout, up to 3" long and about ½" wide, and smooth along the edges. The flowers are compact and much branched at the top, with 5 yellow petals, each about ⅜" long, with many yellow stamens.

Bloom Season: Mid-spring–summer

Habitat/Range: Common in dry, rocky prairies, glades, and pastures; found across the southern half of the Midwest region.

Comments: Unlike most members of the St. John's wort family, round-fruited St. John's wort lacks black dots on the leaves and flowers. St. John's wort is said to have gotten its common name from the red resin that is contained in small, black glands in the flower petals and leaves of some of the species. In the Middle Ages, it was said that this was the blood shed by St. John the Baptist when he was beheaded. The word *wort* is an Old English word for "plant."

PINESAP
Monotropa hypopitys
Heath family (Ericaceae)

Description: Fleshy, single-stemmed plants, 4–12" tall, finely hairy, with alternate scales arranged along the stem and at the bases of the tightly packed flowers. The flowers are about ½" long, with 5 yellow to reddish petals that look tubular but are not fused. Inside the flower are 8–10 stamens. The flowers and the supporting stem are typically the same color. The hanging flowers become upright as the fruits develop into fuzzy round capsules topped by stout styles, often persisting into the next growing season.

Bloom Season: Late spring–midsummer

Habitat/Range: Locally frequent in well-drained acidic soils, often in thick leaf litter of upland forests, bottomland forests, ledges of bluffs, and banks of streams; found throughout the Midwest region.

Comments: Also known as *Hypopitys monotropa*. Because this plant lacks chlorophyll, it derives nutrients from fungi that feed on the roots of decaying plants. Seasonal variation seems to affect the color of the plants, with those blooming in the summer tending to be yellowish, while those in the fall are more pinkish or reddish.

WOOD SPURGE
Euphorbia commutata
Spurge family (Euphorbiaceae)

Description: Several stems may arise from the base, up to 16" tall, with milky sap and light green leaves. The leaves are alternate, stalkless, smooth, up to 6" long, oval, and rounded at the tip. The leaves just below the flowers are often joined at the base. The tiny, greenish-yellow flowers are nested in a cup of small leaves. There are no petals, but a specialized cup-shaped structure holds 9–15 staminate flowers that surround a stalked pistillate flower.

Bloom Season: Mid-spring–midsummer

Habitat/Range: Occasional in moist or rocky woods, ravines, valleys, and low ground along streams; found in the southern half of the Midwest region.

Comments: Nineteen species in the genus *Euphorbia* occur in the Midwest region.

GROUND PLUM
Astragalus crassicarpus var. *trichocalyx*
Bean family (Fabaceae)

Description: Plants usually with several trailing stems, up to 2' long, connected to a thick woody taproot. The leaves are hairy, up to 6" long, and alternating along the stem on short stalks. Each leaf has 7–13 pairs of slightly folded leaflets, each ¾" long and ⅓" wide. The flowers are in small clusters at the ends of branches, with 5–25 flowers in each cluster. Each flower is about ¾–1" long and creamy-white to greenish-yellow. The upper petal is larger and flaring at the tip, below which are two side petals and a lower lip.

Bloom Season: Mid-spring–late spring

Habitat/Range: Locally frequent in dry prairies, loess hill prairies, and rocky woods; found in the southwest quarter of the Midwest region, and westward.

Comments: The fruits are succulent, shiny pods, about 1" in diameter, that become dry and hard when they age. They contain numerous small seeds. When ripe, the fruit has a reddish cast. Widely used for food by Native Americans and early settlers, they are said to taste like raw pea pods. A blue variety of ground plum (*Astragalus crassicarpus* var. *crassicarpus*) can be found on page 280.

CREAM WILD INDIGO
Baptisia bracteata var. *leucophaea*
Bean family (Fabaceae)

Description: A coarse, hairy, bush-like plant with spreading branches, up to 2' tall. The leaves are alternate on the stem and divided into 3 leaflets, each up to 3½" long. The bracts at the base of the leaflets are large and give the appearance of 5 leaflets instead of 3. The flower spike, up to 1' long, droops with numerous creamy-yellow flowers, each about 1" long, and having the arrangement typical of members of the bean family. The seed pods are black, pointed at the tip, and up to 2" long.

Bloom Season: Mid-spring–late spring

Habitat/Range: Common in mesic to dry prairies, sand prairies, sand savannas, mesic to dry upland forests, pastures, and roadsides; found through the Midwest region, but absent in the eastern third and northwest quarter.

Comments: Formerly known as *Baptisia leucophaea*. Native Americans used the plant to treat cuts and certain fevers. The Pawnee pulverized the seeds, mixed the powder with buffalo fat, and rubbed it on the stomach as a treatment for colic. Indian boys often used seed pods as rattles when they imitated their elders doing a ceremonial dance.

PARTRIDGE PEA
Chamaecrista fasciculata
Bean family (Fabaceae)

Description: An annual plant, up to 2' tall, with alternate leaves, each divided into about 20 pairs of leaflets. The leaflets are narrow, less than 1" long, about ⅛" wide, rounded at both ends, with a small bristle at the tip. Near the middle of each leaf stalk, there is a small, saucer-shaped gland. The leaflets fold up at night, and sometimes when touched. There are 1–4 flowers, up to 1½" wide, on slender stalks that emerge at the axil of the leaf and stem. There are 5 yellow petals, with 3 slightly smaller than the other 2, and with a tinge of red at the base of each petal. There are 10 yellow to dark-red stamens.

Bloom Season: Summer–fall

Habitat/Range: Common in upland prairies, savannas, openings of mesic to dry upland forests, pastures, fields, and often in disturbed sandy soils; found through the Midwest region, but absent in the northern quarter.

Comments: Cherokee and early settlers used the root for treating fever, cramps, heart ailments, and constipation. A related species, small-flowered partridge pea (*Chamaecrista nictitans*), differs by having smaller flowers, less than ¾" wide, and 5 stamens. It can be found in the same habitat as partridge pea, but is absent in the northern half of the Midwest region.

WILD SENNA
Senna marilandica
Bean family (Fabaceae)

Description: One to several smooth stems, up to 6' tall, with large, alternate leaves. The leaves are on stalks up to 2" long with a small gland near the base. The leaves are up to 8" long and divided into 8–12 pairs of leaflets, each about 2" long and 1" wide, tapering toward the end, with small, bristle-like points at the tips. The flowers vary from numerous on branched clusters to only 1–4 on stalks emerging from the junction of a leaf and stem. Each flower is about 1" across, with 5 narrow, yellow petals that are often curled, with 10 brownish-red stamens and flattened hairs along the styles. The hanging, flattened pods are up to 4" long and ½" wide.

Bloom Season: Summer

Habitat/Range: Occasional in wet prairies, savannas, open woods, and moist, open areas along rivers and streams; found through the Midwest region, but absent in the northern third.

Comments: Also known as Maryland senna. The Meskwaki ate the seeds, softened by soaking, as a mucilaginous medicine for sore throat. The Cherokee used the bruised root moistened with water for dressing sores. They also used the root in a tea as a cure for fever, and as a laxative. A related species, wild senna (*Senna hebecarpa*), differs by having somewhat hairy stems, leaflets more rounded toward the tip, and spreading hairs along the styles. Occasional in openings along banks of rivers and streams, savannas, and open woods; found through the Midwest region, but absent in the northern half, along with Iowa and Missouri.

RATTLEBOX
Crotalaria sagittalis
Bean family (Fabaceae)

Description: Annual plants, up to 1' tall, with soft, densely hairy stems and leaves. The leaves are alternate, narrow, and up to 3" long and ¾" wide, with a blunt or pointed tip. From 1–4 flowers occur at the ends of short side branches, each flower on a slender stalk, with small, leaf-like bracts. There are 5 long-pointed, green, hairy sepals at the base of the flower. Each flower is yellow, about ⅜" long, with the shape and arrangement typical of members of the bean family. The fruit is an inflated pod up to 1¼" long, initially light green, ripening to a purplish-black.

Bloom Season: Late spring–early fall

Habitat/Range: Occasional in upland prairies, sand prairies, savannas, openings of mesic to dry upland forests, old fields, pastures, and open disturbed ground; found in the southwest quarter of the Midwest region, and rare to absent in parts of the northwest quarter.

Comments: When the pod ripens, the seeds rattle freely within the pod; hence, the common name. The kidney-shaped seeds have been used as a substitute for coffee, but are poisonous to pigs and horses.

PENCIL FLOWER
Stylosanthes biflora
Bean family (Fabaceae)

Description: A small, wiry-stemmed plant, often branched at the base, hairy, up to 8" tall. The leaves are alternate, divided into 3 leaflets, each up to 2" long and ½" wide. There are widely scattered bristles along the leaf margins. The flowers are nested in leafy clusters at the tops of branches and are arranged in the style typical of the bean family. The orange-yellow flowers are about ¼" long.

Bloom Season: Late spring–summer

Habitat/Range: Common in dry prairies, sand prairies, glades, and rocky, open woods; found in the southern third of the Midwest region.

Comments: Pencil flower is named for the similarity of the flower's orange-yellow color to the paint on a Ticonderoga #2 wood pencil.

167

GOLDEN CORYDALIS
Corydalis aurea
Fumitory family (Fumariaceae)

Description: An annual or biennial plant 4–20"
tall, with multiple stems from the base that are
prostrate, with the branches upright. The leaves
are compound and fern-like, with leaflets deeply
divided, covered with a waxy bloom that often gives
a bluish-green or gray-green cast. The flowers are
tubular, ½–¾" long, with up to 20 bright golden-
yellow flowers. Each flower has 4 petals, with an
upper and lower petal and 2 inner petals that are
barely seen. On the top petal, there is a slightly
curved, smooth, nectar spur at the rear about half
as long as the rest of the flower, and at the front, a
broad ruffled lip. Flower stalks are about ¼" long.

Bloom Season: Late spring–early summer

Habitat/Range: Occasional in rocky prairies, openings of dry upland forests, sandstone glades, banks
of streams, bluff outcrops, and disturbed sites;
found through the Midwest region, but absent in
southern Michigan, Indiana, and Ohio.

Comments: Another species, small-flowered
corydalis (*Corydalis micrantha*), has somewhat
smaller stems, 4–12" tall, and flowers that are
½" long or less. Occasional in upland prairies,
openings of dry to mesic upland forests, banks
of streams, ledges of bluffs, and disturbed sites;
found in the Midwest region, but absent in the
northern third, along with Indiana and Ohio.

PALE CORYDALIS
Corydalis flavula
Fumitory family (Fumariaceae)

Description: A delicate, low-growing annual
plant, much branched, up to 10" tall. The leaves
are green, fern-like, alternate, the lowermost on
long stalks, the uppermost on short or no stalks.
There are several yellow to pale yellow flowers
clustered at the end of a stalk, with flowers ¼–⅜"
long. Each flower has 4 petals, with an upper and
lower petal and 2 inner petals that are barely seen.
The upper petal has a nectar spur on the back and
an irregular, wavy, or toothed crest at the front.
Flower stalks are ⅜–¾" long.

Bloom Season: Spring

Habitat/Range: Common in bottomland forests,
mesic upland forests, at the base of bluffs, and
along banks of streams; found in the southern half
of the Midwest region.

Comments: The genus name, *Corydalis*, is of Greek
origin, meaning "crested lark" (referring to the spur
on the top of the flower), and the species name,
flavula, is Latin for yellow.

YELLOW SCREWSTEM

Bartonia virginica
Gentian family (Gentianaceae)

Description: Delicate, slender, wiry annual plants, up to 1' tall, with the stem sometimes curving or spiraled. The leaves are reduced to small pairs of pointed, opposite scales along the stem. The flowers are arranged toward the top of the stem on erect stalks. Flowers are about ⅛" long, with 4 needle-like sepals, and a greenish-white to pale yellow, urn-shaped corolla with 4 small pointed to rounded lobes. A stout green stigma protrudes in the center.

Bloom Season: Midsummer–fall

Habitat/Range: Occasional in acidic sites in wet swales, wet meadows, swamps, bogs, and in moss on shaded sandstone cliffs; found through the Midwest region, but absent in the western third, and eastward.

Comments: Another species, screwstem (*Bartonia paniculata*), differs by having alternate scales on the stem. Occurs in similar habitats; found in a few locations throughout the Midwest region, where it is rare or endangered, and absent in Iowa and Minnesota; then, southward and eastward.

GIANT HYSSOP

Agastache nepetoides
Mint family (Lamiaceae)

Description: A stout-stemmed plant, up to 6' tall, with a sharply 4-sided stem and branching near the top. The leaves are opposite, coarsely toothed along the margins, thin, lance-shaped, up to 6" long and 3" wide, reduced in size upward, with fine hairs on the lower surface. The cluster of flowers is cylindrical along a stalk up to 8" long. The flowers are pale yellow, small, about ⅓" long, numerous, with 2 lips and 2 pairs of long stamens curved in opposite directions.

Bloom Season: Summer–fall

Habitat/Range: Occasional in open woods, low, moist, or mesic woods, at the base of bluffs, borders of woods, and thickets; found through the Midwest region, but absent in the northern third.

Comments: The genus name, *Agastache*, is from the Greek words *agan*, meaning "very much," and *stachys*, meaning an ear of wheat, in reference to the flower spikes. The species name, *nepetoides*, is in reference to the similarity in appearance of this plant to catnip (*Nepeta*). The small, pale yellow flowers are not very showy, and there are only a few flowers in bloom at the same time.

RICHWEED
Collinsonia canadensis
Mint family (Lamiaceae)

Description: A mostly unbranched plant with a hairless square stem, 2–4' tall. The leaves are opposite, 2–6" long and 1½–4" wide, broadest at the middle and tapering at both ends, coarsely toothed along the margins, and stalked. The flowers are in branches at the top of the stem that form a display, 8" long and 6" across. Each flower is about ½" long, tubular, with 2 yellow lips. The upper lip has 2 upper lobes and 2 lateral lobes that are rounded in shape. The lower lobe is broad at the base and heavily fringed along its outer lip.

Bloom Season: Midsummer–fall

Habitat/Range: Uncommon in mesic upland forests, wooded ravines, bottomland forests, and banks of streams; found in the eastern half of the Midwest region, as well as in southern Missouri and southern Illinois; then, south and east.

Comments: The foliage when crushed has a lemon-citronella fragrance. Native Americans used the leaves for pain relief from sores, bruises, burns, wounds, and sprains. It was also used for its antidiarrheal and antirheumatic properties, as well as for a stimulant and tonic.

SPOTTED BEEBALM
Monarda punctata
Mint family (Lamiaceae)

Description: The often showy, pinkish-purple bracts obscure the dull yellow flowers of this plant. This annual or short-lived perennial reaches a height up to 3', with a finely hairy stem and toothed, opposite leaves on short stalks. The leaves are about 3½" long and up to 1" wide. The flowers are arranged in whorls, with 1–5 whorls stacked one above the other, separated by a whorl of pinkish-purple, leaf-like bracts. Each pale yellow, tubular flower is about 1" long and dotted with dark spots. The lower lip has 3 lobes.

Bloom Season: Summer–fall

Habitat/Range: Occasional in sand prairies, sand savannas, and pastures and fields in sandy areas; found through the Midwest region, but absent in the southern third.

Comments: Also known as horsemint. Native Americans used leaf tea for colds, fever, flu, stomach cramps, coughs, and bowel ailments. Historically, doctors used this mint as a stimulant and diuretic.

YELLOW DOGTOOTH VIOLET

Erythronium americanum
Lily family (Liliaceae)

Description: Often forming large colonies, the smooth, fleshy plants are up to 10" tall, with brown mottled leaves, 2½–6" long and ½–2" wide, of equal width throughout their length and tapering at both ends. A single stalk emerges from a pair of leaves with a solitary nodding flower at the top. Single-leaved plants do not produce flowers. The yellow flowers are about 1" long and 1½" wide, with 6 petals that tend to curve backward and 6 long stamens in the center, with rusty red anthers.

Bloom Season: Spring

Habitat/Range: Occasional in moist woods, wooded ravines, shaded bluffs, and along stream banks; found through the Midwest region, but absent in the western quarter.

Comments: This plant is also called "yellow trout lily," because the mottled leaves resemble the sides of a brown or brook trout. Dogtooth is so named for the shape of the corm, a type of root. Another species of yellow dogtooth violet (*Erythronium rostratum*) differs by having flowers that tilt up and out rather than nodding, and with spreading petals that do not curve backward. Both have similar habitats, but *Erythronium rostratum* is found only in the southern half of the southwest quarter of the Midwest region, and southward.

YELLOW STAR GRASS

Hypoxis hirsuta
Lily family (Liliaceae)

Description: Small, hairy plants producing yellow, star-like flowers with grassy leaves; hence, the common name. When flowering begins, the plants are about 5" tall; as they mature, they may reach up to 1' in height. The long, grass-like leaves are about 8" long and ¼" wide. The flower stalks are shorter than the leaves, with 2–7 flowers appearing in succession. The flowers are about ½" wide, with 6 yellow petals and 6 yellow stamens.

Bloom Season: Spring; rarely reblooming through summer and fall

Habitat/Range: Common in mesic to dry prairies, savannas, open woodlands, and glades; found throughout the Midwest region.

Comments: The Cherokee made an infusion of the leaves as a heart medicine, and the corm was used to treat ulcers. Various species of bees, flies, and beetles visit the flower to feed on its pollen, and small rodents feed on the corms. The seeds are eaten by bobwhite quail.

171

INDIAN CUCUMBER ROOT
Medeola virginiana
Lily family (Liliaceae)

Description: A colony-forming plant with unbranched stems, up to 2' tall. The leaves are stalkless and in 2 whorls: a whorl of 5–9 leaves near the middle of the stem, and a whorl of 3–5 smaller leaves at the top of the stem. The flowers are on nodding stalks, about ½" wide, with 6 widely spreading, backward-curving, greenish-yellow petals, 6 protruding stamens, and 3 widely spreading styles that are longer than the stamens.

Bloom Season: Late spring–early summer

Habitat/Range: Common in mesic forests, shaded ravines and slopes, and in moist, shaded depressions; found throughout the eastern half of the Midwest region, and eastward.

Comments: Native Americans used the horizontal white tuber, which tastes like cucumber, for food. The Iroquois used an infusion of the crushed dried berries and leaves to treat convulsions in infants. The root is said to be a diuretic.

GREEN TRILLIUM
Trillium viride
Lily family (Liliaceae)

Description: Unbranched plants, up to 20" tall, with a whorl of 3 leaves at the top of a stout, smooth stem. The leaves are attached to the stem without stalks, smooth, lance-shaped, up to 5" long and 2½" wide, with blunt to round, pointed tips, and with the upper surface green and mottled. The flowers arise directly from the stem, with the 3 green sepals widely spreading, and the 3 yellow-green to sometimes purple-green petals upright, each up to 3" long. The 6 purple stamens are also upright.

Bloom Season: Spring

Habitat/Range: Occasional in moist soils of valleys along streams and ravines and moist, wooded slopes; found in the southwest quarter of the Midwest region.

Comments: A closely related species, Ozark green trillium (*Trillium viridescens*), has leaves with sharp, pointed tips and with the upper surface solid green or only slightly mottled; found in the southern part of the southwest quarter of the Midwest region, and southward.

LARGE BELLWORT
Uvularia grandiflora
Lily family (Liliaceae)

Description: A graceful plant, its several single smooth stems, with a whitish coating, emerge from a common base up to 18" tall. The stem is usually branched at the top, but only 1 branch carries flowers and leaves. The leaves are alternate, without teeth, smooth, up to 6" long and 2" wide, with pointed tips, and the base of the leaf surrounds the stem. The flowers are solitary, drooping from a 1"-long stalk, up to 1½" long, with 6 long petals and 6 stamens that are hidden by the petals.

Bloom Season: Spring

Habitat/Range: Common in mesic forests; found throughout the Midwest region.

Comments: Early settlers cooked the upper stem and leaves as greens. The upper stems served as a substitute for asparagus. Canker sores in the mouth were treated with a concoction made from the roots. A closely related species, small bellwort (*Uvularia sessilifolia*), differs by having the base of the leaf not encircling the stem, having smaller leaves, with flowers pale yellow and about 1" long; found through the Midwest region, but absent to rare in the east-central part.

GROOVED YELLOW FLAX
Linum sulcatum
Flax family (Linaceae)

Description: A pale green annual plant, up to 2½' tall, with a stiff stem that branches near the top. The branches have conspicuous grooves or ridges. The tiny leaves are alternate on the stem, about 1" long and only ⅛" wide, pointed at the tip, stalkless, with tiny round glands at the base of the leaf. The flowers are scattered among the branches on short stalks. The flowers are about ¾" across, with 5 pale yellow petals that drop off shortly after flowering.

Bloom Season: Mid-spring–early fall

Habitat/Range: Occasional in dry upland prairies, hill prairies, sand prairies, glades, and open woods; found throughout the Midwest region, but rare in the eastern third.

Comments: A related species, small yellow flax (*Linum medium* var. *texanum*), differs by being a perennial, lacking the small round glands at the base of the leaf, and lacking grooves or furrows on the branches. The habitat and range are similar to grooved yellow flax, but it is absent in the northern third of the Midwest region. Various species of flax have been cultivated since before recorded history for the fibers in their stems, used to make linen, and the oil in their seeds is used to make linseed oil. The seeds were also used for a variety of medicinal remedies.

173

STICKLEAF
Mentzelia oligosperma
Stickleaf family (Loasaceae)

Description: A spreading to erect plant with much-branched, whitish, rough, brittle stems, ½–3' tall, with hooked hairs on the stem and leaves. The leaves are alternate, stalkless, and broadest below the middle, up to 2½" long and 1" wide, with margins coarsely toothed to lobed, blunt, or pointed tips. Flowers arise from leaf axils toward the tips of branches. Each flower is about ¾" wide and open in the morning. The 5 pale yellow to orange petals are about ¼" long, with tips pointed, and 5–40 stamens about as long as the petals.

Bloom Season: Summer

Habitat/Range: Occasional in dry, rocky prairies, glades, and rocky pastures; found in the southwest quarter of the Midwest region.

Comments: The common name refers to the determined way the leaves stick to clothing and fur. When entwined in sheep's wool, the leaves can lower the wool's market value. The *Mentzelia* genus is native to the New World. There are about eighty species of annual (and some perennial) herbs and some shrubs in this genus, sixty-eight of which are found growing in greater North America.

TOOTHED EVENING PRIMROSE
Calylophus serrulatus
Evening primrose family (Onagraceae)

Description: Often woody at the base, with 1 to many smooth to densely hairy branches, up to 1½' tall. The leaves are alternate, stalkless, hairy, narrow, up to 2" long and ⅛" wide, and usually toothed or wavy along the edges. The flowers are solitary, stalkless, and arise at the bases of upper leaves. Each flower is bright yellow, fading to dark yellow to orange, about 1" across. There are 4 petals, each shallowly notched at the tip, and 8 stamens.

Bloom Season: Late spring–summer

Habitat/Range: Occasional in rocky or gravelly prairies, hill prairies, and sand prairies; found in the northwest quarter of the Midwest region.

Comments: Also known as *Oenothera serrulata*. The flowers open in the morning and close in the afternoon, unlike many species in this family that open in the evening and are pollinated by night-flying insects; hence, the common name of "evening primrose."

COMMON EVENING PRIMROSE
Oenothera biennis
Evening primrose family (Onagraceae)

Description: A biennial with a stout, sometimes hairy stem tinged with red, as are parts of the older leaves, up to 7' tall. The basal leaves are stalked, 4–12" long and 1–2" wide, and irregularly toothed along the margins. The stem leaves are alternate, lance-shaped, pointed at the tip, hairy on both sides, toothed along the margins, and up to 6" long and 2" wide. The flowers are numerous along a long column that opens to 2½" across. The 4 yellow petals have a shallow notch at the end. There are 8 yellow stamens.

Bloom Season: Summer–fall

Habitat/Range: Common to abundant in disturbed areas in prairies, at the edges of woods, along streams, pastures, fields, and along roadsides; found throughout the Midwest region.

Comments: The flowers open in the evening and close by mid-morning on sunny days. The flowers emit a creosote smell that particularly attracts night-flying sphinx moths. Native Americans ate the seeds and the first-year roots (the second-year roots are too woody). After this plant was introduced to Europe from North America in the early 1600s, Europeans ate its roots and put the young shoots into salads. The entire plant was prepared and used to treat whooping cough, hiccups, and asthma. A closely related species, northern evening primrose (*Oenothera parviflora*), differs by having gland-tipped hairs along the stem, flowers ¾–1½" across, and flower spikes nodding at the top; found in the northern half of the Midwest region.

SEEDBOX
Ludwigia alternifolia
Evening primrose family (Onagraceae)

Description: A widely branching plant, up to 4'
tall. The leaves are alternate, up to 4" long and
less than 1" wide, broadest at the middle and
tapering to the tip and base. The flowers are
single, on short stalks, and arise at the junction
of the leaf and stem. Each flower is about ¾"
across, with 4 reddish to green, triangular sepals,
4 yellow petals, which fall shortly after flowering,
and 4 stamens. The seed capsules are more or
less square, up to ¼" across, angled or narrowly
winged, and contain numerous small seeds.

Bloom Season: Summer

Habitat/Range: Common in wet open areas in
prairies, wet prairies, along streams and marshes,
and roadsides; found in the southern half of the
Midwest region.

Comments: Also called "rattlebox," in reference to
the unusual box-like seed capsules, which, when
mature, will rattle when shaken. The genus name,
Ludwigia, is in honor of Christian Ludwig, profes-
sor of botany at Leipzig, Germany, in the late 18th
century, and the species name, *alternifolia*, refers
to how the leaves are arranged on the stem.

NARROWLEAF EVENING PRIMROSE
Oenothera fruticosa
Evening primrose family (Onagraceae)

Description: A tall, slender-looking plant, up to
30" tall, and stems few or solitary with sparsely
to densely covered hairs that are sometimes
gland-tipped. The basal leaves overwinter and are
often withered at flowering time, 1–4" long and
¼–1¼" wide, and broadest below the middle. The
stem leaves are alternate, narrow, ¾–2¼" long and
⅛–¾" wide, short-stalked, often with small secondary leaves arising from the leaf axils. The flowers
are 1–2" across, with 4 bright yellow petals that
are broadest toward the tip, and 8 yellow stamens.

Bloom Season: Summer–fall

Habitat/Range: Occasional in openings of dry to
mesic upland forests; found in the eastern half
of the Midwest region, and a few locations in
southern Missouri, and eastward.

Comments: Narrowleaf evening primrose is
widely grown as a garden ornamental, and several
cultivated varieties exist. Another species, small
sundrops (*Oenothera perennis*), is 9–24" tall, with
the top of the stem nodding and yellow flowers ⅓–¾" wide. Occasional in moist to gravelly
soils in open woods, meadows, and fens; found
in the Midwest region in northeast Minnesota,
Wisconsin, Michigan, and eastern Ohio; rare and
scattered in the remaining states.

CUT-LEAVED EVENING PRIMROSE
Oenothera laciniata
Evening primrose family (Onagraceae)

Description: Generally small plants that often sprawl across the ground to a length of ½–2'. The leaves are alternate along the stem, 1–4" long and up to 1" across, with the lower leaves stalked, the upper, stalkless. The leaves are shallowly to deeply lobed along the edges, with sparsely hairy upper surfaces, and densely hairy undersides. The flowers are single in the mid- and upper leaf axils, each about 1" across, with 4 heart-shaped, yellow petals. There are 8 yellow stamens surrounding a yellow cross-shaped style. The 4 narrow sepals hang down below the petals along the long floral tube (ovary), which is characteristic of evening primroses.

Bloom Season: Late spring–summer

Habitat/Range: Common in sand prairies and sandy disturbed ground; found through the Midwest region, but absent in the northern third.

Comments: As with many evening primroses, cut-leaved evening primrose blooms during the night and closes usually by mid-morning the next day. Although native to the United States, this plant can be found in many other places as an introduced species, and sometimes as a noxious weed. It has been reported in Hawaii, Australia, Britain, France, Korea, Japan, and other areas. Many plants from other countries have certainly caused problems in the United States when they were intentionally or accidentally introduced. Unfortunately, this same process can be extended to other parts of the world by way of transport of plants native to the United States.

FOURPOINT EVENING PRIMROSE
Oenothera rhombipetala
Evening primrose family (Onagraceae)

Description: A hairy annual or biennial plant, 1–4'
tall, with stems erect and often branched from
the base. First-year plants have a basal rosette
of stalked leaves that is up to 6" in diameter.
The leaves on the stem are alternate, stalkless,
crowded, gradually reduced up the stem, ½–4"
long and less than ¾" wide, with the margins
entire or toothed and often wavy. The flowers are
densely arranged along a spike about 1' long. The
flowers have 4 yellow petals each ¾–1¼" long and
½–1¼" wide at the end of a 1–2" floral tube, with
8 stamens, and with stigma above the anthers at
flowering time.

Bloom Season: Summer–fall

Habitat/Range: Occasional in sand prairies, banks
of rivers, roadsides, and disturbed sandy ground;
found in the central part of the Midwest region.

Comments: A similar species, sand evening
primrose (*Oenothera clelandii*), is generally
smaller, less than 3' tall, with petals ¼–¾" long,
and the stigma surrounded by anthers at flowering
time. Also found in similar habitat and range as
fourpoint evening primrose.

THREAD-LEAVED SUNDROPS
Oenothera linifolia
Evening primrose family (Onagraceae)

Description: A thin, branching annual, up to 1' tall,
with many narrow, alternate, thread-like leaves.
The leaves are ⅓–¾" long and about ⅛" wide,
with smooth margins and a pointed tip. There are
smaller leaves clustered at the leaf axils. The flowers are less than ½" across, with 4 yellow petals, 8
stamens, and a 4-lobed stigma.

Bloom Season: Mid-spring–midsummer

Habitat/Range: Locally frequent in rocky or sandy
prairies, open woods, and glades; found in the
southwest quarter of the Midwest region, and
southward.

Comments: The flowers of thread-leaved sundrops
open in the evening and usually stay open through
the following midday.

MISSOURI EVENING PRIMROSE

Oenothera macrocarpa
Evening primrose family (Onagraceae)

Description: A low, sprawling to erect plant, up to 15" long. The alternate narrow leaves are several on a stem and up to 5" long and 1" wide. The leaves are long-pointed at the tip, with a tapering base and small, silky hairs. The base of the leaves and the stem are often red. The showy flowers emerge from leaf axils on the upper part of the stem. They are up to 5" across, with 4 large, yellow to bright yellow petals that turn orange when fading, and 8 yellow stamens. The fruit is a brown, papery capsule 3–4" long with 4 broad wings.

Bloom Season: Mid-spring–midsummer

Habitat/Range: Locally frequent in limestone or dolomite dry, rocky prairies and glades; found in the southwest part of the Midwest region.

Comments: Formerly known as *Oenothera missouriensis*. The flowers open in the late evening and close the next day by mid-morning, and are pollinated primarily by night-flying sphinx moths.

PRAIRIE SUNDROPS

Oenothera pilosella
Evening primrose family (Onagraceae)

Description: Unbranched, alternate-leaved plants, up to 2½' tall, with soft hairy stems and leaves. The basal leaves, up to 3" long and 2" wide, overwinter and usually wither at flowering time. The stem leaves are alternate, widest at the middle, up to 4" long and 1" wide. The yellow to deep yellow flowers arise singly at the axils of the leaves. Flowers are about 2" across, with 4 broadly rounded petals with shallow notching at the tips and 8 yellow stamens.

Bloom Season: Late spring–summer

Habitat/Range: Occasional in mesic to wet prairies and wet depressions in upland prairies; found through the Midwest region, but absent in the northwest part.

Comments: Prairie sundrop flowers bloom once during the day, unlike most others in the primrose family, which are one-time night bloomers. The flowers are pollinated primarily by long-tongued bees, butterflies, and skippers.

SMALL YELLOW LADY'S SLIPPER

Cypripedium parviflorum var. *parviflorum*
Orchid family (Orchidaceae)

Description: Stout, unbranched stems, often forming clumps from a single rhizome, up to 22" tall. The stems and leaves are finely hairy, with the base of the 4–6 alternate leaves forming a sheath around the stem. The leaves are pleated with parallel veins and vary from narrow to round, with pointed tips, and are up to 6" long and 3" wide. Each stem has at least 1 flower, but occasionally 2. The flower has 2 twisted narrow petals, 1½–2" long, on either side of an inflated petal, called a "slipper," ¾–1¼" long. Above and below the slipper are 2 broad sepals. The sepals and lateral petals are reddish-purple to brown.

Bloom Season: Mid-spring–early summer

Habitat/Range: Infrequent on wooded slopes and ravines, mesic prairies, wet sand prairies, and seepage areas in prairie wetlands; found in the southern half of the Midwest region.

Comments: Both large and small yellow lady's slippers were widely used in 19th-century America as a sedative for nervous headache, hysteria, insomnia, and nervous irritability.

LARGE YELLOW LADY'S SLIPPER

Cypripedium parviflorum var. *pubescens*
Orchid family (Orchidaceae)

Description: Stout, unbranched stems, often forming clumps from a single rhizome, up to 30" tall. The stems and leaves are finely hairy, with the base of the 3–5 alternate leaves forming a sheath around the stem. The leaves are pleated with parallel veins and vary from narrow to round, with pointed tips, and are up to 9" long and 5" wide. There are 1–2 flowers per stem. Each flower has 2 twisted, narrow petals, 2–3½" long, on either side of an inflated petal, called a "slipper," and 1¼–2¼" long. Above and below the slipper are 2 broad sepals. The sepals and lateral petals are yellowish-green to greenish-brown.

Bloom Season: Mid-spring–early summer

Habitat/Range: An uncommon plant usually occurring in woodlands and wetlands, but occasionally in prairies and some eastern hill prairies; found throughout the Midwest region.

Comments: Native Americans used the powdered root as a sedative, tranquilizer, and a pain reliever. A related variety, northern yellow lady's slipper (*Cypripedium parviflorum* var. *makasin*), differs by having flowers half the size, and sparsely hairy; occurs in the wet to moist soil of swamps, fens, and springy forest edges; found in the northern third of the Midwest region.

LOESEL'S TWAYBLADE
Liparis loeselii
Orchid family (Orchidaceae)

Description: A short, unbranched plant, 3–8"
tall, with an angled stem and 2 upright, smooth,
glossy leaves arising near the base. The leaves
are 1½–4" long and up to 1½" wide, broadest at
the middle, tapering to a point at the end, and
narrowing at the base to rolled sheathing that
surrounds the stem. Nonflowering plants produce
a single leaf. The flowers range from 3–15 and are
alternate along the stem, each with a tiny bract at
the base. Each greenish-yellow flower is ½" wide,
with 3 narrow, petal-like sepals and 2 thread-like
side petals that point forward and flank a broadly
spreading, curled lower lip.

Bloom Season: Mid-spring–early summer

Habitat/Range: Uncommon in mesic bottomland
forests, forested margins of sinkhole ponds, fens,
seeps, bogs, and marshy stream banks; found
throughout the Midwest region, but rare in Indiana
and Missouri; also occurs eastward.

Comments: Loesel's twayblade is also native to
Europe, northern Asia, and Canada. The orchid
has been shown to self-pollinate, when raindrops
push the pollen mass against the stigma surface.
Consequently, there is a greater percentage of fruit
development when rainy periods coincide with the
pollen becoming mature.

GREEN ADDER'S MOUTH
Malaxis unifolia
Orchid family (Orchidaceae)

Description: A delicate plant, 3–8" tall, with a
single leaf attached about mid-stem. The leaves
are egg-shaped to rounded, 1–3" long and ½–1½"
wide, with the base of the leaf wrapping around
the stem. The flowers are located along the upper
part of the stem, with 20–84 tiny, less than ⅛"
long, greenish-yellow flowers on single stalks
up to ⅜" long. There are 3 tiny sepals, 2 curving,
thread-like petals, and a broader lower lip when
fully mature.

Bloom Season: Late spring–midsummer

Habitat/Range: Occasional in open upland forests,
swamps, bogs, and wet thickets; found throughout
the Midwest region, but rare in Iowa, Indiana, and
Ohio; then, eastward and southward.

Comments: The diminutive green adder's mouth
orchid is also found in Mexico, Central America,
and the Greater Antilles (Cuba, Jamaica, and
Dominican Republic). Another species, white
adder's mouth (*Malaxis monophyllos*), has 12–35
greenish-white flowers, each less than ¼" long,
on slender stalks ¹⁄₁₆" long, and the single leaf is
attached near the base of the stem, not midway.
Occurs in moss and peat hummocks in swamps;
found in the northern third of the Midwest region.

181

SMOOTH FALSE FOXGLOVE
Aureolaria flava
Broomrape family (Orobanchaceae)

Description: An erect to arching, smooth-stemmed, partially parasitic plant, 2–5' tall, often with a purplish tinge. Leaves are opposite, stalked, deeply lobed, 2–6" long, somewhat whitish beneath, and with margins smooth to irregularly toothed. The flowers are in pairs along a stalk toward the tip. Each flower is 1¼–2¼" long, yellow, bell-shaped, smooth on the outside and hairy within, with 5 spreading, broadly rounded lobes.

Bloom Season: Summer–fall

Habitat/Range: Occasional in upland forests, woodlands, and borders of glades; found through the Midwest region, but absent in the northwest quarter.

Comments: There are six species in the genus *Aureolaria* in the Midwest region. False foxgloves are pollinated predominantly by bumblebees. Ruby-throated hummingbirds are also attracted to the flowers for their nectar.

LARGE-FLOWERED FALSE FOXGLOVE
Aureolaria grandiflora
Broomrape family (Orobanchaceae)

Description: A shrubby, partially parasitic plant, with dense, short hairs on the branches, up to 3' tall. The leaves are opposite, short-stalked, with the lower leaves deeply cut; the upper leaves are much reduced, with small teeth, or rounded along the margins. The flowers emerge from the leaf axils, 1½–2½" long and ¼–¾" wide, yellow, with a long tube and 5 spreading lobes.

Bloom Season: Midsummer–fall

Habitat/Range: Occasional in dry or rocky woodlands in acidic soils, savannas, and borders of glades; found in the central and southwestern parts of the Midwest region.

Comments: Plants in the genus *Aureolaria* are hemiparasitic, which means they have modified roots called haustoria that seek out the roots of host plants and tap into them for some of their nutrition. They are not totally dependent on them, however, and can perform photosynthesis. False foxglove plants seek out members especially of the white oak group, including white oak, post oak, chinkapin, and bur oak.

DOWNY YELLOW PAINTED CUP

Castilleja sessilifolia
Broomrape family (Orobanchaceae)

Description: Several hairy, unbranched stems arising from a single base, up to 15" tall. The leaves are alternate, stalkless, up to 2" long, narrow with rounded tips or narrowly lobed in 3 segments. The leaves near the base of the stem are often long, narrow, and undivided. Flowers are in a dense, leafy cluster at the top of the stems. The pale yellow flowers are tubular, 1½–2¼" long, with a long, slender upper lip and a shorter lower lip that is lobed in 3 parts.

Bloom Season: Mid-spring–early summer

Habitat/Range: Occasional in dry prairies, hill prairies, rocky hillsides, and sandy soil; found in the northwest quarter of the Midwest region.

Comments: The genus *Castilleja* was formerly in the snapdragon family (Scrophulariaceae). Downy yellow painted cup is partially parasitic, obtaining water and nutrients from other plants by tapping their roots. Host plants include other wildflowers and various native grasses, such as hairy grama and junegrass, as well as eastern red cedar.

SOUTHERN FERN-LEAF FALSE FOXGLOVE

Aureolaria pectinata
Broomrape family (Orobanchaceae)

Description: A much-branched partially parasitic annual, 1½–3' tall, with dense, gland-tipped hairs on the stems and leaves. The leaves are opposite, up to 3" long and 2" wide, lance-shaped, fern-like, with 7 pairs of primary lobes that have secondary shallow lobes or coarse teeth along the edges, and with a pointed tip. There are 1–3 flowers on short stalks arising from leaf axils. Each flower is yellow, tubular, 1–1½" long and ¾–1" wide, with short hairs on the outer surface, and 5 spreading, rounded lobes.

Bloom Season: Midsummer–fall

Habitat/Range: Occasional in mesic to dry upland forests, woodlands, savannas, glades, blufftops, and banks of streams; found in the Midwest region in Missouri, and southward.

Comments: A closely related species of fern-leaf false foxglove (*Aureolaria pedicularia*) differs by having rounded tips of the end lobes, not pointed, and the fruit hairs are less dense and less spreading. Found in dry, sandy soil in open oak woods and savannas, in the central part of the Midwest region, from the southern parts of Wisconsin and Michigan to the northern parts of Illinois and Indiana.

WOOD BETONY
Pedicularis canadensis
Broomrape family (Orobanchaceae)

Description: Several hairy stems emerge from a clump of fern-like basal leaves. The stems are about 6–10" tall when in flower and grow to about 18" tall as they mature. The basal leaves are narrow, deeply divided, and about 6" long. In the spring, they start out as a beautiful wine color before they turn green. Leaves along the stem are much smaller, scattered, and alternate. The flowers are nearly 1" long and densely clustered at the top of the stem. There are 2 lips, with the upper lip yellow or purple, flattened, and curved in a long arch to form a hood. The lower lip is pale yellow to yellow and has 3 rounded lobes.

Bloom Season: Spring

Habitat/Range: Common in mesic to dry prairies, savannas, open woods, glades, and pastures; found throughout the Midwest region.

Comments: Wood betony is also called "lousewort," from the belief that cattle and sheep grazing in pastures with this plant were once expected to become infested with lice. The Meskwaki and Potawatomi boiled the whole plant to make a tea for reducing internal swelling, tumors, and some types of external swelling. The Ojibwa used the plant as a love charm. The chopped-up root was put into food that was cooking without the knowledge of the couple who were to eat it. If they had been quarrelsome, they would once again become lovers. A similar species, swamp lousewort (*Pedicularis lanceolata*), is a larger plant, up to 3' tall, with opposite leaves and shallower lobes; blooms in the fall in moist soils in prairies and wetlands; found throughout the Midwest region.

MULLEIN FOXGLOVE
Dasistoma macrophylla
Broomrape family (Orobanchaceae)

Description: A stout, biennial plant with branching stems, up to 7' tall. The basal leaves are large, up to 10" long, and deeply cut. The basal leaves in early spring are an attractive reddish-purple before turning green. The stem leaves are progressively smaller toward the top of the plant, lance-shaped, and smooth along the margins. The flowers lack stalks and emerge directly from the axil of the leaves and stem. The flower is a short tube, woolly inside, less than ¾" long, with 5 yellow petals and 4 stamens.

Bloom Season: Summer–fall

Habitat/Range: Occasional in dry, mesic, or low woods, and in valleys and ravines, along rocky slopes, and in thickets; found in the southern half of the Midwest region.

Comments: Mullein foxglove was formerly known as *Seymeria macrophylla*. The plant, although rarely seen in large numbers, is a preferred food of white-tailed deer.

SOUTHERN WOOD SORREL
Oxalis dillenii
Wood sorrel family (Oxalidaceae)

Description: Small hairs lying flat along the stem give the plant a grayish appearance. The stems are 6–12" tall. The leaves are alternate or whorled on long slender stalks, compound, with 3 leaflets ½–1" wide that are covered with flattened hairs. The heart-shaped leaflets are clover-like and fold up at night and on cloudy days. Individual flowers are also on long stalks and arranged in a loose cluster at the tips of branches. Each flower is about ½" across, with 5 yellow petals. The fruit is upright, hairy, and attached to stalks that are at right angles to the stem.

Bloom Season: Late spring–fall

Habitat/Range: Common in upland prairies, savannas, edges of woods, pastures, fields, and roadsides; found throughout the Midwest region.

Comments: The leaves and flowers were eaten by Native Americans of various tribes. The powdered leaves were boiled in water and used to expel intestinal worms, to reduce fever, and to increase urine flow. The distinctive sour taste, which comes from oxalic acid, has been used to flavor salads. A similar species, yellow wood sorrel (*Oxalis stricta*), differs by having the fruit stalk upright, hairs that are spreading, and without a grayish cast. It has a similar habitat and range as southern wood sorrel.

185

CELANDINE POPPY
Stylophorum diphyllum
Poppy family (Papaveraceae)

Description: A more or less upright plant, up to 12" long, hairy, with yellow sap and showy yellow flowers. Leaves at the base of the plant and along the stem are up to 6" long and 4" wide, divided into 5–7 segments, with large, irregular teeth along each segment. The flowers are arranged in clusters of 1–4 at the end of stems. Each flower is 1¼–2¼" across and on a hairy stalk ¼–2" long. The 4 petals are bright yellow, ½–2" long, with rounded tips. There are numerous stamens with golden-yellow anthers surrounding a prominent pistil in the center.

Bloom Season: Spring

Habitat/Range: Occasional in mesic wooded slopes and ravines, and rocky banks of streams; found through the Midwest region, but absent in the northwest quarter.

Comments: A yellow dye was made from the root. This is a showy wildflower that adapts well to shaded gardens.

YELLOW PASSION FLOWER
Passiflora lutea
Passion-flower family (Passifloraceae)

Description: A vine up to 15' long that climbs or sprawls with the help of tendrils. The leaves are alternate, with 3 broad, rounded lobes, usually smooth, and up to 4" across. The unusual flowers are single, arising on stalks from the axils of leaves. Individual flowers are small, about 1" across, with several yellowish-green petals and a yellowish-green fringe. There are 5 drooping stamens around the pistil, which has 3–4 curved stigmas. The fruit is oval, smooth, black when ripe, up to ½" long, and contains dark brown seeds with gelatinous coverings.

Bloom Season: Late spring–summer

Habitat/Range: Occasional in moist or rocky woods, wooded slopes, and thickets; found in the southern third of the Midwest region.

Comments: Despite the plant's common name, the flowers are typically more of a greenish-yellow. The young shoots and tendrils of the plant are eaten by wild turkey. Yellow passion flower is the only pollen source used by a specialist bee, *Anthemurgus passiflorae*, which is the sole member of its genus. This rare bee is unusual in that despite its obligate relationship with the plant, it does not pollinate it.

LANCE-LEAVED LOOSESTRIFE
Lysimachia lanceolata
Primrose family (Primulaceae)

Description: A single-stemmed plant, up to 2' tall, with very short side branches. The stem sends out stolons (runners) at the base to produce more plants. The leaves are opposite, closely spaced, and vary in shape, from rounded and stalked on the lower stem to narrow and tapering on the middle and upper parts. The stem leaves are up to 6" long and less than ¾" wide, pointed at the tip, tapering to the base, pale green to whitish on the underside, and with stalks less than ⅝" long. The flowers dangle on long individual stalks, with each flower about ¾" wide. The 5 yellow petals have ragged edges and finely pointed tips.

Bloom Season: Late spring–summer

Habitat/Range: Occasional in mesic to dry prairies, savannas, pastures, and woodlands; found throughout the Midwest region, but absent in the western half of the northwest quarter.

Comments: Another similar species that used to be a variety under *Lysimachia lanceolata* is low-land yellow loosestrife (*Lysimachia hybrida*), which is a taller plant, up to 30", with relatively stout stems, leaf stalks ⅝" long, with long spreading hairs where it attaches to the stem, leaves green on both surfaces and typically ½" wide. Occasional in bottomland forests, wet prairies, margins of swamps, fens, ponds, and lakes; found through the Midwest region, but absent in the eastern third.

NARROW-LEAVED LOOSESTRIFE
Lysimachia quadriflora
Primrose family (Primulaceae)

Description: Slender stems, up to 2' tall, with very narrow, stalkless leaves that are opposite or in whorls on the stem. The leaves are 3" long and less than ¼" wide, with smooth edges that are slightly turned down. The flowers are on long, slender stalks that bend, causing the flower to droop. The flowers are about 1" wide, with 5 broad, yellow petals each about ⅝" long, and margins that are somewhat uneven and often with an extended point.

Bloom Season: Summer

Habitat/Range: Occasional in mesic prairies, low areas in upland prairies, wetlands, and in sandy soils; found throughout the Midwest region.

Comments: Native Americans made tea from loosestrife plants for kidney trouble, bowel complaints, and other problems. Tea from the root was used to induce vomiting. The flowers of the loosestrifes are unusual in that they produce a floral oil, rather than nectar. Insects like the Melittid bee gather the floral oil and pollen, form a ball, and feed it to its developing larvae. The flowers attract few insects otherwise. Another species, whorled loosestrife (*Lysimachia quadrifolia*), has leaves whorled in groups of 4–5, with much wider leaves, each leaf 1¼–4½" long and ½–1½" wide, and flowers about ½" across, with petals red at the base forming a ring around a center column of re-tipped yellow stamens. Occasional in upland woods and savannas; found in the north-central and eastern third of the Midwest region.

FRINGED LOOSESTRIFE
Lysimachia ciliata
Primrose family (Primulaceae)

Description: An often-branched plant, up to 4' tall, with bristly hairs along the leaf stalk and wide leaves. The leaves are opposite, up to 6" long and 2½" wide, rounded at the base, with pointed tips, and often with fine hairs along the margins. The flowers are on long dangling stalks that are attached to the leaf axil. Each flower is 1" wide, yellow, with 5 broad petals that end in ragged, pointed tips, and with a reddish base.

Bloom Season: Summer

Habitat/Range: Common in bottomland forests, wet prairies, swamps, marshes, and moist thickets; found throughout the Midwest region.

Comments: The broad leaves and fringed leaf stalks separate this plant from the other loosestrifes. The genus *Lysimachia* is named in honor of Lysimachus, a king of ancient Sicily, who is said to have calmed a mad ox by feeding it a member of the genus.

SWAMP CANDLES
Lysimachia terrestris
Primrose family (Primulaceae)

Description: A smooth, typically light green plant, 1–3' tall, often with short, upright side branches. The leaves are opposite, stalkless, up to 4" long and ¾" wide, tapering at both ends, and with a smooth margin. The flowers are along the upper part of a 6"-long (or longer) stem. Each flower is ½–¾" wide, with 5 yellow petals and 2 reddish lines down the center of each petal, with 2 reddish dots at each base. There are 5 protruding stamens that are streaked with yellow and red. In late season, some plants produce narrow reddish bulblets at the bases of the leaf stalks that resemble caterpillars.

Bloom Season: Summer

Habitat/Range: Common in open or lightly shaded wet places in swamps, marshes, bogs, wet meadows, and grassy shores; found throughout the northern half of the Midwest region.

Comments: Another species, tufted loosestrife (*Lysimachia thyrsiflora*), has small, yellow flowers in dense round clusters that are at the end of long stalks attached at the leaf axils. There are no flowers at the top of the plant; each flower is about ⅓" wide, with 6 narrow petals often dotted with black glands, and 6 long, yellow stamens that surround an orange center. Common in open or shaded wet areas, swamps, wet prairies, and fens; found through the Midwest region, but absent in the lower third.

MARSH MARIGOLD
Caltha palustris
Buttercup family (Ranunculaceae)

Description: A low, spreading, much-branched plant, up to 2' long, with hollow ridged stems. The leaves are alternate, on stalks 2–6" long, shiny, round, heart-shaped, up to 4" long, and often scalloped along the margins. Flowers are stalked, usually rising above the stems, bright yellow, 1–1½" wide, with 5 or 6 glossy, petal-like sepals, and with distinct veins radiating from the base. In the center is a ring of numerous yellow stamens.

Bloom Season: Spring–early summer

Habitat/Range: Occasional in low, wet woodlands, marshes, open swamps, and seeps; found through the Midwest region, but absent in the southwest quarter, except for one county in Missouri.

Comments: The young leaves and stems of marsh marigold have been cooked in boiling water in two or three changes to remove the bitter taste and pickled in hot vinegar for later consumption, similar to spinach.

SMALL-FLOWERED BUTTERCUP
Ranunculus abortivus
Buttercup family (Ranunculaceae)

Description: Annual, hairless plant, 6–24" tall, with upright branches and shiny leaves. The basal leaves are round to deeply lobed, up to 2" long and 2½" wide, with scalloped edges, and stalks up to 3" long. The stem leaves are alternate, stalkless, and divided into 3 narrow segments that are either toothed or lobed. Flowers are stalked, arising at the base of upper leaves, each ¼" wide, with 5 small, pale yellow petals, and a ring of yellow stamens surrounding a green bulbous center. The seeds are shiny on the surface.

Bloom Season: Mid-spring–early summer

Habitat/Range: Common in mesic upland forests, bottomland forests, margins of ponds, lakes, sinkhole ponds, old fields, ditches, and disturbed areas; found throughout the Midwest region.

Comments: Also known as little-leaf buttercup. A similar species, rock buttercup (*Ranunculus micranthus*), has hairy lower stems and leaf stalks and dull-coated seeds; common in typically drier sites, and found in the southern half of the Midwest region. There are eighteen species of buttercups in the Midwest region.

HAIRY BUTTERCUP
Ranunculus hispidus
Buttercup family (Ranunculaceae)

Description: Sparse to densely hairy plants, up to 1' tall. The basal leaves are up to 4" long, on long stalks and divided into 3 leaflets. The stem leaves lack stalks and are usually divided into 3 narrow, irregular lobes. The stems just below the flowers usually lack hairs. Each flower is ¾–1¼" wide and has 5 waxy, yellow petals and many stamens.

Bloom Season: Spring–early summer

Habitat/Range: Common in rocky, open woods and glades; also, in moist woods, seeps, and along streams in the northern range; found throughout the Midwest region.

Comments: Miami-Illinois Indians used crushed roots of buttercups to treat gunshot or arrow wounds. The Cherokee used the juice from the leaves as a sedative or as a tea for treating sore throats. Modern medical opinion is that these plants are poisonous if taken internally.

EARLY BUTTERCUP
Ranunculus fascicularis
Buttercup family (Ranunculaceae)

Description: Small, hairy plants, 4–12" tall, with distinctive, shiny yellow flowers. Leaves are mostly basal, emerging on hairy stalks up to 4" long. The hairy leaves are divided into 3 segments, which are again divided into smaller lobes. Flowers are about 1" across, with 5 shiny yellow petals that are rounded at the tip and usually streaked with green at the base. Numerous yellow stamens surround the yellowish center that turns green with maturity.

Bloom Season: Late winter–early spring

Habitat/Range: Frequent in dry prairies, savannas, and open woods; found through the Midwest region, but absent in the northern quarter, and rare to absent in the southeast part.

Comments: The common name "early buttercup" is appropriate, because it is typically the first yellow buttercup to bloom in late winter to early spring. As with many buttercups, early buttercup is considered to be a toxic plant that can cause minor skin irritation lasting minutes if touched. If eaten, symptoms include burning of the mouth, abdominal pain, vomiting, and bloody diarrhea. The sap can cause skin redness, burning sensation, and blisters.

PRAIRIE BUTTERCUP
Ranunculus rhomboideus
Buttercup family (Ranunculaceae)

Description: Plants less than 10" tall, with long, soft hairs on the leaves and stems. The basal leaves are on long stalks about 2" long, with leaves about 1½" long and ¾" wide, and with coarse, rounded teeth along the margins as the leaves mature. The stem leaves are usually stalkless and divided into 3 narrow lobes. A single flower is attached to a hairy stalk that arises from the axil of a leaf. The stems and flowers may be only 2–3" tall when they start to flower, but the stems eventually elongate. Each flower is about ¾" across with 5 small, hairy sepals, 5 yellow, glossy petals, and many yellow stamens surrounding a bulbous green center.

Bloom Season: Spring

Habitat/Range: Occurs in dry prairies, hill prairies, sand prairies, and open woodlands; found in the northern half of the Midwest region.

Comments: Prairie buttercup is among the first prairie plants to bloom in the spring. As in many buttercups, prairie buttercup is considered to be a toxic plant. Refer to comments under early buttercup (see page 191) for more details.

CURSED CROWFOOT
Ranunculus sceleratus
Buttercup family (Ranunculaceae)

Description: An annual or short-lived perennial, 6–24" tall, with hollow stems that are light to medium green, smooth, and slightly ribbed. The basal leaves are up to 3" long and wide, on long stalks, and shallow-lobed in 3–5 parts. Stem leaves are alternate, smaller in size, with 3 narrow lobes. The flowers are on stalks that arise from the leaf axils. Each flower is up to ⅓" across, with 5 shiny yellow petals, and a ring of yellow stamens that surround a large cluster of green pistils that are globe-shaped.

Bloom Season: Late spring–fall

Habitat/Range: Locally common in prairie swales, marshes, meadows, seeps, mudflats, pools in wooded areas, ditches, and poorly drained fields; found throughout the Midwest region, but less common in the southern third; also found in Canada, Mexico, Europe, and Asia.

Comments: The plant is more toxic than most buttercups. The sap causes blisters, which is probably where the common name originated. Reportedly during the Middle Ages, beggars would smear the sap of the plant on their faces to create blisters that would solicit sympathy and money from passersby. This plant has also been documented to poison cattle and cause their milk to develop a bitter taste.

SWAMP AGRIMONY
Agrimonia parviflora
Rose family (Rosaceae)

Description: Stout, hairy stems with wand-like branches, up to 6' tall. The leaves are alternate, stalked, up to 12" long, and divided into 11–23 leaflets, with the larger leaflets interspersed with many small ones. The leaflets are hairy, with many teeth along the margins. The flowers are arranged alternately along the stem, small, about ¼" across, with 5 yellow petals and 10 stamens. The flowers develop into bur-like fruits, with hooked bristles that easily cling to clothing and fur.

Bloom Season: Midsummer–early fall

Habitat/Range: Common in wet ground in prairies, wet prairies, savannas, moist woods, marshes, thickets, and along streams; found in the southern half of the Midwest region.

Comments: An herbal tea made from the whole plant has been used to stop internal bleeding; also used for diarrhea, inflammation of the gall bladder, jaundice, and gout. A similar species, tall agrimony (*Agrimonia gryposepala*), differs by having a dense covering of short, glandular hairs along with sparse, long, spreading hairs on the stems and underside of leaves; similar habitat; found in the northern two-thirds of the Midwest region. Another species, downy agrimony (*Agrimonia pubescens*), has both short, dense hairs and sparse, long, spreading hairs on the stem and underside of the leaflets; similar habitat; found in the Midwest region, but absent in the northern third.

COMMON CINQUEFOIL
Potentilla simplex
Rose family (Rosaceae)

Description: A trailing plant, often rooting at the nodes, with a stiff, hairy stem, up to 3' long. The leaves are alternate along the stem, with long stalks. The leaves each have 5 leaflets that are fan-shaped, up to 3" long, with teeth along the margins. The flowers are on long stalks emerging at the axil of the stem and leaf. Each flower is about ½" across, with 5 pointed, green sepals alternating with 5 rounded, often notched, bright yellow petals and 25–30 stamens.

Bloom Season: Mid-spring–summer

Habitat/Range: Common in mesic to dry upland forests, upland prairies, hill prairies, glades, and savannas; also, old fields and pastures and open disturbed areas; found throughout the Midwest region.

Comments: In folk medicine, a tea made from various species of cinquefoil was used for a variety of inflammations, for throat and stomach ulcers, and for fever and diarrhea. As a mouthwash and gargle, the tea was used to treat throat, tonsil, and gum inflammations.

PRAIRIE CINQUEFOIL
Drymocallis arguta
Rose family (Rosaceae)

Description: Stout, single-stemmed plants below the flower clusters, up to 3' tall, with spreading hairs on the stems and leaves. The leaves are alternate, with each leaf composed of 3–11 toothed leaflets. The lower leaves are long-stalked, with the stalks and leaves becoming progressively smaller upward along the stem. The end leaflet is the longest, up to 3". The flowers, each about ¾" across, appear on branched stems, each with 5 pointed, hairy, green sepals about as long as the petals and 5 creamy-white to pale yellow, rounded petals. There are 25 yellow stamens surrounding a yellow, cone-shaped center.

Bloom Season: Late spring–summer

Habitat/Range: Occasional in mesic and dry prairies, hill prairies, sand prairies, and savannas; found throughout the Midwest region, but less common in the southern third.

Comments: Formerly known as *Potentilla arguta*. Prairie cinquefoil's root system is a taproot with short rhizomes at the surface, which allow the plant to form tight clumps. The whole plant, including the root, has been used in tea or as a poultice (moist, warm plant material applied to the skin); to stop bleeding (as an astringent to capillaries); on cuts and wounds; and to treat diarrhea and dysentery.

LONG-LEAF GROUND CHERRY
Physalis longifolia
Nightshade family (Solanaceae)

Description: A colony-forming, upright, branched plant, up to 3' tall. The smooth stems have ridges along their length. The leaves are up to 5" long and 3" wide, thin, alternate, long-stalked, lance-shaped, and smooth to sparsely hairy. The flowers are single on stalks arising from the axil of the leaf and stem. The bell-shaped flowers are about 1½" long and attached to a dangling stalk. The 5-angled, united, pale yellow petals have purple near the base and 5 yellow stamens. The fruit is enclosed in an inflated papery husk.

Bloom Season: Late spring–fall

Habitat/Range: Frequent in wet prairies, wet depressions in prairies, savannas, bottomland forests, mesic upland forests, fields, edges of wetlands, pastures, and roadsides; found throughout the Midwest region.

Comments: Although Native Americans and early settlers ate ground cherries either raw or cooked, today the unripe fruits are considered poisonous. Ground cherries were sometimes used to treat snakebite, and a tea brewed from the plant was said to cure dropsy (edema). Insects, birds, and rodents eat the fruits in late autumn. A closely related species, Virginia ground cherry (*Physalis virginiana*), differs by being smaller, having moderate to densely hairy stems, and leaves that taper at the base; found in similar habitat throughout the Midwest region, but rare in the eastern third. Clammy ground cherry (*Physalis heterophylla*), another species, is also densely hairy and with gland-tipped hairs, 1–2' tall, with leaves broadest and rounded at the base; found throughout the Midwest region.

BUFFALO BUR
Solanum rostratum
Nightshade family (Solanaceae)

Description: An annual, multibranched plant, up to 2½' tall, with star-shaped hairs and abundant yellowish prickles that are purplish at the base. The leaves are alternate, stalked, up to 6" long and 4" wide, with irregular and deeply rounded lobes. There are long, sharply pointed, yellow prickles along the leaf stalk and the major veins on both sides of the leaf. Flowers are stalked, with 5–15 arising from near the ends of branches. Each flower is about ½–1" across, shallowly funnel-shaped, with 5 bright yellow, fused petals that have crinkled or wavy edges. There are 5 large stamens. The fruit is a round berry covered with many prickles and contains many dark seeds.

Bloom Season: Summer–fall

Habitat/Range: Locally common on disturbed portions of dry prairies, hill prairies, pastures, roadsides, and waste areas; native to the western states, buffalo bur has spread throughout the Midwest region and eastward.

Comments: Buffalo bur has also made its way to Eurasia, Australia, and South Africa, where it is regarded as a troublesome weed. The spiny fruit contains alkaloids that are toxic to mammalian herbivores, and its spines can injure their gastro-intestinal tracts and mouthparts. The spiny fruits can also cling to the fur of bison, sheep, and other woolly animals, which aids in their dispersal.

YELLOW VIOLET
Viola pubescens
Violet family (Violaceae)

Description: Small plants, up to 10" tall, with smooth to slightly hairy stems and undersurfaces of leaves. The basal leaves and 2–4 leaves on the upper stem are heart-shaped, up to 2" wide, on long stalks, with rounded teeth along the margins. The flowers are about ¾" across, on long stalks, with 5 bright yellow petals with brown-purple veins near the base.

Bloom Season: Spring

Habitat/Range: Occasional in moist or mesic woods, also on slopes, ravines, and wooded flood-plains; found throughout the Midwest region.

Comments: Yellow violet produces flowers in the spring and small bud-like flowers later in the season, which never open but self-pollinate. This process is known as cleistogamy, and it requires fewer plant resources to produce seeds because development of petals, nectar, and large amounts of pollen is not required. When the forest canopy is more closed, the plant's photosynthesis is limited and less energy is available, so many violet species have adapted to self-pollination as an alternative.

RED AND ORANGE FLOWERS

This section includes red and orange flowers. Because red flowers grade into both pink flowers and purple flowers, those sections should also be checked.

BUTTERFLY WEED
Asclepias tuberosa
Milkweed family (Asclepiadaceae)

Description: Several stout stems may arise from a common base, giving the plant a bushy appearance, up to 2½' tall. The stems are covered with coarse, spreading hairs and lack the milky latex sap that is typical of the milkweed family. The mostly alternate leaves are stalkless, about 4" long and 1" wide, widest in the middle and tapering at both ends, very hairy, and dark green. The flowers are in clusters at the tops of stems and vary from deep red to brilliant orange to yellow. Each flower is less than ¾" long, with 5 reflexed petals below 5 erect hoods. The seed pods are about 6" long and ¾" thick, with fine hairs.

Bloom Season: Late spring–summer

Habitat/Range: Common in upland prairies, glades, savannas, old fields, sandy sites, and roadsides; found throughout the Midwest region.

Comments: Also called "pleurisy root," because it was considered to be a cure for pleurisy (an inflammation of the covering of the lungs). Several tribes revered this plant as a healer. They used the leaves to induce vomiting and the roots to treat dysentery, diarrhea, constipation, lung inflammations, rheumatism, fever, and pneumonia. The roots were also mashed and applied externally to bruises, swellings, and wounds. Butterfly weed is appropriately named for its popularity with butterflies, especially the monarch butterfly. The larvae consume the leaves, while the adults feed on the nectar.

BLANKETFLOWER
Gaillardia pulchella
Aster family (Asteraceae)

Description: An annual or short-lived perennial, up to 2' tall, with freely branching, hairy stems. The leaves are alternate, 1–4" long and ¼–1" wide, and either lacking teeth along the margins, or toothed, or lobed. The showy flower heads are 1–2" across on long stalks, with the 6–16 petal-like ray flowers red or reddish-purple, with yellow tips that are 3-lobed. The tubular disk flowers are purple.

Bloom Season: Late spring–early fall

Habitat/Range: Occasional to common in prairies and disturbed sites to the west and south of the Midwest region, but frequently cultivated and escaped elsewhere.

Comments: Also known as firewheel and Indian blanket, this showy wildflower is often planted as an ornamental in gardens. The common name suggests its resemblance to the rich and warm colors and patterns of the blankets woven by Native Americans. However, some authorities suggest this common name originally referred to the habit of wild populations of these plants to form colonies and blanket the ground. A similar species, common blanketflower (*Gaillardia aristata*), is perennial, up to 3' tall, with flowers up to 3" across, with rays yellow and reddish-purple at the base; rare in prairies in the northwest quarter of the Midwest region, but more common westward; also escaped from cultivation elsewhere in the northern half of the region.

199

SPOTTED TOUCH-ME-NOT
Impatiens capensis
Touch-me-not family (Balsiminaceae)

Description: Annual plants growing up to 5' tall, with branched stems that are somewhat weak and watery. The stems are pale green and translucent, with leaves alternate, oval, thin, and bluish-green. The leaves are up to 3½' long, with long stalks and widely spaced teeth along the margins. Flowers are shaped like a cornucopia, up to 1¼" long, hanging on a slender stalk. The smaller end of the flower is a curved spur, which holds the nectar. The fruit is a slender capsule about 1" long, which splits and propels the seed when touched.

Bloom Season: Late spring–summer

Habitat/Range: Common in moist, low woodlands, at the base of bluffs, low thickets, and banks of streams; found throughout the Midwest region.

Comments: Water sometimes is exuded along the leaf margins in humid conditions and appears as glistening drops, giving rise to its other name, "jewelweed." The Potawatomi and settlers applied the juice of touch-me-not to relieve the itch of poison ivy. Even today, the juice is used to relieve the burning sensation of stinging nettle, which often grows not far from touch-me-not. The juice is also thought to neutralize the oil of poison ivy after contact. Livestock have been poisoned by eating large amounts of the fresh green plants.

CARDINAL FLOWER
Lobelia cardinalis
Bellflower family (Campanulaceae)

Description: The leafy stem is usually unbranched, up to 4' tall, with milky sap. The basal leaves have short stalks and are up to 6" long and about 2" wide. The stem leaves are alternate, stalkless, narrow, and less than 2" long. The leaves are widest in the middle and taper at both ends, with fine teeth along the margins. The crimson flowers are alternately arranged on short stalks along a dense spike at the top of the plant. Each flower is about 1½" long with 2 lips: The upper lip has 2 small, narrow lobes, and the lower lip has 3 lobes. The 5 stamens and style extend from a red central column.

Bloom Season: Midsummer–early fall

Habitat/Range: Locally frequent in wet sites, including open woods, wet meadows, swamps, marshy depressions in prairies, and borders of prairie streams, as well as ditches and wet roadsides. Found through the Midwest region, but absent in the northern part of the northwest quarter.

Comments: The crimson, tubular flowers are a favorite with hummingbirds. The Meskwaki crushed and dried the plant and threw it to the winds to ward off approaching storms. It was also scattered over a grave as the final ceremonial rite. Other tribes used a root tea as treatment for stomachache and intestinal worms, and as an ingredient in a love potion. Leaf tea was used for colds, nosebleeds, fever, headache, and rheumatism.

ROYAL CATCHFLY
Silene regia
Pink family (Caryophyllaceae)

Description: Slender plants, up to 5' tall, with generally smooth stems on the lower part but with sticky hairs near the top. The leaves are opposite and stalkless, with 10–20 pairs along the stem. Each leaf is about 5" long and 3" wide, smooth along the margins, slightly clasping at the base, and blunt to slightly pointed at the tip. The flowers are crimson, tubular, about 1" long, with sticky hairs along the 5-toothed calyx, and with 5 narrow petals with small teeth along the tips. There are 10 stamens extending beyond the petals.

Bloom Season: Late spring–summer

Habitat/Range: Uncommon to rare in mesic to dry upland prairies, savannas, woodlands, borders of glades, and along fencerows in former prairie habitat. Found mostly in the southwest quarter of the Midwest region, rare to endangered in the southeast quarter, and absent in the northern half.

Comments: Royal catchfly is a very showy plant that is becoming rare or eliminated from loss of habitat throughout its range. The bright, tubular flowers attract larger butterflies like the black swallowtail; also, ruby-throated hummingbirds. The plant's showy color and long flowering period make it an excellent butterfly and wildflower garden addition. Plants and seeds are often available from nurseries and companies that sell wildflowers rather than collecting from the wild. The sticky calyx with its gland-tipped hairs traps small insects, giving the plant its common name of "catchfly."

FIRE PINK
Silene virginica
Pink family (Caryophyllaceae)

Description: A plant, up to 2' tall, with several spreading, hairy, sticky stems. The basal leaves are long, narrow, 1½–4" long and ¼–¾" wide, and stalked, while the stem leaves are opposite, narrow, stalkless, and up to 3" long. The flowers, up to 1½" across, are on long stems that arise above the upper leaves. The brilliant red flowers have 5 narrow petals, with a notch at each tip.

Bloom Season: Mid-spring–early summer

Habitat/Range: Occasional in mesic woods, rocky, open woods, ledges, and wooded slopes; found in the southern half of the Midwest region.

Comments: A common name for the genus *Silene* is "catchfly," which refers to the sticky, insect-trapping hairs on the calyx and stem. The bright red flowers of fire pink attract hummingbirds.

WOOD LILY
Lilium philadelphicum
Lily family (Liliaceae)

Description: Stems arise from a small bulb and vary from ½–3' tall, with alternate or opposite leaves on the lower stem and whorls of 4–7 leaves on the upper part of the stem. The leaves are pointed and 2–4" long and less than ½" wide. The 1–3 showy, reddish-orange to red flowers are 3–4" across, upright, with 3 petal-like sepals and 3 petals. Inside the flower, on the lower parts of the sepals and petals, there are purplish spots with patches of yellow. Six prominent stamens and a stigma extend beyond the flower.

Bloom Season: Summer

Habitat/Range: Uncommon in mesic prairies, moist sand prairies, and woodlands; found in the northern half of the Midwest region, and eastward.

Comments: Also known as prairie lily, this showy wildflower is more commonly found in prairies than woods in the Midwest region. Sensitive to disturbance, the presence of prairie lily is an indicator of a high-quality prairie.

MICHIGAN LILY
Lilium michiganese
Lily family (Liliaceae)

Description: A stately plant arising from a bulb, with a smooth, stout stem, up to 6' tall. The lower leaves are in whorls around the stem, while the upper leaves are alternate. The leaves are waxy and thick, up to 5" long and less than 1" wide, broadest near the middle, tapering at both ends, and with the margins of the leaves and midvein roughened. The flowers hang down from long stalks at the top of the stem. There are 1–12 flowers, depending upon the age of the plant and how much sunlight it receives. Each flower is up to 3" wide, with 3 petal-like sepals and 3 petals that all strongly curve back. The orange-yellow to orange-red sepals and petals sometimes fade to yellow on the underside and have many dark purple spots. The 6 reddish-brown stamens and the stigma show prominently, and the anthers are less than ½" in length.

Bloom Season: Early summer–midsummer

Habitat/Range: Occasional in mesic prairies, depressions in prairies, edges of woods, moist thickets, and moist savannas; found throughout the Midwest region.

Comments: Some tribes of Native Americans used the roots to thicken soups, and others used a tea made from the bulbs to treat snakebite. When chewed to a paste, the flower was a treatment for spider bites. A similar species, Turk's cap lily (*Lilium superbum*), differs by having anthers over ½" in length, a 6-pointed, green star on the throats of its flowers, and the margins of the leaves and midvein smooth; rare in moist to dry woods and edges of woods; found in the southern quarter of the Midwest region.

INDIAN PINK

Spigelia marilandica
Logania family (Loganiaceae)

Description: Plants with smooth, square stems, up to 2' tall, with opposite leaves. The leaves are stalkless, lance-shaped, up to 4" long, and lack teeth along the margins. The flowers are showy, bright red with yellow inside, and about 1½" long, tubular, with 5 sharp lobes that flare out.

Bloom Season: Mid-spring–early summer

Habitat/Range: Occasional in moist woods in ravine bottoms and wooded banks along streams; found in the southern part of the southwest quarter in the Midwest region, and southward.

Comments: Native Americans used root tea to expel intestinal worms. The plant was also once used by physicians for worms, especially in children. Side effects include increased heart action, vertigo, convulsions, and possibly death.

YELLOW FRINGED ORCHID

Platanthera ciliaris
Orchid family (Orchidaceae)

Description: A stem from 1½–3' tall with a column of showy, yellow to orange flowers. The leaves are alternate, with 2–5 leaves up to 12" long that are reduced in size progressively upward along the stem. The flowers are clustered at the top of the stem with 30–60 yellow to orange flowers, each about 1" long. There are 3 rounded sepals, with the top sepal forming a hood, 2 small, narrow, slightly fringed upper petals, and a lower lip that is narrow and deeply fringed along the margin. There is a slender spur with nectar that protrudes from the base of the flower.

Bloom Season: Summer–early fall

Habitat/Range: Rare in moist sand prairies, sand flats, acid seeps, and bogs; found in the southeast part of the southwest quarter and the northeast quarter of the Midwest region.

Comments: Also known as orange fringed orchid. The Cherokee made a tea of the plant parts for treating headache. The Seminole used the root for treating snakebite. The pollinators are primarily swallowtail butterflies.

INDIAN PAINTBRUSH
Castilleja coccinea
Broomrape family (Orobanchaceae)

Description: A biennial plant, with single, hairy stems, typically up to about 12" tall. The leaves are alternate, stalkless, yellowish-green, hairy, ¾–3" long, and divided into 3 lobes. The flowers are concentrated in a dense cluster at the top of the stem that elongates as the flowers open. The brilliant red color does not come from the flower but from leafy bracts that arise from under each flower. The inconspicuous flower is greenish-yellow and tubular. Although typically red, Indian paintbrush is sometimes yellow.

Bloom Season: Spring–early summer

Habitat/Range: Common in mesic and dry prairies, sand prairies, savannas, glades, and fens; found throughout the Midwest region, but less common in the southeast part.

Comments: Typical of many members of this family, Indian paintbrush is a partial parasite, sometimes attaching to roots of other plants to obtain nourishment. Native Americans used weak flower tea as a treatment for rheumatism and as a contraceptive; they also used it as a secret love charm in food, and as a poison "to destroy your enemies."

COLUMBINE
Aquilegia canadensis
Buttercup family (Ranunculaceae)

Description: A smooth to slightly hairy plant with openly branching stems, up to 3' tall. The few basal leaves and lower stem leaves have long stalks, with clusters of 3 leaflets, with each leaflet having several deep lobes. The upper stem leaves have 3 leaflets on short stalks with lobed margins. The distinctive flowers are up to 2" long, nodding, and on slender curved stalks. The 5 yellow, triangular petals are attached between the red sepals. Each of the 5 yellow petals ends in a long red spur tipped with a nectar gland. Numerous stamens extend from the flower.

Bloom Season: Mid-spring–early summer

Habitat/Range: Occasional in rocky woods, slopes, and ledges; found throughout the Midwest region.

Comments: The flower is pollinated by hummingbirds, moths, and butterflies, which all have long tongues in order to reach the nectar located at the tip of the spur. Omaha and Ponca men rubbed pulverized seeds on their palms as a love potion before shaking hands with a loved one. This practice also was supposed to make them more persuasive when speaking to a council. The root was chewed or taken as a weak tea for diarrhea, stomach troubles, and uterine bleeding, and as a diuretic.

PINK FLOWERS

This section includes flowers ranging from pale pinkish-white to vivid electric pink to pinkish-magenta. Because pink flowers grade into purple flowers or white flowers, those sections should also be checked.

SPREADING DOGBANE
Apocynum androsaemifolium
Dogbane family (Apocynaceae)

Description: A branching plant with no defined central stalk, 1–3' tall, with green or red stems and milky sap. The leaves are opposite, often drooping, stalked, 1½–4" long and 2½" wide, with oval, rounded bases, bluntly pointed tips, and hairy underneath. The flowers are stalked, in open clusters at the branch tips, bell-shaped, about ⅜" long, pink to white, with pink stripes on the inside, with 5 spreading, triangular lobes that curl back. The fruit is a dangling, slender pod, 2–6" long and ⅛" wide, that ripens from green to a dull red.

Bloom Season: Summer

Habitat/Range: Locally abundant in open woods, woodland edges, sandy woods, thickets, old fields, and roadsides; found throughout the Midwest region.

Comments: Native Americans used the root of this plant to induce sweating and vomiting; also, to treat headache, sluggish bowels, liver disease, indigestion, rheumatism, and syphilis. Spreading dogbane is considered poisonous, but has shown antitumor activity.

CLASPING MILKWEED
Asclepias amplexicaulis
Milkweed family (Asclepiadaceae)

Description: Single, unbranched stems, with milky sap, up to 30" long, often curving upward instead of being totally erect. The plants are smooth, with up to 5 pairs of leaves. The leaves are up to 6" long and 3" wide, with leaf bases frequently overlapping that of the opposite leaf, and with wavy or curly margins. There is typically 1 flower cluster on each plant (sometimes 2), each with 20–40 flowers on long stalks. Each flower is up to ¾" long, with reflexed green to pink petals flanking 5 pink, cuplike hoods. The seed pods are 4–6" long.

Bloom Season: Mid-spring–early summer

Habitat/Range: Occasional in dry upland prairies, sand prairies, and dry open woodlands; found throughout the Midwest region, but absent in the northern quarter, and rare in the eastern third.

Comments: Also known as blunt-leaved milkweed and sand milkweed. The loose cluster of flowers on long stalks gives the resemblance to a starburst fireworks display.

SWAMP MILKWEED
Asclepias incarnata
Milkweed family (Asclepiadaceae)

Description: This smooth-stemmed, branching plant, up to 5' tall, has milky sap and narrow, opposite leaves. The leaves are up to 6" long and 1" wide, pointed at the tip, and narrowed at the base, with short stalks. The flowers are clustered at the tops of branches. Each flower is about ¼" across, with 5 reflexed, pink petals surrounding 5 light pink to whitish hoods. The seed pods are paired, slender, up to 4" long, and tapering at both ends.

Bloom Season: Summer

Habitat/Range: Common in wet prairies, marshes, sloughs, and along streams; found throughout the Midwest region.

Comments: Swamp milkweed is the only milkweed found growing in saturated soils. This milkweed is gaining in popularity as a garden ornamental, especially in rain gardens. The flowers are also very popular with many kinds of insects, including bumblebees, honeybees, and butterflies, including monarch butterflies. New England colonists used swamp milkweed to treat asthma, rheumatism, syphilis, and intestinal worms, and as a heart tonic.

PRAIRIE MILKWEED
Asclepias sullivantii
Milkweed family (Asclepiadaceae)

Description: Sturdy, thick-stemmed, hairless plants, up to 3' tall, with milky sap. The egg-shaped leaves are stalkless, opposite, up to 7" long and 3½" wide, with pointed tips and broad bases. The midrib of the leaf is typically reddish-pink. There are from 1 to several flower clusters near the top of the stem, with each cluster having up to 40 flowers. Each flower is about ½" across with 5 reddish-pink petals that are reflexed, and 5 erect, pink hoods. The fruiting pods are about 4" long and 1½" wide, and typically have soft, pointed projections on the upper half.

Bloom Season: Early summer–midsummer

Habitat/Range: Occasional in mesic to wet prairies; found throughout the Midwest region, but rare to absent in the northern third.

Comments: Also known as Sullivant's milkweed, it is found in high-quality mesic and wet prairies. The species name, *sullivantii*, was named for William Starling Sullivant (1803–1873), a botanist from Columbus, Ohio, who was the leading American bryologist of his time. His studies of bryophytes (mosses and liverworts) formed the basis for further investigations of these plants in the United States.

COMMON MILKWEED

Asclepias syriaca
Milkweed family (Asclepiadaceae)

Description: A robust plant, up to 5' tall, with a stout stem, large leaves, and large flower clusters. The stem is unbranched, with fine hairs and milky sap. The leaves are opposite, thick, leathery, generally oval, hairy, on short stalks, up to 8" long and 4" wide, and with pinkish veins. The pink flowers are about ¼" across, with 5 reflexed petals surrounding 5 spreading hoods, each about ⅛–¼" long, and with 5 tiny, pointed horns arising from them. The fruits are pods up to 4" long, with soft spines on the surface, and filled with numerous seeds, each with silky hairs at one end.

Bloom Season: Late spring–summer

Habitat/Range: Common to abundant in open disturbed areas, including pastures, fields, and roadsides; occasional in prairies, especially degraded prairies; found throughout the Midwest region.

Comments: Native Americans used root tea as a laxative and as a diuretic to expel kidney stones and treat dropsy (edema). The milky latex sap was applied to warts, moles, and ringworm. Common milkweed was also used by early American physicians for treating asthma and rheumatism. A similar species, showy milkweed (*Asclepias speciosa*), differs by having larger flowers and exceptionally long hoods, each about ½" long, that make the flower heads showy; also, its horns are long and slender. Common in moist, sandy, or rocky prairies and along prairie streams; found in the western half of the northwest quarter of the Midwest region, and westward.

210

TWINFLOWER
Linnaea borealis
Honeysuckle family (Caprifoliaceae)

Description: This delicate, evergreen, woody plant is only 3–6" tall and has stems that creep along the ground, rooting at the nodes to form large colonies. The leaves are evergreen, nearly basal, opposite, ¾" long and nearly as wide, oval, with small teeth at the tip, and tapering to a short stalk at the base. The flowers are in pairs, small, nodding, pink, about ½" long, with 2 tiny bracts and a green ovary at the base. The funnel-shaped flower has 5 shallow, pale-tipped lobes and 4 short stamens.

Bloom Season: Late spring–summer

Habitat/Range: Common in woods, swamps, and in moss mats or needle litter; found throughout the northern half of the Midwest region.

Comments: Twinflower is found throughout the Northern Hemisphere in circumboreal habitats from Siberia to Sweden, and across North America. The plant is reportedly named for Carl Linnaeus, born in Sweden in 1707, and considered to be the "Father of Modern Taxonomy." This was Linnaeus's favorite plant, named in his honor by his friend and teacher, Jan Frederik Gronovius.

SKELETON PLANT
Lygodesmia juncea
Aster family (Asteraceae)

Description: Stiff, hairless, much-branched plants, 6–18" tall, with milky to yellowish sap. The lower leaves are small, narrow, alternate, ½–2" long and less than ⅛" wide, while the upper leaves are inconspicuous and scale-like. The flower heads are single at the tops of branches, with each head ½–¾" across and consisting of 5 pink to lavender, petal-like ray flowers, each with 5 small teeth at the tips.

Bloom Season: Summer

Habitat/Range: Common in dry upland prairies, hill prairies, pastures, and roadsides; found in the western half of the northwest quarter of the Midwest region.

Comments: The stems appear leafless, which inspired the name "skeleton plant." Spherical galls are often seen on the stems, caused by the gall wasp. Native Americans used the plant to treat diarrhea, coughs, heartburn, and kidney ailments. Skeleton plant is unpalatable to livestock because of its bitterness.

WIDOW'S CROSS
Sedum pulchellum
Stonecrop family (Crassulaceae)

Description: Small, winter annual plants, up to 8" tall, with fleshy stems and leaves. The leaves are alternate, crowded along the stem, narrow, round in diameter, and up to ¾" long. The lower leaves wither at flowering time. The flowers are densely packed along 3–5 horizontal branches at the top of the stem. Each flower is small, about ⅜" across, with 5 narrow, whitish to pink petals and 5 red-tipped stamens. The stem and leaves often turn red with age and exposure to sun.

Bloom Season: Late spring–midsummer

Habitat/Range: Common in glades with shallow acid soils derived from sandstone, chert, or igneous rock; also, in limestone glades; found in the southwest quarter of the Midwest region.

Comments: A closely related species, Nuttall's sedum (*Sedum nuttallianum*), differs by having yellow petals, with leaves up to ½" long, and is found in the southwest part of the Midwest region on chert and sandstone glades.

SHOWY TICK TREFOIL
Desmodium canadense
Bean family (Fabaceae)

Description: Plants up to 6' tall, branched above, with long, soft hairs on the stem. Leaves are alternate along the stem on stalks ¾" long, with a pair of bracts at the base, and divided into 3 leaflets. The leaflets are hairy, about 3" long and 1" wide, and two to three times longer than broad. The flowers are in elongated clusters, with each flower about ½" long. The bright pink to purplish petals have a large, flaring upper petal, and 2 small side petals flanking a keel-like lower lip. The fruit pods are in 3–5 segments, with hooked hairs along the margins that enable the pods to easily attach to fur and clothing, aiding in their dispersal.

Bloom Season: Midsummer–late summer

Habitat/Range: Frequent in mesic to dry prairies, savannas, open woods, and pastures; found throughout the Midwest region.

Comments: In general reference to tick trefoils: "There is something witch-like about them; though so rare and remote, yet evidently, from those bur-like pods, expecting to come in contact with some traveling man or beast without their knowledge, to be transported to new hillsides; lying in wait, as it were, to catch by the hem of the berry-picker's garments and so get a lift to new quarters" (Henry David Thoreau, 1856).

LARGE-BRACTED TICK TREFOIL

Desmodium cuspidatum
Pea family (Fabaceae)

Description: A mostly smooth plant, up to 6' tall, with large leaves divided into 3 leaflets. A pair of leafy appendages called "bracts" emerge at the base of the leaf stalk. The leaflets are widest at or below the middle, with the middle leaflet being larger, from 2½–5" long and 1–3" wide. The small, pink flowers are bean-shaped, about ⅓" long, and clustered at the tips of branches.

Bloom Season: Summer

Habitat/Range: Dry to moist woods, thickets, and along stream banks; found throughout the Midwest region, but rare to absent in the northern third.

Comments: The genus name, *Desmodium*, is Greek for "chain," referring to sections of single seeds attached together along the pod. The "tick" in the common name refers to the fact that each link in the chain resembles a tick, and "trefoil" refers to the 3 leaflets.

ILLINOIS TICK TREFOIL

Desmodium illinoense
Bean family (Fabaceae)

Description: Plants 3–6' tall, hairy, typically unbranched, with alternate, stalked leaves. The leaves are divided into 3 leaflets, with the middle leaflet up to 4" long and 2" wide, and with the two side leaflets smaller, about 2½" long and 1½" wide. The flowers are loosely clustered along the upper part of unbranched stems. The pink to purplish flowers are about ⅓" across, with a large, flaring upper petal and 2 small side petals flanking a keel-like lower lip. The fruit pods are in 3–6 flattened, hairy segments.

Bloom Season: Summer–early fall

Habitat/Range: Common in dry upland prairies, sand prairies, sandy open woodlands, pastures, and roadsides; found through the Midwest region, but absent in the northern third and the southeast quarter.

Comments: This tall tick trefoil can surprisingly withstand close roadside mowing, emerging with very tall stems between mowings. The stem, leaves, and fruit pods are covered with hooked hairs that easily attach to fur and clothing, aiding in their dispersal.

PERPLEXING TICK TREFOIL
Desmodium perplexum
Bean family (Fabaceae)

Description: A slender-stemmed, hairy plant, up to 3½' tall, with several branches arising from the base. The leaves are alternate, with 3 leaflets. The middle leaflet is stalked and from one and a half to two and a half times longer than it is broad. There are fine hairs flattened on the lower leaf surface. The flowers are small, pink, in loose branches, about ¼" long, and having the shape and arrangement typical of members of the bean family. The light brown seed pods easily attach to fur and clothing, aiding in their dispersal.

Bloom Season: Late summer–fall

Habitat/Range: Common in dry upland prairies, savannas, rocky, open woods, old fields, and pastures; found throughout the Midwest region, but absent in the northern third.

Comments: Formerly called *Desmodium paniculatum* var. *dillenii*. Unfortunately, it has been reclassified by taxonomists on several occasions, which may be the reason for the *perplexum* in its scientific name. The Cherokee chewed the roots of perplexing tick trefoil to treat sore gums.

DOLLARLEAF
Desmodium rotundifolium
Bean family (Fabaceae)

Description: A plant with trailing stems, up to 3' long, with some branching at its base. The distinctive leaves are alternate, stalked, hairy, and divided into 3 nearly round leaflets. The end leaflet is on a long stalk, up to 2½" long and wide, and the side leaflets are on shorter stalks and up to 1½" long and wide. The flowers are in loose clusters on long, hairy stalks arising from the leaf axils. Each flower is about ½" long, has the shape and arrangement typical of members of the bean family, and ranges from pink to pale lavender or white.

Bloom Season: Summer–fall

Habitat/Range: Common in acidic soils in rocky, open, dry woodlands, usually on crests of hills and upper slopes; occurs through the Midwest region, but absent in the west-central and northern third.

Comments: Dollarleaf is a larval host plant for the variegated fritillary butterfly and the southern cloudywing butterfly. The seeds are eaten by ruffed grouse, wild turkey, bobwhite quail, and small mammals. The plants are eaten by white-tailed deer.

SENSITIVE BRIAR
Mimosa nuttallii
Bean family (Fabaceae)

Description: A trailing or sprawling plant, up to 4' long, with angled stems and abundant hooked prickles. The leaves are alternate, stalked, and divided twice, with the numerous individual leaflets less than ½" long. The flowers are densely packed in round clusters, with each cluster about ¾–1" across, on individual stalks arising from the leaf axils. The flower petals are tiny, and the overall pink color and shape comes from 8–10 stamens in each flower. The fruit is a very prickly pod up to 3½" long.

Bloom Season: Late spring–summer

Habitat/Range: Common in dry upland prairies, savannas, openings in dry upland forests, and roadsides; found in the southwest quarter of the Midwest region and in a few scattered populations in the central part.

Comments: Formerly known as *Schrankia uncinata*. The leaflets have sensitive hairs that trigger them to close when touched. Seeds from this plant contain a purgative and have been used in laxatives. Bobwhite quail are known to eat the seeds and wild turkey feed on the leaves. This plant is also appropriately named "devil's shoestrings" by rural children running barefoot through the prickly stems.

TRAILING WILD BEAN
Strophostyles helvola
Bean family (Fabaceae)

Description: A trailing or twining annual vine, up to 5' long, often branching above. The lowest leaves are usually opposite, the rest, alternate. The leaves are on stalks and divided into 3 rounded leaflets, up to 2½" long, sparsely hairy, usually with a large lobe along one of the margins or on both sides. The pink flowers are few to several, clustered along the vine, up to ½" long, and have the shape and arrangement typical of members of the bean family, with the addition of the lower keel having a dark purplish, spur-like projection that curls back and up at the tip. The pods are narrow and up to 4" long.

Bloom Season: Late spring–fall

Habitat/Range: Occasional in upland prairies, wet prairies, sand prairies, savannas, pastures, old fields, and roadsides; found through the Midwest region, but absent in the northern third.

Comments: The closely related small wild bean (*Strophostyles leiosperma*) has silky-gray stems and leaflets; its leaflets are narrow, unlobed, and up to 2" long. The only perennial wild bean (*Strophostyles umbellata*) has somewhat leathery leaflets and lacks lobes and hairs. All three of these wild beans occupy similar habitats, but the latter is only present in the southern third of the Midwest region.

215

GOAT'S RUE

Tephrosia virginiana
Bean family (Fabaceae)

Description: A small plant, up to 2' tall, with 1 to several hairy stems emerging from the same base. The leaves are alternate, hairy, and divided into as many as 15 pairs of leaflets, with a single leaflet at the tip. Each leaflet is up to 1¼" long and ⅜" wide, with a small bristle at the tip. The dense hairs give the plant a gray cast. The flowers are in dense clusters at the tops of stems, with each flower about ¾" long and consisting of a spreading, pale yellow upper petal and 2 pink side petals that flank a yellowish pink, keel-like lip. The fruits are narrow, whitish, hairy, and about 2" long.

Bloom Season: Late spring–midsummer

Habitat/Range: Common in upland prairies, sand prairies, gravel prairies, savannas, dry, rocky woodlands, and glades; found through the Midwest region, but absent in the northern third.

Comments: Native Americans and early settlers made a tea from the roots to treat intestinal parasites. Cherokee women washed their hair in it, believing the toughness of the roots would transfer to their hair and prevent it from falling out. Some early ballplayers rubbed their hands, arms, and legs with goat's rue to toughen them. Native Americans used the root, which contains rotenone (a toxic crystalline substance found in some plant roots and used as an insecticide), to stun fish.

PALE CORYDALIS

Corydalis sempervirens
Fumitory family (Fumariaceae)

Description: A smooth, soft biennial, 1–2½' tall, with hairless, gray-green to blue-green stems that are covered with a waxy bloom. The leaves are alternate, compound, divided into many small leaflets, with rounded, feathery lobes. The lower leaves are stalked, but the upper leaves are stalkless. Flowers hang on slender stalks at the ends of stem branches. Each flower is ⅝" long, with 2 pairs of petals and a short blunt spur at the back. Petals are pale rose to deep pink, with bright yellow lips at the mouth of the tube. The fruit is narrow, with a somewhat lumpy pod up to 2" long.

Bloom Season: Late spring–summer

Habitat/Range: Common in disturbed dry sandy or rocky woods, talus slopes, clearings, and burned areas; found in the northern half of the Midwest region.

Comments: Corydalis plants contain a narcotic alkaloid and should be avoided as an edible or medicinal plant. They have been used historically as an analgesic, a sedative, and an antispasmodic, and some varieties have been used in the treatment of Parkinson's disease.

COMMON ROSE GENTIAN

Sabatia angularis
Gentian family (Gentianaceae)

Description: Annual or biennial plants, up to 2' tall, with smooth, square stems and opposite branches, giving it a candelabra-like appearance. The leaves are opposite, stalkless, up to 1½" long and 1" wide, smooth, and lacking teeth along the margins. The flowers are on individual stalks, up to 1½" across, with 5 rose-pink (rarely white) petals, with a yellow inner ring at the base and 5 stamens with yellow anthers.

Bloom Season: Summer

Habitat/Range: Locally frequent in moist depressions of upland prairies, wet prairies, open woods, and old fields; found in the southern half of the Midwest region.

Comments: Also known as marsh pink. A closely related species, prairie rose gentian (*Sabatia campestris*), differs by being somewhat smaller in stature, with alternate, fewer branches and fewer flowers overall; locally frequent in dry to mesic prairies, sand prairies, and open disturbed sites; found in scattered locations in the southwest quarter of the Midwest region.

WILD GERANIUM
Geranium maculatum
Geranium family (Geraniaceae)

Description: The stems are hairy and sometimes branched, up to 1½' tall. The basal leaves are on long stalks, hairy, about 5" across, and divided into 5–7 lobes, with prominent teeth along the margins. The stem leaves are few, usually 1 opposite pair, hairy, with short stalks, and similar in shape but smaller than the basal leaves. The flowers are in clusters at the top of stems, up to 1½" across, with 5 rose-lavender petals with fine veins, often fading to white at the base, and 10 stamens with yellow tips that turn brown with age.

Bloom Season: Mid-spring–early summer

Habitat/Range: Common in mesic woods; found throughout the Midwest region.

Comments: Wild geranium is considered an astringent (a substance that causes contraction of the tissues and stops bleeding). Chippewa Indians dried and powdered the roots to provide a treatment for mouth sores, especially in children. Both Chippewa and Ottawa tribes made a tea of the plant for treating diarrhea. The Meskwaki brewed a root tea for toothache and painful nerves, and mashed the roots for treating hemorrhoids.

LEMON MINT
Monarda citriodora
Mint family (Lamiaceae)

Description: Annuals with finely hairy, square stems, up to 3' tall. The leaves are opposite, somewhat hairy, stalked, toothed along the margins, up to 3" long and ¾" wide, and broadest at or below the middle, with a sharply pointed tip. The leaves along the upper stem are often in whorls. The flowers are in 2–6 dense clusters, one above the other along the upper stem. Each flower head is surrounded at the base by hairy, leaf-like bracts that are whitish to pinkish and with pointed tips. Each white to pink to pinkish-purple flower is ⅝–1" long, with 2 lips: The lower lip is 3-lobed, and often with purple spots or lines, while the upper lip is strongly arched downward.

Bloom Season: Late spring–midsummer

Habitat/Range: Occasional to frequent in sandy or rocky upland prairies, woodlands, glades, and pastures; found in the southwest quarter of the Midwest region, and further southwest.

Comments: Also called "lemon beebalm." The leaves of lemon mint have a distinctive lemony aroma when rubbed. Teas made from the leaves have been used to treat colds, coughs, fever, and respiratory problems.

FALSE DRAGONHEAD
Physostegia virginiana
Mint family (Lamiaceae)

Description: Single or sparingly branched stems, up to 5' tall. The leaves are opposite, stalkless, narrow, up to 5" long and 1½" wide, with teeth along the margins. The pink flowers are tightly clustered in long spikes at the tops of stems. Each tubular flower is about 1" long, with 2 lips, the upper lip resembling a hood, the lower lip, divided into 3 lobes.

Bloom Season: Late spring–summer

Habitat/Range: Occasional in wet prairies, moist areas in upland prairies, savannas, and moist soil along streams and wet fields; found throughout the Midwest region.

Comments: Also called "obedient plant," because the flowers, when moved to one side, remain in that position. The closely related species, narrowleaf false dragonhead (*Physostegia angustifolia*), differs by having narrower leaves (less than ½" wide) that are also rather thick and stiff; in addition, the flowers along the spike are more loosely spaced. Found in the central and southwest parts of the Midwest region, in similar habitats as false dragonhead.

HAIRY HEDGE NETTLE
Stachys hispida
Mint family (Lamiaceae)

Description: Square-stemmed plants, 1–4' tall, with stiff, downward-pointing hairs along the stem's edges, while the sides are smooth. The leaves are opposite, 1½–5" long and 2½" wide, with a toothed margin, a pointed tip, rounded to somewhat heart-shaped at the base, the upper surface hairy, and a stalk up to ⅜" long. Each pair of leaves is attached to the stem at a right angle to the pair below it. The flowers are whorled around the stem, usually in groups of 6 at the top of the stem. Each flower is ½–¾" long, pink to lavender, with the outer upper lip covered with short hairs that are sometimes gland-tipped. The lower lip has 3 lobes and contains dark purple spots and streaks on the inside. There are 4 dark purple stamens under the upper lip.

Bloom Season: Summer

Habitat/Range: Bottomland forests, mesic prairies, wet prairies, marshes, banks of streams, margins of ponds and lakes, and roadside ditches; found throughout the Midwest region.

Comments: Hairy hedge nettle also goes by the name of *Stachys tenuifolia* var. *hispida*. *Stachys* is one of the largest genera in the mint family. Estimates of the number of species in the genus vary from about 300 to 450, and they are found in Europe, Asia, Afric, Australia, and North America.

219

WOUNDWORT
Stachys palustris
Mint family (Lamiaceae)

Description: A square-stemmed, mostly unbranched plant, 1–3' tall, with hairs along the stem edges and sides. The leaves are opposite, up to 4" long and 1½" wide, with toothed edges, pointed tips, stalkless or up to ⅛" long, and both leaf surfaces covered with short, fine hairs. Each pair of leaves is attached to the stem at a right angle to the pair below it. The flowers are whorled around the stem, usually in groups of 6 at the top of the stem. Each flower is ½–¾" long, pink to lavender, with the outer lip covered with short hairs. The lower lip has 3 lobes and contains dark purple spots and streaks on the inside. There are 4 dark stamens underneath the upper lip.

Bloom Season: Summer

Habitat/Range: Frequent in marshes, bottomland forests, bottomland prairies, fens, margins of ponds and lakes, and roadside ditches; found throughout the Midwest region, but less common in the southwest quarter and eastern third.

Comments: Also known as *Stachys pilosa*. The name "woundwort" derives from the past use of certain species in herbal medicine for the treatment of wounds. Woundwort closely resembles hairy hedge nettle (*Stachys hispida*), but the former has hairs along the stem edges and sides, whereas the latter has hairs along the stem only on the edges, with the sides being smooth.

SMOOTH HEDGE NETTLE
Stachys tenuifolia
Mint family (Lamiaceae)

Description: Square-stemmed plants that are hairy along the ridges and smooth along the sides, usually unbranched, and up to 3' tall. Leaves are 2–6" long and about 1" wide, with the upper surface smooth to sparsely hairy, toothed edges along the margins, and stalks up to 1¼" long. Each pair of leaves is attached to the stem at a right angle to the pair below it. Flowers are in several whorls of 6 along the upper stem. Flowers are about ½" long, with 2 pink lips; the lower lip is broad, spreading, and 3-lobed, with purplish spots.

Bloom Season: Summer

Habitat/Range: Occasional in wet prairies, moist depressions in upland prairies, and sand prairies; found throughout the Midwest region.

Comments: Also known as germander. Native Americans used a leaf tea to induce menstruation, urination, and sweating. The plant was also used to treat lung ailments, intestinal worms, piles, and, externally, as a gargle and antiseptic dressing. A similar species, hyssopleaf hedge nettle (*Stachys aspera*; formerly known as *Stachys hyssopifolia*), has leaves with stalks less than ¼" long. Uncommon in edges of bottomland forests, marshes, banks of streams, and moist disturbed areas; found in the Midwest region in Illinois, northern Indiana, and western Michigan.

WOOD SAGE

Teucrium canadense
Mint family (Lamiaceae)

Description: Usually unbranched plants, up to 4' tall, with fine, downy hair on square stems. The leaves are opposite, stalked, up to 6" long and 2½" wide, widest near the base, tapering to a pointed tip, and with coarse teeth along the margins. The flowers are clustered along a narrow column, with each flower on a short stalk about ⅛" long. Each pink flower is about ¾" long, with the upper lip absent; the lower lip has 2 upper lobes and 3 lower lobes. The central lower lobe is broad, with two smaller side lobes all marked with dark red to purple blotches.

Bloom Season: Late spring–late summer

Habitat/Range: Common in wet prairies, moist thickets, low disturbed open ground, moist areas in pastures, and roadsides; found throughout the Midwest region.

Comments: Also known as American germander. A leaf tea was used to induce menstruation, urination, and sweating. The plant was also used to treat lung ailments, intestinal worms, piles, and, externally, as a gargle and antiseptic dressing.

WILD GARLIC

Allium canadense var. *canadense*
Lily family (Liliaceae)

Description: A plant up to 2' tall, arising from a bulb. The leaves, which emerge mostly from the base of the plant, are long, narrow, flat, and up to 12" long and about ⅛" wide. A single, long stem contains a rounded cluster at the top on individual stalks. Each pink flower has 3 sepals and 3 petals, all identical in size, and 6 stamens. All or some of the flowers are replaced by small, hard, stalkless bulblets that fall to the ground to produce new plants.

Bloom Season: Late spring–early summer

Habitat/Range: Common in often-degraded prairies and openings in forests; also, in old fields, pastures, roadsides, and other disturbed areas. Found throughout the Midwest region, but less common in the northern quarter.

Comments: Wild garlic has strong antiseptic properties. Native Americans and early settlers often applied the plant juices to wounds and burns. The Dakota and Winnebago used the plant to treat bee stings and snakebite. Settlers used the plant for fever, blood disorders, lung troubles, internal parasites, skin problems, hemorrhoids, earache, rheumatism, and arthritis. When Father Marquette made his famous journey from Green Bay to the present site of Chicago, wild garlic was an important part of his food supply.

SHOWY WILD GARLIC
Allium canadense var. *lavendulare*
Lily family (Liliaceae)

Description: A plant, up to 20" tall, arising from a bulb. The grass-like leaves are at the base, and are long, narrow, and flat, up to 12" long and ⅛" wide. A single, long stem contains a rounded cluster of pink flowers at the top on individual stalks that are 3–5 times as long as the flower. Each pink flower has 3 sepals and 3 petals, all identical in size, with 6 stamens that do not extend beyond the petals. Bulblets are absent.

Bloom Season: Mid-spring–early summer

Habitat/Range: Common in upland prairies, glades, rocky, open woodlands, and roadsides; found in the southwest quarter of the Midwest region.

Comments: Formerly known as *Allium mutabile*. Another variety, meadow wild garlic (*Allium canadense* var. *mobilense*), differs by having a shorter stem; it is up to 12" tall, also with pink flowers, but with individual stalks that are two to four times as long as the flower. Found in the southwest quarter of the Midwest region, in similar habitat.

NODDING WILD ONION
Allium cernuum
Lily family (Liliaceae)

Description: A smooth, leafless, thin-stemmed plant, up to 1½' tall, with several shorter, flat, grass-like leaves at the base, up to 16" long. The stem bends at the top, causing the cluster of flowers to nod downward. Each flower is on about a 1"-long stalk. The light pink to deep rose flowers are small, about ¼" long, with 3 sepals and 3 petals, all identical in size.

Bloom Season: Summer

Habitat/Range: Occasional on dry prairies, hill prairies, glades, and rocky roadsides; found in scattered locations across the Midwest region, but absent in the west-central part.

Comments: The Cherokee used this plant's slender bulbs for colds, colic, croup, and fever. After a dose of spotted beebalm (*Monarda punctata*) tea (see page 170), the juice of this wild onion was taken for "gravel" (kidney stones) and dropsy (edema).

PRAIRIE WILD ONION
Allium stellatum
Lily family (Liliaceae)

Description: This plant is very similar to nodding wild onion (*Allium cernuum*), except the upper stem is straight, not bent, and the flowers are upright and not hanging down. The leaves are basal but typically wither and disappear at the time of flowering. The flowers of prairie wild onion are a deep reddish-pink, compared to the pale pink flowers of nodding wild onion.

Bloom Season: Midsummer–fall

Habitat/Range: Frequent in dry prairies, hill prairies, dry, rocky sites associated with limestone, and along rocky roadsides; found mainly in the western third of the Midwest region.

Comments: Also known as autumn onion and cliff onion, this is the characteristic late-summer-early-fall-blooming wild onion in the Midwest region. The flowers attract small flying insects, primarily hoverflies and small bees.

PINK POPPY MALLOW
Callirhoe alcaeoides
Mallow family (Malvaceae)

Description: A spreading plant, ½–2' tall, with a thick, turnip-like rootstock. Stems are few to several and branched from the base. Leaves are alternate, stalked, 1½–4" long and 1–3" wide, with 5–7 lobes. Flowers are single or in small clusters on stalks up to 4" long. Each flower is ¾–1¾" wide, with 5 pale pink to white to pale lavender lobes that are often fringed at the tip. The stamens are numerous and united into a column.

Bloom Season: Late spring–summer

Habitat/Range: Infrequent on rocky or sandy prairies and open woods; found in scattered locations in the central and southwest parts of the Midwest region.

Comments: The flowers have a fragrant odor, and the roots of poppy mallows have been used as a substitute for sweet potatoes. The Osage dug the roots of poppy mallows in late summer or fall and stored them in caches to eat during the winter. The leaves are also edible, and have been used to thicken soups.

MEADOW BEAUTY
Rhexia virginica
Melastoma family (Melastomataceae)

Description: Short plants, up to 2' tall, with exotic-looking flowers, gland-tipped hairs, and square stems with wings. The leaves are opposite, stalkless, up to 2½" long and about 1" wide, with 3 veins along the leaf. The flowers are pink to rose-colored, about ¾" across, with gland-tipped hairs on the buds and calyx. There are 4 broad petals and 8 bright yellow stamens.

Bloom Season: Summer–fall

Habitat/Range: Rare to uncommon in wet, acidic soils in swampy ravines and valleys, seepy areas, margins of upland sinkhole ponds, and in wet depressions in sand prairies; found in scattered locations through the Midwest region, but absent in the west-central and northwest parts.

Comments: A related species, pale meadow beauty (*Rhexia mariana*), lacks the square stem with wings and the hairs on the stem and flowers; it has narrower leaves and pale pink to nearly white flowers. Rare to uncommon, it's found along the southern edge of the Midwest region, and further south.

SHOWY EVENING PRIMROSE
Oenothera speciosa
Evening primrose family (Onagraceae)

Description: A low-growing, either trailing or somewhat upright plant, with stems up to 2' long. The leaves are alternate, narrow, up to 3½" long and 1" wide, with wavy to weakly toothed margins. The flowers emerge on long stalks from the leaf axils. A showy, pink to white flower is up to 3" across, with 4 broad petals that are cleft at the tip. The petals are tinged with yellow at the base and marked with thin, dark pink lines. There are 8 stamens and a longer style, with a narrowly 4-lobed tip.

Bloom Season: Mid-spring–midsummer

Habitat/Range: Locally common in rocky prairies, pastures, roadsides, and disturbed areas with sparse vegetation; found in the southwest quarter and westward in the Midwest region; adventive in the central and southeast portions; absent in the northern half.

Comments: Showy evening primrose is a popular addition to wildflower gardens, but it can spread aggressively by runners and seeds.

PRAIRIE GRASS PINK
Calopogon oklahomensis
Orchid family (Orchidaceae)

Description: A slender, smooth, single-stemmed plant, 4–14" tall, with the flowering stem not exceeding the grass-like leaf. The leaf is up to 13" long and ¼–½" wide. Up to 8 fragrant flowers occur at the top of the stem. The flowers range from vivid electric pink to pale pink, or even white, with 3 petal-like sepals, 1 lower and 2 lateral. There are 3 petals—2 lateral that are narrower and shorter than the sepals, and 1 upper that is flared into a triangular lobe at the end, with dense yellow hairs along its length.

Bloom Season: Mid-spring–midsummer

Habitat/Range: Uncommon in mesic to dry upland prairies and open woods; found in the southwest quarter of the Midwest region, and rare in a few locations in the north-central part.

Comments: Also known as Oklahoma grass pink. This orchid was first recognized as a new species in 1994. A closely related species, grass pink (*Calopogon tuberosus*), has brighter pink to magenta flowers that extend well above the grass-like leaf; this orchid blooms in midsummer, and is found in wetter habitats.

GRASS PINK
Calopogon tuberosus
Orchid family (Orchidaceae)

Description: A slender, smooth, single-stemmed plant, 8–21" tall, with a single, grass-like leaf that emerges from the base and does not exceed the height of the stem. The leaf is up to 13" long and ¼–½" wide. Up to 10 bright pink to magenta flowers occur at the top of the stem. Each flower has 3 petal-like sepals—1 lower and 2 lateral. There are 3 petals—2 lateral that are narrower and shorter than the sepals, and 1 upper that is flared into a rounded lobe at the end, with dense yellow hairs along its length.

Bloom Season: Spring–midsummer

Habitat/Range: Uncommon in wet prairies, meadows, marshes, and bogs; found in the northern half of the Midwest region and in a few scattered locations in the southern half.

Comments: Formerly called *Calopogon pulchellus*, grass pink is closely related to prairie grass pink (*Calopogon oklahomensis*). The latter has the flowering stem not exceeding the grass-like leaf, with pale pink flowers, and is found in dry to mesic upland prairies.

FAIRY SLIPPER
Calypso bulbosa
Orchid family (Orchidaceae)

Description: Small, single-stemmed plant, 3–6" tall, with a single leaf that emerges in the fall, persists over winter, and dies back after flowering in the spring. The leaf is basal, smooth, broadly rounded, 1–2¼" long and ¾–1¼" wide, and lies flat along the ground attached to a slender stalk. The purplish stem is nodding at the tip, with a narrow, pointed, upright bract at the base of the flower. The flower is 1¼" tall and 1" wide, pink, with 2 narrow, pointed, twisting, spreading petals, 3 similar sepals, and a hood that extends out over the lower lip. The broadly cupped lower lip has purple marking and a zone of yellow hairs on the inner surface.

Bloom Season: Mid-spring–early summer

Habitat/Range: Rare and local in moist to wet forests; found in the northern quarter of the Midwest region.

Comments: Another small, single-stemmed orchid is dragon's mouth (*Arethusa bulbosa*), 3–14" tall, with a single narrow, upright, pointed, grass-like leaf, 2–4" long, that develops after the plant flowers. The flower's petals and sepals are similar to that of the fairy slipper, but the lower lip curves out and downward. Dragon's mouth is rare and occurs in wetter habitat, including bogs, swamps, and fens; found in the northern half of the Midwest region, with a few locations in the southeast quarter.

PINK LADY'S SLIPPER
Cypripedium acaule
Orchid family (Orchidaceae)

Description: Plants often growing in groups, 6–17" tall, with a bristly stem that supports a single flower. There are 2 basal leaves, 3½–9" long and 1–3½" wide, finely bristled on the surface, and stalkless. The flowers are large, with a showy, pink, inflated, slipper-like lip, about 1½–2½" long, that is cleft down the middle and covered in fine hairs. There are 2 narrow, twisted petals on each side of the lip and 2 lateral fused sepals behind the lip, with the third sepal forming a hood above the lip. The sepals and petals are brownish-green in color. A green, leaf-like bract at the flower's base arches over the ovary and upper sepal.

Bloom Season: Late spring–midsummer

Habitat/Range: Locally common in open woods, swamps, and bogs; found in the northern half of the Midwest.

Comments: Also known as moccasin flower. This orchid was widely used in the 19th century as a sedative for headache, hysteria, insomnia, and nervous irritability. Native Americans also used the root in a variety of medicines.

SHOWY LADY'S SLIPPER ORCHID
Cypripedium reginae
Orchid family (Orchidaceae)

Description: Unbranched plant, up to 3' tall, with glandular hairs on the stem and leaves. There are 4–12 leaves along the stem, alternate and pleated. The leaves are up to 10" long and 7" wide, with the base of the leaf clasping the stem. One to 2 showy flowers appear at the top of the stem, each with an upright, leaf-like bract, up to 5" long. The flower has a large, pink slipper, up to 2" long, flanked on each side by narrow, white petals. There are 2 white, petal-like sepals fused behind the lip and 1 upper sepal that is erect and broad.

Bloom Season: Summer

Habitat/Range: Uncommon in wet prairies, meadows, marshes, bogs, and swamps; found primarily in the northern half of the Midwest region, and rare in scattered locations in the southern half.

Comments: Showy lady's slipper once earned second place in a poll ranking the most beautiful flowers of the continent. It is the largest and most colorful of the lady's slipper orchids, and its Latin name suggests that it is the "queen" of the lineage. Its rarity is attributed not only to loss of habitat, but also to unsuccessful attempts to transplant and commercially market these sensitive orchids.

ROSE POGONIA
Pogonia ophioglossoides
Orchid family (Orchidaceae)

Description: A slender, single-stemmed plant, 6–18" tall, with a single leaf about halfway up the stem. The leaf is 1½–4" long and up to ¾" wide, broadest at the middle and tapering at both ends, with a pointed tip, and a base that clasps the stem. The flowers are a bright pink, single (rarely double), 1–2" across, with a leaf-like bract behind the flower that emerges at its base. The flower has an upper sepal that stands erect at the top, 2 lateral petals forming a hood just below it, and two side sepals that flare out to the sides. The lip has prominent fringed edges, dark purple mottling, and a yellow and white bearded throat.

Bloom Season: Late spring–early summer

Habitat/Range: Occasional in swamps, wet meadows, bogs, fens, and peaty wetlands; found in the northern third of the Midwest region, and rare elsewhere.

Comments: Also known as snake-mouth orchid. The genus name, *Pogonia,* is from the Greek word meaning "bearded," while the species name, *ophioglossoides*, also from the Greek, means "snake" (*ophis*) and "tongue" (*glossa*). (The reference is to a perceived similarity to the adder's tongue fern rather than to an actual snake's mouth.)

VIOLET WOOD SORREL
Oxalis violacea
Wood sorrel family (Oxalidaceae)

Description: Small plants, up to 6" tall, with numerous 3-parted leaves arising from the base on stalks. The leaflets are slightly to deeply folded, with small notches at the tip, often with spots or blotches of purple on the upper surface, and often solid purple underneath. The flower stems extend past the leaves, with several individually stalked flowers at the top. Each flower is about ½" wide, with 5 pink to violet petals. The throat of the tube is green and contains 5 long, yellow-tipped stamens and 5 shorter stamens.

Bloom Season: Mid-spring–early summer, and sometimes in the fall

Habitat/Range: Common in mesic to dry prairies, savannas, and open rocky woodlands; found through the Midwest region, but absent in the northeast quarter.

Comments: The plant parts contain a sour, watery juice from which the name "sorrel" is derived. Native Americans used powdered leaves boiled in water to help expel intestinal worms. The plant was also used to reduce fever and to increase urine flow. All parts of the plant are edible and have been added to salads for the sour taste; however, using it in moderation is advisable, due to a high concentration of oxalic acid, which can be poisonous.

229

SMOOTH PHLOX
Phlox glaberrima
Phlox family (Polemoniaceae)

Description: Smooth, hairless plants, up to 3' tall, but usually less than 2' in height. The leaves are stalkless, smooth, opposite on the stem, up to 5" long and ⅝" wide, broadest at the base, and gradually tapering to a pointed tip. The fragrant, deep pink to magenta flowers are in a rounded cluster at the top of the stem, each about ½" wide and tubular, opening into 5 broad lobes.

Bloom Season: Late spring–summer

Habitat/Range: Occasional to common in moist to mesic prairies, moist sand prairies, open bottomland forests, seeps, and fens; found primarily in the central part of the Midwest region and in southeast Missouri.

Comments: The genus name, *Phlox,* is derived from the Greek word *phlox,* meaning "flame," in reference to the intense flower colors of some varieties. The species name, *glaberrima,* means "completely glabrous" (without hairs). Smooth phlox is an excellent spring-blooming phlox for the perennial border, wildflower meadow, or native plant garden.

WILD SWEET WILLIAM
Phlox maculata
Phlox family (Polemoniaceae)

Description: An erect, single-stemmed plant, 1–3' tall, hairless, with numerous purple spots or streaks along the stem. The leaves are opposite, stalkless, 2–4" long and ½–¾" wide, widest toward the base, which is rounded to heart-shaped, narrowing at the tip, smooth along the margins, and often with a glossy upper surface. The flowers are arranged in a cylindrical, branched cluster, up to 12" long at the top of the stem. Each flower is about ¾" wide, stalked, narrowly tube-shaped, with 5 pale pink to pinkish-purple lobes. The yellow-tipped stamens remain inside the tube.

Bloom Season: Summer

Habitat/Range: Uncommon in moist soil in wet prairies, meadows, fens, banks of streams, and spring branches; found through the Midwest region, but absent in the northern third.

Comments: Also known as meadow phlox. Wild sweet William is often cultivated as an ornamental. The spotted stems and elongated flower clusters easily distinguish this phlox from other phlox species.

DOWNY PHLOX

Phlox pilosa
Phlox family (Polemoniaceae)

Description: Hairy, usually single-stemmed plants, up to 2' tall, with widely spaced pairs of opposite, stalkless leaves. The leaves are hairy, up to 3" long and ½" wide, broadest at the base, and gradually tapering to pointed tips. The pink to purplish flowers are grouped into loosely branched clusters. Each flower is about ¾" across, with a long tube and 5 rounded lobes. The base of each lobe often has darker pink markings.

Bloom Season: Mid-spring–midsummer

Habitat/Range: Common in mesic to dry prairies, often rocky or sandy, savannas, and glades; found throughout the Midwest region, but absent along the northeast edge.

Comments: Sometimes specimens of downy phlox with white flowers and pink centers are found. The Meskwaki made a tea of the leaves and used it as a wash for treating eczema. They also used the root mixed with several unspecified plants as part of a love potion.

PINK MILKWORT

Polygala incarnata
Milkwort family (Polygalaceae)

Description: Annual plants with a bluish-green or grayish-green stem, about 1' tall, but sometimes up to 2' tall. The leaves are tiny, alternate, very narrow, and less than ½" long. Flowers are in dense clusters at the tops of stems. Each pink to purple (or, rarely, white) flower is about ¼" long and ⅛" wide, with tiny, green sepals, 2 larger, petal-like sepals, and 3 petals united into a tube that ends in 6 lobes that are fringed and cleft.

Bloom Season: Mid-spring–fall

Habitat/Range: Occasional in dry upland prairies, savannas, and glades; found in the southwest quarter of the Midwest region, and rare in the central part.

Comments: Pink milkwort produces seeds with fleshy appendages that are a mechanism for dispersal. The fleshy appendages (or arils) attract ants to carry off the seeds for the nutritious value, thus providing an effective way to disperse these annual plants.

PURPLE MILKWORT
Polygala polygama
Milkwort family (Polygalaceae)

Description: A small, smooth biennial, 6–12" tall, with stems often leaning over or sprawling along the ground. The leaves are alternate, narrow, up to 1¼" long and less than ¼" wide, with pointed tips and tapering bases. The flowers are alternate, short-stalked, in a cluster at the top of the stem. Each flower is ⅛" long and about ¼" wide, rosy pink to purple, with 3 tiny outer sepals, 2 wing-like sepals that appear petal-like and flare out, and 3 petals forming a tube with a fringed tip.

Bloom Season: Late spring–midsummer

Habitat/Range: Locally common in sandy soil in prairies, meadows, and open woods; found in the northern half of the Midwest region, but rare in Iowa and Ohio.

Comments: Also known as racemed milkwort. A similar species, gaywings (*Polygala paucifolia*), differs by being a perennial, being shorter, up to 6" tall, leaves oval- to egg-shaped, 1–1½" long and ½–¾" wide, and with larger flowers, ¾" long; occasional in open woods; found in the northern third of the Midwest region.

FIELD MILKWORT
Polygala sanguinea
Milkwort family (Polygalaceae)

Description: Small annual plants, less than 1' tall, usually with a single, angled stem. The leaves are alternate, widely spaced, narrow, and up to 1¾" long and ⅛" wide. The flowers are in a dense, cylindrical cluster at the tops of branches. The flowers vary from pink to white or greenish and are less than ¼" long. The flowers have 5 sepals, with the upper 1 and lower 2 small and green. The 2 side sepals are larger and pink to white, like the 3 small petals that are united into a small tube in the center, with 8 tiny, yellow-tipped stamens.

Bloom Season: Late spring–fall

Habitat/Range: Frequent in upland prairies, sand prairies, savannas, sand savannas, woodland edges, glades, and abandoned fields; found throughout the Midwest region, but absent along the northern edge.

Comments: Field milkwort has been used to treat respiratory maladies.

PINKWEED
Persicaria pensylvanica
Smartweed family (Polygonaceae)

Description: A hairy, slender-stemmed, widely branching plant, up to 5' tall. The leaves are alternate, short-stalked, up to 6" long and 1½" wide, widest at the base and tapering to a pointed tip. At the base of the leaf stalk is a brown sheath that extends around the stem. The pink to white flowers are packed in a dense, cylindrical cluster, up to about 1½" long. Flowers are about ⅛" long with 5 petals.

Bloom Season: Late spring–fall

Habitat/Range: Common in wet ground bordering streams, gravel bars, disturbed sites, and along roadsides; found throughout the Midwest region.

Comments: Formerly known as *Polygonum pensylvanicum*. Smartweed seeds were a prehistoric food source and are frequently found in archaeological sites, such as a Hopewellian village near Kansas City that was occupied in AD 635–870. The plant has long been eaten as cooked greens, but some species have a taste that is too bitter or peppery; this is what gave rise to the family name of smartweed. There are eleven native species and seven nonnative species in the genus *Persicaria* in the Midwest region.

SMALL-FLOWERED FAMEFLOWER
Phemeranthus parviflorus
Purslane family (Portulacaceae)

Description: Small, succulent plants, up to 6" tall. The leaves are numerous, fleshy, round in diameter, up to 2" long, and arising from the base. A thin, wand-like stalk supports several showy pink to rose-purple flowers, about ⅜" across, with 5 petals and 5–10 pink stamens with bright yellow anthers. The flowers do not open until late in the afternoon.

Bloom Season: Summer

Habitat/Range: Locally common in sandstone glades, and thin, acid soils over bedrock; found in the southern half of Minnesota and in the southern half of Missouri in the Midwest region.

Comments: Also known as small-flowered flower-of-an-hour. Two closely related species are prairie fameflower or rough-seeded fameflower (*Phemeranthus rugospermus*), with petals ⅜" across and 12–25 stamens; rare on thin soil over bedrock; found in the north-central part of the Midwest region. Large-flowered fameflower (*Phemeranthus calycinus*), with petals ½" across and 30 or more stamens, is another species; locally common in sandstone, chert, and igneous glades; found in the southwest quarter of the Midwest region.

SHOOTING STAR
Dodecatheon meadia
Primrose family (Primulaceae)

Description: The leaves spread out from the base of the plant that sends up a flower stalk to 2' tall. The basal leaves are stalked, smooth, up to 8" long and 3" wide, with rounded tips and a base that tapers to the leaf stalk. The flowers are clustered at the top of a smooth stem on numerous arching stalks, each ending in a single flower. The stalks bend over, causing the flowers to droop. The flowers have 5 petals, each about 1" long, that bend back, resembling the fanciful tail of a shooting star. The petals vary in color from white to dark pink, and are joined at their bases by a small, yellowish tube. The 5 stamens, with their dark brown bases, are held together to form a beak-like cone. The flower stalks become upright as fruits develop.

Bloom Season: Mid- to late spring

Habitat/Range: Common in mesic to dry prairies, savannas, rocky hill prairies, and wooded hillsides; found throughout the Midwest region, but rare to absent in the northern third.

Comments: Flowers of the shooting star have a fragrance similar to the odor of grape juice. Pollination of the flower is by bumblebees, which are strong enough to pry open the beak-like cone. Another species, jeweled shooting star (*Dodecatheon amethystinum*), has rose-purple to sometimes-pink flowers and often bluish-green leaves; rare, and with a limited range on wooded bluffs along the Mississippi, Illinois, and Missouri Rivers. Also rare is French's shooting star (*Dodecatheon frenchii*), which has white flowers, and a flat leaf base that abruptly tapers to a stalk; found at the base of shaded sandstone cliffs along the southern quarter of the Midwest region.

QUEEN OF THE PRAIRIE
Filipendula rubra
Rose family (Rosaceae)

Description: A smooth, hollow-stemmed plant with longitudinal ridges, 4–7' tall. The leaves are alternate, compound, and large, with toothed stipules at the base that clasp the leaf stalks. The leaves are sometimes more than 2' long and divided into several narrow, irregularly toothed segments of varying size on the same leaf. The end leaflet is large and deeply divided into 7–9 leaf-like lobes, each up to 4" long, which themselves are sometimes again further lobed and divided. The flowers are in branching, spray-like clusters at the tops of the stems. The deep pink flowers are about ⅜" across, with 5 small, blunt, reflexed sepals and 5 pink petals surrounding numerous stamens.

Bloom Season: Early summer–midsummer

Habitat/Range: Rare and local in moist to wet prairies, prairie seeps, and fens; found in scattered locations across the Midwest region.

Comments: Native Americans and early settlers used this plant for a variety of medicinal applications, including treatment of arthritis, fever, and skin ailments.

PRAIRIE SMOKE
Geum triflorum
Rose family (Rosaceae)

Description: Hairy-stemmed plants, less than 1' tall, with many basal leaves. The basal leaves are hairy, up to 7" long, and divided into as many as 19 toothed segments. A pair of smaller, opposite, deeply divided leaves occur along the middle of the stem. Each stem has 3–6 individually stalked, nodding flowers, ¾–1" long, with 5 triangular, pink to reddish-purple sepals surrounding 5 smaller, pinkish petals. The flowers nod and remain bud-like when young, but become erect and open after pollination. The showy fruits have long, feathery plumes, up to 2" long.

Bloom Season: Mid- to late spring

Habitat/Range: Locally common in dry prairies, gravel hill prairies, and dry fields; found in the northern half of the Midwest region.

Comments: The graceful feathery plumes resemble smoke at a distance; hence, the common name. It is also called "prairie avens." The Blackfeet boiled the plant in water to treat sore or inflamed eyes. A root tea was used as a mouthwash for canker sores and sore throat, and also applied to flesh wounds. It was also scraped, mixed with tobacco, and smoked, to "clear the head."

PRAIRIE WILD ROSE
Rosa arkansana
Rose family (Rosaceae)

Description: A low-growing, prickly shrub, usually less than 2' tall, with reddish stems, alternate, compound leaves, and slender spines. The leaves are divided into 9–11 leaflets, each about 1½" long, broadest near the base, and sharply toothed along the margins. There are 2 prominent stipules along the base of the leaf stalks. Flowers appear on smooth stalks on the upper branches. Each flower is 1½–2" across, with 5 long-pointed, green sepals, and 5 broad, pink petals, each with a notch at the tip. There are numerous yellow stamens attached to the rim of the dome-shaped extension of the receptacle. The fruits are red, round "hips" about ⅜" long.

Bloom Season: Mid-spring–early summer

Habitat/Range: Common in wet, mesic, and dry prairies, hill prairies, sand prairies, savannas, pastures, old fields, and roadsides; found throughout the Midwest region, but with few locations in the eastern third.

Comments: Native Americans used prairie wild rose to treat convulsions, bleeding wounds, eye sores, and as a stimulant and tonic. A closely related species, early wild rose (*Rosa blanda*), has nearly spineless new branches, 5–7 leaflets per leaf, and pale pink to rose flowers. Occasionally found in upland prairies, bottomland prairies, and sand prairies in the northern half of the Midwest region.

CAROLINA ROSE
Rosa carolina
Rose family (Rosaceae)

Description: A low-growing, prickly shrub, usually less than 2' tall, with alternate, compound leaves and slender spines. The leaves are divided into 5–7 leaflets, each about 2" long, broadest in the middle, and sharply toothed along the edges. There are 2 prominent stipules along the base of the leaf stalks. Flowers appear on bristly stalks on the upper branches. Each flower is 2½–3" across, with 5 long-pointed, green sepals and 5 broad, pink petals, each with a notch at the tip. There are numerous yellow stamens attached to the rim of the dome-shaped extension of the receptacle. The fruits are red, round "hips" about ⅝" long.

Bloom Season: Mid-spring–summer

Habitat/Range: Common in mesic to dry prairies, hill prairies, sand prairies, savannas, pastures, old fields, and roadsides; found throughout the Midwest region, but absent in the western half of the northwest quarter.

Comments: Also known as pasture rose, this low-growing, woody shrub is technically not a wildflower, but its showy flowers can easily be mistaken for one. The fruit, known as rose hips, contains about 100 times more vitamin C than an orange.

236

PRAIRIE ROSE
Rosa setigera
Rose family (Rosaceae)

Description: A prickly shrub that acts more like a vine that can grow 4–12' long, with short, stout spines that are not very numerous. The leaves are divided into 3—and sometimes 5—leaflets, each about 2–3" long, slightly broader at the base, and with finely toothed margins. There are 2 prominent stipules along the base of the leaf stalks. Flowers appear on stalks that lack bristles. Each flower is about 2½–3" across, with 5 long-pointed, green sepals and 5 broad, pink petals, each with a notch at the tip. There are numerous yellow stamens attached at the base of a small column of pistils in the center. The fruits are red, round "hips" about ⅜" long.

Bloom Season: Late spring–summer

Habitat/Range: Common in upland prairies, thickets at the edges of prairies, savannas, fencerows, and old fields; found throughout the southern half of the Midwest region.

Comments: Also known as climbing wild rose. Prairie rose is sometimes cultivated, and has been used in horticultural crosses with European roses.

ROUGH BUTTONWEED
Diodia teres
Madder family (Rubiaceae)

Description: Annual plants, somewhat creeping along the ground, with square, branching, hairy stems, up to 2' long. The leaves are opposite, stalkless, narrow, up to 1¼" long and ¼" wide, with pointed tips and a pronounced central vein. At the junction of the leaves, there is a pair of whitish, papery stipules with bristles along the edges. The flowers are small, about ¼" across, stalkless, and attached in groups of 1–3 at the axis of the leaf and the stem. The tubular flower has 4 pink petals and 4 small stamens.

Bloom Season: Summer–fall

Habitat/Range: Common in dry prairies, sand prairies, and pastures in dry, usually acid soils, such as sand, or thin soil over sandstone; found throughout the southern half of the Midwest region.

Comments: A closely related species, large buttonweed (*Diodia virginiana*), has stems that spread across the ground and white flowers, ⅜" across. It occurs in wet prairies, depressions in sand prairies, wet soil along streams, and roadsides; found across the southern quarter of the Midwest region.

237

PINK VALERIAN
Valeriana pauciflora
Valerian family (Valerianaceae)

Description: Upright plants, 12–30" tall, with two types of leaves. The leaves at the base of the stem are 2–3" long, long-stalked, undivided, broadly heart-shaped, and with wavy margins. The leaves along the stem are on short stalks and divided into 3–7 leaflets, with the end leaflet the largest. There are large, irregular teeth along the margins. The pink flowers are clustered at the top; each flower has a tube about ½" long that opens to five short lobes.

Bloom Season: Late spring–early summer

Habitat/Range: Locally common in mesic forests in valleys and along well-drained stream terraces; found in the southern third of the Midwest region, but absent in Missouri.

Comments: The delicate, pink, tubular flowers arranged in a cluster at the top of the stem makes this plant easy to identify when encountered. Pink valerian commonly forms colonies from runners that take root to form new plants.

ROSE VERBENA
Glandularia canadensis
Vervain family (Verbenaceae)

Description: A low, spreading plant with hairy stems, up to 2' long and 1' tall, often with several stems arising from the base and rooting at the lower nodes. The leaves are hairy, stalked, opposite, up to 4" long and 1½" wide, and usually divided into 3 or more lobes, with coarse teeth along the margins. The flowers are arranged in a flat-topped cluster, with each flower about 1" long and ½" wide, and shaped like a narrow tube, with 5 spreading lobes and notched tips. The flowers vary from pink to rose-purple to magenta.

Bloom Season: Spring–fall

Habitat/Range: Occasional in dry, rocky sites in prairies, savannas, woodlands, glades, pastures, and roadsides; found primarily in the southwest quarter of the Midwest region, and adventive elsewhere.

Comments: Also called "rose vervain," and formerly known as *Verbena canadensis*. Another closely related species, Dakota verbena (*Glandularia bipinnatifida*), differs by having leaves 1½–2" long and lobes deeply cut to the midrib; flowers are smaller, about ½" long; adventive, and found in disturbed rocky ground in a few scattered locations across the Midwest region; more common westward.

BLUE AND PURPLE FLOWERS

This section includes flowers ranging from pale blue to deep indigo and from lavender to violet. Because purple flowers grade into pink flowers, that section should also be checked.

HAIRY WILD PETUNIA
Ruellia humilis
Acanthus family (Acanthaceae)

Description: Plants with hairy, squarish stems, often branched, usually less than 12" tall. The leaves are opposite, on very short stalks less than ⅛" long or stalkless, about 2" long and 1" wide, with long hairs along the veins and leaf margins. The showy, light lavender to purple flowers emerge from the leaf axils on the upper half of the plant. Each flower is 1½–2" long and wide, tubular, and flaring to 5 broad lobes. The mouth of the flower is marked with dark purple lines.

Bloom Season: Late spring–early fall

Habitat/Range: Common in dry prairies and rocky, open woodlands; found throughout the Midwest region, but rare to absent in the northern third.

Comments: The genus name, *Ruellia*, honors Jean de la Ruelle (1474–1537), French herbalist and physician to Francois I (1494–1547), who was king of France from 1515 until his death in 1547. The species name, *humilis*, means "low-growing." The individual flowers of hairy wild petunia open in the morning and fall off by evening. A similar species, smooth wild petunia (*Ruellia strepens*), has smooth to sparsely hairy stems and leaves, leaf stalks about ⅝" long, and stems up to 3' tall; grows in moister sites, including mesic or lowland woods, and borders of streams; found in the southern half of the Midwest region.

JACK-IN-THE-PULPIT
Arisaema triphyllum
Arum family (Araceae)

Description: This plant, up to 18" tall, has a leaf divided into 3 leaflets, which is attached to a smooth, green stalk. Each leaflet is lance-shaped, smooth, up to 7" long, and lacks teeth along the margins. The flower stalk branches off from the leaf stalk near the base. The flowers are wrapped in a tube-like, green sheath called a "spathe," which folds over at the top. The underside of the hood or flap is typically purplish-green with white stripes. Inside the spathe, the flowers are crowded together along the lower end of a cylindrical, purple or green column, called a "spadix." The flowers lack petals or sepals. In the autumn, a cluster of shiny orange-red fruit is arranged along a thick head.

Bloom Season: Spring–early summer

Habitat/Range: Common in mesic upland forests and along lower slopes and in ravines; occurs throughout the Midwest region.

Comments: The Chippewa used the bulb-like underground stem, called a "corm," to treat sore eyes, and the Pawnee applied a powder made from the corm to the head or temples for headache. The corm was also used to treat snakebite, ringworm, stomach gas, rheumatism, and asthma, and it was also boiled or baked for food. If eaten raw, however, the corm's calcium oxalate crystals render it poisonous.

BLUE STAR
Amsonia tabernaemontana
Dogbane family (Apocynaceae)

Description: A branched, smooth plant, up to 3' tall, with milky sap. The leaves are alternate, firm, somewhat leathery, up to 6" long and 2" across, with a dull surface on the upper leaves. Numerous flowers are arranged at the tops of stems. Each flower is star-shaped, light blue, about ½" across, with 5 lobes. Near the base of each lobe, there is a small patch of white or pale yellow. The narrow seed pods are about 4" long and are upright. The plants turn an attractive pale yellow in autumn.

Bloom Season: Spring–early summer

Habitat/Range: Occasional in woods, low, moist ground, and roadsides; found in the southwest quarter of the Midwest region, in southwest Indiana, and southward.

Comments: The genus *Amsonia* was named for Charles Amson, an 18th-century physician of Gloucester, Virginia, by friend John Clayton, a botanist. The species name, *tabernaemontana*, was named for Jacob Theodore von Bergzabern, physician to the Count of the Palatine at Heidelberg, and author of the celebrated *Neuw Kreuterbuch (New Herb-book)* (1588), who Latinized his name to Jacobus Theodorus Tabernaemontanus, which means "tavern in the mountains." A similar species, shining blue star (*Amsonia illustris*), has a shiny surface on the upper leaves and seed pods that hang down. Occasional on gravel bars, rocky, open places along streams, and openings of dry upland forests; found in the southwest quarter of the Midwest region.

SKUNK CABBAGE
Symplocarpus foetidus
Arum family (Araceae)

Description: Plants with foul-smelling flowers and large, cabbage-like leaves that grow up to 20" long and 12" wide. The large leaves emerge from the base near the end of flowering. Each leaf has a heart-shaped base and is hairless, with wavy edges and a network of connected veins. The flowering part has a short stalk and a green to purplish-brown, pointed hood, called a "spathe," 3–6" long, that encloses a dense cluster of flowers. The cylindrical, fleshy column, called a "spadix," has tiny male flowers at the top and small, greenish-yellow female flowers below. There are no petals or sepals. The fruits are bright scarlet and about ⅜" thick.

Bloom Season: Late winter–early spring

Habitat/Range: Occasional in wet woods, swamps, seepy areas, often forming large colonies; found through the Midwest region, but absent in the southwest quarter.

Comments: Being one of the first to flower in the spring, skunk cabbage can produce enough heat while growing to melt through snow. The flowers produce a rotting smell that attracts early-season scavengers, such as carrion flies, for pollination. Native Americans used the root for cramps, convulsions, whooping cough, and toothache. Early physicians used the root as an antispasmodic for epilepsy, spasmodic coughs, and asthma; externally in lotion for itching, and to treat rheumatism; as a diuretic; and as an emetic, in large doses. Today, the roots are considered toxic, and eating the leaves can cause burning and inflammation.

WILD GINGER
Asarum canadense
Birthwort family (Aristolochiaceae)

Description: A low-growing plant, up to 6" tall, with 2 leaves emerging on hairy stalks from the base. The dark green leaves are round, heart-shaped, as much as 7" across when fully grown, hairy, and leathery, with a shiny surface. A single purplish-brown to maroon flower, about 1" across, emerges from the base of the 2 leaves on a hairy stalk. The flower is bell-shaped and lacks petals, but has 3 pointed sepals that curve backward. The inside of the tube is creamy-white, with a ring of 12 stamens that surround 6 reddish styles.

Bloom Season: Mid- to late spring

Habitat/Range: Common, often forming colonies, in mesic upland forests and along lower slopes, ravines, and in valleys; found throughout the Midwest region.

Comments: The Meskwaki considered the root of wild ginger to be one of the most important native seasonings. They also thought its use eliminated the danger of poisoning when eating an animal that had died of unknown causes. They also chewed the root and spit it on bait to improve their chances of catching fish. Settlers used the root as a spice substitute for tropical ginger. In frontier medicine, it was used to treat several ailments but is now considered by the Food & Drug Administration to be nephrotoxic (toxic to the kidneys) and contains the potent carcinogen aristolochic acid.

PURPLE MILKWEED
Asclepias purpurascens
Milkweed family (Asclepiadaceae)

Description: Slender plants with stout stems, up to 4' tall, with milky sap and opposite leaves. The leaves are thick, up to 8" long and 4" wide, tapering at each end, on short stalks, and with fine hairs on the underside. The smaller side veins are at right angles to the central vein, which is also typically red. The flowers are in large, round clusters at the top of the stem. Each deep-reddish-purple flower is about ½" long and ⅓" wide, and has 5 reflexed petals surrounding 5 upright hoods, each with a tiny, pointed horn arising from it. The fruit pods are about 6" long and ¾" thick, with fine hairs on the surface, and filled with numerous seeds, each with silky hairs at one end.

Bloom Season: Late spring–midsummer

Habitat/Range: Frequent in rocky, open prairie thickets, along prairie/woodland edges, savannas, and roadsides; found across the southern two-thirds of the Midwest region.

Comments: Milkweeds have a long medical history, but they have also been used for food. The young shoots were cooked as an asparagus substitute. The flowers, buds, and immature fruits were cooked in boiling water, which had to be changed a few times in order to remove the bitter-tasting toxins. During World War II, the milky latex from milkweeds was tested as a rubber substitute, and the plumes of the seed heads were collected by schoolchildren and others as part of the war effort. The fluffy material was used as a substitute in life preservers when there was a shortage of kapok, the silky down surrounding the seeds of the kapok tree, found in Africa and tropical America.

CLIMBING MILKWEED
Matelea decipiens
Milkweed family (Asclepiadaceae)

Description: A climbing or trailing hairy vine, up to 6' long, with milky sap and opposite, heart-shaped leaves, up to 5" long, tapering to an abruptly pointed tip. The maroon flowers are in clusters on stalks that arise from the leaf axils. Each flower has 5 upright petals, with each petal up to ¾" long. The seed pods are up to 4" long and ¾" thick, with numerous short projections along the surface.

Bloom Season: Late spring–early summer

Habitat/Range: Occasional in rocky, open woods, edges of glades, often in valleys and thickets along streams; found in the southwest quarter of the Midwest region.

Comments: A similar species, Baldwin's climbing milkweed (*Matelea baldwyniana*), has white petals; occasional in glades and rocky, open woods; found in the southwest quarter of the Midwest region.

TALL THISTLE
Cirsium altissimum
Aster family (Asteraceae)

Description: A tall, branching biennial to short-lived perennial plant, up to 8' tall, with stems that have ridges along their length and are often covered with spreading hairs. The alternate leaves grow up to 18" long and 8" wide. The leaves are usually not lobed, but have coarse teeth along the leaf margins that end in spines. The undersides of the leaves have whitish, woolly hairs. The flower heads are at the ends of long stalks. The bracts at the base of the flower heads are flat and green, with a white stripe down the middle, somewhat resembling fish scales. At the end of each bract is a short spine. The flower heads are 1½–2" across, with numerous tubular disk flowers, each about 1" long, with 5 narrow purple to pink lobes, each about ⅜" long.

Bloom Season: Midsummer–fall

Habitat/Range: Occasional in upland prairies, open woods, old fields, and along roadsides; found throughout the Midwest region.

Comments: Thistles are an important part of the common goldfinch's nesting season. Considered late nesters, goldfinches wait until the seeds ripen in August and then collect the downy filaments to line the bowls of their nests, which are surrounded by strands of plant material. Also, the thistle seeds are eaten by the adults and regurgitated to the young back at the nest.

245

FIELD THISTLE
Cirsium discolor
Aster family (Asteraceae)

Description: Stems branched near the top, somewhat hairy, spineless, up to 8' tall, with spiny leaves. The leaves are alternate, up to 9" long and 3" wide, divided into several narrow lobes that are often divided further, with small spines all along the edges, longer spines at the lobe tips, and leaf margins turned downward. The undersides of the leaves are densely covered with white hairs. The flower heads are 1½–2" across on individual, leafy stalks. Each flower head has numerous overlapping, spiny, green bracts with a white stripe that resembles fish scales. There are numerous pinkish-purple disk flowers, each about 1¼" long, with 5 narrow lobes, each about ¼" long.

Bloom Season: Midsummer–fall

Habitat/Range: Common in prairies that have had a history of grazing or some other disturbance, open woods, pastures, old fields, and roadsides; found through the Midwest region, but absent in the northern part of the northeast quarter.

Comments: Another thistle, prairie thistle (*Cirsium hillii*), is a much shorter plant, up to 3' tall, with leaves hairy underneath but not whitened, deeply lobed, and toothed along the edges, with numerous spines. The large flower heads are 2–4" wide, with many overlapping, green, spiny bracts surrounding many small, pale purple disk flowers, each with 5 lobes. Found locally frequent in dry prairies, but rare and declining over its range in the Midwest region, and absent in the southern third. Another short thistle, Flodman's thistle (*Cirsium flodmanii*), is spineless, has stems, and is less than 2' tall, arising from horizontal roots. The upper leaf surface has lightly covered, cobwebby hairs, while the lower surface is velvety white from a dense mat of hairs; the leaf margins have deep lobes that are triangular-shaped and extend to the leaf midrib. Occurs in moist prairies, meadows, and pastures; found in the northwest part of the Midwest region and westward.

SWAMP THISTLE
Cirsium muticum
Aster family (Asteraceae)

Description: A biennial with well-branched, spineless stems, 3–8' tall, and alternate leaves, up to 1' long. The leaves are deeply lobed, with spine-tipped teeth along the margins. Flower heads are on individual stalks at the tip of stem branches. Each flower head is 1–1½" wide, with an overlapping series of narrow, spineless, hairy bracts below a dense cluster of tubular flowers. Each flower has 5 pink to purple lobes and 2 extended, thread-like style branches.

Bloom Season: Midsummer–fall

Habitat/Range: Locally common in the moist soil of swamps, fens, bogs, and open woods; found throughout the Midwest region, but less common in the southern third, and rare in Iowa.

Comments: Of the thistles in the Midwest region, what sets swamp thistle apart are the spineless bracts, their cobwebby hairs, and its wetlands preference. Swamp thistle is a host for some species of butterflies and moths, including the swamp metalmark butterfly (*Calephelis muticum*), a species that is currently being reviewed as a potential species of concern in the United States. The butterfly lays its eggs on the swamp thistle, and when the eggs hatch, the flowers are the only food source for the caterpillars.

MIST FLOWER
Conoclinium coelestinum
Aster family (Asteraceae)

Description: Downy, branching, purplish stems, up to 18" tall, that can spread by underground runners. The leaves are opposite, on short stalks, oval to triangular, with large teeth along the margins. The flower heads are in flat-topped clusters, 1–3" across, at the tops of stems. Each head has 35–70 bright blue or purplish disk flowers, each with 5 lobes and an extended style that is divided into 2 parts.

Bloom Season: Summer–fall

Habitat/Range: Occasional to locally common in moist ground along streams, spring branches, ditches, and low areas in pastures; found throughout the southern third of the Midwest region.

Comments: Formerly known as *Eupatorium coelestinum*. Also called "wild ageratum," because it is similar to the annual ageratum grown in gardens. In a pasture or meadow, when viewed from a distance, the color and shape of the flower clusters resemble mist.

NARROW-LEAVED PURPLE CONEFLOWER
Echinacea angustifolia
Aster family (Asteraceae)

Description: A short, coarsely hairy plant, ½–2' tall, with mostly basal leaves, and with the stem leaves widely spaced. Leaves are alternate, with long stalks at the base and stalkless along the stem, up to 8" long and ½–1½" wide, with smooth margins, hairy and rough to the touch. The flowers are single at the end of stout, hairy stems, with 15–20 pink to light purple ray flowers, each ¾–1½" long and about ¼" wide, and with 3 slightly notched tips. In the center is a large, round to conical, orange to brown disk, with numerous 5-lobed disk flowers. The pollen on the anthers is white.

Bloom Season: Early summer–midsummer

Habitat/Range: Common in dry, especially rocky prairies, open, rocky woodlands, and rocky slopes; found in the western part of the northwest quarter of the Midwest region, and further westward.

Comments: Also known as Kansas snakeroot and black Sampson, among other names. Narrow-leaved purple coneflower was the most widely used medicinal plant of the Plains Indians. Primarily the root, but also the entire plant, was used as a painkiller, and to treat a variety of ailments, including toothache, coughs, colds, sore throat, and snakebite.

PALE PURPLE CONEFLOWER
Echinacea pallida
Aster family (Asteraceae)

Description: A stout-stemmed, showy plant, up to 3' tall, with coarse, bristly hairs on the stem and leaves. The leaves at the base are on long stalks, up to 10" long and 1½" wide, tapering at both ends, with parallel veins running along the length of the blade. The stem leaves are few, smaller, with short stalks. The flower heads are single on long stalks, with several drooping, pale purple petals, each about 3½" long, surrounding a purplish-brown, dome-shaped central disk. The pollen on the anthers is white.

Bloom Season: Late spring–midsummer

Habitat/Range: Common in mesic and dry prairies and savannas; found in the southwest quarter and the west-central parts of the Midwest region.

Comments: Native Americans used the root to treat snakebite, stings, spider bites, toothache, burns, hard-to-heal wounds, flu, and colds. It is widely used today in pharmaceutical preparations. A similar species, glade coneflower (*Echinacea simulata*), has reddish-purple petals and yellow pollen on the anthers (see inset photo); common in dolomite glades; found in the southwest quarter of the Midwest region.

PURPLE CONEFLOWER

Echinacea purpurea
Aster family (Asteraceae)

Description: A showy plant, up to 4' tall, with branching stems and rough hairs on the stems and leaves. The basal leaves are on long stalks, coarsely toothed, up to 6" long and 3" wide, broadest at the base, and tapering to a pointed tip. The stem leaves are alternate, on shorter stalks, coarsely toothed, and smaller. The large flower heads are at the ends of long stalks, and up to 5" across. The 10–20 purple, petal-like ray flowers are up to 3" long and ¾" wide, with 3 notched teeth at each tip, and surround a cone-shaped central disk. The cones are golden-red when in flower.

Bloom Season: Late spring–fall

Habitat/Range: Occasional in moist areas in prairies, savannas, and woodland edges; found through the Midwest region, but absent in the northern third.

Comments: Native Americans used the root to treat snakebite, bee stings, headache, stomach cramps, toothache, and sore throats in people, and distemper in horses. Some tribes discovered that the plant was like a burn preventative, enabling the body to endure extreme heat. They used the plant's juice in sweat baths and in ritual feats, such as immersing hands in scalding water or holding live coals in the mouth. Purple coneflower is a long-blooming ornamental widely used in wildflower gardens.

ELEPHANT'S FOOT
Elephantopus carolinianus
Aster family (Asteraceae)

Description: A branching plant, up to 3' tall, with large basal leaves in proportion to the size of the plant. The leaves are alternate, up to 8" long and 4" wide, with rounded teeth along the margins, and a leaf base that abruptly ends a long leaf stalk. The large basal leaves are often absent at the time of flowering. The upper leaves are smaller and lack stalks. Below the flower cluster are 1–3 leaf-like bracts. Each cluster has 2–5 small flower heads that have only disk florets, each about ⅜" long, which are violet to lavender to almost white.

Bloom Season: Late summer–fall

Habitat/Range: Common in wooded lowlands in valleys, ravines, at the base of bluffs, and along streams; found across the southern third of the Midwest region.

Comments: *Elephantopus* is Greek for "elephant foot," which may describe the basal leaves of these mainly tropical plants. Although the basal leaves of the three species in North America are large, they in no way match the feet of a pachyderm.

SPOTTED JOE-PYE WEED
Eutrochium maculatum
Aster family (Asteraceae)

Description: Stems unbranched, up to 6' tall, green with purple spots or sometimes purple throughout, with widely spaced whorls of 4–6 coarsely toothed leaves. Each leaf is broadest near the middle, up to 9" long and 2" wide, and tapering to a pointed tip. The numerous flower heads are in flat to shallowly rounded clusters at the top of the plant. Flower heads lack petal-like ray flowers and are made up of 8–20 pink to purplish disk flowers, each about ⅓" long. Conspicuous, thread-like, purple styles extend from the flower heads.

Bloom Season: Late spring–early fall

Habitat/Range: Locally common in moist, often sandy soils, wet prairies, wet sand prairies, marshes, and fens; found throughout the Midwest region, but uncommon in the southern third.

Comments: Formerly known as *Eupatorium maculatum*. Native Americans used tea from the plant as a diuretic for dropsy (edema), painful urination, gout, and kidney infections. Root tea was used for fever, colds, chills, diarrhea, and liver and kidney ailments.

JOE-PYE WEED
Eutrochium purpureum
Aster family (Asteraceae)

Description: A tall, slender plant, sometimes growing to a height of 10'. The stem is solid, not hollow, and green, but it may be tinged with purple, especially at the nodes where the leaves are attached. The large, thin leaves are in whorls of 3–5, on short stalks, and up to 12" long and 3" wide, tapering at both ends, with numerous small teeth along the margins. The tiny, fragrant flower heads are in large, dome-like clusters 6" across or more. Each cylindrical flower head contains 3–7 petal-like ray flowers that vary from pink to purple to almost white.

Bloom Season: Midsummer–fall

Habitat/Range: Occasional in low, moist ground, moist wooded slopes and edges, savannas, and borders of streams; found through the Midwest region, but absent in the northeast quarter.

Comments: Legend has it that Joe Pye, a Native American herb doctor of the Massachusetts Bay Colony, used this plant to treat fever; hence, the common name. The Iroquois and, more recently, people in some areas of Appalachia used parts of these plants to treat urinary disorders. Chippewa mothers bathed fretful children in a tea made from this plant to bring restful sleep. It was also traditional for Meskwaki men to nibble the leaves to ensure success in courtship. Another species, hollow Joe-Pye weed (*Eutrochium fistulosum*), has hollow, purplish stems with a whitish coating, and often more than four leaves, in a whorl; occasional in low, wet ground; found in scattered locations across the southern half of the Midwest region.

WOODLAND BLUE LETTUCE
Lactuca floridana
Aster family (Asteraceae)

Description: Slender annual or biennial plants, up to 7' tall, with milky sap. The leaves have deep lobes, up to 10" long and 4" wide, hairless, with the tip broadly triangular, and the base tapering to a stalk edged with leafy tissue. The flower heads are numerous, on widely branching stems, light blue, small, and about ½" across. Each head has 11–16 petal-like ray flowers and 14–17 bracts at the base.

Bloom Season: Late summer–fall

Habitat/Range: Occasional in moist to wet open woods, stream banks, and disturbed sites; found through the Midwest region, but absent in the northern third.

Comments: The genus name, *Lactuca*, is from the Latin word *lac*, meaning "milk," in reference to the plant's milky sap. The species name, *floridana*, means "of Florida." The young leaves have been eaten as part of salads and as cooked greens. The milky sap is bitter. A similar species, tall blue lettuce (*Lactuca biennis*), can grow up to 13' tall, with each flower head having 15–30 light-blue petal-like ray flowers and 23–25 bracts at the base. Occasional in moist woods, thickets, swamps, and along stream banks; found throughout the Midwest region, but absent in the southwest quarter.

BLUE LETTUCE
Lactuca tatarica
Aster family (Asteraceae)

Description: Plants with white, latex, smooth, hollow stems, up to 3½' tall, with a deep rootstock and branching rhizomes. Leaves are stalkless, up to 8" long, linear, hairless, with smooth edges and a whitish underside. The flowers are in branches at the top of the stem. Each flower is about 1" across, with 19–21 light blue, petal-like ray flowers and no disk flowers.

Bloom Season: Summer

Habitat/Range: Occasional in dry prairies, loess hill prairies, and open, disturbed areas; found in the northwest quarter of the Midwest region, and westward.

Comments: Also known as *Lactuca pulchella*. Blue lettuce has a wide distribution. It is also found in Canada, Europe, and Asia. Among the Zuni people of New Mexico, the dried root gum of blue lettuce has been used as chewing gum.

ROUGH BLAZING STAR
Liatris aspera
Aster family (Asteraceae)

Description: A single-stemmed plant that is hairy or smooth, up to 4' tall, arising from a corm. The basal leaves are short-stalked and up to 16" long and 2" wide. The stem leaves are progressively shorter upward along the stem. The flower heads are alternately arranged and loosely spaced along a wand-like spike, up to 1½' long. The bracts on the flower head are rounded, with white to purplish, papery tips. The flower heads are up to 1" across, with 16–35 small, purple disk flowers, each with 5 lobes and 2 conspicuous, purple, thread-like style branches.

Bloom Season: Midsummer–fall

Habitat/Range: Common in prairies, hill prairies, savannas, rocky, open woods, and glades; found throughout the Midwest region, but less frequent in the southeast quarter.

Comments: The Meskwaki used rough blazing star for bladder and kidney troubles. The Pawnee boiled the leaves and root together and fed the tea to children with diarrhea. Root tea was used as a folk remedy for kidney and bladder ailments, gonorrhea, and colic, and was gargled for sore throats. The root was mashed and applied to treat snakebite.

CYLINDRICAL BLAZING STAR
Liatris cylindracea
Aster family (Asteraceae)

Description: There are few flower heads on this stiff, short-stemmed plant, which may grow up to 2' tall. The grass-like leaves are stalkless, smooth, up to 10" long and ½" wide, but becoming progressively smaller upward along the stem. The flower heads are alternate and cylindrical-shaped along the upper stem, about ¾" long and ½" wide, and on short stalks. The bracts are smooth, flat, and not extending outward. The flower heads have 10–35 small, purple disk flowers with 5 narrow, pointed tips that curl backward, and a long style with 2 thread-like, purple style branches that protrude ½" from the flower head.

Bloom Season: Midsummer–early fall

Habitat/Range: Occasional in dry prairies, sand prairies, hill prairies, savannas, rocky, open woods, and glades; found throughout the Midwest region, but rare to absent in the southeast quarter.

Comments: The genus name, *Liatris*, may have come from the Gaelic *liatrusis*, meaning "spoon-shaped," in reference to the shape of the tuberous roots on some species. The species name, *cylindracea*, means "cylindrical," for the shape of the flower head. There are ten species of *Liatris* in the Midwest region.

DOTTED BLAZING STAR
Liatris punctata
Aster family (Asteraceae)

Description: Growing up to 3' tall, these plants often have several unbranched, hairless stems arising from a common base. Leaves are numerous along the stem, alternate, up to 5" long and less than ¼" wide. The leaf margins usually have a row of tiny hairs and many tiny, round dots on the underside. Flower heads are in dense, wand-like spikes, each up to 1' long, with many cylindrical, ½"-long heads. Each head is surrounded at the base by an overlapping series of flat-topped, dotted bracts. The flower heads have 4–8 tiny, lavender to reddish-purple disk flowers, each with 5 lobes and 2 long, thread-like style branches.

Bloom Season: Midsummer–fall

Habitat/Range: Common to locally abundant in dry, often rocky prairies, sand prairies, hill prairies, rocky woodlands, and roadsides; found in the western part of the northwest quarter of the Midwest region and westward.

Comments: The Kiowa considered dotted blazing star to be one of the "ancient" foods, and because of its ability to withstand drought, it was still an important part of their diet in the 1930s. A closely related species, narrow-leaved blazing star (*Liatris mucronata*; also known as *Liatris punctata* var. *mucronata*), differs by lacking the row of tiny hairs along the leaf margins; it also lacks the tiny, round dots on the underside of the leaf and on the bracts. Common in dolomite glades; found in the southwest part of the southwest quarter of the Midwest region.

TALL BLAZING STAR
Liatris pycnostachya
Aster family (Asteraceae)

Description: Hairy, slender, unbranched spikes, up to 5' tall, arising from a corm. The leaves are alternate, stalkless, and numerous, with the lower leaves sometimes over 1' long and up to ½" wide, gradually reducing in size ascending the stem. The numerous flower heads are in a long, dense spike, often over 1' long, at the top of the stem. Each small flower head is about ¼" across, with hairy, outward-curving bracts. There are 5–10 purple disk flowers, each with 5 lobes and 2 prominent thread-like style branches protruding from each flower.

Bloom Season: Midsummer–fall

Habitat/Range: Common in mesic to dry prairies; found throughout the Midwest region, but rare to absent in the eastern half.

Comments: Also known as gayfeather. Edwin James, botanist for Stephen Long's expedition of the Great Plains, reported from near St. Louis on June 27, 1819, that the gayfeather, "here called pine of the prairies, which was now in full bloom, has a roundish tuberous root, of a warm, some-what balsamic taste, and is used by the Indians and others as a cure [for] gonorrhea." Cultivated varieties are grown for the cut-flower market. The flowering spikes can be air-dried for use in winter arrangements.

SAVANNA BLAZING STAR
Liatris scariosa var. *neuwlandii*
Aster family (Asteraceae)

Description: A single-stemmed plant, 2½–5' tall, with moderate to dense hairs and numerous alternate, widely spread leaves arranged densely around the stem. The basal and lower leaves are stalked, about 12" long and 1½" wide, while the leaves ascending the stem are stalkless and less than 3" long. The flower heads are stalked and arranged along the upper part of the stem. The flower head at the tip of the stem is the first to bloom, and a descending order of blooming follows to the bottom, as is typical for other blazing stars. Each flower head is 1–2" across, with 25–80 purple disk flowers and no petal-like ray flowers. The two-branched styles in each disk flower extend outward, giving the flower heads a shaggy appearance.

Bloom Season: Midsummer–fall

Habitat/Range: Uncommon to rare in savannas and savanna/prairie borders; found rare to absent in the western half and uncommon in the eastern half of the Midwest region.

Comments: As the common name implies, savanna blazing star is a classic savanna species. It doesn't compete well with prairie grasses, so it grows in partial shade in savannas, where it is less favorable for prairie grasses. This plant can be found moving into degraded prairies where the grasses are decreased. When fire is applied to the prairie as a management tool, grasses increase while savanna blazing star decreases. In the Midwest region, the decline in savannas directly relates to the decline of this very showy wildflower.

DENSE BLAZING STAR
Liatris spicata
Aster family (Asteraceae)

Description: Slender, unbranched, and hairless plants, with narrow spikes, up to 4' tall, arising from a corm. The leaves are alternate, stalkless, and numerous, with the lower leaves up to 16" long and about ½" wide, gradually reducing in size up the stem. The numerous flower heads are in a long, dense spike, about 1' long, at the top of the stem. Each small flower head is about ¼" across, hairless, and having bracts with their tips flat against the head, often bluntly rounded. There are 4–8 purple disk flowers, each with 5 lobes and 2 prominent, thread-like style branches protruding from each flower.

Bloom Season: Midsummer–early fall

Habitat/Range: Locally frequent in mesic to wet prairies and moist sandy areas; found rare to absent in the western half and scattered in the eastern half, with the highest occurrences in the northeast quarter of the Midwest region.

Comments: Dense blazing star is also known as marsh blazing star, button snakeroot, and prairie gayfeather. The Cherokee used the plant to relieve pain in the back and limbs, and the Menominee used it for a "weak heart." The plant was also used to treat swelling, abdominal pain, and snakebite. Currently, the plant is used for a sore throat by gargling, and as a tea; it is also used as an herbal insect repellent, and in potpourri. Dense blazing star is a garden flower in many countries around the world, grown for its showy purple flowers.

SCALY BLAZING STAR
Liatris squarrosa
Aster family (Asteraceae)

Description: Often hairy, single-stemmed plants, up to 2½' tall, with narrow, somewhat rigid leaves. The lower leaves are up to 10" long and ½" wide, but are progressively smaller upward along the stem. The flower heads are few to solitary, each about ½" across, and emerging from the upper leaf axils. The bracts below the flower head overlap, with pointed tips that look spine-like or scaly. Each flower head has 20–40 small, purple disk flowers that are tubular, with 5 lobes and 2 prominent, thread-like style branches protruding from each flower. The flower heads toward the top of the stem tend to be larger, with more disk flowers.

Bloom Season: Summer–early fall

Habitat/Range: Frequent in dry, often rocky prairies, savannas, open woods, and glades; found primarily in the west-central and southwest quarters of the Midwest region.

Comments: Scaly blazing star was used as a diuretic, a tonic, and a stimulant. It was also used to treat gonorrhea, kidney trouble, and uterine diseases.

SOUTHERN PRAIRIE ASTER
Eurybia hemispherica
Aster family (Asteraceae)

Description: A smooth-stemmed plant, 8–30" tall, with alternate, grass-like leaves, up to 8" long and ¼" wide. Flower heads emerge from leaf axils and are clustered at the top of the stem, 1–2" across, with 15–35 blue or violet, petal-like ray flowers surrounding 40–80 yellow disk flowers.

Bloom Season: Late summer–fall

Habitat/Range: Occasional in high-quality mesic to dry prairies, and less commonly, in open woodlands; found in the southwest quarter of the Midwest region, and southward.

Comments: Formerly known as *Aster paludosus* ssp. *hemisphericus*. The showy flowers are noticeably larger than what might be expected for a plant of this size.

GLAUCOUS WHITE LETTUCE

Prenanthes racemosa
Aster family (Asteraceae)

Description: Tall, slender plants, up to 5' in height, with unbranched, hairless leaves and stems, and milky sap. The lower leaves are alternate, up to 10" long and 3" wide, with long, winged stalks. The middle leaves are mostly clasping the stem while the upper leaves are stalkless. The flowers are in tightly packed clusters along the upper portion of the stem. Each cylindrical flower head is about ½" long, with 9–16 pinkish to lavender to purple, petal-like ray flowers. The purplish bracts and stems of the flower head are densely hairy.

Bloom Season: Midsummer–fall

Habitat/Range: Occasional in wet prairies, meadows, low, ground-bordering streams, and in moist sandy soil; found in the northern half of the Midwest region.

Comments: Also known as *Nabalus racemosus.* The stem has a white, waxy coating (glaucous), which accounts for part of the common name. One feature that easily distinguishes glaucous white lettuce from rough white lettuce (see page 31) is that the former has basal leaves that persist at flowering, while the latter has basal and lowermost stem leaves usually withered or absent by flowering time. Also, glaucous white lettuce prefers low, wet ground, while rough white lettuce occurs in dry prairies and savannas. The bitter roots of this plant were once used to treat snakebite; hence, its other name, rattlesnake root.

FLAX-LEAVED ASTER
Ionactis linariifolius
Aster family (Asteraceae)

Description: Plants with more than one stem emerging from a base, less than 2' tall, with stiff, roughish, minutely hairy leaves. The leaves are alternate, stalkless, narrow, up to 1½" long and ⅛" wide, and tapering to a fine point. Several flower heads are at the tops of stems on short individual stalks. Each flower head is up to 1¼" wide, with 10–20 satiny, purple, petal-like ray flowers surrounding 20–40 yellow disk flowers.

Bloom Season: Late summer–fall

Habitat/Range: Occasional in sand prairies and dry prairies, savannas, and dry, rocky woodlands in acid-based soils over sandstone; found in the southwest quarter and north-central part of the Midwest region.

Comments: Formerly known as *Aster linariifolius*. Another common name, stiff-leaved aster, references the leaves' stiffness and their tendency to break rather than bend when folded.

WOODLAND ASTER
Symphyotrichum anomalum
Aster family (Asteraceae)

Description: Plants with stiff, erect stems, up to 4' tall. The leaves are alternate, the lower leaves lance-shaped, up to 3½" long and 1½" wide, heart-shaped at the base, with a wing of tissue along the leaf base. The upper leaves are lance-shaped, smaller, and without leaf stalks. The flower heads are ½" across, with numerous bracts at the base that curve downward. Each head has 30–45 bright lavender, petal-like ray flowers surrounding a yellow disk.

Bloom Season: Late summer–fall

Habitat/Range: Occasional in dry upland prairies, glades, rocky, open woods, and on thinly wooded bluffs; found in the southwest quarter of the Midwest region.

Comments: Formerly known as *Aster anomalus*. The flowers and fruits of woodland aster are eaten by wild turkey, and the leaves, by white-tailed deer.

SMOOTH BLUE ASTER
Symphyotrichum laeve
Aster family (Asteraceae)

Description: Single-stemmed plants, up to 3' tall, with smooth leaves and a noticeable silvery to bluish-green cast to the leaves and stem. The leaves at the base of the stem are rounded and stalked, with a leafy fringe along two sides of the leaf stalk. The stem leaves are alternate and somewhat clasp the stem. There are several flowers on stalks, about 2" long, at the upper end of the stem. The flower heads are about 1" across, with up to 25 bluish-purple, petal-like ray flowers surrounding a yellow disk.

Bloom Season: Late summer–fall

Habitat/Range: Occasional in mesic to dry prairies, hill prairies, savannas, and open woods; found throughout the Midwest region.

Comments: Formerly known as *Aster laevis*. The attractive silvery to bluish-green stem and leaves contrasting with the numerous bluish-purple rays and yellow disks account for the many cultivated garden varieties that have been developed from this aster.

NEW ENGLAND ASTER
Symphyotrichum novae-angliae
Aster family (Asteraceae)

Description: Showy plants, up to 6' tall, with branching stems that have gland-tipped hairs toward the tip. The leaves are alternate, numerous, up to 4" long and 1" wide, hairy, with pointed tips and leaves clasping the stem. Several flower heads are clustered along the upper stems. The flower stalks and bracts at the base of each flower head are covered with gland-tipped hairs. Each head is about 1½" across, with over 40 bright purple, petal-like ray flowers surrounding a yellow disk that turns reddish-purple with age. The flowers can also be pinkish-purple or pale lavender.

Bloom Season: Late summer–fall

Habitat/Range: Locally common in mesic to wet prairies, fens, edges of woods, old fields, pastures, and roadsides; found throughout the Midwest region.

Comments: Formerly known as *Aster novae-angliae*. The Meskwaki burned the plant and blew the smoke up the nose of an unconscious person to revive him or her. Other tribes used root tea for diarrhea and fever. This is the tallest aster in the Midwest region, and is easily grown in gardens and wildflower plantings.

261

AROMATIC ASTER
Symphyotrichum oblongifolium
Aster family (Asteraceae)

Description: Fragrant, hairy plants, up to 2½' tall, with spreading branches. The leaves are alternate, crowded, hairy, up to 3" long and less than 1" wide, with clasping bases and a rough surface. The flower heads are at the end of short branches, with numerous, small, leaf-like bracts along their length. Each flower head is 1" across and has 20–40 purple, petal-like ray flowers surrounding 30–50 yellow disk flowers.

Bloom Season: Late summer–fall

Habitat/Range: Occasional in upland prairies, hill prairies, glades, and open woods; found throughout the Midwest region, but absent in the northeast quarter, and rare in the southeast quarter.

Comments: Formerly known as *Aster oblongifolius.* Aromatic aster takes on a shrubby look with hundreds of attractive flowers when grown in the garden and given full sun. It continues to bloom well after the first frost. And, according to one reference, aromatic aster is used as a lotion for protection from witches!

SKY BLUE ASTER
Symphyotrichum oolentangiensis
Aster family (Asteraceae)

Description: This species has rough, slightly hairy stems, up to 3' tall. The leaves are alternate, thick, sandpapery on both sides, and lack teeth (or mostly so) along the margins. The basal leaves have long stalks and are lance-shaped, narrowing to a pointed tip, with heart-shaped leaf bases, and up to 5" long and 2" wide. The stem leaves are much smaller and lack stalks. The flower heads are in spreading clusters at the tops of stems. Each head is about 1" across, with 10–25 blue, petal-like ray flowers surrounding 15–28 yellow disk flowers.

Bloom Season: Late summer–fall

Habitat/Range: Common in mesic to dry prairies, sand prairies, savannas, rocky upland forests, and glades; found throughout the Midwest region.

Comments: Formerly known as *Aster oolentangiensis* and *Aster azueus.* John Leonard Riddell (1807–1865) was a science lecturer, botanist, geologist, medical doctor, chemist, microscopist, numismatist, politician, and science-fiction author in the United States. He originally described this flower in 1835, and named it *Aster oolentangiensis* after the Olentangy River, where he found it near Worthington, Ohio. Riddell originally misspelled the name of the river with two O's, and that remains unchanged because the older species name had precedence.

SPREADING ASTER
Symphyotrichum patens
Aster family (Asteraceae)

Description: This plant has slender, hairy, somewhat brittle stems, up to 2½' tall. The leaves are alternate, sandpapery, hairy, lance-shaped, up to 2" long and 1" wide, with bases clasping the stem. The flower heads are single on branches arising from the leaf axils. Each head is about 1" across, with about 15–25 blue, petal-like ray flowers surrounding a yellow disk.

Bloom Season: Late summer–fall

Habitat/Range: Occasional in usually acidic soils in rocky prairies, savannas, glades, and rocky, open woods; found along the southern third of the Midwest region.

Comments: Formerly known as *Aster patens*. The genus name, *Symphyotrichum*, comes from the Greek word *symph*, meaning "coming together," and *trich*, possibly in reference to the flower anthers. *Symphyotrichum* replaces *Aster* in the New World. The species name, *patens*, means "spreading."

WILLOWLEAF ASTER
Symphyotrichum praealtum
Aster family (Asteraceae)

Description: Plants up to 5' tall, often growing in dense colonies. The leaves are alternate along the stem, up to 5½" long and about ¾" wide, and about the same width along the length of the leaf. The lower surface has conspicuous net-shaped veins. Numerous flower heads are clustered in a pyramid-like column near the top. The flower heads are about 1" wide, with 20–25 pale lavender, petal-like ray flowers surrounding 20–35 yellow disk flowers.

Bloom Season: Late summer–fall

Habitat/Range: Frequent in wet prairies, moist depressions in upland prairies, fens, open thickets, and other moist places; found throughout the Midwest region, but rare in the northeast quarter.

Comments: Formerly known as *Aster praealtus*. Willowleaf aster is named for its long, linear, willow-like leaves. The species name, *praealtum*, means "very tall."

SWAMP ASTER
Symphyotrichum puniceum
Aster family (Asteraceae)

Description: Light green stems turning reddish-purple with age, up to 6' tall, with sparse to dense, stiff, white hairs in lines along its surface. The leaves are mostly dark green, often shiny, with short hairs underneath along the central vein. Leaves are 2–8" long and ¼–1¼" wide, with basal leaves having winged sheathing stalks that wither away by flowering time, along with lower stem leaves. Stem leaves are stalkless, with bases that clasp the stem, and pointed tips. The flower heads are stalked, on branching clusters at the top of the stem, each 1–1½" across, with 30–60 pale violet to bright blue-violet, petal-like ray flowers surrounding 30–70 yellow disk flowers.

Bloom Season: Late summer–fall

Habitat/Range: Occasional in wet prairies, fens, swamps, bogs, and edges of moist woods; found throughout the Midwest region, but in scattered locations in the southwest quarter.

Comments: Formerly known as *Aster puniceus.* Swamp aster is also called purple-stemmed aster, red-stalked aster, red-stemmed aster, and glossy-leaved aster. This aster is similar to New England aster, but occurs in wetter sites, has hairs with fine lines along the stems, and lacks gland-tipped hairs. Native Americans used the roots of swamp aster to treat fever, colds, typhoid, pneumonia, and toothache.

SILKY ASTER

Symphyotrichum sericeum
Aster family (Asteraceae)

Description: Attractive plants with widely branching stems, up to 2½' tall. The leaves are alternate, somewhat stiff, up to 1¾" long and ½" wide, with soft, silky hairs that lie flat on both sides of the leaves, giving them a silvery-green color. Numerous flower heads are in an open cluster at the tops of stems. Each head is about 1¼" across, with 15–30 violet-purple, petal-like ray flowers surrounding 15–35 yellow disk flowers.

Bloom Season: Late summer–fall

Habitat/Range: Occasional in dry or sandy prairies, hill prairies, glades, and edges of woods; found throughout the western half of the Midwest region.

Comments: Formerly known as *Aster sericeus.* Silky aster is very attractive, with its violet-purple rays contrasting intensely with the silvery-white foliage. Compared to most other American asters, the flowers appear disproportionately large for the plant's size. It is a good plant for dry open spaces in native plant gardens, rock gardens, or butterfly gardens.

SHORT'S ASTER

Symphyotrichum shortii
Aster family (Asteraceae)

Description: Single to multiple stems arise from the base, up to 4' tall, and are smooth to moderately hairy. The leaves are alternate, 2–6" long and 1–2" wide, on 1" hairy stalks on the lower part of the stem, and often stalkless along the upper part. Each leaf is toothless, pointed at the tip, narrowly heart-shaped at the base, smooth on the upper surface, and sparsely to moderately hairy underneath. Each flower head is stalked, ¾–1" wide, with 10–20 lavender to pale blue-violet, petal-like ray flowers that surround a yellow central disk.

Bloom Season: Late summer–fall

Habitat/Range: Common in dry to mesic, often rocky upland forests, forest edges, and bluffs; found through the Midwest region, but absent in the northern third and in Missouri.

Comments: Formerly known as *Aster shortii.* Short's aster is named for C. W. Short, an early-19th-century physician who practiced in the Louisville, Kentucky, area. Short's goldenrod (*Solidago shortii*) is also named for him. This is an endangered goldenrod found only in one location in Indiana, and in Kentucky.

ARKANSAS IRONWEED

Vernonia arkansana
Aster family (Asteraceae)

Description: From 1 to several stems arise from the base, up to a height of 4', with willow-like leaves. The leaves are alternate, stalkless, up to 6" long and ½" wide, gradually tapering at both ends, and with small teeth along the margins. The flower heads are few in number but large, from ¾–1¼" across, with each head containing from 50–120 small, reddish-purple disk flowers. Petal-like ray flowers are absent. The bracts at the base of the flower head are long and curled, a distinctive characteristic that is unique to this ironweed.

Bloom Season: Midsummer–fall

Habitat/Range: Common in upland prairies, bottomland prairies, savannas, fens, glades, stream banks, and gravel bars; found in the southwest quarter of the Midwest region.

Comments: Formerly known as *Vernonia crinita*. The genus name, *Vernonia*, honors botanist William Vernon, who collected the plant in Maryland in 1698. The species name, *arkansana*, means "of Arkansas," probably indicating where it was first found.

WESTERN IRONWEED

Vernonia baldwinii
Aster family (Asteraceae)

Description: Stems with relatively long, spreading, or often bent hairs, up to 5' tall. The leaves are alternate, up to 7" long and 2½" wide, broadest near the middle, tapering at both ends, densely hairy underneath, and toothed along the margins. The flower heads are numerous, up to ½" across, with up to 30 small, purple disk flowers. There are no petal-like ray flowers. A series of small, overlapping bracts with pointed, often-spreading tips are at the base of the flower head.

Bloom Season: Summer–fall

Habitat/Range: Common in upland prairies, hill prairies, savannas, woodlands, glades, and pastures; found in the southwest quarter and the west-central area of the Midwest region; also, in a few scattered locations in the central part.

Comments: A closely related species, tall ironweed (*Vernonia gigantea*; formerly *Vernonia altissima*), differs by having smooth to minutely hairy stems and leaves, with the bracts along the cup of the flower heads blunt instead of pointed, and not spreading; common in wet prairies, fens, bottomland forests, swamps, pastures, and roadsides; found in the southern half of the Midwest region.

PRAIRIE IRONWEED
Vernonia fasciculata
Aster family (Asteraceae)

Description: Mostly unbranched, green to reddish-purple stems, up to 4' tall, with smooth, hairless stems and leaves. The leaves are alternate, up to 6" long and 1" wide, finely toothed along their edges, widest at the middle and tapering at both ends. Each leaf has numerous tiny pits on the underside. Flower heads are in a dense, rounded cluster at the top of the stem. Each flower head is about ¾" across, with 10–26 bright, reddish-purple disk flowers. There are no petal-like ray flowers. The bracts at the base of the flower heads are green to purplish-brown, flattened and rounded at the tip, somewhat resembling fish scales, and with white, cobwebby hairs around the edges.

Bloom Season: Midsummer–fall

Habitat/Range: Common in wet prairies and wet depressions in upland prairies, fens, marshes, and other moist places; found throughout the Midwest region, but absent to rare in the eastern third.

Comments: Also known as smooth ironweed because its stems, leaves, and flower heads are glabrous (smooth). The species name, *fasciculata*, is from the Latin word for "clustered, grouped together."

MISSOURI IRONWEED
Vernonia missurica
Aster family (Asteraceae)

Description: A densely hairy, single-stemmed plant, up to 6' tall. The stem has long, crooked, or often bent to tangled hairs toward the tip. The leaves are up to 8" long and 2½" wide, with long, crooked hairs on the lower surface. The leaf margins range from coarsely toothed to entire. The flower heads are in clusters on several branches at the top of the stem. Each flower head is ½–¾" across, with 34–60 bright reddish-purple disk flowers. There are no petal-like ray flowers. Numerous bracts, each rounded to a bluntly pointed tip, surround the flower head.

Bloom Season: Midsummer–fall

Habitat/Range: Common in dry and wet prairies, savannas, woodlands, glades, old fields, and pastures; found in the southern half of the Midwest region, but rare in Ohio.

Comments: The species name, *missurica*, is in reference to the Missouri River. Missouri ironweed is a good late-season nectar source. Butterfly visitors include monarchs, painted ladies, sulfurs, swallowtails, whites, and others. Like milkweeds, ironweeds are bitter to the taste, so herbivorous animals like white-tailed deer and cattle will avoid consuming it.

WILD COMFREY
Cynoglossum virginianum
Borage family (Boraginaceae)

Description: An attractive plant with large leaves and a hairy, wand-like stem, up to 2½' tall. The basal leaves and lower stem leaves are up to 1' long, on stalks, broadest along the middle, tapering at both ends, and rough-hairy. The upper stem leaves are smaller, lack stalks, and clasp the stem. The flowers are on short, branching clusters at the top of the stem, with each cluster in a tight coil, unwinding and elongating with maturity. The bluish-white flowers are about ½" across, with 5 rounded lobes and 5 stamens.

Bloom Season: Mid-spring–early summer

Habitat/Range: Common in moist or rocky woods, on slopes, and in ravine and valley bottoms; found throughout the Midwest region.

Comments: Cherokee used root tea for "bad memory," cancer, and milky urine. A related species, common hound's-tongue (*Cynoglossum officinale*), is a downy-covered biennial with a branched stem; it is leafy to the top and has lance-shaped leaves, dark purple to reddish-purple flowers, and a musty odor. This plant is a native of Europe that has spread across the Midwest region. It is found in old fields, disturbed soil, eroded slopes, and along roadsides.

BLUEBELLS
Mertensia virginica
Borage family (Boraginaceae)

Description: The pale, smooth, fleshy stem grows up to 2' tall, with alternate blue-green leaves along the stem. The basal leaves are about 8" long and 5" wide, and on long stalks. The lower leaves are somewhat oval, up to 6" long and 1–3" wide, and with a winged stalk. The upper stem leaves are smaller. The flowers are in loose clusters, hanging from smooth, slender stalks. Each flower is trumpet-shaped, up to 1¼" long, with 5 petals united to form a long tube. The flower buds are initially pink and open to a light blue.

Bloom Season: Spring–early summer

Habitat/Range: Occasional in mesic woods and lower slopes, and terraces along streams and in valleys; found throughout the Midwest region, but uncommon to rare in the northern third.

Comments: Where bluebells are found, they often grow in dense colonies, carpeting the forest floor with a crisp porcelain blue, but the plants disappear completely by midsummer. A similar species, northern bluebells (*Mertensia paniculata*), has smaller flowers, about ½" long, with hairy leaves, sepals, and flower stalks; found in the northern half of the northwest quarter of the Midwest region. (The populations of the two species do not overlap.)

PURPLE CRESS

Cardamine douglassii
Mustard family (Brassicaceae)

Description: Single-stemmed plants with spreading hairs, 4–12" tall. There are 1–2 basal leaves, 1–2" long and wide, that are normally present at flowering. The alternate leaves along the stem are up to 2" long and 1" wide, usually broadest at the middle, with blunt teeth to wavy margins. Flowers are arranged along the upper part of the stem, each ½–¾" across, with 4 petals, 4 sepals, and several stamens. The petals are pale purple to white and broadest at the end.

Bloom Season: Early spring–mid-spring

Habitat/Range: Occasional in wet to mesic bottomland forests and areas along seeps and springs; found through the Midwest region, but rare to absent in the northwest and southwest parts.

Comments: Although the common name describes the flowers as purple in color, they are typically a light pink to purplish-pink to often white. This is one of many spring-blooming plants threatened by the rapidly spreading, nonnative garlic mustard (*Alliaria petiolata*) (see page 351).

PURPLE ROCKET

Iodanthus pinnatifidus
Mustard family (Brassicaceae)

Description: Mostly smooth plants, up to 3' tall. Leaves are alternate, up to 6" long and 1½" wide, thin, smooth, sharply toothed to nearly toothless, and tapering to a winged leaf stalk, often with 1–4 pairs of small lobes along the stalk. The flowers are arranged in an elongated cluster at the top of the stem. Each flower is about ¼" across, with 4 pale violet to nearly white petals and 6 purple-gray stamens. The fruit is a thin pod, from ¾–1½" long.

Bloom Season: Late spring–midsummer

Habitat/Range: Occasional to locally common in moist to wet floodplain forests; found throughout the Midwest region, but rare to absent in the northern third.

Comments: The genus name, *Iodanthus*, is from the Greek *iodes* (violet-colored) and *anthos* (flower). The species name, *pinnatifidus*, is in reference to the often pinnately lobed leaf stalk.

MARSH BELLFLOWER
Campanula aparinoides
Bellflower family (Campanulaceae)

Description: A 3-sided, weak-stemmed plant with milky sap, 6–30" tall, with hooked hairs that grasp onto nearby vegetation in order to gain support. Leaves are loosely alternate, stalkless, narrow, up to 1½" long and less than ⅜" wide, with a pointed tip, tapering at the base, and widely spaced teeth along the margins. The flowers are single on sometimes-nodding, slender stalks at the ends of branching stems. Each flower is ¼–½" long, white to pale blue, bell-shaped, with flaring petals that are pointed at the tip, fused at the base, and with white stamens.

Bloom Season: Summer

Habitat/Range: Occasional in moist soil of meadows, swamps, bogs, fens, and along shores; found throughout the Midwest region, but absent in southern Illinois and southern Indiana; also, a few relict populations occur in southern Missouri.

Comments: The genus name, *Campanula,* is derived from the Latin word *campana,* for "bell," which refers to the shape of the flower. The species name, *aparinoides,* is from the Greek word *aparine,* for the plant known as cleavers (*Galium aparine*), because the leaves resemble those of cleavers. The Iroquois concentrated the essence from boiled stems, and it was given to young women to induce childbirth.

HAREBELL
Campanula rotundifolia
Bellflower family (Campanulaceae)

Description: Slender, erect to loosely ascending plants, up to 20" tall, with slender, alternate leaves. The basal leaves are long-stalked, almost round, with toothed edges and heart-shaped bases. The stem leaves are stalkless, up to 3" long and less than ½" wide, becoming grass-like on the upper stem. Flowers occur at the top of the plant on slender stalks, causing the flowers to nod. Each flower is about ¾" long and pale blue to violet to bright purple. The cup-like flowers have 5 flaring, pointed lobes. A long style extends from the center, and its tip splits into 3 parts.

Bloom Season: Late spring–early fall

Habitat/Range: Local in dry hill prairies, open sandy woodlands, savannas, cliffs, and meadows; found in the northern half of the Midwest region.

Comments: The common name, which is of European origin, may relate to the fact that this plant is sometimes found in areas inhabited by rabbits (hares). *Campanula rotundifolia* occurs throughout the northern United States, Canada, and southward in the intermountain region to near the Mexican border. It has a near-circumpolar distribution in the Northern Hemisphere, from about latitude 40 degrees N to about 70 degrees N, extending in Europe from northernmost Scandinavia to the Pyrenees and the French Mediterranean coast. It also occurs on the southern coasts of Greenland and Iceland.

AMERICAN BELLFLOWER
Campanulastrum americanum
Bellflower family (Campanulaceae)

Description: A tall, slender, annual plant, up to 6' in height, with ridges along the stem. The leaves are alternate, stalked, 3–6" long and 1–2" wide, lance-shaped, with fine teeth along the margins. The flowers emerge at the leaf axils and are about 1" across, with 5 pointed, spreading, blue petals. A white ring is present at the base of the petals. The style is long and curves upward.

Bloom Season: Summer–fall

Habitat/Range: Common in moist, open woods and borders of woods, wooded streamsides, and thickets; found through the Midwest region, but absent in the northern quarter.

Comments: Formerly known as *Campanula americana*, and also called "tall bellflower." The Meskwaki used leaf tea to treat coughs and tuberculosis, and the crushed root to treat whooping cough.

KALM'S LOBELIA
Lobelia kalmii
Bellflower family (Campanulaceae)

Description: A small, delicate plant, 4–16" tall, with milky sap. The leaves are alternate, very narrow, up to 2" long and ¼" wide, mostly linear, with tiny teeth widely spaced along the margins. The basal leaves are broader and more rounded. The flowers are on stalks, ¼–1" long, with small leaves growing at the base of each stalk. Each flower is ¼–½" long, pale blue, tubular, with 5 pointed lobes. There are 2 smaller upper lobes, 3 spreading lower lobes, and a white center.

Bloom Season: Summer–fall

Habitat/Range: Common in wet, open sites in shallow marshes, wet meadows, fens, and sandy shores; found in the northern half of the Midwest region.

Comments: Kalm's lobelia was used by the Iroquois to treat abscesses and earache, and to induce vomiting to remove the effect of a love medicine.

DOWNY LOBELIA
Lobelia puberula
Bellflower family (Campanulaceae)

Description: Erect, single-stemmed plants, 1–3'
tall, covered with dense hairs that are sometimes
curved and spreading. The leaves are alternate,
stalkless, 1–4" long and ⅜–¾" wide, broadest
at the middle, with a pointed tip, tapered at the
base, sharply toothed along the margins, and both
surfaces densely hairy. The flowers are in a spike,
4–12" long, at the top of the stem where the flowers are generally arranged on one side of the stem.
Each flower is ½–¾" long, blue to rarely white, the
outer surface with short, spreading hairs, tubular,
with 5 pointed lobes. There are 2 smaller upper
lobes, 3 spreading lower lobes, and a white center.

Bloom Season: Late summer–fall

Habitat/Range: Occasional in dry to mesic open
woods, meadows, and old fields; found in the
southern quarter of the Midwest region, and
southward.

Comments: The genus name, *Lobelia,* honors Mat-
thias de l'Obel (1538–1616), a French physician
and botanist, who with Pierre Pena wrote *Stirpium
Adversaria Nova* (1570), which detailed a new
plant classification system based upon leaves. The
species name, *puberula,* refers to the soft, downy
hairs on the stem.

GREAT BLUE LOBELIA
Lobelia siphilitica
Bellflower family (Campanulaceae)

Description: Unbranched stems, up to 3' tall, with
milky sap. The leaves are alternate, stalkless, up
to 6" long and 1½" wide, widest in the middle
and tapering at both ends, with teeth along the
margins. The flowers are crowded along the upper
part of the stem on short stalks, with leafy bracts
at the base of the stalks. Each flower is ¾–1" long,
deep blue, with pale stripes along the outside of
the tube, and 2 lips. The upper lip is split into 2
upright lobes, and the lower lip into 3 spreading
lobes with a white base.

Bloom Season: Midsummer–fall

Habitat/Range: Occasional in moist depressions
in upland prairies, wet prairies, fens, and along
streams and seepage areas; found throughout the
Midwest region.

Comments: The Meskwaki used great blue lobelia
in love medicines. The roots were finely chopped
and mixed into the food of a quarrelsome couple
without their knowledge. This, the Meskwaki
believed, would avert divorce and make the pair
love each other again. Other tribes used root tea
for syphilis and leaf tea for colds, fever, upset
stomach, worms, croup, and nosebleed.

PALE SPIKED LOBELIA
Lobelia spicata
Bellflower family (Campanulaceae)

Description: Slender, smooth, single-stemmed plants, up to 3' tall, with milky sap, and ridges along the stem. The leaves are alternate, narrow, up to 3½" long and 1" wide, with teeth along the margins. The pale blue flowers are on short stalks that alternate along the stem. There is a small, leaf-like bract at the base of each stalk. The flowers are about ½" long and ½" wide, with 2 lips; the small upper lip has 2 lobes that are stiffly erect, while the broad lower lip has 3 larger, spreading lower lobes. There are 2 yellowish spots at the base of the lower lobes.

Bloom Season: Mid-spring–summer

Habitat/Range: Common in prairies, savannas, glades, open woodlands, and old fields; found throughout the Midwest region.

Comments: Native Americans used a tea of the plant to induce vomiting. Root tea was used to treat trembling by applying the tea to scratches made in the affected limb.

INDIAN TOBACCO
Lobelia inflata
Bellflower family (Campanulaceae)

Description: An annual plant, ½–2½' tall, with angular hairy stems. The leaves are alternate, 2–3" long, ½–1½" wide, broadest below the middle, bluntly toothed at the tip, tapering at the base, with the margins irregularly toothed, and the upper surface smooth while the lower surface is hairy. The flowers are arranged along the upper part of the stem and attached at the leaf axils. Each flower is about ¼" long, pale blue or white, tubular, with 5 pointed lobes. There are 2 smaller upper lobes, 3 spreading lower lobes, and a yellow center with white hairs.

Bloom Season: Midsummer–fall

Habitat/Range: Common in openings of dry to mesic upland forests, bottomland forests, old fields, pastures, roadsides, and disturbed areas; found throughout the Midwest region.

Comments: Indian tobacco is distinctive because its calyxes become conspicuously inflated from the developing seed capsules. Native Americans smoked leaves for asthma, bronchitis, sore throat, and coughs. The foliage was burned by the Cherokee as a natural insecticide to smoke out gnats. The plant is considered toxic.

VENUS' LOOKING-GLASS

Triodanis perfoliata
Bellflower family (Campanulaceae)

Description: A slender, mostly unbranched annual, up to 18" tall, with stems angled and hairs along the ridges. The leaves are roundish, about 1" long and nearly as wide, and clasp the stem with a heart-shaped base. There are tiny teeth along the margins, and the veins are fan-shaped. Several star-shaped flowers arise from the leaf axils, stalkless, about ½" across, with 5 blue petals. Those flowers on the lower stalk do not open but produce the seed.

Bloom Season: Mid-spring–summer

Habitat/Range: Common in often gravelly or sandy soils in prairies, glades, open woodlands, pastures, old fields, and roadsides; found throughout the Midwest region, but uncommon to absent in the northern quarter.

Comments: The Cherokee took a liquid compound of the root for indigestion. The Meskwaki used it as an emetic (a substance that causes vomiting), to make one "sick all day long," and to smoke it at ceremonies. A closely related species, small Venus' looking-glass (*Triodanis biflora*), has leaves that are longer than they are broad, do not clasp the stem, and with only 1–2 flowers with petals at the top of the stem. Small Venus' looking-glass occupies similar habitats and is found in the southwest quarter of the Midwest region.

COMMON HORSE GENTIAN

Triosteum perfoliatum
Honeysuckle family (Caprifoliaceae)

Description: Stems with gland-tipped hairs, up to 3' tall, with thick, dark green leaves that encircle the stem. The hairy leaves are opposite, stalkless, up to 10" long and 4" wide, broadly lance-shaped, with those in the middle of the stem distinctly fiddle-shaped. The flowers emerge at the leaf axils on short stalks. Each cluster typically has 3–4 maroon flowers that are tubular, up to ¾" long, with 5 overlapping petals, and a conspicuous light green style protruding from the tube. The fruit is about ½" across and resembles little oranges in color and shape.

Bloom Season: Late spring–midsummer

Habitat/Range: Common in dry open woods and savannas; found through the Midwest region, but absent in the northeast quarter.

Comments: Native Americans made a tea of this plant for treating fever, and the roots were mashed and applied to painful swellings. The Pennsylvania Dutch collected the orange fruits and dried the seeds, then roasted and ground them as a coffee substitute. A similar species, red-fruited orange gentian (*Triosteum aurantiacum*), has hairs without gland tips, leaf bases that narrow and do not encircle the stem, and orange-red fruit; found throughout the Midwest region.

SLENDER DAYFLOWER
Commelina erecta
Spiderwort family (Commelinaceae)

Description: A perennial plant, up to 3' tall, with branching, upright stems. The leaves are lance-shaped with parallel veins, up to 6" long and 1½" wide, and with ear-like lobes where the leaf base joins the stem. The flowers emerge from folded spathe-like bracts, 1 at a time. Each flower, which lasts but a day, is up to 1" across, with 2 rounded blue petals and 1 smaller white petal. There are 6 yellow-tipped stamens.

Bloom Season: Late spring–fall

Habitat/Range: Common on gravel bars, sandbars, mud banks of streams, rocky, wooded slopes, and exposed bluffs and glades; found in the southwest quarter and south-central part of the Midwest region.

Comments: Slender dayflower is native to much of the world, including the Americas, Africa, and western Asia. The native dayflowers have been used in salads and as cooked greens. The young leaves and stems can be added fresh to salads or boiled for 10 minutes and served with butter. A similar-looking weedy species, Asiatic dayflower (*Commelina communis*), can be found on page 354.

VIRGINIA DAYFLOWER
Commelina virginica
Spiderwort family (Commelinaceae)

Description: Tall stems ascending up to 4½', with thick rhizomes and sometimes rooting at the nodes. The leaves are alternate, 3–8" long and 1–2" wide, broadest toward the base, sometimes rough to the touch, with leaf sheaths at the base that encircle the stem and contain a fringe of stiff, reddish-brown hairs. The flowers are mostly clustered at the tips of the stems, with folded, spathe-like bracts ¾–1¼" long that are fused in the lower third. The flowers are about ½" wide, with 3 rounded, blue petals and 6 stamens. Each flower lasts but a day.

Bloom Season: Midsummer–fall

Habitat/Range: Locally frequent in bottomland forests, banks of streams, swamp edges, sloughs, and ditches; found in the lower third of the Midwest region, and southward.

Comments: The genus *Commelina* is named for brothers Jan (1629–1692) and Kaspar (1667–1731) Commelin, distinguished Dutch botanists. The species name, *virginica*, is named for the state. This is the only dayflower in the Midwest region that produces a rhizome.

OHIO SPIDERWORT

Tradescantia ohiensis
Spiderwort family (Commelinaceae)

Description: Thin plants, up to 3' tall, with smooth, bluish to silvery-green stems and leaves. The arching leaves are alternate, up to 15" long and about 1" wide, and tapering to a long point, with a sheath that wraps around the stem. The flowers are in a tight cluster at the top of the stem. Each flower is about 1½" across, with 3 blue to purple, rounded petals and 6 yellow-tipped stamens covered with long, purple hairs.

Bloom Season: Late spring–midsummer

Habitat/Range: Common in mesic to dry prairies, savannas, woodlands, pastures, and roadsides; found through the Midwest region, but absent in the northern quarter.

Comments: Also called "common spiderwort," it was once thought to be a cure for spider bites. Native Americans used the stems as potherbs. Each showy flower lasts but a day.

BROAD-LEAVED SPIDERWORT

Tradescantia subaspera
Spiderwort family (Commelinaceae)

Description: A somewhat hairy plant, up to 3' tall, with a zigzag stem and long, arching leaves. The leaves are up to 12" long and 2" across, hairy, and gradually tapering toward the tip. The flowers are in clusters arising from the axils of the upper leaves. Each flower is about 1" across, with 3 purple petals, and with 6 stamens on feathery stalks.

Bloom Season: Summer–fall

Habitat/Range: Occasional in moist woods, at the base of bluffs, and in wooded valleys along streams; found in the southern half of the Midwest region.

Comments: Also known as zigzag spiderwort. The name "spiderwort" comes from the hairs along the stamens, which resemble a spiderweb.

VIRGINIA SPIDERWORT
Tradescantia virginiana
Spiderwort family (Commelinaceae)

Description: A smooth-stemmed plant, up to 16" tall, with 2–5 leaves along the stem. The leaves are up to 12" long and less than 1" wide, becoming wider toward the base to form a sheath that clasps the stem. The flowers are blue, purple, or reddish-purple, and occur in a cluster at the end of the stem just above 2 bracts that are about the same size as the lower leaves. Each flower is about 1" across with 3 rounded petals. There are 3 hairy, green sepals beneath the petals. Each flower has 6 bright yellow stamens with purple hairs along their length.

Bloom Season: Mid- to late spring

Habitat/Range: Occasional in sandy or rocky prairies and rocky woodlands, and mesic to dry upland forests; found in the southern half of the Midwest region; also, rare in Michigan.

Comments: The Lakota made a jelly-like, blue paint from the flowers, which was used for decorative purposes. A closely related species, long-bracted spiderwort (*Tradescantia bracteata*), is shorter, up to 12" tall, has dense hairs on the flower stalks and sepals, and broad bracts longer and wider than the lower leaves. Occurs in upland prairies, sand prairies, and edges of woods; found in the western half of the Midwest region.

LEAD PLANT
Amorpha canescens
Bean family (Fabaceae)

Description: A small shrub, up to 3' tall, with grayish hairs on a stem that becomes woody with age. The leaves are stalked, up to 4" long, and divided into as many as 51 leaflets. The leaflets are covered with gray hairs, giving the plant a lead-gray color, which was thought to indicate the presence of lead ore below in the soil. Each leaflet is up to ¾" long and ½" wide. The tiny, purple flowers are in a spike-like mass along the upper part of the stem. Each flower has a single ¼"-long petal curling around 10 orange-tipped stamens.

Bloom Season: Late spring–summer

Habitat/Range: Occasional in high-quality mesic to dry prairies, savannas, glades, and rocky, open woods; found through the Midwest region, but absent in the eastern third.

Comments: Native Americans used the dried leaves for smoking. A tea was made for treating pinworms and was used externally for eczema. The Omaha powdered the dried leaves and blew them into cuts and open wounds to help promote scab formation. A closely related species, indigo bush (*Amorpha fruticosa*), is a larger shrub, up to 10' tall, lacking hair, with 11–31 leaflets, each up to 2" long and over 1" wide. It is common in thickets along streams and in prairie draws; found throughout the western half of the Midwest region, and with scattered locations in the eastern half.

GROUNDNUT
Apios americana
Bean family (Fabaceae)

Description: A climbing or sprawling vine with milky sap and widely spaced, stalked, alternate, divided leaves. The leaves have 3–7 leaflets on short stalks, each up to 3" long and ½" wide, with smooth edges along the margins, broadly rounded bases, and pointed tips. Flowers are in dense clusters on short stalks emerging at the base of leaves. The flowers are fragrant, up to ½" long, with a light pinkish upper hooded petal that is divided into 2 wings, 2 smaller maroon side petals, and a strongly upward-curved, keel-like middle petal. The fruits are wavy pods, 2–4" long.

Bloom Season: Summer–fall

Habitat/Range: Moist soil in prairies, thickets, moist woods, borders of marshes, ponds, lakes, and streams; found throughout the Midwest region.

Comments: Groundnuts were important food sources of the Osage, Pawnee, and many other tribes. The Osage gathered them in late summer and fall and stored them in caches for winter use. Also an important food of New England colonists, the pilgrims were dependent on the potato-like tuber for their survival that first winter. The tubers can be used in soups or stews, or fried like potatoes, with three times the protein of the latter. The seeds in summer can be eaten cooked like peas.

GROUND PLUM
Astragalus crassicarpus var. *crassicarpus*
Bean family (Fabaceae)

Description: Plants usually with several trailing stems, up to 2' long, connected to a thick, woody taproot. The leaves are hairy, up to 6" long, and alternating along the stem on short stalks. Each leaf has 7–13 pairs of slightly folded leaflets, each ¾" long and ⅓" wide. The flowers are in small clusters at the ends of branches, with 5–25 flowers in each cluster. Each flower is about ¾–1" long and varies in color from purple and violet to bluish- or pinkish-red. The upper petal is larger and flaring at the tip, below which are two side petals and a lower lip.

Bloom Season: Mid- to late spring

Habitat/Range: Locally frequent in dry prairies, loess hill prairies, and rocky woods; found in the western third of the Midwest region.

Comments: The fruits are succulent, shiny pods about 1" in diameter that become dry and hard when they age. They contain numerous small seeds. When ripe, the fruit has a reddish cast and was widely used for food by Native Americans and early settlers. They are said to taste like raw pea pods. A creamy-white to greenish-yellow variety of ground plum (*Astragalus crassicarpus* var. *trichocalyx*) can be found on page 164.

BENT MILK VETCH
Astragalus distortus
Bean family (Fabaceae)

Description: A low-growing legume with several finely hairy stems that mostly lie along the ground, up to 12" long. The leaves are alternate, stalked, up to 5" long, and divided into 11–25 leaflets. Each leaflet is mostly oval, up to 1" long, smooth above, and sparsely hairy below. The mostly lilac-purple flowers are in clusters of 5–20 at the top of the stem. Each flower, which has the structure typical of the bean family, is about ½" long. The seed pod is up to 2" long, and bent; hence, the common name.

Bloom Season: Mid-spring–early fall

Habitat/Range: Occasional on glades, dry open woods, and edges of bluffs; found in the southwest quarter of the Midwest region.

Comments: There are approximately 364 species in the genus *Astragalus* in mostly the western part of the United States, but 12 of them also occur in the Midwest region. Many species of milk vetch, which is also called "locoweed," accumulate and store selenium, making them toxic to livestock.

BLUE WILD INDIGO
Baptisia australis var. *minor*
Bean family (Fabaceae)

Description: Smooth, branched, shrub-like plants, up to 4' tall. The leaves are alternate, divided into 3 leaflets, each less than 2" long. The flowers are on stalks and attached along a stem that stands well above the leaves. Each deep blue to purple flower is about 1" long, with a notched upper petal, 2 small side petals, and a middle keel-shaped lip. The seed pods are black, hairless, and about 2" long, with a pointed tip.

Bloom Season: Late spring–early summer

Habitat/Range: Occasional in upland prairies and glades; found in the southwest quarter of the Midwest region and adventive elsewhere, usually escaping from cultivation.

Comments: Native Americans used root tea as an emetic (to induce vomiting) and a purgative (to clear the bowels). Externally, it was used as a wash for inflammations, cuts, wounds, bruises, and sprains, and in a compress for toothache. The Cherokee used the plant as a source of blue dye for cloth.

BUTTERFLY PEA

Clitoria mariana
Bean family (Fabaceae)

Description: A smooth, twining (but not climbing) plant, up to 3' long. The leaves are stalked and divided into 3 leaflets, with the center leaflet on a long stalk. The leaflets are up to 3½" long and 1½" wide, broadest at the base, and tapering to a pointed tip. There are 1–3 flowers on short stalks attached along the stem. The showy, lavender to pale blue flowers are about 2" long, with purple markings along the center of the large upper petal (the *banner*), which is pointed downward.

Bloom Season: Late spring–fall

Habitat/Range: Occasional in acidic soils in low or upland rocky woods or borders of glades; found along the southern third of the Midwest region, and southward.

Comments: Flowers late in the season may pollinate without opening. There are thirty-five species of the genus *Clitoria*, mostly native to warm regions of the world.

PURPLE PRAIRIE CLOVER

Dalea purpurea
Bean family (Fabaceae)

Description: Slender, leafy plants, up to 2' tall, with 1 to several stems arising from a common base. The leaves are divided into 3–9 shiny, narrow leaflets, each about 1" long and ⅛" wide. The flowers are densely packed in a cylindrical head, 1–2" long, at the tops of the branches, with the flowers opening in a circle around the head from bottom to top. Each reddish-purple flower is about ¼" long, with a large petal, 4 smaller petals, and 5 orange stamens.

Bloom Season: Late spring–early summer

Habitat/Range: Common in mesic to dry prairies, hill prairies, sand prairies, savannas, and glades; found through the Midwest region, but absent in the eastern third.

Comments: Native Americans used the plant medicinally by applying a tea made from the leaves to open wounds. The Pawnee took root tea as general preventive medicine. The tough elastic stems were gathered to make brooms. A closely related species, silky prairie clover (*Dalea villosa*), has densely hairy leaves and stems, leaves with 9–25 leaflets, flowers pink to reddish-purple, densely packed in a 4"-long cylindrical head; found in sand prairies and pastures in the northwest part of the Midwest region.

VEINY PEA
Lathyrus venosus
Bean family (Fabaceae)

Description: A vinelike plant, up to 3' long, with angled stems, and stalked, alternate, compound leaves ending in branched, coiled tendrils. Each compound leaf has a pair of leafy appendages (stipules) where the leaf stalk attaches to the stem, the upper appendage being longer than the lower, and both being pointed. Leaves are divided into 4–7 pairs of leaflets, broadest at the middle and tapering at both ends. There are usually more than 6 flowers per cluster. Each flower is ½–¾" long and about ⅜" wide, pinkish-purple, with a broad, upright petal, 2 smaller side petals, and a keel-like lower lip. The upper lip has distinct darker veination.

Bloom Season: Late spring–midsummer

Habitat/Range: Occasional in dry to mesic upland forests, ledges and blufftops, margins of lakes, and along roadsides; found in the northern half of the Midwest region, and also in southern Missouri.

Comments: A closely related species, marsh vetchling (*Lathyrus palustris*), has compound leaves in 2–4 pairs of leaflets, usually a winged stem, fewer flowers per cluster, and usually found in wetter ground; frequent in marshes, swamps, and wet meadows; found more commonly in the northern half of the Midwest region, and less so in the southern half.

AMERICAN VETCH
Vicia americana
Bean family (Fabaceae)

Description: Sprawling vines, up to 3' long, with alternate compound leaves with a tendril at the end of each leaf that winds around other plants for support. Each leaf typically has 4–7 pairs of leaflets, each about 1½" long and ½" wide, oval- to egg-shaped, toothless, and hairless. There are prominent, sharply toothed stipules at the bases of the leaf stalks. There are 3–10 flowers in loose clusters arising from leaf axils in the upper part of the stem. Each flower is ½–1" long, purplish-blue to purple, tubular, with an erect, flaring upper petal, two smaller side petals and a keel-like lower lip.

Bloom Season: Mid-spring–midsummer

Habitat/Range: Occasional in prairies, edges of mesic upland forests, and open woodlands, usually in somewhat moist areas; found in the northern half of the Midwest region.

Comments: American vetch is much more common and widespread across the western states, where it is a common understory plant in many types of forest and other habitats, such as chaparral, and provides forage for wild and domesticated animals. The Iroquois women used an infusion (soaking the plant to make a tea) of roots as a love medicine. The Navajo used an infusion of the plant as an eyewash, and made smoke for a horse to inhale to increase the horse's endurance.

VIOLET BUSH CLOVER

Lespedeza frutescens
Bean family (Fabaceae)

Description: A bushy plant with weak stems that tend to lean, usually not more than 18" tall. The leaves are alternate, stalked, and divided into 3 somewhat oval leaflets. Each leaflet is about 1½" long and ¾" wide. The flowers are in sparse clusters at the ends of slender branches. Each violet- to rose-colored flower is about ⅜" long, with a spreading upper petal, 2 smaller side petals, and a protruding lower lip. The single seed pods are small, flattened, and up to ¼" long.

Bloom Season: Midsummer–early fall

Habitat/Range: Common in mesic to dry prairies, hill prairies, savannas, rocky woodlands, and glades; found in the southern half of the Midwest region.

Comments: Formerly known as *Lespedeza violacea*. The seeds are eaten by songbirds, ruffed grouse, bobwhite quail, wild turkey, and greater prairie-chicken. The plants are eaten by white-tailed deer.

SLENDER BUSH CLOVER

Lespedeza virginica
Bean family (Fabaceae)

Description: A narrow-stemmed plant, up to 3' tall, with hairy, branching stems. The leaves are numerous, stalked, divided into 3 narrow leaflets, each of which is up to 1½" long and less than ¼" wide. The flowers are in dense clusters interspersed with leaves on the upper part of the stem. Each pink to purple flower is about ¼" long, with a spreading upper petal, 2 smaller side petals, and a lower protruding lip. The upper petal has a dark red blotch near its base.

Bloom Season: Late spring–early fall

Habitat/Range: Common in mesic to dry prairies, sand prairies, glades, savannas, and open woods; found in the southern half of the Midwest region.

Comments: A closely related species but extremely rare, prairie bush clover (*Lespedeza leptostachya*), is federally listed as threatened. The plants have a silver cast, with widely spaced, slender leaflets and open clusters of pale pink to creamy-white flowers that bloom from midsummer to early fall. They occur in dry prairies and hill prairies with sandy or gravelly soils; found in the northwest quarter of the Midwest region.

WILD LUPINE
Lupinus perennis
Bean family (Fabaceae)

Description: Hairy-stemmed plants, up to 2' tall, with alternate, stalked, compound leaves. The leaves are hairy and divided into 7–11 leaflets, radiating from a central point. Each leaflet is up to 2" long and ½" wide, with round tips, and often with a sharp point at the apex. The flowers are in a spiked cluster, up to 8" long. Each stalked, blue or purple flower is about ½" long, with a fan-shaped upper petal that is often blue and white, 2 side petals, and an extended lower lip. Both upper and lower lips have darker blue veins running along their length. The seed pod is up to 2" long, hairy, and turns black when mature.

Bloom Season: Mid-spring–early summer

Habitat/Range: Locally common in sand savannas, sand woodlands, and somewhat degraded sand prairies where grasses are decreased; found in the northern half of the Midwest region.

Comments: Wild lupine is the host plant for the Karner blue butterfly caterpillar. Habitat loss has led to the decline in wild lupine plants, the food larval source, and that has put the Karner blue butterfly on the federal endangered species list. Native Americans drank cold leaf tea of wild lupine to treat nausea and internal hemorrhage. A fodder was used to fatten horses and make them "spirited and full of fire." The seeds are considered poisonous.

SAMPSON'S SNAKEROOT
Orbexilum pedunculatum
Bean family (Fabaceae)

Description: A slender, sparingly branched plant, up to 3' tall, the leaves are alternate, stalked, and divided into 3 leaflets. Each leaflet is up to 3" long and ½" wide, with the center leaflet on a longer stalk. The flowers are in cylindrical clusters at the top of long stalks. Individual flowers are light blue to bluish-purple, about ¼" long, with a spreading upper petal, 2 smaller side petals, and a lower protruding lip. The fruits are hairy, flat pods, less than ¼" long, with wrinkled surfaces and a strongly curved beak at the end.

Bloom Season: Late spring–early summer

Habitat/Range: Common in acidic soils in dry upland prairies, sand prairies, savannas, rocky, open woodlands, and glades; found in the southern third of the Midwest region.

Comments: Formerly known as *Psoralea psoralioides*.

PURPLE LOCOWEED
Oxytropis lambertii
Bean family (Fabaceae)

Description: A very short-stemmed plant, 4–16" tall, with silky hairs and a stout taproot. The stem is reduced to a small crown at ground level where the leaves emerge. The leaves are on short stalks with 7–19 leaflets, each ¼–1½" long and less than ¼" wide. Flowers are on leafless stalks that combined are up to 8" tall. Each flower is silky-hairy, about ¾" long, with purple or rose petals. The upper petal forms a notched hood, while the side petals flank a pointed, keel-like lower lip.

Bloom Season: Mid-spring–early summer

Habitat/Range: Locally frequent in dry, rocky prairies, loess hill prairies, and open wooded slopes; found in the western half of the northwest quarter of the Midwest region, and westward.

Comments: Like many species of locoweeds, purple locoweed accumulates and stores selenium from the soil, making it toxic to livestock if accumulated in substantial amounts. Although it is known to have deleterious side effects, the Navajo were known to make a tea for constipation and they also ate it, parched or mushed, for food.

SILVERY SCURF PEA
Pediomelum argophyllum
Bean family (Fabaceae)

Description: A silvery-looking, bushy plant, up to 3' tall. The stems and leaves are covered with dense, shiny, white hairs that give the plant a silvery appearance. The leaves are alternate, on stalks up to 2" long, and compound, with each leaf consisting of 3–5 oval to narrow leaflets, ½–2" long and ¾" wide, with all leaflets radiating from a single point. The flowers are in open spikes from upper leaf axils, with 2–8 deep blue to purplish-blue flowers whorled around the stem. Each flower is less than ¼" wide, with a flaring upper petal and 2 side petals flanking a protruding lower lip.

Bloom Season: Summer

Habitat/Range: Occasional in dry, rocky prairies, hill prairies, and open woodlands; found in the western half of the northwest quarter of the Midwest region, and westward.

Comments: Formerly known as *Psoralea argophylla*. The Meskwaki used a tea from the root to cure chronic constipation. The Cheyenne made a tea from the leaves and stems to cure a high fever. Meriwether Lewis of the Lewis and Clark Expedition reported that "a decoction of the plant is used by the Indians to wash their wounds."

PRAIRIE TURNIP
Pediomelum esculentum
Bean family (Fabaceae)

Description: A much-branched plant, up to 18"
tall, with long, white, spreading hairs on the stem
and leaves. The leaves are alternate, on long, hairy
stalks, and fan-shaped, with 5 leaflets, each about
2" long. The undersides of the leaflets are densely
hairy. The flowers are tightly clustered at the tops
of stems. Individual flowers are about ½" long,
dark bluish, with a flaring upper petal and 2 side
petals flanking a protruding lower lip. The flowers
turn from blue to white with age.

Bloom Season: Late spring–early summer

Habitat/Range: Occasional in dry prairies, often
with rocky soil, glades, and open, rocky woods;
found in the western third of the Midwest region,
and westward.

Comments: Formerly known as *Psoralea esculenta*.
The prairie turnip was considered the most
important food of Native Americans who lived on
the prairies. The plants were so valued that their
presence influenced the tribes' selection of hunting grounds. The tuberous roots, which are said to
taste like turnips, were also a favorite of the now-
extinct Plains grizzly bear. The plant's medicinal
uses included a root tea for treating sore throat,
chest problems, and gastroenteritis.

SCURF PEA
Psoralidium tenuiflorum
Bean family (Fabaceae)

Description: A bushy plant, up to 3' tall, with gray-
hairy stems. The leaves are alternate and stalked,
with usually 3 leaflets, each up to 2" long and less
than ½" wide. The flowers are in loose clusters
on long stalks that arise from the leaf axils. Each
flower is about ⅜" long, bluish-purple to purple in
color, with a flaring upper petal and 2 side petals
flanking a protruding lower lip.

Bloom Season: Late spring–summer

Habitat/Range: Occasional in mesic to dry prairies,
savannas, glades, and sandy or rocky, open woods;
found in the central and southwest quarters of the
Midwest region, and westward.

Comments: Formerly known as *Psoralea tenuiflora*.
The Lakota made a root tea to treat headache, and
they burned the root as incense to repel mosquitoes. The Dakota took the tops of the plants and
made garlands that were worn on very hot days to
protect the head from the heat of the sun.

CLOSED GENTIAN
Gentiana andrewsii
Gentian family (Gentianaceae)

Description: Unbranched stems, up to 2½' tall, with stalkless, smooth leaves that are opposite along the stem. The upper leaves are usually the largest, up to 5" long and 1½" wide, with pointed tips, parallel veins running down the leaf, and a fringe of small hairs along the margin. The flowers occur in 1–3 clusters along the stem, with a whorl of leaves and leaf-like bracts below each cluster. Each flower is about 1½" long, deep blue, with petals that remain closed except for a tiny, fringed opening at the top. Each flower has 5 lobes, with an interconnecting membrane between each lobe that extends slightly beyond the lobe, creating the fringed appearance.

Bloom Season: Late summer–fall

Habitat/Range: Infrequent in mesic prairies, seepage areas, fens, and moist areas in woodlands; found throughout the Midwest region.

Comments: This plant is also called "bottle gentian" for the shape of the flowers. Bumblebees are the primary pollinators because they are strong enough to force their way into the tightly closed flowers. A closely related species, soapwort gentian (*Gentiana saponaria*), has the 5 lobes of each flower with an interconnecting membrane between each lobe that is of equal length, or slightly below, each lobe. This gentian is infrequent to rare in mesic sand prairies, sandy woods, and savannas; found primarily in the central part of the Midwest region, with a few locations in the south-central part.

DOWNY GENTIAN
Gentiana puberulenta
Gentian family (Gentianaceae)

Description: Stout, unbranched stems, up to 12" tall, with shiny, pointed, opposite leaves. The leaves are without stalks, broadest toward the base, up to 2" long and 1" wide, with minute hairs along the margins. The showy flowers are in dense clusters of 3–10. Each flower is deep blue to bluish-purple, up to 1½" long and about as wide, with 5 spreading lobes that alternate with small fringed segments. The base of the petals is white with dark blue stripes or streaks.

Bloom Season: Late summer–fall

Habitat/Range: Locally frequent in mesic to dry prairies, savannas, and open woods; found throughout the Midwest region, but rare in the eastern third.

Comments: Downy gentian is one of the last flowers to bloom in the fall, even surviving the first frosts. The flowers can remain closed on overcast days or can begin closing within minutes when shaded by a large passing cloud. The Winnebago and Dakota took root tea as a tonic. The Meskwaki used the root to treat snakebite.

STIFF GENTIAN
Gentianella quinquefolia
Gentian family (Gentianaceae)

Description: Annual or biennial plants, up to 16" tall, with 4-sided stems and several upper branches. The leaves are opposite, stalkless, up to 2½" long and 1" wide, broadest at the base, clasping the stem, and abruptly tapering to a pointed tip. The flowers are lilac to pale lavender to blue, tubular, upright, up to 1" long, and mostly closed at the top, with 5 bristle-tipped lobes.

Bloom Season: Late summer–fall

Habitat/Range: Infrequent in hill prairies, upland savannas, thinly wooded slopes; also, bottomland forests, banks of streams, seepages, and wet meadows; found through the Midwest region, but absent in the northern third.

Comments: Formerly known as *Gentiana quinquefolia*, this genus has now been reserved for the perennial gentians. Root tea was once used as a bitter tonic to stimulate digestion and weak appetite. Also used for treatment of headache, hepatitis, jaundice, and constipation.

FRINGED GENTIAN
Gentianopsis crinita
Gentian family (Gentianaceae)

Description: Annual or biennial plants, up to 2' tall, stems hairless, slightly 4-angled, with few to several side branches. The leaves are opposite, stalkless, clasping the stem at their bases, up to 2½" long and ¾" wide, tapering to a pointed tip, hairless, smooth along the margins, and with a glossy surface. The flowers are on single, slender stalks, 2–7" long, near the top of the plant. The flowers are royal blue to blue-violet, trumpet-shaped, 1½–2" long and 1" wide, with 4 broadly rounded, spreading lobes that have long, delicate fringes around the edges.

Bloom Season: Late summer–fall

Habitat/Range: Uncommon in moist depressions in prairies, wet to moist sand prairies, fens, open wooded swamps, and stream banks; found in the northern half of the Midwest region.

Comments: Fringed gentian flowers open on sunny days, but generally remain closed on cloudy days. Ants are highly attracted to the nectar of these flowers because of their taste and nutritional value, so in response, some specialists believe the fringe along the petal lobes provides a measure of protection so that only pollinators like bees and bumblebees are allowed. Another species, lesser fringed gentian (*Gentianopsis virgata*), is a smaller plant overall, 3–18" tall, with shorter fringes on the flowers, less-spreading petal lobes, and smaller, more-linear leaves, 1–1½" long and ¼–⅓" wide; occasional in wet woods, banks of streams, wet meadows, and thickets; found in the northern half of the Midwest region.

WOOLLEN BREECHES

Hydrophyllum appendiculatum
Waterleaf family (Hydrophyllaceae)

Description: Biennial plants, often forming dense colonies, with hairy stems, often branched, and up to 2' tall. The leaves are alternate, fan-shaped, up to 6" long and about as wide, with 5–7 shallow lobes, hairy, and coarsely toothed along the margins. The upper surface of the leaves is often mottled gray or light green. The flowers are in loose clusters at the tops of long, hairy stems. Each pinkish-purple to lavender flower is up to ½" across, on slender, hairy stalks, with 5 petals and 5 stamens that are equal to or extend just beyond the petals.

Bloom Season: Mid-spring–midsummer

Habitat/Range: Common in moist woods; also, on steep, rocky slopes, at the base of bluffs, and in wooded valleys; found through the Midwest region, but absent in the northern third.

Comments: A closely related species, broadleaf waterleaf (*Hydrophyllum canadense*), a perennial, lacks hairs and has the upper leaves often above the flowers, which are white; occasional in moist woods; found through the Midwest region, but absent in the northwest quarter.

VIRGINIA WATERLEAF

Hydrophyllum virginianum
Waterleaf family (Hydrophyllaceae)

Description: Plants often form dense colonies, with smooth stems, up to 2' tall. The lower leaves are alternate, deeply divided into 5–7 opposite lobes, with the lower pair of lobes quite separate from the others. The upper leaves are closer to being fan-shaped, with the lobes not all deeply cut. The flowers are in loose, rounded clusters, about 2" across on long stems, with the heads extending beyond the leaves. Individual flowers are violet to white, up to ½" long, and shaped like a tiny, fluted, narrow bell. The 5 petals are joined toward their bases, with the 5 stamens extending well beyond the petals, giving the flowers a rather hairy appearance.

Bloom Season: Mid-spring–early summer

Habitat/Range: Common in moist or low woods in ravines, at the base of bluffs, and in valleys along streams; found throughout the Midwest region.

Comments: Native Americans used root tea as an astringent (a substance that causes tissue to contract) to stop bleeding and to treat diarrhea and dysentery. The Iroquois used the tender young leaves as greens. Another species, large-leaved waterleaf (*Hydrophyllum macrophyllum*), has hairy stems, leaves that are deeply divided into 9–13 lobes, and white flowers; common in moist woods and ravines; found in the southeast quarter of the Midwest region.

PHACELIA
Phacelia bipinnatifida
Waterleaf family (Hydrophyllaceae)

Description: A biennial, 8–20" tall, with spreading hairs on the stem and branched above. Leaves are alternate, 5" long and 3" wide, hairy, deeply divided into 3–5 leaflets, with coarse teeth, and often covered with white blotches. The blue to lavender flowers are clustered at the top of stems with each flower about ½" across, and with 5 hairy stamens that extend beyond the 5 petals.

Bloom Season: Mid-spring–early summer

Habitat/Range: Occasional in moist woods, wooded slopes, ravines, and low areas along streams; found across the southern third of the Midwest region.

Comments: The genus name, *Phacelia*, is from the Greek *phakelos*, meaning a "bundle," relating to the clustered arrangement of the flowers. There are 200 species of annual and perennial phacelias from the Andes to North America, with 8 species occurring in the Midwest region.

HAIRY PHACELIA
Phacelia hirsuta
Waterleaf family (Hydrophyllaceae)

Description: A branched, annual plant, up to 14" tall, with densely spreading hairs on the stems and leaves. The leaves are alternate, divided into 3–7 segments, with rounded lobes and dense hairs on both surfaces and along the margins. The basal leaves have stalks, but the stem leaves are attached directly to the stem. The flowers are about ¾" across, on short stalks, and in loose clusters at the tops of the stems. Each flower is often whitish at the base, with 5 lavender to blue, rounded lobes.

Bloom Season: Spring–early summer

Habitat/Range: Occasional in dry prairies, sand prairies, open woods, glades, roadsides, and open disturbed ground; found in the southwest quarter of the Midwest region, and southward.

Comments: The genus name, *Phacelia*, is from the Greek *phakelos*, meaning "a bundle," relating to the clustered arrangement of the flowers. The species name, *hirsuta*, is from the Latin for "hairy."

MIAMI MIST

Phacelia purshii
Waterleaf family (Hydrophyllaceae)

Description: An annual, 8–16" tall, with weak stems and branches. Leaves are alternate, with the lower leaves on stalks and deeply cut to the central vein. Upper leaves are stalkless and clasp the stem with 3–11 lobes along the leaf. The leaves, stem, and flowers have flattened hairs. The blue to pale lavender flowers have a white center and are about ½" across. The 5 petals are distinctly fringed along the margin.

Bloom Season: Mid-spring–early summer

Habitat/Range: Occasional in bottomland forests, mesic forests, prairies, glades, and banks of streams; found in the southern half of the Midwest region.

Comments: An attractive spring flower with its fringed petals, the name refers to the effect its display produces in the Miami Valley of Ohio. Another species, small-flowered phacelia (*Phacelia gilioides*), is similar to Miami mist, but its flowers are toothed, not fringed, and with hairs on the outer surface of the petals. The habitat is similar to Miami mist; found in the southwest quarter of the Midwest region.

CRESTED IRIS

Iris cristata
Iris family (Iridaceae)

Description: A showy plant, up to 8" tall, with creeping, rootlike rhizomes that can spread quickly to form colonies. The leaves are mostly basal, up to 8" long and 1" wide, usually slightly curved or arching, light green, with parallel veins. The flowers are pale blue, lilac, or lavender, 1–2 on a long stalk, about 2½" across, with 3 smaller petals and 3 larger sepals. The sepals have a yellow or white, bearded ridge outlined by a dark purple margin.

Bloom Season: Mid- to late spring

Habitat/Range: Occasional on lower rocky slopes and in sandy soil bordering streams; found in the southern quarter of the Midwest region, and southward.

Comments: Native Americans used root ointment (prepared in animal fats or waxes) on cancerous ulcers. Root tea was used to treat hepatitis.

SOUTHERN BLUE FLAG
Iris virginica var. *shrevei*
Iris family (Iridaceae)

Description: Spreading rhizomes produce clumps of basal leaves, up to 3' long and 1" wide. The leaves are erect or arch out at the base, bluish-green to green, smooth, with parallel veins along the leaves and pointed tips. The flowers are on smooth, often waxy stems, up to 3' tall, with 1–2 branches. There are 1–4 flowers on a stalk, with each flower up to 3–4" across, pale blue-violet, and with yellow and white markings on the lower half of the petals. Each flower has 3 large, downward-curving sepals, 3 erect petals, ⅔–equal the size of the sepals, 3 stamens, and 3 petal-like style branches within the flower. The fruit is a 3-angled capsule, up to 3" long and 1½" wide.

Bloom Season: Late spring–midsummer

Habitat/Range: Locally frequent in wet prairies, marshes, fens, and roadside ditches; found through the Midwest region, but absent in the northern quarter.

Comments: The Cherokee pounded the root into a paste that was then used as a salve for skin ulcers. A tea made from the root was used to treat ailments of the liver, and a decoction (boiling) of the root was used to treat "yellowish urine." It is considered to be one of the iris species used by the Seminole to treat "shock following an alligator-bite." Another species, northern blue flag (*Iris versicolor*), has darker blue to blue-violet petals, smaller petals that are ½–⅔ the size of the sepals; locally frequent in wet meadows and marshes; found in the northern third of the Midwest region, and northward.

PRAIRIE IRIS
Nemastylis geminiflora
Iris family (Iridaceae)

Description: A low-growing plant with grass-like leaves and a showy, sky-blue flower. The leaves are up to 12" long and about ¼" wide. The flowers are on stems about 4" tall, from 1–2 per stem, and up to 2½" across, with 6 sky-blue petals that are actually 3 petals and 3 sepals; the latter are widest near the middle, narrow at the bases, and taper to pointed tips. The bases of the flowers are white and surround 3 yellow to orange stamens. Each flower opens once around mid-morning and closes by mid-afternoon.

Bloom Season: Mid- to late spring

Habitat/Range: Uncommon in mesic to dry prairies, usually over limestone; also, in glades and other rocky sites; found in the southwest quarter of the Midwest region, and southwestward.

Comments: A closely related species, Nuttall's pleatleaf (*Nemastylis nuttallii*), has a taller stem, up to 8", narrower leaves, less than ¼" wide, smaller flowers, less than 2" across, which are more purple in color and open in late afternoon and close during the night; uncommon on prairies, glades, and dry upland woods; found in the southwest quarter of the Midwest region, and southward.

NARROW-LEAF BLUE-EYED GRASS
Sisyrinchium angustifolium
Iris family (Iridaceae)

Description: Small, clump-forming plants, up to 12" tall, with winged stems, each about ⅛" wide, that appear to branch at the top. The grass-like leaves are green in shaded areas but appear bluish or grayish-green in the sun. The flower stalks are winged. The flower clusters are each attached on 1–4 long stalks arising from 1 leaf-like bract. Each flower is deep blue-violet, with a yellow center, about ½" across, with 3 sepals and 3 petals, all looking like petals. The tips of the sepals and petals vary, from rounded with a hair-like point, to notched, to shallowly toothed.

Bloom Season: Late spring–early summer

Habitat/Range: Uncommon in mesic upland prairies and more frequent in prairie/woodland borders, savannas, bottomland forests, and stream banks; found through the Midwest region, but absent in the northwest quarter.

Comments: The deep blue-violet flowers of narrow-leaf blue-eyed grass give this species a distinctive look, along with its denser display of blooms. This plant makes for a popular addition to wildflower plantings and rock gardens. Another species, mountain blue-eyed grass (*Sisyrinchium montanum*), has flower stems winged with finely toothed edges and flowers larger, about ¾" across; occasional in sandy fields and meadows; found in the northern third of the Midwest region, and westward. A species similar to mountain blue-eyed grass is needle-pointed blue-eyed grass (*Sisyrinchium mucronatum*), but the latter lacks wings on the flower stalks, which are smooth; also found in similar habitats and range.

PRAIRIE BLUE-EYED GRASS

Sisyrinchium campestre
Iris family (Iridaceae)

Description: Small, clump-forming plants, with stems not branching at the top, up to 12" tall, with pointed, upright, grass-like leaves. The flower stems are flat, about ⅛" wide, with 2 narrow wings, and typically longer than the leaves. Several flowers, each on a slender stalk, emerge from a long-pointed, leaf-like bract at the top of the stem. Each flower is light to dark blue or white (see page 59 for white version) with a yellow center, about ½" across, with 3 sepals and 3 petals, all looking like petals. The tips of the sepals and petals vary, from rounded with a hair-like point, to notched, to shallowly toothed.

Bloom Season: Mid-spring–early summer

Habitat/Range: Common in dry upland prairies, savannas, rocky, open woods, and glades; found throughout the Midwest region, but absent in the eastern third.

Comments: A similar species, eastern blue-eyed grass (*Sisyrinchium albidum*), has 3–4 leaf-like bracts surrounding a single flower cluster at the top of the stem. Flowers are white or pale violet; habitat is similar to prairie blue-eyed grass; found through the Midwest region, but absent in the western third.

DOWNY WOOD MINT

Blephilia ciliata
Mint family (Lamiaceae)

Description: Plants with square, unbranched stems covered with downy hair, up to 2' tall. The leaves are opposite, without stalks, up to 3½" long and 1½" wide, broadest at the base and tapering to a pointed tip, with fine hairs on the undersurface and small, scattered teeth along the margins. The basal leaves remain green throughout the winter. The pale pink to lavender to pale purple flowers are packed in a tight cluster, with up to 3 clusters stacked one above the other. The flowers are about ½" long, hairy, with 2 lips; the upper lip is arching, while the lower lip has 3 lobes and reddish spots.

Bloom Season: Late spring–summer

Habitat/Range: Occasional in mesic to dry upland forests, glades, old fields, and along roadsides; found through the Midwest region, but absent in the northern third.

Comments: Also known as Ohio horse mint. The Cherokee used a preparation of the fresh leaves for headache. The aromatic leaves can be used as tea when steeped in hot water.

HAIRY WOOD MINT
Blephilia hirsuta
Mint family (Lamiaceae)

Description: Plants with square, sometimes-branched stems covered with long white hairs, 1½–2½' tall. The leaves are opposite, on hairy stalks about 1" long, about 3½" long and 1½" wide, broadest below the middle and tapering to a point, with dense hairs on the undersurface and numerous teeth along the margins. The white to lavender flowers are packed in a tight cluster, with several clusters or whorls stacked one above the other. The flowers are about ½" long, hairy, with 2 lips; the upper lip is arching, while the lower lip has 3 lobes and reddish spots.

Bloom Season: Summer

Habitat/Range: Occasional in mesic upland forests, bottomland forests, and banks of streams; found throughout the Midwest region, but rare to absent in the northern third.

Comments: Hairy wood mint is found to have a fainter, less pleasant odor than downy wood mint. That being the case, hairy wood mint is more heavily foraged by insects, making the species less desirable as a garden ornamental.

WILD MINT
Mentha arvensis
Mint family (Lamiaceae)

Description: Plants with square, usually single stems that are erect to somewhat sprawling, ½–2' tall, hairy, and with a strong minty fragrance. The leaves are opposite, short-stalked, lance-shaped, 1–2½" long and ½–1" wide, toothed along the margins, pointed at the tip, and hairy underneath. A pair of leaves on the stem is at a right angle to that above and below. The flowers are about ⅛" long in clusters of about 20 above the axils of the leaves. Each white to pink to lavender flower has an upper lip notched into two parts, and a lower lip with 3 lobes, with darker spots on the inside of the tube. Four long stamens extend beyond the tube.

Bloom Season: Summer

Habitat/Range: Common in bottomland forests, marshes, spring branches, springy seeps, fens, and other moist soil areas; found throughout the Midwest region, but less common in the southern third.

Comments: Also known as *Mentha canadensis*. One native and seven nonnative members of the *Mentha* genus are found in the Midwest region, and there is some evidence that the North American native wild mint is an old hybridization with European mint species that were brought over by early settlers. North American tribes used this plant for more than 100 different medicinal purposes, as well as to make tea and to flavor food.

CALAMINT
Clinopodium arkansanum
Mint family (Lamiaceae)

Description: A sparse, low-growing mint, with smooth, branching, square stems, up to 12" tall, and very fragrant. The stem leaves are opposite, stalkless, slender, less than ½" long and ⅛" across, and often with a smaller pair of leaf-like bracts emerging from each leaf axil. The basal leaves are round and rose-purple underneath. The flowers are in clusters of 2–3, on stalks attached at the leaf axils. Each flower is tubular, but somewhat flattened, hairy on the outer surface, about ⅜" long, with 2 pale lavender lips. The upper lip has 2 small lobes, and the lower lip is larger, with 3 lobes.

Bloom Season: Late spring–fall

Habitat/Range: Common in limestone and dolomite glades and ledges, mesic gravel prairies, sandy savannas, and rocky areas along springs; found in the southwest quarter of the Midwest region, and in scattered populations throughout the eastern half.

Comments: Formerly known as *Calamintha arkansana* and *Satureja arkansana*. A leaf tea has been used for colds, fever, coughs, indigestion, kidney and liver ailments, and headache. The essential oil, which can be lethal if taken internally, has been used as an insect repellent, but may cause dermatitis. Another species, wild basil (*Clinopodium vulgare*), is taller, up to 24", with leaves that are 1–2" long and 1" wide, with flowers in clusters of about 30. Occasional in upland woods and woodland edges, meadows, and rock outcrops; found in the north-central and eastern third of the Midwest region.

DITTANY
Cunila origanoides
Mint family (Lamiaceae)

Description: A low, much-branched, wiry plant, up to 1' tall, sometimes with fine hairs along the square stem. Leaves are opposite, stalkless, hairless, up to 1½" long, broadest at the base, tapering to a pointed tip, and usually with a few teeth along the margins. The flowers are in clusters arising from the leaf axils. Each lavender flower is ¼–⅓" in length and has 2 lips: The smaller upper lip has 2 lobes, while the larger lower lip has 3. The lips have purplish dots. There are 2 stamens and 1 style that extend well beyond the lips of the flower.

Bloom Season: Midsummer–fall

Habitat/Range: Common in thin acidic soils over sandstone in dry, rocky, or open woods on upper slopes and edges; found across the southern third of the Midwest region.

Comments: In late autumn, during hard freezes, dittany produces "frost flowers." These are ribbons of ice oozing out of cracks at the base of the stem. Sap from still-active roots freezes as it emerges from the dead stem, growing like a white ribbon as more fluid is pumped out. Another plant known for its frost flowers is white crownbeard (*Verbesina virginica*).

ROUGH FALSE PENNYROYAL
Hedeoma hispida
Mint family (Lamiaceae)

Description: A summer annual, 3–16" tall, with a square stem and moderately to densely covered with mostly downward-curled hairs. The leaves are opposite, narrow, about ¾" long and ⅛" wide, toothless, hairy, with a blunt tip, stalkless, and mildly aromatic. The flowers are in whorls around the leaf axils along the stem. Each flower is blue to purple, about ¼" long, tubular, with a notched upper lip and a 3-lobed lower lip that has a white spot at the base. The calyx is green, tubular, distinctly ribbed, and bristly-hairy, with sharply pointed teeth.

Bloom Season: Late spring–summer

Habitat/Range: Common in openings of dry upland forests, savannas, prairies, glades, banks of streams, pastures, and roadsides; found through the Midwest region, but uncommon in the eastern third.

Comments: A tea made from the leaves has been used to treat colds. A similar species, American pennyroyal (*Hedeoma pulegioides*), differs by having leaves broader in the middle, about 1" long and ¼" wide, with a few irregular teeth along the margins. The calyx is smooth or with fine hairs and triangular lobes, and the leaves are strongly scented. Found through the Midwest region, but absent in the northern third. Although ingesting the concentrated essential oil can be lethal, a leaf tea has traditionally been used for colds, fever, coughs, indigestion, kidney and liver ailments, headache, and insect repellent.

HORSEMINT
Monarda bradburiana
Mint family (Lamiaceae)

Description: A square-stemmed plant, up to 1½'
tall, with 1 to several unbranched stems emerging from the base. The leaves are opposite, hairy,
without stalks, up to 2½" long and 1¼" wide,
broadest at the base, narrowest at the tip, and
slightly toothed along the margins. The flowers are
in a round cluster at the top of the stem, with 5
leafy, triangular-shaped bracts below each cluster.
The bracts are often faded pink or purple and have
fringed margins. The lavender flowers are up to
1½" long, ending in 2 lips—the lower, broad and
recurving, the upper, arching upward with stamens
protruding. The lower lip has numerous purple
spots.

Bloom Season: Mid-spring–early summer

Habitat/Range: Common in rocky upland woods,
borders of upland prairies and glades, bluffs, thickets, and along roadsides; found in the southwest
quarter of the Midwest region, and southward.

Comments: Also called "beebalm," and formerly
known as *Monarda russeliana*. A tea can be prepared from horsemint leaves, which are aromatic
when crushed.

WILD BERGAMOT
Monarda fistulosa
Mint family (Lamiaceae)

Description: The plants have square stems and a
fragrant aroma, characteristics typical of the mint
family. The stems branch and are up to 5' tall, with
the upper stem usually covered with fine hairs.
The leaves are opposite, on short stalks, up to 5"
long and 2" wide, widest at the base, narrowing
to a long, pointed tip, and sometimes with fine to
coarse teeth along the margins. The flowers are
numerous in dense, round heads, 1–2" across at
the tops of the stems. The tubular, purple to lavender flowers have 2 long lips—the upper, narrow
and hairy, with 2 protruding stamens, the lower,
broad, 3-lobed, with 2 notches at the tip.

Bloom Season: Late spring–summer

Habitat/Range: Common in prairies, savannas,
borders of glades, dry, rocky woods, pastures, old
fields, and along roadsides; found throughout the
Midwest region.

Comments: Many Native American tribes made
tea from the flower heads and leaves to treat
colds, fever, whooping cough, abdominal pain, and
headache, and to act as a stimulant. The Lakota
wrapped boiled leaves in a soft cloth and placed
it on sore eyes overnight to relieve pain. Chewed
leaves were placed on wounds under a bandage to
stop the flow of blood. Wild bergamot is still used
today in herbal teas.

LANCELEAF SELF-HEAL
Prunella vulgaris var. *lanceolata*
Mint family (Lamiaceae)

Description: The stems are hairy and slightly creeping but mostly erect, up to 12" long. The leaves are opposite, hairy, lance-shaped, tapering at the base, and up to 4" long and 1½" wide, with some small teeth along the margins. The lower leaves have stalks. The light purple flowers are in elongated clusters at the tops of stems. Each flower is about ½" long, with the upper lip forming a hood that is darker in color. The lower lip has 3 lobes, with the center lobe rounded and fringed at the tip.

Bloom Season: Late spring–summer

Habitat/Range: Common in open woods, low woodlands, banks and gravel bars of streams, pastures, old fields, and along roadsides; found throughout the Midwest region.

Comments: Also known as heal-all. Many Native American tribes used the aromatic self-heal for treating sore throat, hemorrhages, diarrhea, stomach troubles, fever, boils, urinary disorders, liver ailments, gas, colic, and gynecological problems. A closely related species, common self-heal (*Prunella vulgaris* var. *vulgaris*), was introduced to the United States from Europe by early settlers. It differs by having upper leaves rounded at their base and about half as broad as they are long. The native self-heal has leaves that taper at their base and narrower leaves, about a third as broad as they are long. This nonnative is found scattered across the Midwest region, mostly in more-disturbed sites.

BLUE SAGE
Salvia azurea var. *grandiflora*
Mint family (Lamiaceae)

Description: A slender, sometimes-branched plant, up to 5' tall, with short hairs along the four-sided stems. The leaves are widely spaced along the stem, opposite, short-stalked, narrow, up to 4" long and 1" wide, with a few teeth along the margins. The flowers are in whorls along the upper stem, with up to 8 flowers in a whorl. Each flower is blue with a white center, tubular, about 1" long, with 2 lips: The upper lip is narrow, hooded, and contains the two stamens, while the lower lip is broad, with 2 lobes.

Bloom Season: Summer–early fall

Habitat/Range: Common in dry prairies, savannas, and glades; found in the southwest quarter of the Midwest region, and absent or escaped from cultivation elsewhere.

Description: The genus name, *Salvia*, comes from the Latin word *salvere*, meaning "to feel well and healthy; to heal," which is the verb related to *salus* (health, well-being, prosperity, or salvation), in reference to the healing properties of some species in the genus. The species name, *azure*, means "sky blue," for the azure-blue flowers. The attractive, sky-blue flowers are pollinated by bumblebees. Another species, lance-leaved sage (*Salvia reflexa*), is an annual, shorter, 1–2' tall, with smaller, light blue flowers, each about ⅓" long, and smaller leaves, 1–2" long and ¼–½" wide; occasional in sandy or rocky prairies, wet prairies, upland and bottomland forests, and banks of streams; found native in the western third of the Midwest region, and adventive elsewhere.

CANCER WEED

Salvia lyrata
Mint family (Lamiaceae)

Description: A hairy plant with a single, square stem, up to 2' tall. The basal leaves have long stalks, up to 8" long and 3" wide, with wavy to lobed margins. There is usually 1 smaller pair of stem leaves attached without stalks. The flowers are in a series of whorls on the upper part of the stem, with about 6 flowers in a whorl. Each flower is about 1" long, light blue, with the upper lip much shorter than the lower lip.

Bloom Season: Mid-spring–early summer

Habitat/Range: Occasional in moist or rocky, usually open woods, sandy or gravelly soils along streams, and pastures; found in the southern quarter of the Midwest region, and southward.

Comments: Also called "lyre-leaved sage" for the unusual shape of its basal leaves that somewhat resemble a U-shaped, stringed musical instrument of the harp class. Native Americans used the root in a salve to treat sores. Tea from the whole plant was used for coughs, colds, nervous debility, and, taken with honey, for asthma. It was also used as a folk remedy for cancer and warts.

DOWNY SKULLCAP

Scutellaria incana
Mint family (Lamiaceae)

Description: This plant has fine, downy hairs that cover the square stems, which are up to 3' tall. The leaves are opposite, stalked, with the largest up to 6" long, occurring toward the center of the stem. The lance-shaped leaves have rounded bases, coarse, blunt teeth along the margins, and soft, downy hairs on the underside. The flowers occur along several stalks. Each purplish-blue flower is about 1" long with 2 lips: The upper lip is a hood, while the lower lip is divided into 3 lobes, with a white center.

Bloom Season: Summer–fall

Habitat/Range: Occasional in mesic to rocky, open woods, wooded slopes, and banks along streams; found in the southern half of the Midwest region.

Comments: A closely related species, heart-leaved skullcap (*Scutellaria ovata*), has heart-shaped leaf bases, stems with conspicuous soft hairs, and flowers ⅜–1" long. It is common in rocky, open woods and glades; found in the southern half of the Midwest region. Another commonly encountered species, mad dog skullcap (*Scutellaria lateriflora*), has flowers that are not on stalks; instead, 1–3 flowers emerge from the leaf axils, each ¼–⅓" long. It is found in meadows and low, wet woods in valleys along streams; found throughout the Midwest region.

307

SMALL SKULLCAP
Scutellaria parvula
Mint family (Lamiaceae)

Description: A short, slender plant, up to 8" tall, with a hairy, square stem. The leaves are opposite, stalkless, hairy, less than 1" long and about ¼" wide, lance-shaped, rounded at the base, and blunt-tipped. The flowers are opposite each other on short stalks that emerge from the leaf axils. Each flower is about ⅜" long, purple, and hairy, with a tube ending in a small, hooded upper lip and a broad, lobed lower lip. The lower lip has a white center with purple spots.

Bloom Season: Late spring–midsummer

Habitat/Range: Common in upland prairies, savannas, open woodlands, glades, and pastures, often in sandy or rocky sites; found throughout the Midwest region, but rare in the northeast part.

Comments: The genus name, *Scutellaria*, comes from the Latin word *scutella*, meaning "a small dish or saucer," in reference to the shape of the persistent calyx after the flowers fade. The species name, *parvula*, means "little, small." The common name, skullcap, alludes to the resemblance of the calyx to miniature medieval helmets. The Meskwaki used small skullcap in the treatment of diarrhea. Another species of small skullcap, *Scutellaria leonardii*, is now considered by many to be a variety of *Scutellaria parvula*.

FALSE PENNYROYAL
Trichostema brachiatum
Mint family (Lamiaceae)

Description: Aromatic, annual plants, less than 18" tall, with branching stems that are 4-sided and hairy on the upper part. The leaves are opposite, and the pairs are at right angles to the one above and below. Each leaf is up to 2" long and ¾" wide, with short stalks, broadest in the middle and tapering at the end. Each leaf has parallel veins along its length and surfaces that are moderately to densely covered with gland-tipped hairs. Flowers are stalked, with 1–3 flowers per cluster at the base of upper stem leaves. Each flower ranges from pink to purple, about ¼" across, with petals fused at the base to form a tube that opens to 5 tiny lobes, the lowermost slightly longer than the others.

Bloom Season: Midsummer–early fall

Habitat/Range: Frequent in thin-soil areas of upland prairies, savannas, glades, rock outcrops, blufftops, banks along streams, and rocky pastures; found throughout the Midwest region, but rare in the northern third.

Comments: Formerly known as *Isanthus brachiatus*; also known as fluxweed. According to *Culpeper's Complete Herbal* (1880) by English physician Nicholas Culpeper (1616–1654), fluxweed was used for stomach ailments, and even has bone- and sore-healing properties.

BLUE CURLS

Trichostema dichotomum
Mint family (Lamiaceae)

Description: A much-branched, annual plant, up to 2' tall, with square stems, and covered with dense, gland-tipped hairs. The leaves are opposite, broadest in the middle to lower half, up to 2½" long and ¾" wide, with usually smooth margins, and tapering at the base to a short stalk about ½" long. The flowers are about ¾" long, lavender-blue, with the upper lip having 4 short, spreading lobes, while the lower lip is much longer, and with a patch of white with purple spots. The 4 stamens are long and curve downward.

Bloom Season: Late summer–fall

Habitat/Range: Occasional on acidic soils of rocky, open woods and glades; also on sandy soils along streams; found throughout the lower half of the Midwest region.

Comments: The attractive flowers, with their lavender-blue corolla and long, curving stamens, must be viewed up close to be appreciated.

WILD HYACINTH

Camassia scilloides
Lily family (Liliaceae)

Description: A stout-stemmed plant emerging from a bulb, growing up to 2' tall. The stem is bare, with long, narrow, grass-like leaves, up to 1' long and ⅓" wide, emerging from the base. The leaves are often partially folded along their lengths. At the top of the stem is a cluster 4–12" long and 1¼–2" wide of up to 50 stalked flowers, each about 1" across, displaying 6 petals (3 petal-like sepals and 3 petals) varying in color from pale blue to lilac, and, rarely, pure white. There are 6 yellow-tipped stamens.

Bloom Season: Mid- to late spring

Habitat/Range: Common in mesic and dry prairies, open woodlands, glades, and rocky, open slopes; found throughout the southern half of the Midwest region.

Comments: A closely related species, prairie hyacinth (*Camassia angusta*), has stems up to 3' tall, a flower cluster 4–12" long and ¾–1¼" wide, from 50–100 flowers in a cluster, each flower ¾" wide, and petals deep lavender to pale purple; infrequent to rare in mesic to dry upland prairies, savannas, sometimes in rocky areas; found in the southwest quarter and central part of the Midwest region, and southwestward.

PURPLE TRILLIUM

Trillium recurvatum
Lily family (Liliaceae)

Description: Unbranched, stout-stemmed plants, up to 18" tall, with a whorl of 3 leaves at the top. The leaves are broadest in the middle and tapering at both ends, 3–6" long, smooth, 1½–3½" wide, and mottled on the surface. The bases of the leaves are stalked. The single flower is attached to the top of the stem without a stalk. The 3 green sepals are curved down, while the 3 maroon petals are upright and surround the 6 stamens.

Bloom Season: Mid- to late spring

Habitat/Range: Common in mesic upland forests along lower slopes, valleys, and ravine bottoms; found through the Midwest region, but absent in the northern third.

Comments: Purple trillium is sometimes known to have greenish-yellow petals. Several North American tribes used the root as a treatment for open wounds and sores, menstrual disorders, menopause, and internal bleeding, as an induce-ment to childbirth, and as an aphrodisiac. Frontier physicians used the crushed fresh leaves to treat snakebite, stings, and skin irritations.

WAKE ROBIN

Trillium sessile
Lily family (Liliaceae)

Description: Plants with smooth, stout stems, up to 10" tall, with a whorl of 3 leaves at the top. The leaves are oval, rounded, or pointed at the tip, rounded at the base, smooth, up to 4" long and 3½" wide, without stalks, and usually mottled on the surface. A single, stemless flower arises just above the leaves, up to 1½" long. The 3 green sepals are spreading, up to 1" long, while the 3 maroon to brown petals point upward, enclosing the 6 stamens.

Bloom Season: Mid- to late spring

Habitat/Range: Common on rocky, wooded slopes and low, moist bottoms of ravines and valleys; found throughout the southern half of the Midwest region.

Comments: Sometimes known to have greenish-yellow petals, wake robin has been used much the same as purple trillium.

FALSE HELLEBORE
Veratrum woodii
Lily family (Liliaceae)

Description: Plants with long, slender stems, up to 6' tall, with ribbed or pleated basal leaves. The basal leaves are broadest at the middle and tapering at both ends, up to 12" long and about 3" wide, and somewhat clasping the stem. The stem leaves are few and narrow. The upper stem is widely branched, hairy, with several flowers on short stalks each about ½" long. Each maroon flower is up to ¾" wide, with 3 petals and 3 sepals, all the same size, and with a pair of dark red glands at their bases.

Bloom Season: Midsummer–fall

Habitat/Range: Occasional to locally common on north- or east-facing wooded slopes; found in the southwest quarter of the Midwest region, and rare in the remaining southern half of the region.

Comments: Also known as *Melanthium woodii*. Although false hellebore is a perennial, it can go for several years without flowering. All parts of the plant are considered highly toxic. Most grazing animals avoid the plant because of its sharp, burning taste. A similar species of false hellebore has been used in pharmaceutical drugs to slow the heart rate, to lower blood pressure, and to treat arteriosclerosis.

CLAMMY CUPHEA
Cuphea viscosissima
Loosestrife family (Lythraceae)

Description: A sparsely branched annual, up to 2' tall, with sticky, purplish hairs. The stalked leaves are opposite on the stem, broadest below the middle, and from ¾" to 2" long. There are 1–2 small, purple to purplish-red flowers arising at the junctions of the upper stem and leaves. The flower is about ½" long, tubular, with 6 tiny petals of unequal size, with the upper 2 larger than the lower 4, and 12 stamens.

Bloom Season: Midsummer–fall

Habitat/Range: Occasional in dry soil in open woods, bluffs, sand prairies, and banks of streams; found throughout the southern half of the Midwest region.

Comments: Formerly called *Cuphea petiolata*, clammy cuphea (or blue waxweed) was used to treat infant cholera in the late 1800s. This plant has recently been tested for its potential cancer-fighting properties.

WINGED LOOSESTRIFE
Lythrum alatum
Loosestrife family (Lythraceae)

Description: A smooth, loosely branching plant, up to 2' tall, with squarish stems that may support shallow wings or flaps of tissue. The leaves are opposite on the lower stem and alternate above, narrow, up to 2" long and ½" wide, progressively smaller toward the top, broadly round at the base, and pointed at the tip. The flowers, up to ½" across, arise singly from the upper leaf axils. Each flower has a narrow tube with 6 lavender to reddish-purple petals and 6 purplish-brown stamens.

Bloom Season: Summer

Habitat/Range: Common in wet prairies, depressions and seepage areas, and along streams in upland prairies; found throughout the Midwest region.

Comments: The native winged loosestrife should not be confused with the introduced purple loose-strife (*Lythrum salicaria*) (see page 361). Purple loosestrife is much taller, up to 4' high, hairy, with whorled or opposite leaves and tall spikes of red to purple flowers that appear in clusters.

BUSH'S POPPY MALLOW
Callirhoe bushii
Mallow family (Malvaceae)

Description: Plants with densely hairy stems, up to 30" tall. The basal leaves are on hairy stalks, 4–9" long, with each leaf 1½–4" long, hairy, and divided into 5–7 narrow, deep, finger-like lobes that are coarsely toothed. The stem leaves are 1–4" long, stalked, hairy, triangular-shaped, with 3–5 lobes that are sparsely to coarsely toothed along the margins. The flowers are stalked, arising from leaf axils, cup-shaped, about 2–2½" across, with 5 reddish-purple petals, each about 1" long, and a central column containing stamens and styles.

Bloom Season: Summer

Habitat/Range: Uncommon to rare in upland prairies, glades, and woodland edges; found in the southwest quarter of the Midwest region.

Comments: Bush's poppy mallow is named for Benjamin Franklin Bush (1858–1937), an American botanist and ornithologist credited with discovering the plant. Bush was an expert on the flora of Jackson County, Missouri, in which Kansas City is located. His lifelong research into the plant life of that area made it into one of the best-known botanical regions in the United States at that time. In addition to Missouri, he also traveled extensively throughout Arkansas, Oklahoma, and Texas.

FRINGED POPPY MALLOW
Callirhoe digitata
Mallow family (Malvaceae)

Description: A smooth, widely branching, spindly plant, up to 4' tall, with a whitish coating on the stems that can be rubbed off. The leaves are alternate, stalked, and divided into 5–7 narrow, deep, finger-like lobes. Each lobe can be further divided and is usually less than ¼" wide. The flowers are on long stalks, with each flower 1½–2" across. The 5 petals are bright magenta, with ragged or fringed outer edges and a central column containing stamens and styles.

Bloom Season: Late spring–summer

Habitat/Range: Occasional in upland prairies, glades, and open areas; found in the southwest quarter of the Midwest region.

Comments: The genus name, *Callirhoe*, honors the daughter of a minor Greek deity, Achelous, a river god. The species name, *digitata*, means "shaped like an open hand," referring to the leaves.

CLUSTERED POPPY MALLOW
Callirhoe triangulata
Mallow family (Malvaceae)

Description: Stems single or multiple from the base, weakly erect to ascending to prostrate, and 16–40" tall (or long). The stem and leaves are densely covered with star-shaped hairs. The basal leaves are stalked, up to 4" long, triangular-shaped, and with scalloped margins. The stem leaves are alternate, up to 4" long, becoming smaller along the upper stem, triangular-shaped, and with 3–5 shallow lobes. There are clusters of short-stalked flowers at the stem tips that arise from the upper leaf axils. Each flower is 1–2½" wide, with 5 reddish-purple petals and a central column containing the stamens and styles.

Bloom Season: Summer

Habitat/Range: Uncommon to rare in sand prairies and sand savannas; found in the central section of the Midwest region.

Comments: The genus name, *Callirhoe*, honors the daughter of a minor Greek deity, Achelous, a river god. The species name, *triangulata*, means "with three angles," referring to the lower leaves.

PURPLE POPPY MALLOW
Callirhoe involucrata
Mallow family (Malvaceae)

Description: A low, spreading plant with hairy, branched stems, up to 3' long. The leaves are alternate, stalked, 1½–3½" long and 1–3" wide, and deeply divided into 3–5 lobes, arranged like the fingers of a hand. The flowers arise from the junction of a leaf and a stem and are on stalks, up to 8" long and numerous. Each flower is cup-shaped, deep reddish-purple, about 2–2½" long, with 5 large petals surrounding numerous stamens and styles that are united into a column.

Bloom Season: Late spring–midsummer

Habitat/Range: Occasional in dry upland prairies, especially in sandy soil, glades, and open woodlands; found in the southwest quarter of the Midwest region, and westward; also adventive in the lower half of the central region.

Comments: The Dakota and Lakota dried the root and used it in a smoke treatment, inhaling the fumes from the smoldering root to treat head colds. The Dakota also boiled the root and drank the tea for internal pains, or used it externally to bathe aching body parts.

WILD FOUR O'CLOCK
Mirabilis nyctaginea
Four o'clock family (Nyctaginaceae)

Description: The stems are nearly square, some-what hairy, branching, up to 4' tall, with widely spaced opposite leaves. The leaves are short-stalked, 2–4" long and 1–3" wide, with smooth margins, heart-shaped, and with pointed tips. The flowers are in open-branched clusters at the tops of the stems. As many as 5 flowers are seated upon a shallow, green, cup-shaped platform, which is 5-lobed and ¾" across. Each flower is about ½" across with no petals, and 5 pink to red, petal-like sepals, which form a spreading bell shape, with 5 notches and 3–5 yellow-tipped stamens. The flowers open in late afternoon and close the next morning.

Bloom Season: Late spring–early fall

Habitat/Range: A weedy species, occasional in upland prairies, especially in sandy soils, disturbed open ground, pastures, and roadsides; found throughout the Midwest region, but adventive in the eastern quarter.

Comments: The Ponca chewed the root and spit it into wounds to heal them. The Pawnee ground the dried root and applied it as a remedy for sore mouth in teething babies. Some tribes pounded the root and used it to treat swellings, sprains, and burns. The plant is considered poisonous. A closely related species, white four o'clock (*Mirabilis albida*), has densely hairy stems, narrower leaves, about ½" wide, without stalks, and white-lilac to pinkish flowers. Occurs in prairies, sand prairies, glades, and dry disturbed sites; found throughout the Midwest region, but adventive in the eastern half.

FIREWEED
Chamaenerion angustifolium
Evening primrose family (Onagraceae)

Description: Unbranched plants, 3–7' tall, with green or reddish stems and often with stiff hairs toward the top. The leaves are alternate, stalkless, narrow, 2–8" long and up to 2" wide, mostly smooth along the margin, and tapering at both ends. The flowers are in a spike-like cluster on the upper part of the stem. Each flower is about 1" across, with 4 broadly spreading, magenta to purplish petals, 8 stamens, and a downward-curving style. Behind the flower is a long, slender ovary that resembles the short flower stalk. The fruit is a slender, upright pod that turns red as the seed ripens.

Bloom Season: Summer

Habitat/Range: Common in moist soil, woodland edges, lightly shaded areas, and rocky slopes, often appearing after a disturbance like a burned wooded area; found in the northern half of the Midwest region.

Comments: Formerly known as *Epilobium angustifolium*. North Americans used the stem fibers to make thread and fishing nets. The greens of young plants have been cooked and eaten. Another species, not to be mistaken for fireweed, is hairy willow herb (*Epilobium hirsutum*), a branched, densely hairy Eurasian weed with mostly opposite leaves and notched petals. It occurs in moist disturbed areas in the Great Lakes region.

PUTTY ROOT
Aplectrum hyemale
Orchid family (Orchidaceae)

Description: This orchid has a leafless stem, up to 1½' tall, and produces 1 leaf, emerging from the root, that withers away by flowering time. The evergreen leaf appears from September through early May. The leaf is broadest at the middle and narrowing at both ends, up to 6" long and 3" wide, blue-green, with narrow, white, parallel veins, and strongly ribbed or pleated. The flowers are stalked and attached along the upper 8" of the stem. Each greenish-maroon flower is about ½" long, with 3 sepals and 3 petals. The top sepal and 2 lower side sepals flare open and outward. The 2 side petals and lower lip petal form a semi-opened, tubed flower in the center. The lower petal is a 3-lobed lip with a wavy edge.

Bloom Season: Late spring–early summer

Habitat/Range: Occasional in moist woods and in ravines and valleys; found through the Midwest region, but absent in the northern quarter.

Comments: The name for putty root is derived from the sticky juice from the corm (bulb-like underground structure), which was once used to glue broken pottery. Another common name, Adam-and-Eve, comes from the plant's production of a new corm every year that is connected by a slender branch to the old one. Native Americans mashed the corm and applied it to boils. Root tea was formerly used for bronchial troubles.

SPOTTED CORAL ROOT

Corallorhiza maculata
Orchid family (Orchidaceae)

Description: A yellow, brown, or purplish, single-stemmed plant, 6–20" tall, with no green color. The leaves are reduced to 1 or more yellowish, pointed, alternate, sheathing scales along the stem. The 6–50 flowers are alternate, each about 1" long and ½" wide, with a central sepal, flanked by 2 lateral, spreading sepals that are slightly longer than the two petals. The lower lip is white, with 1 large central lobe, and 2 much smaller side lobes, all with purple spots.

Bloom Season: Summer

Habitat/Range: Occasional in mesic upland forests and swamps; found throughout the Midwest region, but absent in the southwest quarter.

Comments: Another orchid species, striped coral root (*Corallorhiza striata*), has purple-striped sepals and petals and a smooth-edged lower lip; occasional in mesic upland forests; found in the northern quarter of the Midwest region.

FALL CORAL ROOT

Corallorhiza odontorhiza
Orchid family (Orchidaceae)

Description: Single-stemmed, brown to purplish, up to 1' tall, and lacking green color. Leaves are reduced to 3 alternating, sheathing scales along the stem. There are 5–15 flowers, each about ⅜" long, that alternate along the stem. Each small, purplish-brown flower has the sepals and petals joined together to form an upper hood and a conspicuous lower lip that is white, with small purple dots, and crinkled along the margin.

Bloom Season: Late summer–fall

Habitat/Range: Uncommon in woods and wooded slopes; found throughout the Midwest region, but absent in the northern quarter.

Comments: Also called "autumn coral root," this is one of the smallest-flowered orchids in the Midwest region. Lacking chlorophyll, the plants must obtain their nutrients from decaying organic matter through the aid of soil fungi.

SPRING CORAL ROOT

Corallorhiza wisteriana
Orchid family (Orchidaceae)

Description: Single-stemmed, brown to purplish, up to 16" tall, and lacking green color. Leaves are reduced to 3 alternating, sheathing scales along the stem. There are 5–25 purplish-brown flowers, each about ⅜" long. Each small, purplish-brown flower has the sepals and petals joined together to form an upper hood and a conspicuous lower lip that is white with small, purple dots, and wavy along the margin.

Bloom Season: Spring

Habitat/Range: Occasional in mesic upland forests; found in the southern third of the Midwest region.

Comments: Orchids in the genus *Corallorhiza* have coral-shaped roots, as the name implies. Lacking chlorophyll, the plants must obtain their nutrients from decaying organic matter through the aid of soil fungi. A similar orchid that blooms in the spring is northern coral root (*Corallorhiza trifida*), which has greenish-yellow stems and flowers; each flower has 2 petals and 1 sepal forming a loosely formed upper hood, with 2 lateral sepals spreading out and downward, and a lower lip that is white, sometimes speckled with purple dots. Occasional in upland forests, swamps, and bogs; found in the northern third of the Midwest region.

SHOWY ORCHIS

Galearis spectabilis
Orchid family (Orchidaceae)

Description: A single, stout-stemmed plant, up to 10" tall, with a pair of shiny leaves emerging from the base. The leaves are broad and up to 7" long and up to 3½" wide. From 2–10 flowers are located along the upper part of the stem, with each flower ¾–1" long. The flowers are two-toned, with the purple upper hood being composed of 2 small petals and 3 petal-like sepals, while the lower lip is white with crinkled edges. A stout, white spur projects downward from the base.

Bloom Season: Mid-spring–early summer

Habitat/Range: Occasional in moist woods and wooded ravines; found through the Midwest region, but absent in the northern quarter.

Comments: Formerly known as *Orchis spectabilis*. The genus name, *Galearis*, is from the Greek *galea*, meaning "hood," in reference to the combining of the sepals and petals formed above the lower lip.

LARGE WHORLED POGONIA
Isotria verticillata
Orchid family (Orchidaceae)

Description: Small plants, 6–10" tall, with a single, smooth, purplish, hollow stem and a root system that can send up new plants that form colonies. The leaves are in a whorl of 5–6, each 1¼–2" long and ½–¾" wide, smooth, broadest in the middle and tapering at both ends. The flower is on top of a stalk, ¾–1½" tall, that emerges from the upper stem. Each flower has 3 narrow, widely spreading sepals, 1¼–2½" long, that are yellowish-green and purplish toward the tips. The lateral petals are smaller, ½–¾" long, and form a yellowish-green hood. The lip is ½–¾" long, yellowish-green, with the lateral lobes purple-tinged, the middle lobe often white and broadly rounded, with a yellow-green crest that is sometimes purple.

Bloom Season: Mid-spring–early summer

Habitat/Range: Rare in dry and mesic upland forests, lower slopes and bottoms of ravines, and bogs; found in the Midwest region in southeast Missouri, Indiana, Michigan, and Ohio.

Comments: A much rarer whorled pogonia, often referred to as the rarest orchid east of the Mississippi River, is small whorled pogonia (*Isotria medeoloides*), which has green stems, does not form colonies, with a yellowish-green to green flower, sepals ⅝–1" long, only slightly longer than the petals, and a lip about ½" long. Occurs in mesic upland forests; found historically in the Midwest region in southeast Missouri, southwest Illinois, southern Ohio, and eastward.

CRESTED CORAL ROOT
Hexalectris spicata
Orchid family (Orchidaceae)

Description: A smooth, leafless plant, 10–25" tall, with a yellowish-brown to purplish stem. There are 8–25 flowers, stalked, along a spike at the upper end of the stem. Each flower is about ¾" long, yellow to yellow-brown, with purple-brown stripes running the length of the 2 petals, 3 sepals, and the lip, which also has 3 lobes with a crested center and bright purple veins.

Bloom Season: Midsummer–fall

Habitat/Range: Uncommon in dry upland forests and blufftops and edges of glades; found in the southern quarter of the Midwest region.

Comments: Crested coral root orchid lacks chlorophyll and subsists entirely on nutrients obtained from mycorrhizal fungi in the soil.

TWAYBLADE
Liparis liliifolia
Orchid family (Orchidaceae)

Description: A smooth, hairless plant, 4–8" tall, with a pair of glossy green leaves arising from the base. Sterile plants have a single leaf. The leaves are broadest at or below the middle, about 4" long and 3" wide, with smooth margins and parallel veins. The flowers are purplish-brown, 5–20, with a broad, showy lip that is somewhat translucent, about ⅝" long, and pointed at the tip. Two thread-like petals hang below the lip. The 3 sepals are greenish-yellow and slender; the upper sepal is extended back, the lower two, extended out below.

Bloom Season: Late spring–midsummer

Habitat/Range: Found in mesic woods, rocky, open woods, edges of glades, and along stream banks; found throughout the Midwest region, but rare in the northern third.

Comments: Also called "lily-leaved twayblade." The genus name, *Liparis*, means "glossy," and refers to the glossy luster of the leaves, while the species name, *liliifolia*, draws attention to the lily-like leaves. Twayblade has been found to successfully inhabit recently disturbed sites, such as after selective timber harvest, construction of forest trails and roads, forest edge creation by clearing, and tree plantations.

PURPLE FRINGELESS ORCHID

Platanthera peramoena
Orchid family (Orchidaceae)

Description: A striking orchid with a smooth stem, up to 3' tall. There are 2–5 leaves along the stem, each from 4–8" long and about 2" wide, progressively reduced in size upward. A cylindrical cluster of 30–50 reddish-purple flowers, each 1" long and ¾" wide, is found at the top of the stem. The flower lip is divided into 3 fan-shaped lobes, with the middle lobe notched. The upper sepal and 2 upper petals form a small hood, while the 2 lower sepals form the sides of the flower. A 1" spur reflexes downward from the rear of the flower.

Bloom Season: Summer–fall

Habitat/Range: Uncommon in low, moist woods along streams, and wet meadows; found throughout the southern half of the Midwest region.

Comments: Formerly known as *Habenaria peramoena*. This is a very showy orchid; unfortunately, it does not bloom every year. This is typical of many orchids in the genus *Platanthera* that seem to rest a year or more after flowering, in order to gain energy to bloom again.

PURPLE FRINGED ORCHID

Platanthera psycodes
Orchid family (Orchidaceae)

Description: A smooth, green, single-stemmed plant, 1–2½" tall, with leaves up to 8" long and 2¾" wide at the base. The leaves are alternate, oval with pointed tips, toothless, clasping at the base, and becoming progressively smaller ascending the stem, ending with bracts near the flowers. The flowers are alternate along a compact spike along the upper part of the stem. Each flower is ½–¾" long, lavender to rose-purple, with 3 petal-like sepals that form a hood, 2 lateral petals, and a lower lip deeply divided into 3 segments with fringed tips, white at the base, and a curving, tubular spur underneath.

Bloom Season: Late spring–midsummer

Habitat/Range: Occasional in mesic forests, meadows, marshes, swamps, stream banks, and shorelines; found in the northern half of the Midwest region, and rare in the southeast quarter.

Comments: Formerly known as *Habenaria psycodes*. The genus name, *Planthera,* means "broad anther," while the species name, *psycodes*, which is a misspelling of *psychodes*, means "butterflylike," probably alluding to the shape of the flowers.

CRANEFLY ORCHID
Tipularia discolor
Orchid family (Orchidaceae)

Description: A slender, fragile-looking plant, 14–18" tall, that produces a single leaf that overwinters and dies back in the spring. The winter leaf is about 2½" long and 2" wide, broadest at the base, dark green above with purple spots, purple below, pleated, and with a 1½" stalk. The stem leaves are reduced to a few sheathing bracts. There are 20–40 flowers on a purplish-brown stem. Each small flower is about ⅜" long, purplish-green, with sepals and petals similar, each about ⅛" long; the lip, also about ⅛" long, is translucent, pale purple, 3-lobed, with the middle lobe having 2 small notches at the tip.

Bloom Season: Summer

Habitat/Range: Uncommon in mesic upland forests, flatwoods, and on top of forested, shallow sand dunes in southeast Missouri; found in the southern quarter of the Midwest region.

Comments: The genus name, *Tipularia*, references the crane fly genus *Tipula*, because the flowers appear to resemble crippled crane flies. The species name, *discolor*, means "of two colors," and relates to the 2-toned leaves. Another orchid that has a leaf that overwinters and dies back before flowering is putty root (*Aplectrum hyemale*) (see page 317).

ROUGH FALSE FOXGLOVE
Agalinis aspera
Broomrape family (Orobanchaceae)

Description: An annual, slender-stemmed plant, 8–24" tall, with slightly rough stems and short, stiff hairs. Leaves are opposite, stalkless, and narrow, 1–1½" long and less than ⅛" wide, with sharp-pointed tips and smaller leaf clusters in the leaf axils. The flowers are bell-shaped, reddish to deep purple, with prominent lobes, minutely hairy, and ¾–1" long. The throat of the flower has 2 pale yellow lines and reddish or purplish spots.

Bloom Season: Late summer–fall

Habitat/Range: Occasional in dry upland prairies, hill prairies, sand prairies, and open woods; found in the western half of the Midwest region.

Comments: Another species, eared false foxglove (*Agalinis auriculata*), has moderately to densely hairy stems and leaves, with leaves up to 2" long and ¾" wide, and 1–2 small, outward-pointing lobes near their rounded bases. Each flower is densely hairy and ¾–1¼" long; uncommon in dry to mesic prairies and savannas; found in widely scattered locations across the Midwest region, but absent in the northern third. Also, rough-stemmed false foxglove (*Agalinis gattingeri*) has flowers single or in small open clusters just at the branch tips; uncommon in prairies, upland forests, and savannas; found in the central and southwest quarters of the Midwest region, and rare elsewhere.

FASCICLED FALSE FOXGLOVE
Agalinis fasciculata
Broomrape family (Orobanchaceae)

Description: Stems ridged to 4-sided, with moderate to dense hairs, 2–3' tall, and somewhat bushy, with numerous short side branches. The primary leaves have clusters (or fascicles) of secondary leaves arising from their bases. Leaves are linear, somewhat arching, up to 1½" long and less than ⅛" wide, with pointed tips, smooth edges, and a prominent vein along the middle. The showy flowers are on short stalks at the leaf junctions, or at the tips of stem branches. The flowers are pink to purplish-pink or purple, up to 1" across, with hairs along the flaring tubular portion and the 5 lobes. The lobes are fringed along the margins and joined above a whitish throat, with purple to reddish-purple spots.

Bloom Season: Late summer—fall

Habitat/Range: Occasional to uncommon in mesic to dry upland prairies, open woodlands, and sandy open ground; found in the southwest quarter of the Midwest region.

Comments: Like other members of the genus *Agalinis*, slender false foxglove is hemiparasitic (half or partially parasitic) on a variety of host plants, particularly grasses and sedges. Foxgloves use a special structure called a haustoria to connect its roots with those of its host plants, for the purpose of obtaining nutrients; in addition, the plant also has green tissues, and performs photosynthesis.

SLENDER FALSE FOXGLOVE

Agalinis tenuifolia
Broomrape family (Orobanchaceae)

Description: A much-branched, annual plant, less than 2' tall, with narrow ridges along the main stem. The leaves are opposite, very narrow, up to 3" long and often less than ⅛" wide, with smooth edges. The upper leaves have smaller secondary leaves emerging from the same axils. Single flowers arise from the leaf axils on slender stalks about ½–¾" long. Each rose-purple flower is less than ½" long and ¾" across, and funnel-shaped, with a short tube opening to 5 rounded lobes. There are purple spots and 5 hairy stamens in the mouth of the flower.

Bloom Season: Midsummer–early fall

Habitat/Range: Occasional in mesic to dry prairies, sand prairies, savannas, glades, and moist sandy areas; found throughout the Midwest region.

Comments: Another species similar in appearance, purple false foxglove (*Agalinis purpurea*), is easily separated by its short flower stalk, less than 3" long; frequent in wet prairies, moist sand prairies, sand savannas, and openings in sandy woodlands; found throughout the Midwest region.

BLUEHEARTS

Buchnera americana
Broomrape family (Orobanchaceae)

Description: A hairy, single-stemmed plant, up to 3' tall. Leaves are 2–4" long, opposite, stalkless, broadest at the base and tapering to a pointed tip, hairy, with a few coarse teeth along the margins. Flowers are in pairs along a spike at the tip of the stem; each reddish-purple flower is about ⅝" across and about ½" long, tubular, with 5 widely spreading lobes.

Bloom Season: Summer–early fall

Habitat/Range: Occasional in mesic to dry prairies, glades, and savannas; found in the southwest quarter of the Midwest region, and southward.

Comments: The genus name, *Buchnera*, is in honor of Johann Gottfried Buchner, an 18th-century German botanist. Like the false foxgloves, bluehearts are hemiparasitic, meaning they are able to grow independently without a host, but grow more strongly with a host. They also attach to their host plant by a structure on its roots called a haustoria.

PASSION FLOWER
Passiflora incarnata
Passion flower family (Passifloraceae)

Description: A vine, up to 20' long, which climbs or sprawls with the help of tendrils. The leaves are alternate, with 3 broad, toothed lobes, usually smooth, and up to 5" across. The unusual flowers are single, arising on stalks from the axils of leaves. Individual flowers are up to 3" across, with several petals and a purple fringe. There are 5 drooping stamens around the pistil, which has 3–4 curved stigmas. The fruit is oval, smooth, yellow when ripe, up to 2" long, and contains many seeds with gelatinous coverings.

Bloom Season: Late spring–fall

Habitat/Range: Occasional in low, moist, open woods, ditch banks, fencerows, and along roadsides; found in the southern third of the Midwest region, and southward.

Comments: Also known as maypops, which comes from children in the South stomping on the fruit to make it pop. Native Americans used the root to treat boils, cuts, earache, and inflammation. A tea was made from the plant to soothe the nerves. The fruit is edible.

MONKEY FLOWER
Mimulus alatus
Lopseed family (Phrymaceae)

Description: Smooth, often-branched plants, up to 3' tall, with squarish stems, or at least ridges or wings, down the sides. The stems are also winged with strips of green tissue. The leaves are opposite, stalked, up to 4" long and 2" wide, broadest toward the base, tapering at the tip, and toothed. The flowers are on stalks arising from the leaf axils. Each flower is about 1" long, pale violet, hairy, with 2 lips: the upper, small, the lower, broad, with 3 lobes. The upper lip has a pair of lobes that fold backward laterally, while the lower lip has 3 well-rounded lobes that spread outward. In the mouth of the flower, there is a patch of yellow that is surrounded by a narrow band of white.

Bloom Season: Summer–fall

Habitat/Range: Occasional along borders of streams, spring branches, swamps, ponds, and in low, wet woods; found in the southern half of the Midwest region.

Comments: The common name refers to the flower's resemblance to a grinning monkey's face. A related species, Allegheny monkey flower (*Mimulus ringens*), has leaves without stalks, with the base clasping the stem, flowers up to 1½" long, and angles of the stem without wings (strips of green tissue). The habitat is similar, and its range is throughout the Midwest region.

LOPSEED
Phryma leptostachya
Lopseed family (Phrymaceae)

Description: The stems are hairy, angled, up to 3' tall, and branched in the upper half. The leaves are opposite, up to 6" long and 4" wide, stalked, egg-shaped, coarsely toothed, hairy, with a pointed tip and tapering at the base. The flowers are opposite along the spikes that arise from the leaf axils, and below every flower are 3 tiny bracts. Each flower is ¼" long and wide, lavender to pale purple, tubular, with 1 short top lobe that turns up and 3 longer bottom lobes that extend out. The fruit is a seed that hangs down close to the stem; hence, the common name.

Bloom Season: Summer

Habitat/Range: Common in bottomland forests, mesic upland forests, banks of streams, and bases and ledges of bluffs; found throughout the Midwest region.

Comments: Native Americans gargled root tea or chewed the root for sore throat and drank the tea for rheumatism. The root has been poulticed (mashed and applied to the body) to treat boils, carbuncles, sores, and cancers. The plant is also considered insecticidal.

ROSE TURTLEHEAD
Chelone obliqua var. *speciosa*
Figwort family (Scrophulariaceae)

Description: An upright, usually unbranched plant, up to 3' tall, with angled stems. The leaves are opposite along the stem, broadest at the middle, toothed along the margin, up to 6" long and 1½" wide. The reddish-purple flowers are clustered at the top, each about 1" long. The upper lip of the flower has two lobes, which extend over the 3-lobed lower lip that has a small, yellow beard inside the lip.

Bloom Season: Midsummer–fall

Habitat/Range: Uncommon in low areas in wet soil, marshes, and wet woods; found in the south-central part of the Midwest region.

Comments: Also called "pink turtlehead," the common name is very fitting, especially when viewing the profile of the flower. A leaf tea was said to stimulate appetite; also, it was used as a folk remedy for worms, fever, jaundice, and as a laxative.

BLUE TOADFLAX
Nuttallanthus canadensis
Plantain family (Plantaginaceae)

Description: Annual to biennial plants with smooth, slender stems, up to 18" tall. The leaves are alternate on the upper stem and opposite or whorled below, narrow, up to 1½" long and ⅛" wide, toothless, hairless, with pointed tips, and no leaf stalk. The light blue to blue-violet flowers are in a loose cluster along the upper part of the stem. Each flower is about ½" long, with 2 lips: The upper lip has 2 lobes, and the lower lip has 3 lobes, with a 2-humped, white spot at the base. A long, down-curved spur emerges from the back of the flower.

Bloom Season: Mid-spring–summer

Habitat/Range: Occasional in sandy soils, including sand prairies, glades, and savannas; found throughout the Midwest region, but rare to absent in the southeast quarter.

Comments: Formerly known as *Linaria canadensis.* A closely related species, southern blue toadflax (*Nuttallanthus texanus*), has larger flowers (up to 1" long). It shares a similar bloom season and habitat as blue toadflax, but is found in the southwest quarter of the Midwest region, and southwestward.

LARGE BEARDTONGUE
Penstemon grandiflorus
Plantain family (Plantaginaceae)

Description: A stout, unbranched, waxy plant, up to 3' tall, often with a bluish-green color. The leaves are opposite, thick, stiff, stalked below, stalkless and clasping above, up to 3" long and 2" wide. The flowers are stalked and in 2–6 clusters, each with 2–3 flowers along the upper part of the stem, with a pair of small leaves below each cluster. Each bluish-lavender to pale blue flower is tubular, inflated, and hairless, about 2" long, with 2 upper lobes that are slightly shorter than the 3 lower lobes. The mouth of the flower has faint reddish to magenta lines.

Bloom Season: Mid-spring–midsummer

Habitat/Range: Locally common in dry prairies with sandy to loamy soils, and hill prairies; found in the northwest quarter of the Midwest region, introduced or escaped from cultivation eastward.

Comments: The Pawnee drank a tea made from the leaves for chills and fever. The Kiowa made a tea from the boiled roots as a cure for stomach-ache. The Dakota boiled the root and used it to treat pains in the chest.

SLENDER BEARDTONGUE
Penstemon gracilis
Plantain family (Plantaginaceae)

Description: Slender, single-stemmed plants, 12–18" tall, hairy, and reddish on the upper part. The leaves are opposite, up to 3" long and ½" wide, narrow, tapering to a pointed tip, widest at the base, somewhat clasping the stem, and with tiny teeth along the margins. The flowers are in groups of 2 or more on short stalks in a spike-like cluster along the upper part of the stem. Each flower is about ¾" long, pale lavender to purple, tubular, with 5 lobes; the upper 2 lobes are the shortest and turn up, while the lower 3 lobes extend out and down. Gland-tipped hairs are present on the surface, while the inside tube is white at the center, with dark purple veins running along the inside, and a bearded flap down the center. There are 5 yellow-tipped stamens that turn dark brown at maturity.

Bloom Season: Late spring–midsummer

Habitat/Range: Locally common in sandy or rocky prairies and rocky, open woods; found in the northwest quarter of the Midwest region, and westward.

Comments: Slender beardtongue was first described for science in 1818 by the noted English botanist-naturalist Thomas Nuttall (1786–1859). The Lakota used the roots to treat snakebite.

HAIRY BEARDTONGUE
Penstemon hirsutus
Plantain family (Plantaginaceae)

Description: Several stems often arise from a single rhizome, 15–30" tall, hairy on the lower stem and with gland-tipped hairs on the upper stem and branches. The leaves are opposite, hairy, 2–4½" long, broadest at the middle and tapering at both ends, with teeth along the margins. The flowers are on branches at the top of the stem, with gland-tipped hairs covering the stalks and flowers. Each flower is about 1" long, pale lavender, with 2 upper lobes and 3 lower lobes. The 3 lower lobes push upward, partially closing the mouth, which has a large, bearded, yellow flap down the center.

Bloom Season: Late spring–midsummer

Habitat/Range: Occasional in gravelly or sandy soils in prairies, wooded slopes, bluffs, and along stream banks; found in the eastern two-thirds of the Midwest region.

Comments: A similar-looking species, smooth beardtongue (*Penstemon calycosus*), differs by having leaves and stems essentially smooth, while the branches, flower stalks, and flowers are covered with fine, white hairs, and the flower's 3 lobes do not push upward. Occasional in open rocky woodlands, woodland borders, savannas, and prairies; found in the central and southeast parts of the Midwest region.

CLEFT PHLOX
Phlox bifida
Phlox family (Polemoniaceae)

Description: A phlox forming open mats, up to 6" high, with wiry, hairy stems. The leaves are opposite, stalkless, very narrow, up to 2" long and less than ¼" wide, hairy, and lacking teeth along the margins. The flowers are light blue to white, up to 1" across, on slender, hairy stalks. The tubular flowers have 5 narrow lobes that have deep notches at the tips.

Bloom Season: Mid- to late spring

Habitat/Range: Occasional on rocky or dry upland woods, upper slopes of ravines, ledges of bluffs, sand prairies, sand savannas, and hill prairies; found in the central part and southwest quarter of the Midwest region.

Comments: Another species, creeping phlox (*Phlox subulata*), forms dense mats, with leaves ¼–¾" long, and a shallow notch at the tip of each lobe; weedy in sandy or rocky soil and escaped from gardens; native to the eastern United States, and adventive with scattered locations in the northern half of the Midwest region.

BLUE PHLOX
Phlox divaricata
Phlox family (Polemoniaceae)

Description: This plant has finely hairy stems, up to 1½' tall, unbranched, with 1 to several stems arising from the base. The leaves are opposite, widely spaced, stalkless, lance-shaped, up to 3" long and ½" wide, finely hairy, and lacking teeth along the margins. The blue to blue-violet flowers are on slender stalks in loose clusters about 3" across at the top of the stems. Each flower is up to 1" across, tubular, 5-lobed, with the tips either rounded or slightly notched.

Bloom Season: Mid-spring–early summer

Habitat/Range: Common in rocky or moist woods on slopes, ravines, and valley bottoms; found through the Midwest region, but absent in the northern quarter.

Comments: The overwintering green leaves and the flowering tops are eaten by white-tailed deer. Ruffed grouse occasionally eat the seed-filled capsules. In pioneer medicine, leaf tea was used to treat eczema and to purify the blood. Root tea was taken to treat venereal disease.

PERENNIAL PHLOX

Phlox paniculata
Phlox family (Polemoniaceae)

Description: A showy, late-blooming phlox, up to 5' tall. The leaves are opposite, stalkless, up to 6" long and 1½" wide, broadest along the middle and narrowing at both ends, with the side veins prominent. The flowers are often in large, pyramidal clusters at the tops of stems. Each flower is pinkish- to reddish-purple, on short stalks, up to ¾" across, with a short-hairy tube about 1" long, 5 lobes, and with 1 of the yellow stamens extending just beyond the mouth of the flower.

Bloom Season: Midsummer–fall

Habitat/Range: Occasional in moist soil in low woods along streams and in valleys; native to the southern half of the Midwest region, and adventive from garden escapes in the northern half.

Comments: Also called "summer phlox" and "garden phlox," the latter because of its popularity as a garden plant, and the many horticultural varieties that have been developed from it.

JACOB'S LADDER

Polemonium reptans
Phlox family (Polemoniaceae)

Description: Low, weak-stemmed plants, up to 15" tall, with hollow stems. The alternate leaves are up to 12" long, with each leaf divided into 3–13 leaflets, which form a "ladder." The leaflets are up to 1½" long and ½" across, widest in the middle and tapering at both ends. The flowers are on slender stalks in a loose cluster at the top of the stem. Each bell-shaped flower is about ½" across and often nodding. The 5 pale blue petals are united for about half their length.

Bloom Season: Mid-spring–early summer

Habitat/Range: Common in moist, low, or rocky woods at the base of bluffs and slopes and in ravines and valleys; found throughout the Midwest region, but absent in the northern quarter.

Comments: The Menominee tribe used this plant to treat eczema and skin sores. The Meskwaki and Potawatomi used it for treating hemorrhoids. Root tea was used to induce sweating and to treat fever, snakebite, bowel complaints, and bronchial afflictions.

ROUND-LOBED HEPATICA

Anemone americana
Buttercup family (Ranunculaceae)

Description: Stems are absent in this low-growing plant, with basal leaves that overwinter. The leaves are on hairy stalks, 3-lobed, with blunt or rounded tips, leathery, and up to 3" long and wide. The flowers are single, on long, somewhat hairy stalks up to 8" tall. Each flower is about 1" across and can vary in color from purple to lavender to white. The 6–10 "petals" are actually sepals. There are 3 large, hairy bracts, each up to ½" long, oval- to egg-shaped, with a blunt or rounded tip.

Bloom Season: Spring

Habitat/Range: Occasional in upland woods, moist, rocky, wooded slopes, and ravine bottoms; found in the southwest quarter and the northern half of the Midwest region.

Comments: Formerly known as *Hepatica nobilis* var. *obtusa*. Another common name, "liverleaf," refers to the overwintering leaves that turn a deep reddish-brown, the color of liver. The Chippewa gave root tea from this plant to children who had convulsions. Leaf tea was used as a treatment for liver ailments and poor indigestion, and as a laxative. A closely related plant, sharp-lobed hepatica (*Anemone acutiloba;* formerly known as *Hepatica nobilis* var. *acuta*), is almost identical, except that it has sharp-pointed leaves. Occurs in similar habitat, and found throughout the Midwest region.

CAROLINA LARKSPUR
Delphinium carolinianum
Buttercup family (Ranunculaceae)

Description: The stems of this plant are wand-like, with soft hairs, and up to 3½' tall. The stalked leaves are mostly on the lower half of the stem. The leaves are fan-shaped, with 3–7 narrow segments that are often divided once or twice again. The short-stalked flowers are alternately arranged along the upper stem. Each flower is about 1" long and shaped like a cornucopia, consisting of 5 white to blue or purple, petal-like sepals, with the upper sepal curved back and upward in a long, tubular spur, 2 lateral, spreading sepals, and 2 lower sepals. There are 4 smaller petals, with the upper 2 petals extending backward into the sepal spur, while the other 2 petals are each split into 2 hairy lobes.

Bloom Season: Late spring–early summer

Habitat/Range: Frequent in upland prairies, savannas, and glades; found in the western half of the Midwest region.

Comments: Most of the plants belong to subspecies (ssp.) *virescens*, with flowers white or pale blue to bright blue, with leaf stalks ⅛" long, and with most basal leaves present at flowering time. Subspecies (ssp.) *carolinianum* has flowers that are pale to deep blue or purple, or blue and white, with leaf stalks ¼–½" long, and with most basal leaves absent at flowering time. Both subspecies occupy similar habitat, but ssp. *carolinianum* is less common and found primarily in the southwest quarter of the Midwest region.

BLUETS
Houstonia caerulea
Madder family (Rubiaceae)

Description: A small, mat-forming winter annual, with stems usually less than 6" tall. The leaves are opposite, few in number, mostly at the base, spatula-shaped, less than ½" long, and narrowed to a stalk almost as long as the leaf. The flowers are at the ends of stalks, about ½" across, sky-blue and tubular, with 4 pointed lobes and a yellow center.

Bloom Season: Spring

Habitat/Range: Occasional, sometimes locally abundant in sand prairies, sand savannas, sandstone glades, and sandy areas along streams; found in the central part and southern third of the Midwest region.

Comments: Formerly known as *Hedyotis caerulea*. Bluets are also known as azure bluets and Quaker ladies. The flower's yellow center is distinctive among bluet species.

DWARF LARKSPUR
Delphinium tricorne
Buttercup family (Ranunculaceae)

Description: A single-stemmed, rather succulent plant, with fine, downy hairs, that begins flowering at 6–10" tall but may reach 18" later in the season. The basal and alternate stem leaves are shaped like a hand, with 5–7 deep lobes; the basal leaves are on stalks. The flowers are loosely clustered along the top of the stem. Each flower is up to 1½" long, stalked, with 5 showy sepals, 1 of which is developed into a spur, up to 1" long. The 4 petals are small and inconspicuous. The flowers vary from blue to violet to white.

Bloom Season: Mid-spring–early summer

Habitat/Range: Common in moist or rocky woods, on lower slopes, and in valley and ravine bottoms; found in the southern half of the Midwest region.

Comments: Larkspurs are poisonous to most mammalian herbivores. Most poisoning takes place in the spring, when the plants are fresh and green.

SMALL BLUETS
Houstonia pusilla
Madder family (Rubiaceae)

Description: A small, mat-forming winter annual, with stems usually less than 4" tall. The leaves are opposite, few in number, mostly at the base, and less than ½" long. The blue, pink, or sometimes white flowers are at the ends of stalks, about ¼" across, with a tubular shape, 4 pointed lobes, and a reddish-purple center.

Bloom Season: Late winter–mid-spring

Habitat/Range: Locally common in the open, sandy soils of prairies, woodlands, glades, pastures, cemeteries, and lawns; found in the central part and southern third of the Midwest region.

Comments: Formerly known as *Hedyotis crassifolia*. Small bluets often form a carpet of blue in yards and cemeteries in early spring.

BLUE-EYED MARY
Collinsia verna
Snapdragon family (Scrophulariaceae)

Description: A slender, weak-stemmed winter annual, up to 12" tall, often covering large areas on the forest floor. The upper stem leaves are opposite, stalkless, up to 2" long and ¾" across, widest at the base, tapering to a pointed tip, and somewhat toothed along the margins. The lower stem leaves have stalks, are more rounded, and lack teeth. The flowers emerge in whorls in axils of the stem; each flower has a slender stalk, each about 1½" long. The flower is ½–¾" across, with 2 lips. The upper lip is white with 2 lobes, the lower, blue with 3 lobes. The center lower lobe forms a pouch in which the stamens and the pistil are hidden.

Bloom Season: Mid-spring–early summer

Habitat/Range: Locally common in moist, low woodlands in ravines and valley bottoms along streams; found across the southern half of the Midwest region.

Comments: A closely related species, violet collinsia (*Collinsia violacea*), has narrower leaves and the lower lip is colored violet; occasional in drier sites, including upland prairies, sand prairies, glades, and dry open woods; found in the southern half of the southwest quarter of the Midwest region, and westward.

EASTERN FIGWORT
Scrophularia marilandica
Snapdragon family (Scrophulariaceae)

Description: A stout, square-stemmed plant, up to 7' tall, with multiple branches. The leaves are on stalks up to 2½" long, opposite, up to 6" long and 3" wide, with heart-shaped leaf bases, pointed at the tip, and with teeth along the margins. The tiny flowers are in a loose cluster. Each flower is about ¼" long and wide, reddish-purple, shaped like a scoop, with 2 larger upper lobes, 2 short lateral lobes, and one greenish-yellow lower lobe. There are 4 fertile stamens with yellow anthers and 1 infertile stamen with a reddish-purple anther.

Bloom Season: Summer–fall

Habitat/Range: Occasional in low, moist woods, borders of woods, and along stream banks; found through the Midwest region, but absent in the northern quarter.

Comments: Also called "carpenter's square" for the grooved, 4-angled stem. Native Americans used root tea to treat fever and piles, and as a diuretic and a tonic. It is also a folk remedy for treating sleeplessness in pregnant women, restlessness, anxiety, and cancer. A similar species, lanceleaf figwort (*Scrophularia lanceolata*), lacks a heart-shaped leaf base, has shorter leaf stalks, an infertile stamen with a green anther, and gland-tipped hairs along the stem. Occasional in open woods, at the edges of woods, and in open fields; found through the Midwest region, but absent in the southern third.

BLUE VERVAIN
Verbena hastata
Vervain family (Verbenaceae)

Description: Tall, slender plants, up to 6', with rough hairs, and ridges along the stems. The leaves are opposite, stalked, up to 7" long and 2" wide, pointed, and coarsely toothed along the margins. The larger leaves have a pair of spreading basal lobes. Flowers are densely packed, blue to purplish-blue, about ⅜" long and ¼" across, with 5 spreading, rounded lobes fused at the base, forming a short tube.

Bloom Season: Summer–fall

Habitat/Range: Common in wet prairies, fens, wet woodlands, borders of streams, edges of ponds, along roadsides, and other wet areas, especially where the soil is disturbed; found throughout the Midwest region.

Comments: The Omaha used the leaves for a beverage tea. The Meskwaki used the root as a remedy for fits. The Chippewa took the dried, powdered flowers as a snuff to stop nosebleed. During the American Revolution, doctors used blue vervain to induce vomiting and to clear respiratory tracts of mucus. Early settlers used a leaf tea as a spring tonic, known as "simpler's joy" (*simpler* is an old term for an herbalist).

NARROW-LEAVED VERVAIN
Verbena simplex
Vervain family (Verbenaceae)

Description: Short, slender plants, 12–18" tall, hairy, with ridges along the stems. The leaves are opposite, stalkless, somewhat hairy, narrow, up to 3½" long and ½" wide, with sparse teeth, and tapering at both ends. The flowers are crowded along a spike at the top of the stem. Each flower is dark lavender to purple, small, about ¼" long, hairy, with a short tube and 5 spreading, rounded petals.

Bloom Season: Late spring–summer

Habitat/Range: Common in upland prairies, glades, other open rocky sites, pastures, along roadsides, and open disturbed areas; found throughout the Midwest region, but rare or absent in the northern third.

Comments: Another species, creeping vervain (*Verbena bracteata*), is an annual or biennial that produces several hairy, spreading stems, up to 12" long, forming a low mat on the ground. The hairy leaves are deeply lobed. The small flowers are purplish-blue, ⅛" across, and densely packed along a thick spike at the end of branching stems. Common in disturbed portions of upland prairies, old fields, pastures, and along roadsides; found throughout the Midwest region.

HOARY VERVAIN
Verbena stricta
Vervain family (Verbenaceae)

Description: Stout, densely hairy plants, up to 4' tall, branching in the upper half, and with square stems. The leaves are opposite, with very short stalks, gray-hairy, tips rounded, up to 4" long and 2½" wide, and toothed along the margins. The flowers are crowded along 1 to several narrow spikes at the top of the plant. Each purple to purplish-blue flower is about ⅜" long and ¼" across, with 5 spreading, rounded lobes.

Bloom Season: Summer–early fall

Habitat/Range: Common in degraded upland prairies, hill prairies, old fields, pastures, old urban areas, roadsides, and other disturbed sites; found throughout the Midwest region.

Comments: The genus name, *Verbena*, comes from a Latin name used for some plants in religious ceremonies and in medicine. The species name, *stricta*, means "erect" or "upright." Hoary vervain is one of the showiest of the vervains because of its larger flowers and exceptionally hairy stems and leaves, giving the plant a silvery cast. Cattle and other herbivores generally avoid this plant because of its hairy nature and bitter taste.

JOHNNY-JUMP-UP
Viola bicolor
Violet family (Violaceae)

Description: A small, slender, annual plant, up to 6" tall. The leaves are alternate, the lowermost nearly circular, the upper ones, narrower, up to ¾" long, rounded, and on long stalks. At the base of each leaf, there is a deeply divided, leaf-like stipule. The flowers are on stalks arising from the axils of leaves. The flowers are violet, lavender, or white, up to ¾" long, with 5 petals. The base of the petals is white, with a beard of hairs and purple lines. There is usually a yellow throat that is best developed on the lower petal.

Bloom Season: Spring

Habitat/Range: Common in disturbed upland prairies, margins of hill prairies, glades, savannas, pastures, fallow fields, gardens, lawns, and open disturbed areas; found in the southern half of the Midwest region.

Comments: Formerly known as *Viola rafinesquii*. Johnny-jump-up was once considered to have originated from Europe, but is now accepted as part of the native flora, although it has weedy tendencies. The flowers look like miniature pansies, often forming dense carpets in lawns and in cemeteries. The common name refers to the quick growth of this plant in the spring. As in other members of the violet family, Johnny-jump-up contains quantities of methyl salicylate (oil of wintergreen) in its taproot.

CLEFT VIOLET
Viola palmata
Violet family (Violaceae)

Description: A stemless plant with leaves and flower stalks emerging from the base. The leaves are hairy or smooth, about 2–4" across, on long stalks, and deeply 3- to 11-lobed, with the earliest leaves being more heart-shaped. The flowers are on long stalks, large, up to 1" across, blue-violet to white, or sometimes streaked, or blotched violet and white, with 5 petals; the 2 side petals have small tufts of white hairs at their bases, while the lower petal has several dark purple lines on a white background that function to guide pollinators to the short nectar spur in the back of the flower.

Bloom Season: Mid-spring–early summer

Habitat/Range: Occasional in moist to dry open woods, wooded slopes, thinly wooded bluffs, and stream banks; found through the Midwest region, but absent in the northwest quarter.

Comments: Formerly known as *Viola triloba*, cleft violet is very mucilaginous, and has been used in the South—where it was known as wild okra—to make soup. The bruised leaves were used to soften and soothe the skin.

MARSH VIOLET
Viola cucullata
Violet family (Violaceae)

Description: A small, hairless plant, 4–6" tall, that forms colonies from short-branched rhizomes. The leaves are basal, up to 3½" long and wide, broadly rounded, with a blunt tip, an indented base, small, rounded teeth along the margins, and stalks up to 4" long. The flowers are solitary at the tips of stalks up to 7" long. Each flower is ¾–1" across, light blue to violet, with 5 petals that are white at the base. The 2 lateral petals have short, white hairs with swollen tips, while the lower, smaller petal has a patch of white with radiating purple veins running down it. The sepals are narrow and have sharply pointed tips.

Bloom Season: Mid-spring–early summer

Habitat/Range: Occasional in wet areas, including acid seeps, fens, marshes, swamps, bogs, borders of rocky streams, and at the base of bluffs; found throughout the northern half of the Midwest region, and infrequent in the southern half.

Comments: A similar species, northern blue violet (*Viola nephrophylla*), has the 2 lateral petals with short, white, slender hairs, lacking swollen tips, and the sepals broad with blunt tips; occasional in similar habitats; found throughout the Midwest region, but rare in the southeast quarter.

BIRD'S FOOT VIOLET
Viola pedata
Violet family (Violaceae)

Description: Small, sparse violets, up to 6" tall, with leaves and flowers emerging from the same base. The leaves are ¾–1½" long and wide, with narrow, deeply cut segments resembling a bird's foot, and are often further divided into smaller lobes. The bare flower stems extend above the leaves and are sharply curved at the top, each with a single flower. The flowers are about 1½" across, with 5 petals; the lowest petal is white at the base, with purple lines. The orange stamens form a column in the center of the flower. There are two color variations, one with all 5 petals pale lilac or lavender, the other, with the upper 2 petals deep velvety purple, and the lower 3, pale lilac to lavender.

Bloom Season: Spring; also, in fall

Habitat/Range: Common in rocky or sandy soils in prairies, hill prairies, sand prairies, black-soil prairies, savannas, glades, and dry open woods on upland slopes and ridges; found throughout the Midwest region, but rare to absent in the southeast quarter.

Comments: It has been reported that compared to other violets, the more-horizontal position of the flowers of bird's foot violet are more attractive to butterflies and skippers, which makes it easier for them to land on. The caterpillars of various fritillary butterflies feed on the foliage and flowers. One specific fritillary, the regal fritillary, may prefer this violet species over others as a larval food source.

PRAIRIE VIOLET
Viola pedatifida
Violet family (Violaceae)

Description: Small plants, up to 6" tall, with individual leaves and single flowers on stalks emerging from the base of the plant. The leaves are 1–3" long and wide, with each leaf divided into 3 deeply lobed, narrow segments that are further divided into smaller segments. The slightly irregular flowers barely appear above the leaves on single stalks. The purple to blue-purple flowers are about ¾" across, with 5 slightly irregular petals. The 3 lower petals are white near the base, with the 2 side petals having a tuft of white hairs, and the lower petal with dark purple lines. The stamens are arranged in a tight group within the flower.

Bloom Season: Spring; also, in fall

Habitat/Range: Local in dry prairies, hill prairies, and savannas; found throughout the Midwest region, but rare to absent in the eastern third and north-central parts.

Comments: Prairie violet is similar in appearance to bird's foot violet, but differs in having the leaf segments further divided into narrower lobes; flowers about ¾" across compared to 1½" across for the latter; and tufts of hairs at the base of the 2 side petals, while the latter lacks hairs.

ARROW-LEAVED VIOLET
Viola sagittata
Violet family (Violaceae)

Description: Plants up to 6", with single flowers arising on stalks above the leaves. The leaves, which emerge from the base on long stalks, are up to 3" long and about 1½" wide, shaped like an arrowhead, with small lobes generally toward the base. The flowers are ¾–1" across, with 5 blue-violet to purple petals that are white at the base. The 3 lower petals have white tufts of hairs at their base, with the lowest petal also showing dark purple veins.

Bloom Season: Spring–early summer

Habitat/Range: Common in dry to moist prairies, sand prairies, and open woodlands; found throughout the Midwest region.

Comments: Arrow-leaved violet's species name, *sagittata*, is derived from the Latin word *sagitt(a)*, meaning "an arrow," referring to the leaves, the shape of which easily distinguishes it from the other violets.

341

COMMON BLUE VIOLET
Viola sororia
Violet family (Violaceae)

Description: The plant forms a mound of leaves and flowers on usually hairy stalks, less than 6" tall. The leaves are less than 3" across, about as wide as—or wider than—it is long, rounded at the base, with rounded teeth along the margins, and often hairy on both surfaces. The flowers are on long, smooth (or hairy) stalks, with each flower about ¾" across, with 5 bluish-purple to purple petals. The mouth of the petals is white, with a tuft of white hairs at the base of each side petal, and several purple lines over white on the bottom petal.

Bloom Season: Spring–early summer

Habitat/Range: Occasional in upland prairies, savannas, and glades, and more frequent in rocky or dry open woods, wooded slopes along streams, pastures, lawns, and disturbed areas; found throughout the Midwest region.

Comments: The plants have been used as salad ingredients, as cooked greens, soup thickener, tea, and candy. A closely related species, Missouri violet (*Viola missouriensis*), has leaf blades that are triangular-shaped, longer than they are wide, flat at the base, sharply toothed along the margins, and with a lighter shade of blue-violet flowers, each about ½–¾" across. Common along the borders of wet prairies and bottomland forests, upland forests, marshes, and other wet areas; found through the Midwest region, but absent in the northern third and southeast quarter.

WEEDS

As the Midwest region began to be settled by Europeans—and, later, by Asians—hundreds of years ago, they brought with them either deliberately or accidentally seeds and plants from their homeland. Over time, hundreds of these often-aggressive nonnative species have become established in the Midwest region, as well as across the United States. Their presence has led to the degradation of many natural communities by overcrowding and outcompeting native plants. Many of these nonnative species are more in harmony and not as aggressive in their European and Asian native environments because the animals that feed upon them are present. This section includes some invasive weeds that one can encounter in the Midwest region.

POISON HEMLOCK
Conium maculatum
Parsley family (Apiaceae)

Description: A robust biennial with large, highly dissected leaves, reaching a height of up to 9'. The branching, furrowed stems are smooth, with purple spots and hollow centers. The leaves are up to 14" long, highly dissected into numerous leaflets, and almost fern-like. The numerous flowers are produced in loose, flat-topped clusters, 4–5" across. Each flower is about ⅛" across with 5 white petals

Bloom Season: Late spring–summer

Habitat/Range: Common in disturbed ground, fields, pastures, fencerows, low ground, and along roadsides and railroads; introduced from Europe and found throughout the Midwest region.

Comments: This is the infamous plant that was used to put Socrates to death in 399 BC. All parts of the hemlock, especially the green, almost ripe seeds, are deadly poisonous, and may also cause contact dermatitis.

QUEEN ANNE'S LACE
Daucus carota
Parsley family (Apiaceae)

Description: A biennial with a large taproot and stout, branching, hairy stems, up to 4' tall. Both basal and stem leaves are large and finely divided on long, hairy stalks. Tiny flowers, each about ⅛" across and with 5 white petals, are tightly grouped in clusters, which in turn form a larger umbrella-shaped cluster about 4" across. In the center, there is often 1 purple flower. As the flowers fade, the feather-like stalks curl into a tight, bird's-nest shape supporting numerous oval, bristly, dried fruits that are up to ⅛" long.

Bloom Season: Late spring–summer

Habitat/Range: Common in fields, waste ground, roadsides, and disturbed prairies; introduced from Europe and Asia; found throughout the Midwest region.

Comments: Also known as wild carrot.

WILD PARSNIP
Pastinaca sativa
Parsley family (Apiaceae)

Description: A stout, smooth-stemmed, biennial plant, up to 5' tall, with grooves along the stem. The leaves are alternate and divided into leaflets, each up to 3" long, that are round and lobed, with teeth along the margins. The flowers are in large clusters, 5–8" across, on long stalks, and shaped like an umbrella. There are numerous tiny, yellow flowers, each with 5 petals that curl under, 5 yellow stamens, and a greenish-yellow center.

Bloom Season: Late spring–summer

Habitat/Range: A common weed, found in disturbed portions of upland prairies, pastures, fallow fields, old fields, roadsides, and open, disturbed sites; native to Europe; found throughout the Midwest region.

Comments: The sap from this plant reacts with sunlight to form a toxin and can cause a skin rash similar to that of poison ivy on some individuals, with the affected area remaining reddened for several months.

HEDGE PARSLEY
Torilis arvensis
Parsley family (Apiaceae)

Description: A hairy, much-branched plant, up to 2½' tall. The leaves are finely dissected and resemble parsley. The small flowers, each about ⅛" across, with 5 white, notched petals, occur in flat-topped clusters on long stalks that extend well above the leaves. The fruit is densely covered with hooked bristles that attach to clothing and fur.

Bloom Season: Summer

Habitat/Range: Common in disturbed sites and fields and along roadsides and railroads; native to Europe; found throughout the Midwest region, but less common in the northwest quarter (although increasing in numbers).

Comments: Hedge parsley was formerly known as *Torilis japonica.*

MUSK THISTLE
Carduus nutans
Aster family (Asteraceae)

Description: A sturdy biennial with a spiny, winged stem, up to 7' tall. First year's leaves spread over the ground, radiating out from a central core, and overwinter, sending up branching stems the second year. Leaves are alternate, up to 10" long and 4" wide, smooth, deeply lobed, with spiny tips. The flower heads are about 2" across, solitary, somewhat nodding at the ends of very long, spineless stalks, with numerous reddish-purple disk flowers. The bracts are large, triangular, green or tinged with purple, and in many layers that spread out and away from below the flower head.

Bloom Season: Summer–fall

Habitat/Range: A common weed, which can spread into upland prairies from adjacent road-sides, old fields, pastures, and open, disturbed sites; native to Europe and Asia; found throughout the Midwest region.

Comments: A related species, plumeless thistle (*Carduus acanthoides*), has more numerous and smaller flower heads, about 1" across, and spines along the flower stalks. Plumeless thistle resembles bull thistle (*Cirsium vulgare*), but the latter has larger flowers, about 1½" across, and hairier leaves. Plumeless thistle occupies similar range, habitat, and origin as musk thistle.

SPOTTED KNAPWEED
Centaurea stoebe
Aster family (Asteraceae)

Description: A biennial or short-lived perennial plant, with several stems emerging from the base, up to 3' tall. The basal leaves are up to 6" long and densely hairy, with shallow to deep lobes. The stem leaves are deeply divided into narrow, finger-like lobes, with the leaves toward the top simple and not divided. The flower heads, each about 1" across, are at the ends of loosely arranged branches. The flower heads are pink to purple, with the outer ray flowers enlarged. The bracts at the base of the flowers have dark spots on their tips.

Bloom Season: Summer–fall

Habitat/Range: Common in disturbed open ground, fields, and along roadsides; native to Europe; found throughout the Midwest region.

Comments: Formerly known as *Centaurea maculosa*. This plant is a noxious weed that overwhelms native plants. The plant is being studied for possible cancer-causing agents in its sap.

CANADA THISTLE
Cirsium arvense
Aster family (Asteraceae)

Description: Plants spreading to form large colonies from deep lateral roots that send up new stems, up to 4' tall, that are spineless. Leaves are alternate, spiny, lobed, and 2–7" long. There are numerous pale pink flowers, each less than 1" across, with bracts at their bases that emerge with spineless tips. Male and female flowers are on separate plants, unlike other thistles in the region.

Bloom Season: Summer–fall

Habitat/Range: A common weed that invades prairies, fields, roadsides, and other disturbed open ground; native to Europe, Asia, and North Africa; found across the Midwest region, but less common in the southwest quarter.

Comments: The names "Canada thistle" and "Canadian thistle" are in wide use in the United States, despite being a misleading designation (it is not of Canadian origin).

BULL THISTLE
Cirsium vulgare
Aster family (Asteraceae)

Description: A biennial plant growing from a fleshy root, with much-branched, stout, hairy stems and with wings along the margins that are narrowly spined, 2–5' tall. The leaves extend along the stem as spiny wings. Basal leaves are 4–16" long and the stem leaves are 1–6" long, deeply lobed, with crinkled margins and spines. Flower heads are reddish-purple to purple, 1–1½" wide, and covered with numerous long, yellow-tipped spines at their bases.

Bloom Season: Summer–fall

Habitat/Range: A common weed that can invade prairies, fields, roadsides, and other disturbed open ground; native to Europe, Asia, and North Africa; found throughout the Midwest region.

Comments: Here is an excellent example of the value of one scientific name compared to the common names for this single plant species: spear thistle, bank thistle, bird thistle, black thistle, blue thistle, boar thistle, bull thistle, bur thistle, button thistle, common bull thistle, common thistle, Fuller's thistle, green thistle, plume thistle, roadside thistle, Scotch thistle, and swamp thistle.

ORANGE HAWKWEED
Hieracium aurantiacum
Aster family (Asteraceae)

Description: Single-stemmed plants with milky sap, 6–24" tall, with both stems and basal leaves covered in long hairs. The basal leaves are 2–5" long and up to 1" wide, pointed or rounded at the tip, and lacking teeth. There are often 1–2 small leaves alternately attached on the lower part of the stem. The flowers are in a compact cluster on short, hairy stalks at the top of the stem. Each flower is ¾–1" wide, deep red-orange to orange to yellow-orange, often with a yellow center, and with bracts behind the flower densely covered with glandular hairs.

Bloom Season: Early summer–fall

Habitat/Range: Common in disturbed prairies and woods, woodland edges, old fields, and along roadsides; found in the northern half of the Midwest region; native to the alpine regions of central and southern Europe.

Comments: Also known as devil's paintbrush. Orange hawkweed is highly invasive and continues to spread effectively through its wind-dispersed, dandelion-like seed, and vegetatively by solons and shallow rhizomes.

TALL HAWKWEED
Hieracium piloselloides
Aster family (Asteraceae)

Description: Typically single-stemmed plants with milky sap, 14–40" tall, with both stems and basal leaves covered with a waxy coating. The basal leaves are upright, 3–7" long and ¼–1" wide, with a waxy coating on both surfaces and sparse hairs. The upper stem, flower stalks, and flower bracts have dark, gland-tipped hairs. The flowers range from 5–30 in a loose cluster. Each flower is about ¾" wide and yellow.

Bloom Season: Summer

Habitat/Range: Common in sandy woodlands, meadows, prairies, old fields, and roadsides; found in the northern half of the Midwest region; native to Europe.

Comments: Also known as glaucous king devil because of the waxy coating on the stem and leaves; also, early farmers referred to tall hawkweed as king devil because the weeds were a troublesome invader of fields. A similar species, yellow hawkweed or meadow hawkweed (*Hieracium caespitosum*), is 1–3' tall and has leaves with a dull surface, and not a waxy coating, and a dense flower cluster at the top of the stem. Also occurs in disturbed soil; found through the Midwest region, but absent in the southwest quarter (for now); native to Europe.

OX-EYE DAISY
Leucanthemum vulgare
Aster family (Asteraceae)

Description: Plants are often multistemmed, to 2½' tall, with basal leaves round to spoon-shaped, toothed, and on stalks. The stem leaves are widely spaced, narrow, deeply cut along the margins, and lack stalks. The flower heads are up to 2" across, with about 30 white, petal-like ray flowers surrounding a central disk of numerous bright yellow tubular flowers.

Bloom Season: Late spring–summer

Habitat/Range: A common weed that occurs in fields, pastures, roadsides, and open, disturbed areas, and can invade degraded, often unburned prairies; native to Europe and Asia; found throughout the Midwest region.

Comments: Although attractive at first glance, ox-eye daisy is difficult to control or eradicate because plants can regenerate from root fragments. They can be persistent not only in degraded natural communities but also in lawns, pastures, and fields; and they have been shown to carry several crop diseases.

COMMON TANSY
Tanacetum vulgare
Aster family (Asteraceae)

Description: A tall, strong-scented plant, up to 5' tall, with ridges along the stems and alternate, fern-like leaves. The leaves are compound, up to 8" long and 4" wide, and divided into 4–10 pairs of leaflets. The flowers are in flat clusters, up to 4" wide, at the top of the plant, with 20–200 yellow flower heads, each about ¼" wide. The disk flowers are tubular, with 5 upright lobes. There are no petal-like ray flowers.

Bloom Season: Midsummer–fall

Habitat/Range: Locally common in disturbed soil along prairie edges, weedy meadows, rocky shores, old fields, ditches, roadsides, and pastures; found across the Midwest region; native to Europe.

Comments: Common tansy has had a long history and wide diversity of uses. It was first recorded in the 8th century AD as being cultivated by Benedictine monks in Greece for the treatment of intestinal worms, rheumatism, fever, sores, and digestive problems. It was also used as an insect repellent and a flavoring in foods. However, today it is considered lethal; just ½ ounce can kill in 2–4 hours if ingested. It is now illegal to sell this herb as food or medicine.

BLUEWEED
Echium vulgare
Borage family (Boraginaceae)

Description: Mostly single-stemmed plants, up to 3' tall, with bristly hairs on the stems and leaves. The basal leaves are stalkless, long, and narrow, up to 6" long. The stem leaves are progressively smaller up the stem. The flowers are on the upper stems in crowded, curled spikes. Each flower is funnel-shaped, about ¾" long, with 5 uneven petals. The pink buds turn to purple flowers when open.

Bloom Season: Late spring–fall

Habitat/Range: Locally common in open, disturbed ground, fields, along roadsides, and gravel bars in streams; a native of Europe; found throughout the Midwest region in scattered locations, and spreading.

Comments: Also called "viper's bugloss." *Bugloss* is an English word given to several plants of the borage family. *Viper* refers to the resemblance of the seed to the head of a viper snake. In early folk medicine, a leaf tea was used for fever, headache, nervous conditions, and pain from inflammation. The hairs may cause a rash.

GARLIC MUSTARD

Alliaria petiolata
Mustard family (Brassicaceae)

Description: A biennial plant, up to 3' tall, with few branches. The leaves, when crushed, have the odor of garlic. Leaves are alternate on the stem, up to 2½" long, broadest at the base, narrow at the tip, and coarsely toothed along the margins. First-year plants have just a rosette of smaller, round- or kidney-shaped leaves with scalloped edges. The flowers are in a rounded cluster, about 1–3" across, at the top of each stem that elongates as the plant matures. Each flower is about ⅓" across, with 4 white petals. Fruit pods are narrow, 4-sided, and up to 2½" long.

Bloom Season: Mid-spring–early summer

Habitat/Range: Locally common in moist woods, ravines, edges of woods, and banks along streams; native to Europe; found throughout the Midwest region.

Comments: Garlic mustard spreads rapidly, with each plant producing thousands of minute seeds. Once established, this aggressive weed forms dense stands that smother spring wildflowers and lowers the diversity of woodlands. The first year's growth produces a single, heart-shaped leaf that overwinters. Hand-pulling is the easiest way to eradicate this exotic pest through successive visits.

YELLOW ROCKET

Barbarea vulgaris
Mustard family (Brassicaceae)

Description: A biennial plant, branched, smooth, and up to 2' tall. The basal leaves are up to 6" long and 2½" wide, deeply lobed, with the end leaflet larger than the rest, and on long stalks. The upper leaves are alternate, toothed, and usually without a stalk. The flowers are crowded together at the end of branches, in a cluster about 1–1½" wide that elongates as the plant matures. Each flower is about ⅜" across with 4 bright yellow petals. The fruit has elongated pods, up to 1½" long.

Bloom Season: Mid-spring–early summer

Habitat/Range: Common in idle and cultivated fields, pastures, edges of woods, disturbed prairies, wet ground near streams, and along roadsides; a native of Europe; found throughout the Midwest region.

Comments: Yellow rocket was introduced into the United States early. The Cherokee ate the greens as a "blood purifier." Leaf tea was used to treat coughs and scurvy, and to stimulate appetite. Studies indicate this plant may cause kidney malfunction, so internal use should be avoided.

DAME'S ROCKET

Hesperis matronalis
Mustard family (Brassicaceae)

Description: Usually a single, hairy-stemmed biennial to short-lived perennial plant, up to 4' tall. The leaves are alternate, up to 6" long and 2" wide, lance-shaped, hairy, sharply toothed, with short stalks, or stalkless. The flowers are arranged along stalks that arise from the upper leaf axils. Flowers are fragrant, showy, about 1" across, with 4 white to pink to lavender to deep purple petals.

Bloom Season: Late spring–early summer

Habitat/Range: Locally common in moist ground in woods, edges of woods, meadows, and roadside ditches; a native of Europe, it escapes from homesites, where it is grown as an ornamental; found throughout the Midwest region.

Comments: Dame's rocket is a well-known flower of old-fashioned gardens and English cottage gardens. Twenty-four species are known, from the Mediterranean region to central Asia.

SOAPWORT

Saponaria officinalis
Pink family (Caryophyllaceae)

Description: Often forming colonies, these plants have stems that are sometimes branched and up to 2' tall. The leaves are opposite, stalkless, smooth, up to 4" long and 1½" wide, with 3–5 conspicuous veins along the leaves, and often with wavy margins. The flowers are fragrant, in open clusters at the top, with each flower about 1" across. Each flower has a long tube and 5 petals that vary from pink to white, with a notch at the end of each petal.

Bloom Season: Summer–fall

Habitat/Range: Common on gravel bars and sandbars along streams, woodland edges, disturbed ground, and along roadsides and railroads; a native of Europe that escaped as a garden plant; found throughout the Midwest region.

Comments: Also called "bouncing bet." A soapy, green lather can be made from the plant by rubbing the leaves and stems in water. This natural cleanser, saponin, was used to wash fabrics and tapestries as far back as in ancient Greece. Later, soapwort was also used to produce a "head" on beer. The plant has been used to treat asthma, jaundice, gout, syphilis, rheumatism, coughs, and bronchitis. If taken in large doses or over a prolonged period, it can cause severe irritation to the gastrointestinal tract.

COMMON ST. JOHN'S WORT
Hypericum perforatum
St. John's wort family (Clusiaceae)

Description: A multibranched plant, 1–3' tall, with green to reddish-brown stems that are sharply ridged below each leaf. The leaves are opposite, stalkless, 1–2" long and ¼" wide, slightly broadest in the middle, tapering to rounded ends, and with scattered, tiny, translucent dots along the lower surface. The flowers are on short stalks at the ends of upper stems in clusters. Each flower is about ¾–1" across, with 5 yellow petals that have tiny, black dots along the edges. There are numerous stamens that also may be dotted.

Bloom Season: Early summer–fall

Habitat/Range: Common in mesic upland forests, bottomland forests, prairies, glades, banks of streams and spring branches, old fields, pastures, roadsides, and other disturbed sites; found throughout the Midwest region; native to parts of Europe and Asia, it has spread to temperate regions worldwide as an invasive weed.

Comments: The plant has been used medicinally for treating external ulcers, wounds, sores, cuts, and bruises, and as a tea in folk remedies for bladder ailments, depression, dysentery, and worms. The biologically active compound, hypericin, may cause photodermatitis (skin burns) when applied to some individuals who are then exposed to sunlight. There are similar-looking St. John's worts that are native to the Midwest region, so be sure to review them in the Yellow Flowers section of this book.

ASIATIC DAYFLOWER
Commelina communis
Spiderwort family (Commelinaceae)

Description: An often-sprawling, annual plant, 1–3' long, which often roots at the nodes. The leaves are alternate, hairless, 5" long and 2" wide, broadest at or below the middle, with pointed tips, and at the base, a sheath that wraps around the stem up to 1" long. The flowers are about ½–1" across on stalks and with folded, spathe-like bracts, up to 2" long, that are open from the top to the base. Each flower has 2 blue upper petals that are round, a much smaller, white lower petal, 3 sterile upper stamens, and 3 smaller, lower stamens that are fertile. All stamens have a maroon spot at the tip.

Bloom Season: Midsummer–fall

Habitat/Bloom: Common along edges of mesic upland and bottomland forests, banks of streams, fields, gardens, moist roadsides, and other disturbed sites; found throughout the Midwest region; native throughout much of East Asia.

Comments: Each flower lasts but a day; hence, the common name. In China, leaf tea is gargled for sore throat, flu, tonsillitis, urinary infections, and dysentery.

COMMON TEASEL
Dipsacus fullonum
Teasel family (Dipsacaceae)

Description: A tall, stout biennial, with very prickly, branched stems, up to 8' tall. The basal leaves appear the first year and are up to 12" long and 3" wide. The second-year stem leaves are opposite and stalkless, or sometimes slightly fused to the stem at the very base, up to 12" long and 3" wide, broadest at the base, narrowing to a pointed tip, with rounded teeth along the margins and lacking prickles, except underneath, along the midvein. The flowers are pink to lavender, 4-lobed, and densely packed along a cylindrical head at the top of long stalks. At the base of each flower head, there are several narrow, prickly bracts, each about 6" long, that curve upward, surrounding the spike.

Bloom Season: Summer–fall

Habitat/Range: Forming large colonies along roadsides, ditches, fields, waste areas, mesic prairies, and woodland edges; a native of Europe; found throughout the Midwest region.

Comments: A similar species, cut-leaved teasel (*Dipsacus laciniatus*), has opposite leaves that form a cup-like structure around the stem, long, narrow lobes along the margins, and white flowers. Both species of teasel share similar bloom dates, habitat, and range.

LEAFY SPURGE
Euphorbia virgata
Spurge family (Euphorbiaceae)

Description: Stems are single or multiple from the base, hairless, often branched above the midpoint, up to 3' tall, and forming colonies from rhizomes. The leaves are alternate, narrow, 1–3" long, and pointed at the tip. The upper stems have a branched array of paired, round, yellow bracts, about ¼" wide, that look like petals, surrounding a small cluster of greenish-yellow flowers.

Bloom Season: Late spring–fall

Habitat/Range: Forming dense stands in prairies, pastures, fields, and disturbed soil that are very difficult to eradicate; native to Europe and Asia; found throughout the Midwest region, but uncommon in the southern third (for now).

Comments: According to the organization Flora of North America, populations long thought to be *Euphorbia esula* are more appropriately treated as leafy spurge (*Euphorbia virgata*), although some believe that both occur in North America. *Euphorbia virgata* differs by having a somewhat pointed tip at the end of a leaf that is long and narrow along its length, while *Euphorbia esula* has a rounded tip at the end of a leaf that is wider above the middle.

SERICEA LESPEDEZA
Lespedeza cuneata
Bean family (Fabaceae)

Description: A single-stemmed plant, up to 5' tall, with many erect, leafy branches that are green to ashy in color. The stem has flattened hairs along its length. The leaves are divided into 3 leaflets, each ¼–1" long. The lower 2 leaves have stalks, with the end leaflet stalkless, or nearly so. The flowers are in clusters of 2–3 in the upper leaf axils. The flowers are about ¼" long, with a pale creamy color, and arranged in the pattern typical of members of the bean family. There are conspicuous purple or pink markings in the center of the fan-like upper petal.

Bloom Season: Summer–fall

Habitat/Range: Often forming dense stands in prairies, woodlands, and gravel bars in streams; also along roadsides and in disturbed open ground; native to eastern Asia; found in the southern half of the Midwest region (for now).

Comments: A common aggressive weed, it was first introduced into the United States in the early 1900s to aid in soil-erosion control. It has become a major nuisance and is difficult to eradicate.

BIRD'S FOOT TREFOIL
Lotus corniculatus
Bean family (Fabaceae)

Description: A sprawling plant, up to 2' long, with branching stems upright toward the tips. The leaves are divided into 5 leaflets, each up to ¾" long, with 2 lower leaflets some distance below the 3 upper leaflets. The flowers are clustered on a long stalk that arises from a leaf axil. The flowers are golden-yellow, about ¾" long, and arranged in the pattern typical of members of the bean family. The seeds form in slender, upright pods.

Bloom Season: Late spring–fall

Habitat/Range: Common along roadsides, fields, and pastures; native to Europe; found throughout the Midwest region.

Comments: This common weed has been planted as a forage crop; later, it was marketed as "good for erosion control," and planted along roadsides, where it sometimes invades prairie pastures.

BLACK MEDIC
Medicago lupulina
Pea family (Fabaceae)

Description: A sprawling, annual plant that sometimes grows up to 20" long. The branching stem has soft hairs with alternate leaves divided into 3 leaflets. The leaflets are up to ¾" long with very shallow teeth along the margins. The flowers are crowded together in dense heads, up to ¾" long, with the heads attached to a long stalk that emerges from the leaf axil. The flowers are small, with 5 yellow petals in an arrangement typical of the bean family.

Bloom Season: Mid-spring–summer

Habitat/Range: Locally common in disturbed prairies, glades, edges of bottomland forests, and banks of streams; also found in disturbed ground, lawns, fields, and along roadsides; native to Eurasia and Africa; found throughout the Midwest region.

Comments: Black medic was introduced to the United States for livestock forage, but generally has a low yield. There are six species of black medic in the genus *Medicago* in the Midwest region, including alfalfa (*Medicago sativa*). None are native to the United States.

WHITE SWEET CLOVER
Melilotus albus
Bean family (Fabaceae)

Description: This legume, depending on conditions, grows as an annual or biennial. The branching, smooth stems can be up to 6½' tall. The leaves are alternate, grayish-green, divided into 3 leaflets, with each leaflet about 1" long, oval, rounded at the tip, and finely toothed. The flowers are white, fragrant, about ⅜" long, clustered on 4" stalks, with 5 petals in an arrangement typical of the bean family.

Bloom Season: Late spring–fall

Habitat/Range: Very common, aggressive, and difficult to eradicate; occurs in prairies, glades, fields, roadsides, and open, disturbed ground; native to Europe and Asia; found throughout the Midwest region.

Comments: Some botanical authorities consider white sweet clover to be a different color form of yellow sweet clover, and believe that both should be called *Melilotus officinalis*. In fact, white sweet clover has distinct characteristics that differentiate it from yellow sweet clover, including being slightly larger in size, with grayish-green foliage, a network of raised nerves on the surface of the fruits, and blooming about two weeks later.

YELLOW SWEET CLOVER
Melilotus officinalis
Bean family (Fabaceae)

Description: This legume, depending on conditions, grows as an annual or biennial. The branching, smooth stems can be found up to 5' tall. The leaves are alternate, green, divided into 3 leaflets, with each leaflet about 1" long, oval, rounded at the tip, and finely toothed. The flowers are yellow, fragrant, about ⅜" long, clustered on 4" stalks, with 5 petals in an arrangement typical of the bean family.

Bloom Season: Late spring–fall

Habitat/Range: Very common, aggressive, and difficult to eradicate; occurs in prairies, glades, roadsides, fields, and open, disturbed ground; native to Europe and Asia; found throughout the Midwest region.

Comments: Some botanical authorities consider yellow sweet clover and white sweet clover to be the same species (*Melilotus officinalis*), but yellow sweet clover has distinct characteristics, including being slightly smaller in size, with green foliage and a network of flat nerves on the surface of the fruits, and blooming about two weeks earlier.

CROWN VETCH
Securigera varia
Bean family (Fabaceae)

Description: Densely spreading plants, up to 4' long, with branched, smooth stems. The leaves are alternate and divided into 15–25 leaflets. Each leaflet is up to ¾" long, narrow, abruptly pointed at the tip, lacking hairs, and smooth along the margins. The flowers are in dense clusters (like a crown), on long stalks arising from the axils of the leaves. Each flower is about ½" long, with 5 pink and white petals in an arrangement typical of the bean family.

Bloom Season: Late spring–summer

Habitat/Range: A common, aggressive weed that often escapes into prairies, glades, forests, edges of streams and gravel bars, fields, and disturbed sites; native to Europe, Asia, and Africa; found throughout the Midwest region.

Comments: Formerly known as *Coronilla varia*. Crown vetch has often been planted to control erosion, especially along roadsides, but it has been found to actually increase erosion. This is because it provides no cover in contact with the ground, so the soil remains bare even though there is dense foliage above it.

RED CLOVER
Trifolium pratense
Bean family (Fabaceae)

Description: Multibranched stems, up to 2' tall, occurring in open clumps, with widely spaced leaves. The leaves are alternate, divided into 3 rounded leaflets, up to 2" long and ¾" wide, stalkless, with sparse hairs along the margins, which are sometimes finely toothed. There is typically a V-shaped pattern on the leaf surface. The pinkish-red flowers are in round, dense clusters about ¾–1" across, with 5 petals in an arrangement typical of the bean family.

Bloom Season: Mid-spring–fall

Habitat/Range: Very common, planted as a forage or cover crop that often escapes into disturbed or degraded prairies, glades, banks of streams, margins of wetlands, pastures, roadsides, and open, disturbed ground; native to Europe and Asia; found throughout the Midwest region.

Comments: Red clover is grown in more areas of the world than any other species of *Trifolium*. It has been in cultivation since the third and fourth centuries, probably beginning in Spain. Once established, it is difficult to eradicate.

WHITE CLOVER
Trifolium repens
Bean family (Fabaceae)

Description: Low-growing plants with fibrous roots and sometimes short rhizomes. Stems are 4–12" long and rooting at the nodes. The leaves are alternate and divided into 3 broadly oval to nearly round leaflets, each about ½" in diameter, with finely toothed edges. Sometimes there is a white crescent across the middle of the leaflets. The flowers are round, about ½" across, white, on smooth stalks about 3" long, with 5 petals in an arrangement typical of the bean family.

Bloom Season: Mid-spring–fall

Habitat/Range: Very common, planted as a forage or cover crop that often escapes into disturbed or degraded prairie, edges of bottomland forests, and margins of wetlands, where it can be very persistent; also found in pastures, roadsides, lawns, and open, disturbed ground; native to Europe, western Asia, and northern Africa; found throughout the Midwest region.

Comments: When white clover was introduced in North America, it was known to Native Americans as "white man's foot grass."

BLACKBERRY LILY
Belamcanda chinensis
Iris family (Iridaceae)

Description: A stout flower stalk, up to 3' tall, supports attractive orange flowers, each of which lasts but a day. The leaves are alternate, up to 12" long and 1" wide, with parallel veins along the length of the blade. The flowers are clustered at the top of the stem. Each lily-like flower is up to 2" across, with 3 sepals and 3 petals of similar size that are orange, with darker orange to brownish-purple spots. The fruit capsule splits open to reveal shiny black, fleshy seeds resembling a blackberry.

Bloom Season: Summer

Habitat/Range: Occasional in rocky, open woods, hillsides, glades, edges of bluffs, roadsides, and old homesteads; found in the southern two-thirds of the Midwest region; a native of Asia that was introduced as a garden plant and has escaped.

Comments: Although the flowers resemble lilies, the leaves along the stem are typical of irises. The orange rhizome distinguishes this iris from other irises.

GROUND IVY
Glechoma hederacea
Mint family (Lamiaceae)

Description: A creeping mint with branched stems, rooting at the nodes, and growing up to 6' long in a single year. The leaves are opposite, stalked, round, up to 1½" across, with rounded teeth along the margins. The flowers emerge from the axils of the stem and leaf. Each flower is up to ¾" long, with 2 purple-blue to reddish-blue lips that are divided into lobes. The lower lip is much larger than the upper, with 3 lobes, and usually with dark spots and streaks on the center lobe.

Bloom Season: Mid-spring–midsummer

Habitat/Range: Common in low woodlands, valleys, banks along streams, lawns, fields, and along roadsides; a native of Europe, introduced as a ground cover for residences, and now spread throughout the Midwest region.

Comments: Also known as gill-over-the-ground. The first report of ground ivy in North America was from the eastern United States in 1814.

ORANGE DAYLILY
Hemerocallis fulva
Lily family (Liliaceae)

Description: The leafless flower stalks are up to 5' tall and produce flowers that last but a day. The leaves are at the base, narrow, up to 2' long and ½" wide, with pointed tips. The flowers are clustered at the top, orange with yellow centers, and up to 4" across. There are 3 petals and 3 slightly smaller sepals. The 6 stamens are long and curve upward.

Bloom Season: Late spring–summer

Habitat/Range: Locally common along roadsides and edges of woods where it has escaped from cultivation around homesites; a native of Europe and Asia; found throughout the Midwest region.

Comments: The plants have been eaten in salads, in fritters, as a cooked vegetable (sometimes as a substitute for asparagus), and as a seasoning. In China a root tea is used as a diuretic, and also to treat jaundice, nosebleed, and uterine bleeding. Recent Chinese reports warn that the roots and young leaf shoots are considered potentially toxic because the toxin accumulates in the body and adversely affects the eyes, even causing blindness in some cases. Their studies also warn that the roots contain colchicine, a carcinogen.

STAR OF BETHLEHEM

Ornithogalum umbellatum
Lily family (Liliaceae)

Description: These showy plants with their star-shaped flowers and grass-like leaves colonize disturbed sites. From underground bulbs, the leaves emerge to a length of about 12". The margins of the leaves are curved inward, with a white stripe down the middle. The flowers are on stalks, up to 12" tall, with each stalk bearing 3–7 flowers. The flowers are about 1" across and have 6 white petals with a green stripe down the back of each petal.

Bloom Season: Mid-spring–early summer

Habitat/Range: Common in disturbed areas along roadsides, open fields, grassy areas, and shaded banks along streams; also, mesic upland and bottomland forests; a native of Europe; found throughout the Midwest region, but widely scattered across the northern third.

Comments: This exotic plant is very aggressive, producing bulbs at a rapid rate, and is very difficult to eradicate once established. The leaves and bulbs are poisonous, containing toxic alkaloids, and should be kept away from children and domestic animals.

PURPLE LOOSESTRIFE

Lythrum salicaria
Loosestrife family (Lythraceae)

Description: Hairy, square-stemmed, branching plants, up to 6' tall, with opposite leaves, but occasionally in whorls of 3 or 4. The leaves are stalkless, about 4" long and 1" wide, smooth along the margins and slightly hairy. The flowers are purple or pinkish-purple and densely packed in spikes up to 20" long. Each flower is about ½–¾" across, with 6 petals that have a wrinkled appearance and a dark vein down the middle.

Bloom Season: Summer–fall

Habitat/Range: A common, aggressive weed in wet prairies with standing water, edges of wetlands, lakes, and streams, ditches, and roadsides; native to Europe and Asia; found throughout the Midwest region.

Comments: Purple loosestrife often occurs in dense stands that shade out native flora. The plant was introduced to the east coast of North America in the early 1800s by immigrants as an ornamental and herb. It eventually spread into the Midwest and established a strong presence in the 1970s. Difficult to eradicate, each plant can produce thousands of seeds a year that can lay dormant in the soil for many years. It can also reproduce from roots and broken stems.

HELLEBORINE
Epipactis helleborine
Orchid family (Orchidaceae)

Description: Plants with light green, hairy stems, 1–3' tall, with 3–7 alternate leaves and up to 50 flowers. Leaves are 1½–6" long and ½–3" wide, oval to broadest at the middle, and narrowing at both ends, with the base clasping the stem, hairless and toothless. There are prominent, parallel veins along the length of the leaf, and slightly wavy edges along the margins. The flowers are stalked and loosely to densely arranged along the upper length of the stem. Each flower is ½–¾" wide, varying in color from pale yellow or green to pink to deep reddish-purple, with the lower petal forming a bowl that is constricted toward the tip. The 2 side petals are broad with pointed tips and flare out, while the 3 light green sepals form a triangle behind the flower.

Bloom Season: Midsummer–fall

Habitat/Range: Locally common in disturbed soil in mesic woods, woodland edges, banks of streams, and roadsides; found in Michigan, in forests bordering the Great Lakes, and in scattered locations elsewhere in the Midwest region, where it has escaped from cultivation; native to Europe, Asia, and northern Africa.

Comments: Helleborine is pollinated by several species of wasps, bees, and ants, particularly the common wasp. Flowers release a sweet nectar to attract wasps, which has an intoxicating effect on them. The nectar contains naturally occurring oxycodone, as well as another narcotic-like opioid, in minute amounts.

MONEYWORT

Lysimachia nummularia
Primrose family (Primulaceae)

Description: Creeping stems, up to 3' long, that grow flat on the ground, branching at the base and rooting at the nodes. The leaves are opposite, shiny, evergreen, stalked, round, ¾–1" long and wide, hairless, but with small, black-dotted glands. The flowers emerge from leaf axils, each ¾–1" across, yellow, with 5 round petals, the surfaces of which are often speckled with deep red dots. There are 5 yellow stamens.

Bloom Season: Late spring–summer

Habitat/Range: Locally common in bottomland forests, banks of streams, and spring branches, margins of lakes and ponds, roadsides, and moist disturbed areas; native to Europe; found throughout the Midwest region.

Comments: Also known as creeping Jenny, moneywort was brought to the United States as a horticultural item for garden landscapes, but it can spread rapidly and crowd out other plants. The plant has been used in Chinese medicine to treat gallstones, urinary bladder stones, and gout.

TALL BUTTERCUP

Ranunculus acris
Buttercup family (Ranunculaceae)

Description: Strong, upright stems, 10–40" in height, and taller than any native buttercup in the Midwest region. The basal leaves are up to 6" long and 6" wide, and deeply divided into 3–5 lobes, with each lobe further divided. The basal leaves and lower stem leaves have stalks up to 10" long. The stem leaves are alternate, along the lower half of the stem, and smaller in size. The flowers are on stalks up to 6" long. Each flower is ½–1" across, with 5 broad, shiny yellow petals and numerous stamens that surround a greenish center.

Bloom Season: Late spring–summer

Habitat/Range: Common along edges of woods, fields, meadows, stream banks, pastures, roadsides, and other disturbed areas; found throughout the northern half of the Midwest region and in scattered sites in the southern half; native to Europe and Asia.

Comments: Besides the United States, tall buttercup is an introduced species across much of the world. In New Zealand, it is a serious pasture weed costing the dairy industry hundreds of millions of dollars. It has become one of the few pasture weeds that has developed a resistance to herbicides.

MOTH MULLEIN
Verbascum blattaria
Snapdragon family (Scrophulariaceae)

Description: A biennial plant with a slender form, up to 5' tall. The stem is either single or branched, and smooth on the lower part, with round, gland-tipped hairs above. The basal leaves are large, tapering to the base, and toothed along the margins. The leaves along the stem are smaller, alternate, and somewhat clasping, or simply lacking a stalk. The flowers, about 1" across, are loosely spaced along the branch. The 5 petals are either white or yellow, with 5 stamens displaying woolly filaments that are violet to reddish-brown.

Bloom Season: Late spring–fall

Habitat/Range: Common in pastures, fields, rocky, open places, waste ground, woodland edges, gravel bars along streams, and roadsides; native to Europe and Asia; found throughout the Midwest region, but less invasive in the northwest quarter.

Comments: Both white- and yellow-flowering moth mulleins appear equally as common. Looking at the flower, with some imagination, one may see a moth; hence, the common name; others say it is so-called because the flowers attract moths.

WOOLLY MULLEIN
Verbascum thapsus
Snapdragon family (Scrophulariaceae)

Description: This stocky biennial can reach a height of 6', with large, woolly leaves and a spike of densely packed yellow flowers. The first year's leaves form a basal rosette, with each leaf up to 15" long and 5" across, with soft, woolly hairs. The second year, a flower stalk emerges with alternate leaves scattered along the stem. The leaf bases extend down the stem forming wings. The short, tubular flowers open to about 1" across, with 5 yellow lobes.

Bloom Season: Late spring–summer

Habitat/Range: Common in disturbed portions of prairies and edges of marshes, banks of streams and rivers, old fields, pastures, disturbed ground, and along roadsides; native to Europe, Asia, and northern Africa; found throughout the Midwest region.

Comments: Woolly mullein has been introduced throughout the temperate world, and is estab-lished as a weed in Australia, New Zealand, tropical Asia, Hawaii, Chile, the Caribbean, Argentina, and, of course, North America.

GLOSSARY

Alternate—Placed singly at different heights on the stem or axis (see "Opposite") (see page xiv, figure 2).

Annual—A plant completing its life cycle, from seed germination to production of new seeds, within a year, and then dying.

Anther—The pollen-bearing part of a stamen (see page xvi, figure 8).

Axil—The angle between the upper part of a leaf and the stem from which it grows.

Banner—The usually erect, spreading upper petal in many flowers of the bean family (Fabaceae) (see page xvi, figure 9).

Basal—At the base or bottom of; generally used in reference to leaves at the base of the plant (see page xiv, figure 4).

Biennial—A plant that completes its life cycle in two years, normally not producing flowers during the first year.

Bract—A reduced or modified leaf, often associated with flowers (see page xvii, figure 10).

Bristle—A stiff hair, usually erect or curving away from its attachment point.

Bulb—An underground plant part derived from a short, usually rounded shoot that is covered with scales or modified leaves.

Calyx—The outer set of flower parts, composed of the sepals, which may be separate or united; usually green (see page xvi, figure 8).

Capsule—A dry fruit that releases seeds through splits or holes.

Clasping—Surrounding or partially wrapping around a stem or branch.

Cluster—Any grouping or close arrangement of individual flowers that is not dense and continuous.

Compound leaf—A leaf that is divided into two to many leaflets, each of which may look like a complete leaf but which lacks buds. Compound leaves may have leaflets arranged along an axis like the rays of a feather or radiating from a common point like the fingers on a hand (see page xv, figures 6–7).

Corm—A fleshy, bulblike base of a stem, usually underground.

Corolla—The set of flower parts interior to the calyx and surrounding the stamens, composed of the petals, which may be free or united; often brightly colored (see page xvi, figure 8, and page xvii, figure 10).

Disk flowers—Small, tubular flowers in the central portion of the flower head of many plants in the aster family (Asteraceae) (see page xvii, figure 10).

Disturbed—Referring to habitats that have been impacted by actions or processes associated with human settlement, such as ditching, grading, or long intervals of high-intensity grazing.

Erect—Upright, standing vertically, or directly perpendicular from a surface.

Escape—A plant that has been cultivated in an area and subsequently spread from there into the wild.

Family—A group of plants having biologically similar features, such as flower anatomy, fruit type, and so on, and common ancestry, such as the family Liliaceae, encompassing lilies, onions, wild hyacinths, and trilliums.

Fen—A specialized wetland permanently supplied with mineralized groundwater.

Flower head—As used in this guide, a dense and continuous group of flowers, without obvious branches or space between them; used especially in reference to the aster family (Asteraceae) (see page xvii, figure 10).

Fruit—The ripened ovary of a flowering plant, containing seeds.

Genus—A group of related species, such as the genus *Solidago*, encompassing the goldenrods (see "Specific epithet").

Glade—An opening in the forest with bedrock at or near the surface with drought-resistant plants.

Gland—A bump, projection, or round protuberance, usually colored differently than the object on which it occurs, and often sticky or producing sticky or oily secretions.

Herbaceous—Having the character of an herb, which is a plant lacking persistent woody parts above the ground.

Hood—The curling or folded, petal-like structures interior to the petals and exterior to the stamens in milkweed flowers (*Asclepias* species); because most milkweeds have reflexed petals, the hoods are typically the most prominent feature of the flowers.

Hooded—Arching over and partially concealing or shielding.

Horn—A small, round, or flattened projection from the hoods of milkweed flowers (*Asclepias* species).

Keel—A sharp lengthwise fold or ridge, referring particularly to the two fused petals forming the lower lip in many flowers of the bean family (Fabaceae) (see page xvi, figure 9).

Leaf—A flat outgrowth of a stem capable of manufacturing food for the plant and usually green (see "Photosynthesis").

Leaflet—A distinct, leaf-like segment of a compound leaf.

Lobe—A segment of an incompletely divided plant part, typically rounded; often used in reference to leaves.

Margin—The edge of a leaf.

Mesic—Referring to a habitat that is well-drained but generally moist through most of the growing season.

Midrib—The central or main vein of a leaf.

Node—The portion of the stem where one or more leaves are attached. Buds are commonly borne at the node, in the axils of the leaves.

Opposite—Paired directly across from one another along a stem or axis (see "Alternate") (see page xiv, figure 1).

Ovary—The portion of the flower where the seeds develop, usually a swollen area below the style (if present) and stigma (see page xvi, figure 8).

Palmate—Lobed, veined, or divided from a common point, like the fingers of a hand (see page xv, figure 6).

Parallel—Side by side, approximately the same distance apart for the entire length; often used in reference to veins or edges of leaves.

Pedicel—The stalk of a single flower (see page xvi, figure 8).

Perennial—A plant that normally lives for three or more years.

Petal—An individual segment or part of the corolla, often brightly colored (see "Corolla") (see page xvi, figure 8).

Photosynthesis—The process in which the energy of sunlight is used by organisms, especially green plants, to synthesize carbohydrates from carbon dioxide and water, releasing oxygen as a by-product.

Pinnate—A compound leaf, where smaller leaflets are arranged along either side of a common axis (see page xv, figure 7).

Pistil—The seed-producing, or female, unit of a flower, typically consisting of the ovary, style, and stigma; a flower may have one to several separate pistils (see page xvi, figure 8).

Pod—A dry fruit that splits open along the edges.

Pollen—The fine, dust-like grains discharged from the male part of the flower and typically necessary for seed production.

Prickle—A small, sharp, spine-like outgrowth emerging from the outer surface.

Ray flowers—The flowers on the flower heads of members of the aster family (Asteraceae) that have a single, strap-shaped corolla, resembling one flower petal. Ray flowers may surround the disk flower in a flower head, or in some species, such as dandelions, the flower heads may be composed entirely of ray flowers (see page xvii, figure 10).

Recurved—Curved backward or outward.

Reflexed—Abruptly bent or curved downward.

Rhizome—An underground stem, usually lateral and producing shoots and roots.

Root—An underground organ that anchors a plant in the soil and absorbs water and nutrients.

Rosette—A dense cluster of basal leaves from a common undergound part, often in a flattened, circular arrangement.

Sepal—An individual segment or part of the calyx; typically green, but sometimes enlarged and brightly colored (see page xvi, figures 8–9).

Shrub—A persistent woody plant with several stems from the base.

Simple leaf—A leaf that has a single, leaf-like blade, although this may be lobed or divided (see page xv, figure 5).

Specific epithet—The second portion of a scientific name, identifying a particular species; for instance, in wild geranium (*Geranium maculatum*), the specific epithet is *maculatum*.

Spike—An elongated, unbranched cluster of stalkless or nearly stalkless flowers.

Stalk—As used in this guide, the stem supporting the leaf, flower, or flower cluster.

Stalkless—Lacking a stalk; a stalkless leaf is attached directly to the stem at the leaf base.

Stamen—The pollen-producing, or male, unit of a flower, typically consisting of a long filament with a pollen-producing tip (the anther) (see page xvi, figure 8).

Stigma—The portion of the pistil receptive to pollination; usually at the top of the style, and often appearing fuzzy or sticky (see page xvi, figure 8).

Stipule—A bract or leafy structure occurring in pairs at the base of the leaf stalk.

Stolon—A modified stem elongated and arching or creeping above the ground, rooting at the nodes or at the tip and giving rise to new plants.

Style—The portion of the pistil between the ovary and the stigma; typically a slender stalk (see page xvi, figure 8).

Succulent—Thickened and fleshy or juicy.

Tendril—A slender, coiled, or twisted filament with which climbing plants attach to their support.

Toothed—Having small lobes or points along the margin (as of a leaf).

Tubular—Narrow, cylindrical, and tube-like.

Variety—A group of plants within a species that has a distinct range, habitat, or set of characteristics.

Vine—A plant with long, flexible stems trailing on the ground or climbing on other plants.

Whorl—Three or more parts attached at the same point along a stem and often surrounding the stem; usually referring to leaves (see page xiv, figure 3).

Winged—Having thin bands of leaf-like tissue attached edgewise along the length of a stem or leaf stalk.

Wings—The two side petals flanking the keel in many flowers of the bean family (Fabaceae) (see page xvi, figure 9).

Winter annual—An annual plant that begins its growth from seed in the fall and produces basal leaves that overwinter.

SELECTED FURTHER READING

Adelman, Charlotte, and Bernard Schwartz. 2013. *Prairie Directory of North America*. 2nd ed. New York: Oxford University Press. (A comprehensive source for locating North American public prairies, grasslands, and savannas in the United States, Canada, and Mexico.)

Foster, Steven, and James A. Duke. 1990. *A Field Guide in Medicinal Plants*. New York: Houghton Mifflin. (Provides illustrations and descriptions of medicinal plants and their uses.)

Illinois Wildflowers; http://illinoiswildflowers.info/. (This website provides photographs and descriptions of many wildflowers that occur in the state, along with their uses by animals, especially insects.)

Kartesz, J. T. The Biota of North America Program (BONAP). 2013. *North American Plant Atlas*. Chapel Hill, North Carolina. http://bonap.net/NAPA/Genus/Traditional/County. (The maps provided list the flora of North America by genus and species at the county level.)

Minnesota Wildflowers: A Guide to the Flora of Minnesota. https://www.minnesotawildflowers.info/. (This website provides photographs and descriptions of wildflowers that occur in the state.)

Mohlenbrock, Robert H. 2013. *Vascular Flora of Illinois*. 4th ed. Carbondale: Southern Illinois University Press. (A guide to over 3,400 species of flora from Illinois, with taxonomic keys and brief descriptions.)

Peterson, Lee Allen. 1977. *A Field Guide to Edible Wild Plants*. New York: Houghton Mifflin. (Provides illustrations and descriptions of edible plants and their preparation and uses.)

Swink, Floyd, and Gerould Wilhelm. 1994. *Plants of the Chicago Region*. 4th ed. Indianapolis: Indiana Academy of Science. (A checklist of the plants of the Chicago region, with keys, notes on local distribution, ecology, and taxonomy, including tallgrass prairie plants.)

USDA Plants Database. https://plants.sc.egov.usda.gov/java/. (Provides standardized information about the vascular plants, mosses, liverworts, hornworts, and lichens of the United States and its territories.)

Wilhelm, Gerould, and Laura Rericha. 2017. *Flora of the Chicago Region: A Floristic and Ecological Synthesis*. Indianapolis: Indiana Academy of Science. (A guide to plants of the Chicago region, along with illustrations, dot distribution maps, and taxonomic keys, including tallgrass prairie plants.)

Yatskievych, George. 1998. *Steyermark's Flora of Missouri*. Vol. 1. Jefferson City: Missouri Department of Conservation. (A major revision of the original *Flora of Missouri*, with keys, descriptions, and illustrations to over 800 species of ferns, fern allies, conifers, and monocots.)

———. 2006. *Steyermark's Flora of Missouri*. Vol. 2. St. Louis: Missouri Botanical Garden Press. (This volume contains treatments of more than 900 species of dicots in the families Acanthaceae through Fabaceae.)

———. 2013. *Steyermark's Flora of Missouri*. Vol. 3. St. Louis: Missouri Botanical Garden Press. (This volume contains treatments of 1,235 species of dicots in the families Fagaceae through Zygophyllaceae.)

INDEX

ABOUT THE AUTHOR

After completing master's degrees in botany and zoology at Southern Illinois University, Carbondale, Don Kurz spent the next thirty-four years working to inventory, acquire, protect, and manage natural areas, endangered species sites, and other special features in the Midwest. For twenty-two years, he was employed by the Missouri Department of Conservation, where he held various supervisory positions in the Natural History Division, including that of natural history chief, which he maintained until his retirement from the department in 2002.

Don is now a part-time writer and nature photographer specializing in landscapes, wildlife, insects, and plants. His photos have appeared in calendars and magazines such as *Natural History*, as well as numerous wildflower books, including Falcon Publishing's *Tallgrass Prairie Wildflowers* and *North Woods Wildflowers*. He is also author of Falcon Publishing's *Prairie Wildflowers, Ozark Wildflowers*, and *Scenic Driving the Ozarks, including the Ouachita Mountains*, along with the Missouri Department of Conservation's *Shrubs and Woody Vines of Missouri, Shrubs and Woody Vines of Missouri Field Guide, Trees of Missouri*, and *Trees of Missouri Field Guide*. His other guides, published by Tim Ernst Publishing, are *Arkansas Wildflowers, Illinois Wildflowers*, and *Missouri's Natural Wonders Guidebook*.